CONVERSION
AS
TRANSFORMATION

CONVERSION
AS
TRANSFORMATION

Lonergan, Mentors, and Cinema

Dominic Arcamone

PICKWICK *Publications* · Eugene, Oregon

CONVERSION AS TRANSFORMATION
Lonergan, Mentors, and Cinema

Pickwick Publications
An Imprint of Wipf and Stock Publishers
199 W. 8th Ave., Suite 3
Eugene, OR 97401

www.wipfandstock.com

PAPERBACK ISBN: 978-1-5326-7892-9
HARDCOVER ISBN: 978-1-5326-7893-6
EBOOK ISBN: 978-1-5326-7894-3

Cataloguing-in-Publication data:

Names: Arcamone, Dominic, author.
Title: Conversion as transformation : Lonergan, mentors, and cinema. / Dominic Arcamone.
Description: Eugene, OR : Pickwick Publications, 2020. | Includes bibliographical references and index(es).
Identifiers: ISBN 978-1-5326-7892-9 (paperback) | ISBN 978-1-5326-7893-6 (hardcover) | ISBN 978-1-5326-7894-3 (ebook)
Subjects: LCSH: Conversion. | Lonergan Bernard J. F.
Classification: BX4705.L7133 A73 2020 (paperback) | BX4705.L7133 A73 (ebook)

Manufactured in the U.S.A.   01/23/20

Contents

Acknowledgments

I WANT TO THANK my wife, Anita, for her patience and gift of listening during the making of this manuscript. I would also like to thank my colleagues, both at work and more broadly, who helped me in various ways: Tom and Anna Hall; Maree Ataya; Natasha and Dennis Carroll; John Collins; and Robert Dueweke. Lastly, I would like to thank Neil Ormerod, who introduced me to the work of Bernard Lonergan so many years ago, and for all who are part of the Lonergan scholarly community.

Introduction

WELCOME TO THIS BOOK. These chapters will introduce a framework that hopefully will help negotiate the gift and task of fully human transformation. The insights of this book do not contain everything that might illuminate such an enterprise. Thousands of libraries contain books about human transformation. This book contains some insights that have helped people along the path to transformation, and I hope that the reader might also find a similar resonance. These insights come out of a lifelong love for the Catholic Christian wisdom of God, nurtured from birth in a faith community.

Since this book is about transformation, the intention is to explore the dimensions of living by which our relationship with God, each other, and the world change from a diminished vision to a complete understanding and essential commitment. The goal of spiritual transformation is authenticity, and it is not easy to achieve. However, we cannot avoid it since to live an authentic life is an invitation to all and not the task of a chosen elite. It is what we are all meant to accomplice to realize our full humanity. Authenticity is not an abstract task or a series of moral statements. Authenticity is concrete, dynamic, and existing in the here and now. It requires living out the drama of human existence with meaning and purpose within our context and historical circumstances. For some, the particular context in which we live may be conducive to truly human living. For others, the context provides a stiff challenge to the task of becoming authentic.

We are all embedded in time and in a set of historical arrangements. On the one hand, through our circumstances, our interactions with others, and our ongoing dramatic response to them, we are already formed as persons. We have adopted a set of meanings and values or heritage. On the other hand, we feel the need and summons to respond to the invitation of ongoing transformation toward authenticity to change current distortions and provide a better environment for growth in the future. The movement toward authenticity within a Christian understanding grounds the religious insight that God has ordered creation in such a way that nothing is complete from the beginning. In all creation, there must be change and growth with the tendency hopefully toward a better state. When we come to examine our relationship with God, many would admit that, for too long, the context in the secular West has been one where at best we have loved the idea of God instead of being-in-love with God. At worst, we have witnessed a widespread assertion of the irrelevance of God. God is the source and end of human transformation, and yet some people in our communities of faith have been content to find security in doctrines and ideas.

More troubling still is the cultural insight of T. S. Eliot, stated some fifty years ago and still valid for today: "The trouble of the modern age is not merely the inability to believe certain things about God which our forefathers believed, but the inability to feel God and man as they did."[1] People have lost a feeling for God and toward God. It would seem that God is missing but not missed. For many, God is not believable and not real. The dominant cultural narrative is that the autonomy of the individual, the will to control, and self-fulfillment are the keys to unlocking inner happiness. In his poem, *Burnt Norton*, T. S. Eliot diagnoses the unease on the faces of people passing by. He speaks of the flicker of light in their eyes strained, distracted, and without concentration.[2] Eliot warns us that the society we have created, and ourselves influenced by it, is full of distractions, and so, we can become deformed and entombed in a spiritual numbness with no real purpose. There is a kind of restlessness, more like an agitation, that contributes to a personal and cultural unease.

Building on Eliot's insights, Michael Paul Gallagher diagnoses three wounds of the modern cultural consciousness that gives rise to this agitation. These are the wounds of memory, of belonging, and of religious imagination.[3] First, the wound of memory points to the malady that the people of this age suffer through an absence of rootedness in any one tradition, the collapse of collective memory, and the lack of appreciation for a unified view of life. The modern person picks and chooses bits

---

1. Eliot, *On Poetry and Poets*, 25.

2. Eliot, *Four Quartets*, 17.

3. Gallagher, "Christian Identity in a Postmodern Age," 150–52.

and pieces of traditions from a smorgasbord of spiritualities, ideas, and lifestyles, usually based on personal satisfaction. Often, they are unaware as to the origin of specific traditions or how they fit into a richer view of life. There remains little to no effort in the broader society to unify these diverse strands, often finding them at odds with one another.

Second, the wound of belonging points to a relational fragmentation within our societies. In an age where we use and access an explosion of social media platforms, people still find themselves without communities of support. If there is a connection, it exists superficially without a commitment to others. This wound points to a hurting affectivity. Trust breaks down between people. A spiritual loneliness marks out our inner space.

Third, there is the wound of religious imagination. Imagination is vital for human living. Jesus in the gospels calls on his listeners to imagine. A saturation of consumerist images and sounds that dominate the current cultural space stifles our power to imagine a different promise and future. The result is a society that bombards and shapes our desiring toward egocentric goals. Since we cannot imagine a different future, many opt to look after themselves. The key message is that self-fulfillment counts above all else. As a consequence, our image of ourselves and God shrinks. Human transformation is needed, and the challenge to authenticity remains. If a transformation is to occur, it must address the whole person.

These chapters will bring three aspects into dialogue to best understand and appreciate transformation: first, the insights of Bernard Lonergan; second, mentors transformed in their lives despite personal setbacks and challenges; third, the drama of cinema to illustrate transformation. First, these chapters draw primarily upon the insights of the Canadian Catholic philosopher and theologian, Bernard Francis Lonergan (1904–1984) and those individuals who have found their own insights about religion, transformation, and human living enriched by him. A community of women and men have appropriated his writings and continued the creative collaboration he worked so hard to achieve, so that we might all live more authentically. Lonergan reaches up to human transformation through some key insights, especially, in the notion of conversion. By conversion, Lonergan means a transformation of the whole person through a radical change to their meanings and values upon which we take a position about what is authentic and what is not, what is worthwhile and what is not, guiding us to better dialogue with others. Conversion is not a once and forever experience but a process over a long period with cumulative and progressive sequences of development on all levels of life.

Second, I will reflect on the lives of people who have transformed their lives. Their transformed lives reflect a change to their religious, moral, affective, intellectual, and psychic dimensions. The circumstances of their lives, their explicit or implicit response to the grace of God, the decisions they made, and the values they espoused, their quest for truth and reality, and their affective responses to people and events unveil to us their soul in the process of transformation. We could say of them that they exhibit holiness, conscience, clear thinking, and a passionate commitment to people. Some have deeply felt the pull of moral responsibility, while others are just trying to get the basics of living right. All hold a fire in their belly to live the drama of human existence. They are not always perfect human beings, but they are willing to be transformed into more authentic people and transform other individuals or social structures. For this reason, they can be a symbol of hope for each of us.

Thirdly, I will illustrate transformation through cinema. The medium of film has demonstrated powerfully and imaginatively many aspects of human transformation in the modern era.[4] The art of cinema is also the art of storytelling. People who love movies look to many aspects within the film: themes, genre, actors, style, script, music, storyline, directors, and locations. However, there is a place for asking where our values, including our commitment to religious faith, and cinema generally might intersect. The primary concern of these chapters is evaluating the religious and existential dimensions of the protagonists, and what they might communicate to us and challenge in our lives. In each film, the reader would profit from watching the whole film to understand more thoughtfully the proper context of the scenes presented and to evaluate more thoroughly the feelings, thinking, decisions, and actions of the protagonists.

Each of the films communicates protagonists going through the process of human transformation. They experience transformation through a deeper appreciation of the true God or by embracing authentic values or by exercising more critical thinking, and a commitment to

---

4. The films studied in this book can be obtained from most streaming services, including Justwatch.com. Justwatch is available in European countries, South Africa, North America, South America, Asian Countries, Australia, and New Zealand. Visit the website for more information.

intellectual integrity, or demonstrating the power of love. These films also point to the power of real desire that enhances the lives of individuals and their communities. Finally, these films highlight the importance of psychological healing as a must so that people might live healthy lives. As far as possible we are meeting people at a particular part of their story which has the potential to speak to our story. Therefore, there remains the possibility of identifying with some aspect of a protagonist and their circumstances. Individually, we meet them at a point of transformation when they are stepping out of their taken-for-granted life and are open to something more, which enhances their fuller humanity or leads to an openness to the mystery that surrounds us all.

Chapter 1 explores the importance of authoring one's life and its link with the subject, subjectivity, consciousness and intersubjectivity. Lonergan's notion of self-appropriation guides us to a very unique form of self-discovery. Self-discovery becomes more than self-understanding, but also the way to become more authentic. The act of self-discovery puts us all on a path of being able to tell our story with our voice, not only as a story of what has passed but also a story of what is present and, more importantly, what anticipations, desires, and hopes we hold for the future. By telling our story, we will be in a better position to know where we are standing and so transform. There is a benefit to examining ourselves through the lens of escape, quest, and love dimensions of our story by exploring the protagonists in a set of films known as the *Three Color* Trilogy.

Chapter 2 begins the task of presenting a framework for understanding transformation by introducing some of Lonergan's terms. Lonergan begins from a new paradigm for understanding transformation. This paradigm requires the turn to the subject. There are a number of terms to this framework: horizon, insight, feelings and values, self-esteem, conversion, sublation, and dialectic, the experience of desire, the innate natural desire to know, value, and love and the influence of elicited desire in our lives. These terms help us to better understand the central theme of this book, conversion as transformation.

Chapter 3 focuses religious conversion. Since the approach is from the perspective of interiority and ourselves as subjects, religious experience is explained from the viewpoint of Lonergan's two paths of development and his notion of realms of meaning. Religious experience and religious conversion are interrelated as well as the impact of religious conversion on the sinner and the victim of sin. Chapter 4 describes religious

conversion by delving into the lives of several people who have experienced the power of God in their lives, who have come to know God, and
whose lives have changed for the better. Lonergan asserts that meaning
is embodied and carried in relationships, in art, in symbols, in language
and especially in the lives and deeds of people.[5] The films, *Babette's Feast*
and *As it is in Heaven*, illustrate the nature of religious experience. Chapter 5 examines religious conversion through a specifically Christian lens
to elucidate the personal experience of the disciples of Jesus through the
categories of the awakening of desire, the desolation of desire, and the
transformation of desire. To further examine a Christian perspective, the
relationship between religious conversion and belief, trust and beauty is
also examined. The life of St Therese of Lisieux in an imaginary conversation with Fredrich Nietzsche, who is often referred to as the father of
modern atheism, highlights some of the essential aspects of Christian
conversion speaking to non-believers.

In chapter 6, I explain the meaning of moral conversion both in
its individual and social dimensions, the relationship between religious
conversion and moral conversion, the scale of values, and the importance
of developing the cardinal virtues in our lives. Chapter 7 examines moral
conversion through the lives of saintly people especially St Augustine
and Franz Jaggerstatter. The films *The Mission* and *Romero* illustrate how
moral conversion and religious conversion are closely linked.

Chapter 8 unpacks the importance of affective conversion and the
centrality of love as an art. The damaging effects of self-esteem and social
exclusion cry out for healing. It is important to identify the kind of conditions in which this wounding can heal: communicative communities,
communities of faith and pastoral care, spiritual friendship, restoring
esteem, and compassionate solidarity. The film, *Dead Poets Society*, illustrates the centrality of affectivity and our loving commitment to others.

Chapter 9 explains intellectual conversion, the search for truth,
knowledge, and objectivity, illustrating this form of conversion through
two films, *Dail M for Murder* and *Twelve Angry Men*. It is the contention
of this book that intellectual conversion is one of the most important
forms of conversion for our time due to the debasement of objectivity
and the rise of the will to power.

Chapter 10 explores the importance of psychological conversion
under two forms: conversion from neurosis and psychic conversion.

5. Lonergan, *Method*, 57.

Neurosis usually is accompanied by damaged self-esteem. Terror, rage, and addiction can grip the human heart, robbing it of vitality. Psychological conversion addresses the problem of neurosis. To better appreciate psychic conversion, the place of the psyche and its relationship to the organism and the human spirit is explained. and the need to reverse the impact of repression. Through the film *Ordinary People*, the importance of moving from damaged esteem to positive self-esteem, from neurosis to functioning humanity is illustrated. Chapter 11 argues the link between the pathology of the psyche and the pathology of the human spirit and explores their healing by the power of love. The importance of psychotherapy is illustrated through the autobiographical account by Marie Cardinal and her journey through mental disorder. Using the film trilogy, *The Godfather*, I give an account of a man whose character descends through a pathology of the spirit into a pathology of the psyche.

Chapter 12 brings together religious, moral, intellectual, affective and psychic conversion as dimensions of transformation, to address one of the most severe challenges of our time, ecological conversion. Drawing on the insights of Pope Francis's inspirational document, *Laudato Si'* the needed aspects of ecological conversion are brought into focus. Chapter 13 illustrates through the cinematic trilogy, *The Lord of the Rings*, the difference between an integral ecology and ecocide.

Lastly, chapter 14 presents some touchstones that help us understand what ongoing conversion as transformation might mean interiorly. Finally, the book has been written in a formal style, using second person and third person grammar, however some of the quoted authors have written their texts in the first person. These authors have stepped in the first person in an effort to convey an interior and storytelling approach.

1

Authoring Our Life, Telling Our Story

THE TASK OF THIS book is to help the reader appreciate a possible framework for understanding human transformation. This framework will give some understanding as to how we might better attune ourselves to our feelings, questions, and understandings of truth and reality. By yoking ourselves to the truth, we will be better able to evaluate what is worthwhile, choose responsibly, and be in love. The long-term goal is to author the drama of our lives more profoundly. The first step to authoring our drama is to know ourselves and the person we are becoming. To know ourselves requires that we often ask and answer questions truthfully: Who do we think we are? To whom or to what do the parts of our life belong? Where is our life going? What kind of spontaneous concerns and cares are vital to us and can these widen? What place does critical thinking have in our lives? What do we value and how do we contribute to the human good? To what and to whom are we committed? Why do we do what we do? Do we believe in God or is God merely an idea that does not impact personally? What must we do to transform so as to become a better person?

AUTHORING OUR LIFE

Lonergan is keenly aware that authoring our own lives is a crucial task. Lonergan is convinced that life is a drama and our first work of art is our living.[1] We are to form ourselves into the most splendid and beautiful

---

1. Lonergan, *Insight*, 210.

work that we can be. However, unlike a work of art, our lives are subject to the limitations of embodiment, death, time, and place. We discover that the human drama is never about memorizing some role by merely imitating others. It is not just developing skills handed on to us by someone else in order to cope. The human drama implies that "each of us is burdened with the task of deciding what kind of person we wish to be in the context of the drama of our life."[2] To author our lives authentically into a work of art, we need a new paradigm by which to grasp reality and our place in it. A paradigm offers a framework for getting to what is real and valuable for human living. A new paradigm usually arises when the old one no longer works. Lonergan's paradigm begins with the turn to the subject.[3] This shift means that new terms arise to understand the making of ourselves: subjectivity and self-constitution, authenticity and self-transcendence, intersubjectivity and consciousness.

First, there is the complexity and richness of subjectivity. Tony Kelly states that the desire to understand reality needs to be firmly connected to an inward journey through an exploration of the dimensions of human consciousness and its "endless differentiation."[4] Some of these dimensions include the "objectivity of the scientist, the creativity of the artist, the unutterable experience of the mystic, and in everyday communication and action that makes up the ordinary human world."[5] The turn to the subject indicates a significant shift in the way we express our identity and subjectivity. When questions arise concerning personal identity, values, and commitments, the conscious subject couches their answer in the language of "I am." This language expresses our self-understanding in terms of our successes and failures, our hopes and fears, our sufferings and joys, our awareness of ourselves as a knower and doer, our freedom and responsibility. By contrast, a previous language would have answered questions about identity by stating "man is a rational animal," thus focusing on our common potential to be rational whether we are asleep or awake, children or adults, men or women, people with no learning or people who have attained a doctorate.[6]

2. Braman, *Meaning and Authenticity*, 51.

3. Lonergan, *Collection*, 222–23.

4. Kelly, *Expanding Theology*, 34–35.

5. Kelly, *Expanding Theology*, 35.

6. Lonergan, *Topics in Education*, 80.

Second, there is self-constitution. The transition to being a subject shifts our focus from the objects we make to the way that our discoveries, deeds, and decisions make us. By our decisions and actions, we change as subjects. This transition is a shift to subjectivity, from the object that we desire to know to the subject who acts. There is a shift from outcomes to process. Lonergan states:

> There are from the very nature of the case two periods in human life. In the first period, one is concerned with objects, with coming to do things for oneself, to decide for oneself, to find out for oneself. This is all about objects. But this process of dealing with objects makes one what one is. One develops habits, becomes a certain kind of man or woman by one's actions. But there is that reflective moment in which one discovers that one is not merely dealing with objects but also making oneself. There arises the question of finding out for oneself what one is to make of oneself, of deciding for oneself what one is to be, and of living in fidelity to one's decisions. Such existential commitment is a disposal of oneself.[7]

Third, authoring one's life as a subject will be more or less challenging depending on what may be required for authenticity to come about. There exists the simple person who lives a good and upright life in love with God, neighbor, and the land, aided by a close-knit community who follow the same path. He has pursued a way of life handed down from generation to generation and this way has worked for him. His authenticity is an unreflective imitation of a moral upbringing and religious obedience to the doctrines of faith which are touchstones for his love of God.

Alternatively, authenticity can be a hard-fought struggle to win back one's life free of illusion, pretense, self-deception, false pride and arrogance, surrounded by a community that does not support an authentic life.[8] Moreover, any form of emotional disturbance can prevent or slow down the desire for understanding, assured judgments, and good decisions. Anxiety, grief, fear, and threat can curtail the smooth flowing of our operations. All of these contexts bring enormous challenges, require courage, and invite hope in God. For this reason, Lonergan contrasts between becoming an authentic subject and the life of the drifter. The drifter goes along with the status quo and so "is content to think and say

---

7. Lonergan, *Philosophical and Theological Papers*, 171.
8. Lonergan, *Insight*, 500–502.

what everyone else is thinking or saying."[9] The individual as drifter has not developed. He has not yet chosen a path of self-discovery and not asked questions that search for the motivations of his action. He has not established a mind of his own and not yet cultivated the inward skills to critique factual and moral errors or prejudices. He has not yet found a will of his own. The drifter exists in a community that is more or less a light of integrity in its meanings and values. The community can maintain the drifter in his inauthenticity, preferring that he goes on performing the outworking of some distorted tradition just like everyone else does. In this case, both individuals and communities must transform.

Fourth, Lonergan succinctly states that self-transcendence moves us toward an authentic authoring of our lives.[10] Self-transcendence is the process of going beyond the self that one is to the self that one may become. Through self-transcendence, we go beyond myths and illusions about reality and values and reach up for what is real and truly good. Self-transcendence happens when the innate operations or acts within human consciousness form the basis of all intelligent and responsible living. Lonergan points to degrees of self-transcendence through which we become a subject more and more. We grow in self-transcendence through the symbolism of dreams where we first sense ourselves as subjects and not objects. We advance in self-transcendence when our memories recall pleasures, our imaginations anticipate fears, and we launch into action. While awake, we question and wonder, moving us into a world of inquiry, meaning, and judgments when we discover the truth through sufficient evidence for our insights. We come to the world of responsibility in which making our lives worthwhile and changing the world becomes a deliberate task. Finally, we fall in love, whether the domestic love of husband and wife, the love of our neighbor, and, ultimately, the love of God, thus, overcoming our egocentric concerns.[11] Self-transcendence is at the heart of becoming authentic.

Fifth, whenever we set ourselves the task of authoring our lives, we do so in concert with other people. Lonergan uses the term intersubjectivity to give weight to the importance of our encounter with others.[12] We acquire beliefs about life, judgments about reality, and spontaneous

---

9. Lonergan, *Third Collection*, 200.

10. Lonergan, *Method*, 104.

11. Lonergan, *Third Collection*, 200.

12. Lonergan, *Method*, 57–61.

concerns through community and family. These learnings shape our affective response to one another. The process of encounter is important since persons can mutually exchange who they are to another in such a way that the exchange transforms each other through their mutual sharing. It is only within communities that the individual becomes a person. If the self that the person is becoming outstretches the accepted meanings of the community, then his capacity for active becoming will depend on the ability of the community to be renewed and the capacity of individuals working together to renew.[13]

Sixth, Lonergan's turn to the subject requires an understanding of the nature of human consciousness. Louis Roy speaks about three kinds of consciousness: consciousness-in, consciousness-of, and mystical consciousness.[14] Consciousness-in is the form of consciousness we experience in daily living, a presence to self that permeates all our acts and affective states since we are consciously feeling and acting when dreaming and awake. Consciousness-in is not the same as knowledge. To illustrate consciousness-in, we could think about being caught up watching a movie and not noticing the time fly. We are conscious through the movie, but it may take some reflection to impart to someone else what we know about the film. The activities of experiencing, understanding, judging, and evaluating are operating in our conscious self. However, there is a difference between our conscious performance and knowing our conscious performance. To be a conscious performing subject is not the same as knowing the world or ourselves. To be a conscious performing subject is "being myself more and more fully."[15] This growth in conscious self-awareness and knowledge is a continuous challenge.

The path to objective knowledge whether of ourselves or the world begins in asking questions about our conscious performance. Asking questions about our conscious performance brings us to a second form of consciousness, consciousness-of. In this case, consciousness-of is both conscious and intentional at the same time. Intentionality means that consciousness is heading toward answering questions.[16] It is through consciousness-of that we know both the object to be understood and our conscious activities, even when the object to be understood is ourselves.

13. Lonergan, *Collection*, 227.

14. Roy, *Engaging the Thought*, 142–43

15. Moore, "New Life," 147.

16. Roy, *Engaging*, 144.

Consciousness-of is another term for what Lonergan calls self-appropriation which is examined thoroughly in the next section. Finally, there is mystical consciousness which pertains to religious experience, and chapter 3 will explore its nature.

SELF-DISCOVERY AND SELF-APPROPRIATION

All of us gather up and memorize much knowledge on a host of subjects during our lives. We spend an enormous amount of time on our devices, watching our televisions, or reading print media to know what is going on in an array of subjects. When it comes to the task of authoring our lives, we cannot merely accept the insights of others. We must seek our insights through a process of self-discovery and self-knowledge. We must adhere to the warning of the ancient oracle of Delphi "know thyself." In the previous section, it was noted that we can apply the operations of consciousness as intentional to the operations of consciousness as conscious.

Lonergan's response to the oracle's dictum is self-appropriation. He defines it as the effort to discover who we are, the kind of person we are, and, through this effort, take on the task of being present to ourselves as we respond to the world or ourselves.[17] The word introspection for such a process is not helpful since it suggests looking at one's mind in a spirit of cold detachment. By contrast, self-appropriation is grasping what is happening in human consciousness through a sustained and heightened self-awareness when the person engages concretely in living.[18] Lonergan states that we apply "the operations as intentional to the operations as conscious" whether we are asking questions about ourselves or the world.[19]

Brian Cronin states that knowing ourselves is taking possession of our mind and "taking responsibility for what we do with it."[20] It exists not only to improve our self-understanding but also as the means to a radical transformation of ourselves and the activities within consciousness.[21] Mark Morelli states that self-knowledge "enables us to conduct ourselves more attentively, intelligently, reasonably, deliberately, and responsibly.

17. Lonergan, *Lonergan Reader*, 352.
18. Lonergan, *Method*, 11–14.
19. Lonergan, *Method*, 14.
20. Cronin, *Phenomenology*, 29.
21. Doran, *Theology*, 159.

It enables us to elevate our spontaneous and unreflective commitment to the level of deliberate and reflective commitment."[22] To date, many of us may not have undertaken a serious reflection on our conscious performance. However, as stated, conscious performance and knowledge of our performance are two different things. Robert Doran reminds us that we can be "conscious and ignorant, conscious and questioning, conscious and in error—conscious and not knowing. In all of these operations and states, one is aware of oneself operating and being disposed in such and such a fashion. This awareness is not reflexive. It is not self-knowledge."[23] This fact alone makes our performance fragile and easily derailed. Morelli asserts that, while we may be conscious in our performance, "being conscious in our performance is not *being attentive* to our performance, *inquiring about* our performance, *describing* our performance, *discovering relationships* among the various elements of our performance, or *knowing what we're doing* when we're performing. If we don't know ourselves as conscious performers, we can't claim legitimately to be in possession of ourselves or to be at home with ourselves as conscious performers."[24]

Lonergan states that this second awareness is self-appropriation. Lonergan makes four points concerning self-approriation. He asserts that first, we notice ourselves paying attention, notice ourselves questioning something or ourselves and trying to understand, noticing ourselves finding evidence, noticing ourselves evaluating the truth or otherwise of our insights;[25] second, we understand the unity and relatedness between the operations or activities of consciousness;[26] third, we affirm these operations and verify an invariant pattern;[27] and fourth, we decide to accept this pattern as a norm for living and act according to where it takes us.[28]

Cronin admits to the difficulty of this bifocal gaze: working out some problem while, at the same time, observing the activities of our mind and heart.[29] He suggests a twofold technique for self-appropriation. First, confront the problem, pose questions, struggle with the problem,

22. Morelli, *Self-Possession*, 49.

23. Doran, *Theology*, 68.

24. Morelli, *Self-Possession*, 49.

25. Lonergan, *Method*, 14–15.

26. Lonergan, *Method*, 16.

27. Lonergan, *Method*, 16.

28. Lonergan, *Method*, 16.

29. Cronin, *Phenomenology*, 33.

wait for insights, find a solution, and then relax. Second, "shift our attention back to the experience as it unfolded, including the hints and guesses that point to the solution, the false clues and hunches that lead to a dead end, the flash of insight, the putting down of the pieces of the solution, and the realization that we have solved the problem."[30] This whole approach is grounded in the fact that human consciousness is both conscious and intentional at the same time. As conscious, we are present to ourselves all the time through feeling, thinking, valuing, and acting.[31] As intentional, we are simultaneously reaching out to the world around us or ourselves seeking knowledge of truth and values. Chapter 3 will elaborate the operations of the conscious subject more precisely.

The Challenge and Difficulty of Self-Appropriation

Self-appropriation is a task that bears enormous fruitfulness in self-discovery when we persist. However, it is a challenging and difficult task for many reasons. First, human consciousness is a complex and multi-layered reality. Lonergan refers to this complexity as the "polymorphism of consciousness."[32] When we speak of consciousness being polymorphic, we attest to the fact that our concerns potentially put us in touch with an enormous variety of human experiences, meanings, judgment, and values. Alternatively, each of us can be question free or questioning, wondering or lacking in wonder, critical or uncritical, and evaluative or lacking evaluation. Each of us can react to what is present or, alternatively, be thoughtful with our response.

Second, Lonergan notes that the consciousness of most people is an "undifferentiated" conscious field, a quality readily observed in early childhood.[33] It means that many people make little effort to distinguish between inner and outer activities, process and content, between knowing and knowledge, valuing and values. James Marsh recalls one of his first philosophy teachers stating that "2 percent of people think, 4 percent think that they think, and 94 percent would rather die than think."[34]

---

30. Cronin, *Phenomenology*, 33.

31. Cronin, *Phenomenology*, 31. Cronin provides a comprehensive list of the myriad of mental activities possible.

32. Lonergan, *Insight*, 410–12.

33. Lonergan, *Method*, 84–85.

34. Marsh, "Self-Appropriation as a Way," 312.

The more we distinguish and take time to attend to our subjectivity, the more our consciousness becomes differentiated. Joseph Flanagan likens the process of differentiation to listening to a motet in four voices, each singing in a different register. He states that to "differentiate four simultaneously heard voices is difficult enough, but after attending to and differentiating their melodic, rhythmic, and tonal differences, you must go further and attend to their blending and integrating patterns which are producing the changing textures and harmonies that you are hearing."[35]

There is the differentiation of consciousness that verifies the four levels of consciousness discovered in the process of knowing and valuing, and the activities within each level. By differentiating, we distinguish between a common meaning of the word "experience" and a technical meaning. The seven distinct patterns of experience, with all their various orientations, also create complexity. These include: biological, practical, intellectual, dramatic, aesthetic/artistic, and religious. While the experiential starting point might be difference, our performance can be unreflective and not informed by self-understanding or deliberative and guided by self-understanding. There are also the four differentiated realms of meaning: common sense, theoretic, interiority, and mystical. Lastly, there is the process of conversion as religious, moral, affective, intellectual, and psychological/psychic. The chapters ahead will unpack the meaning and significance of these elements of differentiation. All these elements point to the importance of knowing subjectivity. However, its complexity can leave us with the feeling that the conscious and intentional self is too elusive and too tricky to get to know.

Third, self-appropriation is difficult since we live under the misapprehension that human consciousness is akin to something like a black box flight recorder, unable to be penetrated. In the physical sciences, a black box is a device that we understand in terms of its inputs and outputs without any knowledge of its internal workings. The process by which things happen is rendered opaque. This assumption seems to put a stop to our desire for self-discovery or, at least, favors a discovery of self that looks at outward behavior and actions alone. Such is the mistaken view regarding human consciousness. When combined with our extraverted orientation and the erroneous idea that reality is out there to be observed, the task of self-discovery seems insurmountable.

35. Flanagan, *Quest for Self-Knowledge*, 235.

Fourth, self-appropriation is also very difficult since it is unimaginable. We find it difficult to imagine realms of meaning and operations of consciousness though we have a habit of speaking about them as if they were spatial objects or events. Mistakenly, we tend to think that only what we imagine can be known. It took science years to discover that the objects it was enquiring about need not be imaginable or moving through space/time.[36] Following Lonergan, Matthews states that the acts of consciousness are "a form of unimaginable self-awareness that accompanies and is causally inseparable from our intentional living in the world."[37] It is not like seeing a mountain or hearing a train or tasting a fruit where each gives us a sensible image from which we can experience curiosity, ask questions, seek insights, verify our ideas and come to judgments about what is real.

Personal Story and Self-Appropriation

Despite the difficulties of self-appropriation, our personal story helps us recognize and give shape to the unimaginable acts of consciousness that are involved in all our projects. Our relationship with the world around us comes out of our relationship to ourselves. We begin to understand our circumstances or situation but also our inner responses to them, which have shaped the past, currently form the person we are today, and anticipate the future. Our inner responses are the mark of our character. Through our story, we discover our innate desire for personal identity, wonder, curiosity, meaning, truth, objectivity, values, love, and religious and interpersonal commitment, while drawing from the worlds of work, society, relationships, public, and private. We can say that the operations of consciousness are guided by a number of basic commitments which include our search for meaning, objectivity, knowledge, truth, reality, and value.[38] Even if a person does not believe in the ideas just expressed, their arguments would still be a search for meaning and truth and, thereby, an engagement of these basic commitments.

Through storytelling, we recognize the processes of creativity and healing that have occurred in our lives. The narration relates what excites us, impresses us or disturbs us, what sets a firm determination

36. Hughes, *Transcendence*, 21.
37. Matthews, "On Memoir, Biography," 308.
38. Morelli, *Self-Possession*, 12–14

within us, what makes us ask questions, what helps motivate us toward understanding, and what we decide is genuinely worthwhile and why. The importance of narrating the story of our lives also highlights that meaning and truth are not only discovered but also chosen and made. We are meaning-makers as well as people who discover meaning. We constitute ourselves and the world. However, our meaning-making operates out of a framework of adopted ideas and values, often implicit and mostly unknown. This framework needs to be recognized, and often it needs to transform if we are to become more authentic. Our understanding of reality, judgments about values, and the choices we make can feed into our worldview, reinforcing our thinking, or challenge us to change. They not only improve our world but they change us into the person we are becoming. Finally, when we endeavor to tell our story as truthfully and honestly as we can, we will find that when we read the story back, the story interprets us.

The Responsibility of Telling our Story

Telling our story carries with it a set of responsibilities. We do not tell our story for the sake of the positive feelings that come from being listened to nor for the praise of others. We tell our story to name our experiences, learn our history, broaden our shrunken horizons through insight, transform inwardly, and make the world a better place in some small way. Through telling our personal story truthfully in all its light and darkness, we are better able to decide to choose what is best and, with the will to carry it out, better able to consent to grow authentically as an individual and in a community. The story expresses the journey of our soul through signposting significant events. If this is so, then telling our story truthfully is essential and the first step to personal freedom; therefore, having a language and framework for this task is equally important.

Telling our story is not the same as recording our reminiscences. Alex Nelson proposes that the distinguishing quality of a life story is not necessarily getting the historical details accurate but rather in its capacity to help us move onto a new and next chapter of our lives.[39] While our story may recall the past and reflect on present experiences, we tell it so that we may give an account of ourselves and look forward to transformation. We tell our story so that we may gently confront ourselves amid life

---

39. Nelson, "Imagining and Critical Reflection," 1–3.

by entering more authentically into our circumstances. Our spontaneous concerns shape our anticipations which in turn shape our present, as well as the way we may choose to remember the past. Consequently, a tense unity exists between our concerns and anticipations, our response to the present, and our memory of the past. The crucial point is to tell our story to learn from our life, recognize aspects of change, gain self-understanding, and participate in ongoing formation.

One of the least helpful features of our cultural unease is the possibility of social and personal fragmentation. Within such fragmentation, there is no story to tell. The pace of change in our societies, the explosion of collective knowledge, the diversity in various lifestyles, and the propensity to take a smorgasbord and self-serving approach to our life direction, increases the possibility that our lives will not be unified but fragmented. It would be a mistake to view our decisions and actions as discontinuous moments having no meaning for us as a whole. Reflecting on the insights of Alasdair MacIntyre, William Matthews poses the critical question for a holistic life: "How do actions and conversations add up or cohere in the unity of a human life?"[40] Narrative storytelling becomes a significant means of uniting the parts to the whole. While each of us is occupied in many activities, telling our story is akin to making known and authoring our life as a unity.

Matthew makes it very clear that we do not set out with a design or blueprint for our lives. We may make plans, but life's circumstances may cause us to change direction. The design is something left behind and, when recognized, takes the form of a story.[41] Within those many activities that make up the drama of our lives, only a small portion have truly significant and momentous importance. Only a small number of questions and decisions are indeed life-changing. These are the historical markers of our life. There is a relationship between these events and the values we take hold of in our lives. These significant moments are varied and many. We can point to the experiences of wonder and curiosity toward understanding a field of knowledge. The emergence of a significant insight whether practical, religious, moral, relational or about ourselves are poignant for us. The chance or planned meeting with some person who changes the way we feel about ourselves, think about life, or who shapes what is or is not worthwhile in our lives becomes central. There

40. Matthews, "Fragmented," 206.
41. Matthews, "Fragmented," 215.

are also suffering moments that make us ask specific questions and go searching for the answers.[42]

John Dunne distinguishes between a story of behavior and a story of action.[43] A story of behavior is one where we recount the various situations and incidents of our life in terms of our behavior as a response to a stimulus. Situations become merely the occasions for behavior and behavior simply represents our reaction to stimuli. By contrast, a story of action is one where it has become possible for us to act due to insight. Insight takes place in the moment. Insight comes out of questioning and is self-reflexive. We know that we know. There is insight into your action,[44] insight into your character, insight into your successes and failures,[45] insight into the situation that you find yourself in, insight into the relationship between your life and your time,[46] and insight into the relationship of your life to all time. Whenever one's life is underpinned by insight, it is no longer simply a set of behaviors. It becomes a story of action and character formation. The life of action is a transformation of the story of stimulus and behavior. No doubt for many, our stories are made up of a combination of behaviors and actions following insight. The more that our story is simply behavior as a reaction to stimuli, the less we will know why we do what we do. The fear in the story of behavior is the temptation to control or be controlled simply through reading the stimuli and responding adequately.[47] When our story becomes a life of action, we engage in the sharing and the receiving of insight, and then, all we have to fear is fear itself.

My Story and My Voice

If a critical task in life is to tell our story truthfully, then another task is to speak it in our voice. There was a time when various groups of people could not speak their voice. Indigenous groups under the oppression of colonization cried out for a hearing in their voice, rather than their voices being conveniently suppressed and forgotten. Women asked

42. Matthews, "Fragmented," 219.
43. Dunne, *Way of All the Earth*, 184.
44. Dunne, *Way of All the Earth*, 170.
45. Dunne, *Way of All the Earth*, 172.
46. Dunne, *Way of All the Earth*, 171.
47. Dunne, *Way of All the Earth*, 184.

others, especially men, to hear their voices so that they could attain equal citizenship. The poor and oppressed asked for a hearing of their story so that economic and social rights, as well as just civil and political rights, might be pursued. In all these examples, the question as to who is telling the story becomes relevant. It needs to be one's own story with one's own voice. We cannot be imitating someone else's story in someone else's voice.

In the modern period, the link between knowledge and power has become explicit in our societies. Generally, the more knowledge we have, the more choices we will be. All knowledge comes to us by two means: knowledge acquired and passed on through generations as part of a social heritage and knowledge gained by empirically and immanently understanding the issues ourselves and working through our relevant questions. This insight prompts us to ask these questions: how reliable are the social sources of knowledge that we accept on trust? Have we been given the power to generate our knowledge and story? Is knowledge anything more than a set of opinions held by the most important groups in society? Knowledge gained through our acts of intelligence and responsibility complements the knowledge we gain through social sources which we accept on trust. There have always existed forms of social control that sought to keep people in their place and stop them from generating their knowledge. The breaking of social and cultural barriers has meant that people, once silenced, have found a voice to express a desire for human liberation.

Cynthia Crysdale presents many insights into how women especially have transformed from "receivers" to "discoverers" of their voice and the story of women in Western societies.[48] She presents this progression of discovery in several stages. First, there was a time, surprisingly in recent history, when women could not tell their stories.[49] They were told to keep silent. Silencing often went hand in hand with abuse whether physical, emotional, sexual, or spiritual. Women lived in fear and disesteem. They felt that they did not have the right to speak. They were not encouraged to give voice to their experiences.

Second, it seems that minor breakthroughs happened. If they communicated knowledge of themselves put together by other more powerful

---

48. Crysdale, *Embracing Travail*, 76–82.

49. Crysdale, *Embracing Travail*, 77–78.

groups, usually men, then, they found an acceptance of their story.[50] Tellingly, women were still in the position where their knowledge came from what others said about them, and so identity became a subset of what others thought of them. They were told by others what to say about themselves, what to feel about themselves, what to think about themselves, what their place was in the world, what they were and were not capable of, and even whom they would or would not marry.

Third, even at this point, another breakthrough happened. Women's stories progressed to what was personal, private, and subjectively gained, usually because their own financial and social circumstances or their sense of personal significance changed for the better.[51] They felt enough personal power to speak. Once thrust into positions of responsibility, they began to think that the truth told by others about them was breaking down. Sometimes, however, their personal story came through, but with their violent history of putdowns and suppression biasing their thinking. With the possibility of education, people developed to the point of articulating their story with courage but also with critical judgments, well-argued by reason, and grounded in evidence. They educated themselves in ways of understanding themselves through the lens of economic, political, psychological, feminist, and liberationist frameworks.

Fourth, people developed to the point of acknowledging the worth of both the content of their critical judgments and the discovery of their creative inner processes.[52] They learned the difference between the content of knowledge and the operations of knowing and valuing that answer questions such as: what are we doing when we are knowing? What are we doing when we are evaluating and choosing? They valued their subjectivity. They could judge between what they had learned from others, what their efforts brought by way of learnings, and what was going on interiorly when they were learning anything at all. They came to realize that the truth of the matter was not merely about perception, listening to gut instinct, or memorizing the "right" answers. They grew an interiorly based self-awareness and self-discovery so they would be able to know anything including their consciousness and its operations critically: their feeling, seeing, hearing, sensing, daydreaming, symbolizing, paying attention, understanding, thinking, comparing and contrasting, analyzing,

50. Crysdale, *Embracing Travail*, 78–79.

51. Crysdale, *Embracing Travail*, 79–80.

52. Crysdale, *Embracing Travail*, 80–82.

evaluating, choosing, and deciding. Lonergan asserts that, through this inward process, we become critical and self-critical thinkers, valuers and doers and start to create "the first and only edition" of our lives.[53]

Escape, Quest, and Love Stories

Michael Paul Gallagher believes in the importance of telling our story. To help others in the process of storytelling, he speaks about three kinds of stories going on in our lives at any one time that form the inner kernel of transformation: escape stories, quest stories, and encounter or love stories.[54]

Escape Stories

First, there are escape stories. Lonergan holds a healthy awareness of the challenge each of us has in escaping inauthenticity, both individual or communal, whether through poor personal choices or mistaken ideas absorbed from a distorted, devaluated, and corrupted tradition.[55] Lonergan calls the person's individual flight from understanding, the major inauthenticity and the distortions within traditions, the minor inauthenticity. Escape stories focus on becoming free or regaining lost freedom and on escaping from the false self to the true self. They center on escaping desolate and negative thinking and moving toward. They tell of people seeking release from superficiality to living from the depth of ourselves.

Escape stories move us from a religious faith that thinks about God as "out there" to a religious feeling and wonder that experiences the mystery of God "in here." It shifts us from unworthy and immature images of god to God revealed in the face of Jesus. These stories seek to heal the anxious attainment of perfection by instilling patience with our own shadow. They generate gratitude, hope, and openness to suffering, positive esteem, generosity, and freedom as we move away from destructive anger, a will to control, disesteem, selfishness, and the unfreedom in not seeking God.

We find escape stories in abundance through the Holy Scriptures. The Exodus of God's people from the slavery of Egypt and their entry

53. Lonergan, *Second Collection*, 72.
54. Gallagher, *Free to Believe*, 1–6.
55. Lonergan, *Method*, 80.

into the Promised Land is an escape and freedom story. The captivity of the people of God in Babylon and their second Exile to their return to the city of Jerusalem is an escape story. The Gospel stories of men and women caught in dehumanizing ways of living and then encountering the healing of Jesus are stories about liberation. Escape stories recall the words of Jesus: "no one can serve two masters" (Matt 6:24).[56] At some point, people have felt the need to escape what was not working for them but were unsure where to find freedom and liberation. Just getting to the point of wanting to find liberation can be a significant achievement and revelation. The process of getting past self-deception, denials, avoidances, and rationalizations to the point of acknowledging that "this is not working for me" comes about due to insight. We can feel this desire stirring within first as dissatisfaction with ourselves or the status quo and, then, by observing the edifice of our self-made existence crumble. A period of unhelpful routine living or half-existing is interrupted by unexpected love or suffering which makes us wake up and question our lives.[57] We find that our indolent complacency cannot sustain life and things do not hold together any longer. In the words of W. B. Yeats, "Things fall apart, the center cannot hold."[58]

Quest Stories

Second, there are quest stories. Again, chapter 2 will demonstrate the importance that Lonergan places on understanding the eros of the human mind and, in this case, the desire or quest to know and value. Lonergan's concern is to answer a question: what are we doing when we are knowing and choosing? Quest stories are concerned to help us find focus in our lives and move us from the known to the unknown. In her program, *Conversations*, on the ABC Australian Radio Network, Sarah Kanowski interviewed Helen Lewis.[59] Helen Lewis's father, Mike Lewis, was a cameraman with the British Army Film Unit during the Second World War. In April 1945, Lewis was sent to film the liberation by British and Canadian troops of the Bergen-Belsen Nazi Concentration Camp. He was there for ten days, not only creating an enduring record but also

---

56. All Scriptural texts come from the NRSV.

57. Gallagher, *Free to Believe*, 21.

58. Yeats, *Collected Poems*, 158.

59. Lewis, "Seeing Bergen-Belsen."

as a witness to the horrors wrought by the Holocaust. When Helen was a child, she happened across some photographs her father made while filming the camps. She never told anyone of her discovery and spent decades avoiding the subject of the war with her father. Later in life, Helen undertook academic research on imagery shot in wartime. She wanted to understand the effect of context on the photographer or cinematographer. Helen traced her father's life story, and the events he captured on film. When asked by Kanowski, the interviewer, why she undertook such a work, Helen responded that for her it was *a quest* to find the truth behind the photos of her father and of what happened for him at Bergen-Belsen. Finding the truth about her father was the goal of her quest.

If truth is the purpose of questing, there are at least two different ways of speaking about truth. First, we affirm the truth when we can find evidence for our insights. We do not jump to conclusions or think that our perceptions alone will give up the truth. The evidence for some insight describes what it takes for the idea to be correct. Truth is real knowledge. If it is real knowledge then it is objective and a source of knowledge for others anywhere. Knowledge may be one of the best ways to care for someone pastorally for actual knowledge puts us in touch with reality. False or half-truth leads us to confusion and poor choices. The truth alone stands between us and darkness. However, the task of discovering the truth is challenging and requires quiet determination.

Again, the program *Conversations* on the ABC Radio Network captures the crucial social function of truth when the Australian novelist, Richard Flanagan, speaking of his new book, *First Person*, talks on the topic of truth with the presenter, Richard Fidler. Flanagan shapes the central antagonist of his novel out of the memories of his encounters with a historical person, John Friedrich, one of Australia's most notorious con men. Friedrich was a person who told lies and defrauded people regularly and who was fundamentally egocentric, lacking all ability to engage in the truth. Flanagan is well aware of the vital function of truth as the lens by which to read our lives whether as individuals or in political society. Reflecting on the global situation, Flanagan asserts that truth has come under attack by political commentators. Flanagan clarifies that he is not alluding to the fact that politicians lie. Lying by politicians has always been the case. Instead, it is a question of these lies having a new goal, which is to deny the very concept of the truth. He judges that people have eroded the very idea of objective truth and have replaced it by the voice of sheer power, while disempowering everyone else.

AUTHORING OUR LIFE, TELLING OUR STORY 19

Chillingly, Flanagan states that those who are most powerful will tell the rest of us what the world is and all will have to agree with it. People will no longer have the power to say what the world is. He states that "we are only left with opinion. In the words of Karl Rove, 'we are the Empire now, and we will create our own reality and you will follow that reality.' And that is power saying we will tell you what the world is and you will have to accept it."[60]

Second, we capture another way of understanding the truth in the question: what is our particular truth? This truth is more of an existential question. Truth leads us to ask: What does this knowledge ask us to do? Knowing this truth, what will bring about the human good? It is about what is truly valuable for the individual and society. Margaret Silf offers some insight into the concreteness of existential truth. She speaks about the secondary importance of questions that concern themselves with hypotheticals such as: Where could any of us have been had we picked up specific opportunities presented to us? Where do we wish we could be if we did not have to be in this place? Would people think differently toward us, if our circumstances were different?[61] Silf asks us to put all these considerations aside since "if we do manage to act out of our true reference point, we find that a whole new source of energy breaks open inside of us. We experience *liberation*, freeing us to do the true thing, make the true choice, from a place of power, because there and only there, our own desire, our own who-center, is aligned with God's desire for us."[62] Silf is asserting that what matters is where we are right now in our lives. Where we concretely stand is our right reference point, and where we are now is the place where we will find the truth and God.

In quest stories, we go searching for the truth in a critical and self-critical manner. We might discover religious truth, historical truth, personal truth, or interpersonal truth. We also may need to know scientific truth about the created universe. All these differentiations of truth can work in creative collaboration for the sake of personal and communal transformation. Living informed by truth might impel us toward discovering the reality of climate science as much as deepening religious insights. In terms of knowledge, it is as much about practical ideas that will help us accomplish some critical task as it is about theoretical and

60. Flanagan, "Fredrich and Flanagan." Karl Rove was a Senior Advisor and Assistant to President George W. Bush when Bush decided to invade Iraq.

61. Silf, *Landmarks*, 182–83.

62. Silf, *Landmarks*, 186.

philosophic insights that help explain how the universe works. It may involve an intentional shift to go beyond common sense knowing where the whole focus is practical and move to a more technical knowledge that tries to untangle the knots of more difficult questions. It may involve the personal task of telling our story with all its emotional intensity. However, to find truth implies critical thinking and evidence. To be self-critical requires us to appropriate ourselves so that we can verify that we have asked all the relevant questions regarding our life direction. In turn, this may involve uprooting stubborn interior biases that might prevent the truth from emerging.

If we are searching for religious truth, we might ask: Are there experiential pointers within life that indicate a "hungering" for God? If people get the feeling that life is ultimately unsatisfying, is that dissatisfaction the end of the story? Similarly, if we are searching for personal truth, we might ask: In moments of intense vulnerability when our self-sufficiency breaks down and the unrecognized hunger of the human heart roar to be acknowledged, what is going on within us? To what might such a person be invited? In his poem *Journey of the Magi*,[63] T. S. Eliot puts certain words on the lips of the wise men once they had come to the end of their travels and returned home. Whatever may have been their original religious worldview, there were specific experiential pointers that answered their questions at the manger in Bethlehem. They followed the star patiently and with great difficulty to arrive at Bethlehem. They thought that the lowly stable in Bethlehem would be the end of their quest; however, having returned to their place of origin, they come to realize that their search had only just begun. They found themselves uneasy in their old way of life and had assessed that the discovery of the child left their lives disrupted and ready for transformation. Eliot puts on their lips the moral insight that the truth for them would involve death and rebirth.

Such an experience reminds us of Maria Rainer Rilke who asserts that people who stay with the 'whys' in their lives, find their answers, partially and rarely fully, especially when we ask the right questions. People seek answers to questions and are not satisfied until they receive the answers that most fit. Often, these answers are not absolute certainties nor the kind truth we might find in mathematics. Truth often means growing in approximations. Truthful answers lead us to a point where to go on authentically often means making a commitment that affects the

63. Eliot, *Poems and Plays*, 68.

whole person. However, it is the rupturing power of truth that brings about such commitments. We allow it to get under our skin and we consent to suffer it.

Love Stories

Third, there are love or encounter stories. Lonergan asserts that beyond the desire to know, yet continuous with it and giving it a new direction, is the desire to embrace genuine values and to be attracted to all that is good through expressions of love. For Lonergan, love is the highest way of being a human being.[64] There are many different love stories, and each of us must draw to mind our own love stories. For the religious pilgrim, the Christian fulfillment of all human love is encountering God in Christ moved by his understanding, power, and compassion in such a way as to sense a being-in-love with God. Equally, love stories point to relationships of affectivity between human persons. Indeed, when we examine the language of love, we use the expression "to fall in love" meaning that such an event knocks us off balance, we are no longer in control, and we are drawn by the strangeness of the other. Each of us gives consent to the experience of falling in love through being generously open to a gift. What happens next is an achievement in cooperation with the gift. Jerome Miller proposes that when we fall in love, we are "drawn by the strangeness of the Other, the uncanny wonderment of her which is disarming and impossible to define. The very Otherness of the Other beckons me out of my self. We can see how fundamentally falling in differs from sensuality, where my experience of the Other is subordinate to my experience of the desire she arouses in me. In falling in love, I am carried out of myself towards another who opens up an infinite world to me."[65] The lovers cannot account for their "falling" in love just as the artist cannot account for their inspiration. Miller proposes that the lover acts on us "with a mysterious power and bestows on us an unearned grace."[66]

Chapter 3 will examine the fundamental importance of being in love with God and chapter 8 will explore the quality of affectivity. At this stage we can affirm that there exist a variety of ways that acts of love reveal themselves to us. Richard Flanagan, the author of the Man Booker

64. Lonergan, *Method*, 105–6.
65. Miller, *Way of Suffering*, 30.
66. Miller, *Way of Suffering*, 31.

Prize-winning novel, *The Narrow Road to the Deep North*, relates how a story of love influenced the structure of his prize-winning book. His father recounts the story of a Latvian man living in the town of Longford, Tasmania where Flanagan's father was born. This man had been displaced from his hometown far away through the devastation and ravages of war that swept Eastern Europe. He managed to get back to his Latvian village after the war. He found it razed to the ground and those who were still living told him that his young wife was dead. Flanagan recounts how this man refused to believe that his wife was dead and for the next two years roamed "the wastelands of post-war Europe—the east, the west, the DP centers, [and] the Red Cross camps—for his wife, all to no avail. He finally had to accept the terrible truth: she had perished. The husband immigrated to Australia, came to live in Longford, married and had a family. In 1957 he visited Sydney. One day, while walking down a crowded street, he saw coming towards him his Latvian wife, alive, with a child on either hand. At that moment he had to decide whether he would acknowledge her or walk on by."[67] Flanagan relates that the man chose to walk on rather than stop. Though moved by deep affection and despite many years looking for her, he could only think of the pain that such a meeting would bring to her life and so out of love he kept walking.

The Three Colors Trilogy and Human Stories[68]

The *Three Colors* trilogy (1993–1994) is a set of films that reflect the process of human transformation. The films broadly unfold the threefold typology already described: escape, quest, and love stories. Each of the films explore subjectivity, the search for meaning and love, and the desire for freedom.

Three Colors Blue

The first film in the trilogy, *Three Colors Blue* (1993), is set in Paris, France. It is the story of Julie de Courcy, who is a wife and mother. In the first minutes of the film, Julie, returning home with her celebrated composer husband, Patrice and their young daughter, crashes the car and both her husband and daughter die. Julie is driving though it is clear the accident

67. Flanagan, "On Love Stories."
68. In the French, these are known as the *Trois Couleurs* Trilogy.

is due to a mechanical fault. The consequences of the fateful crash will include a journey of personal discovery for Julie. She will go through grief and an identity crisis. She will embark on a journey to put together her life. Julie will have to sort out where to go and what to do with her life. The audience is thereby launched quickly into Julie's escape story. It is a dramatic plunging into the darkness of grief and the traumatic destruction of her old world. The question that confronts the audience is whether she will be able to escape from this dark world to something new and different yet unknown. By the end of the film, the audience is allowed only a glimpse of a possible new world emerging for Julie.

Several insights into Julie's inner turmoil present themselves. While recovering in hospital, Julie causes a diversion by smashing a window, so that she can get access to the medicine cabinet and swallow a mouthful of pills, in an attempt to suicide. She tries but spits them from her mouth and proceeds to apologize to the nurse who looks at her with compassionate eyes. Julie tells the nurse: "I cannot, I am unable, I broke the window; I am sorry." A family friend, Olivier, who was collaborating with Julie's husband on a musical score for the Unification of Europe Ceremony, brings Julie a small monitor so that she can watch the funeral of her husband and daughter by video link from her hospital bed.

Julie finally comes home from the hospital, and the first thing we notice is that her maid and the gardener are more outwardly upset at the tragic events than Julie herself. Julie's life has been turned upside down. She has become a mixture of numbness and stoicism. Her immediate response is to clear the decks. She puts their large villa and the property up for sale and rids herself of her belongings. In time she proceeds to throw out the musical score. This cleansing is her way of achieving a kind of freedom through being unencumbered, by shaking off the past. It is Julie's way of being in control rather than suffering the questions this tragic disruption brings to her.

All along, some incidents communicate to the audience that Julie is inwardly traumatized and, concurrently, some of her actions are those of a woman trying to break a psychic numbness. For example, she consumes sweet candy popsicles quickly to ingest the sugar, presumably to feel a quick energy high. Julie invites Olivier to have sex with her so that at least she might feel something bodily. She brushes her clenched fist against a hard and rough wall, grazing it and drawing blood. On many occasions, we observe something of Julie's dark interior disposition. When the real estate agent, trying to find her an apartment in the city, asks her what she does for a living, she answers him "nothing." She tells the young man, who witnesses the crash and who wants to give her back a necklace he discovered at the scene, that "nothing is important." Visiting her demented mother, now in a nursing home and unable to recognize Julie, Julie declares that she has no memories, no belongings, and nothing of meaningfulness in her life any longer. Julie has become another version of her mother, except the memory loss comes from suppression and the fear of facing an all-consuming abyss.

Despite her efforts to remain unencumbered, her memory and the people around her pull her back to what she is truly feeling. Every time she goes swimming, the music that she and her husband had been working on, an *Ode for the Unification of Europe*, bursts into her awareness. She cannot prevent it from filling her consciousness both disturbing and exciting her. She finds herself becoming personally involved with one of the apartment block renters, Lucille, who works in an XXX Club performing explicit sexual acts for the audience. A petition goes around the apartment block to have Lucille expelled. Julie will have no part of it. She responds when Lucille has a crisis one night at the Club. Lucille notices her father in the audience and realizes a breach has happened in the psychological anonymity between the audience and sex worker/performer. Julie is concerned enough to ask Lucille why she does this kind of work. Lucille's response indicates a lonely heart.

In another scene, while looking at a montage of photographs of her husband on the wall, Julie discovers photos of her husband together with a young and beautiful woman. She realizes what this could mean: that her husband had been having an affair. Confirmed by Olivier, Julie seeks out the young lady and introduces herself. The woman is in the legal profession. She has been having a relationship with Julie's husband over several years and is pregnant with Patrice's child. Julie's response is to leave the house and property to her and her future child.

Finally, despite at first refusing many offers by Olivier to finish the musical score started by her and her husband, Julie is drawn into the enterprise and together they complete the musical score. The music score comes with a choral piece, a homage to St. Paul's hymn of love (1 Cor 13:1–2, 4–8, 13). The choir sings the words in the language of the original New Testament Greek. In this text, Paul gives weight to the primacy and unrestricted summons of love. These musical lyrics are the closest that the director, Krzysztof Kieslowski, gets to reveal the importance of divine love implicitly at work in the lives of the protagonists.

Julie's story is that of a woman who has a controlled and predictable plan for her life and the life of her family, until the tragic death of her only daughter and husband. The viewer gets the sense that she is generous and kind, dutiful, non-judgmental, modest, and sacrificial, often putting her feelings in second place to the feelings of others. Her life belonged to another moral order prior to the accident. After the accident, her former world has come crashing down, and the audience wonders whether she will ever recover given her trauma. The people and events around her draw her out of her grief and into a new world, where her feelings and commitments matter. In the final scene of the film, Julie is in bed with Olivier making love, and we see for the first time, tears streaming down her face with the words and music of the hymn of love filling her conscious awareness. The audience intuits the possibility that her healing can now begin.

Three Colors White

In the second of the trilogy, *Three Colors White* (1994), set partly in France and mostly in Poland, Karol and Dominique, a married couple, introduce themselves to the audience. At the beginning of the film, they are in a French court where Dominique is suing for divorce from Karol for the non-consummation of their marriage. When asked by the judge what this case is about, Dominique responds that she does not love her husband any longer. It is clear to her that if her husband is not prepared to have a sexual relationship with her, then he is not serious about the marriage, let alone the possibility of creating a family. The audience suspects that the lack of sexual activity have to do with Karol's obsession to be financially successful.

Through a series of events, Karol, now separated from Dominique, is helped by Mikolaj, a fellow Pole, to get back to Poland. In time, Karol proves cunning in buying land off farmers and selling it back to shady entrepreneurs. The action is also risky and reckless. This story is set against a political backdrop of political corruption and the breakdown of the political order in Poland. Karol makes enough money from his risky enterprise to set himself up in business and becomes very wealthy.

The rest of the film concerns Karol's whimsical efforts to get back with his wife. Karol hatches a plot to get Dominque to come to Poland. He orchestrates his death, putting a purchased corpse in the funeral casket.

He devises a scheme in such a way that it later appears to the police that Dominique has murdered her husband to benefit from the will. On the day of the funeral, Karol waits for Dominique in her apartment, naked in her bed. When she arrives, she is wholly startled, thinking him dead. They make love, and Dominique is delighted, supposing that all will be well between them. However, Karol has planned Dominique's downfall. The police arrive, arrest her, and take Dominque to jail. In the final scene, Karol visits Dominique in prison. From the courtyard, they both see each other, Dominique from her prison cell window on the fourth floor and Karol from ground level. She more or less gestures to him: freedom from prison and we will be a married couple again. We leave Karol with tears streaming down his face.

This film is a love story that starts at the place where love stories usually come to an end, the divorce courts. From there, unbeknownst to each of the protagonists, it is the story about two people finding their way back to one another by a strange route. Remembering the day of their marriage becomes for them both an essential aspect of their ultimate desire to reunite. Each recalls their kiss on the steps of the church. For Dominique love must include sexual union, if it is to be married love. We never understand why Karol has become impotent while in France. We suspect that the priority of financial success is an offshoot of his days in Poland when food and money were always limited and the fear of hunger was always there. Later, we can only assume that becoming financially successful gives Karol a boost to his self-esteem and so he feels able to make love to his wife. We are left wondering whether Karol will make affectivity the most important priority of his marriage. Like the story told by Richard Flanagan regarding the Latvian man, love stories are both numerous and different in their texture and context.

Three Colors Red

Three Colors Red (1994) is the third film of the trilogy and is set in Geneva, Switzerland. The central protagonist of the film is Valentine, a university student who does modeling work to pay the bills. Valentine is warm, beautiful, kind, generous, vulnerable, and exudes child-like innocence. She has a moral compass. After accidentally hitting a dog with her car, she tracks down the dog's owner, the retired judge, Joseph Kern. Their relationship becomes vital to the story, with two other connections also introduced to the audience: the relationship between a law student, Auguste, sitting for his exams, and his girlfriend, Karin; as well as the failing relationship between Valentine and her boyfriend, Michel.

The film carries many themes. It is a reflection on the nature of altruism and the limits of love: Can altruism come from a pure self-giving heart or is it merely a disguised form of self-centeredness? Ought we to not waste time trying to rescue people, especially when it causes us to suffer, preferring only to let people find their path, even if it means their self-destruction? It is a reflection on destiny: Is destiny determined or in our own hands or are the lives of people the outcome only of chaos? It prompts us to reflect ethically upon the question of truth in a social setting: Should the truth of people's lives, especially their moral lives, be laid bare to all? Should this be done even if it means violating their privacy and bringing about suffering towards those who love them? At one juncture, Auguste has passed his exams and wants to celebrate with Karin. She cannot be contacted so he goes to her apartment only to find her making love to another man. Karin could not speak the painful truth of her heart to August, namely, that she did not love him anymore. Instead, he discovers this truth in a most shocking way. The film takes the side of being truthful and speaking the truth with love even when relationships are mired in problems rather than avoiding or denying them.

Valentine's meeting with the world-weary and cynical retired judge challenges her to face some of these questions. Valentine is shocked at the thought of having to justify her self-giving, but by the end of the film, she is a fuller and richer person for having done so. The judge presents as someone who has given up on the best in human beings, preferring to take the stance that in the end we are all in the hands of fate and nothing counts. By the end of the film, we sense that the judge has shifted to a place in his life where he can appreciate the importance of love. The developing relationship of friendship between himself and Valentine and his valuing of what she thinks, causes him to confess to the authorities that he has been breaking the law by listening to the phone calls of his neighbors. This first step of his truth-telling helps him to find integrity, and his friendship with Valentine helps him to regain his worth as a human being.

The final scene of the film has the protagonists of all three films, Julie and Olivier, Karol and Dominique, Valentine and Auguste, surviving an English Channel ferry accident. Most of the other passengers have not survived. The audience leaves with this hopeful assurance: despite the tragedies that visit us and destroy our world, and may potentially render us cynical and nihilistic, there is still hope. The circumstances of life may bring us down on our knees, but in all our vulnerability we must find the strength to keep standing. Through relationships of care and trust, we can begin a path of healing. In the face of relationship failures, we will find that the goodwill of people and the desire to change can animate good feelings toward each other. Amid the pain of truth-telling, we are called to live by the truth where our own lives are concerned and, then, exercise a compassionate non-judgmental attitude for the lives of others, remembering that honesty is best spoken in love.

2

Signposts of the Interior Terrain

CHAPTER 1 EXPLORED THE importance of becoming a subject and narrating our escape, quest, and love stories with our voice. This chapter examines a set of terms and their relation to each other that will contribute to a framework for navigating the path towards authentic human transformation.

HORIZON

William Penn once said: "Life is eternal, and love is immoral, and death is the only horizon, and the horizon is nothing save the limit of our sight."[1] Lonergan suggests that the word "horizon" might help us gain some insight into where we are standing.[2] Immediately, the word horizon gives rise to an image: standing on the beach looking out to the visible horizon. From this image, the common understanding of the word horizon is "as far as the eye can see." This understanding is outward focused in which the metaphor of opening our eyes and looking predominates.

For Lonergan, the metaphor of horizon suggests "the scope of one's knowledge and the range of one's interests."[3] It is a metaphor pointing to an inner landscape. He approaches the great variety of human experience through the notion of experiential patterns. Usually, we speak about "experiences" when we are claiming knowledge gained in and through the drama of life. This common meaning to the word covers a range of

1. Penn, "Words About the Dead," 1.

2. Lonergan, *Method*, 235–37.

3. Lonergan, *Method*, 237.

lived events and decisions. For Lonergan, "experience" is a more techni-cal reality. Experiencing is the act of noticing the raw data of the senses or the data of consciousness. In our day to day lives, a person not only has content in their experience but this content enters consciousness according to a pattern.[4] We experience these particular contents since intelligence and imagination select specific patterned experiences out of a whole range of various neurological configurations for conscious repre-sentation as images. Following Lonergan, Patrick Byrne states that these contents are experienced according to one's concerns and interest and "in some order, perspective, relative intensity, and poignancy."[5] Our felt concern orients us toward or away from various experiential patterns. We feel these concerns according to what we love or repel. In other words, what a person likes or hates influences what they think about and allow into their experiential horizon. Further, these concerns, while sponta-neous and felt, become a habit of the mind and heart. What we decide to question, the insights we might have, the judgments we make about reality, the values we judge to be worthwhile, and the decisions we make are all determined "directly or indirectly by the orientation of one's expe-riencing, and therefore, by one's concern."[6] Our concern shapes us toward the kind of "world" we will build for ourselves.[7]

Lonergan names several patterns of experience that orient the flow of consciousness: the biological, aesthetic, artistic, intellectual, the dramatic, the practical, and the religious or mystical.[8] We attend to the biological pattern of experience usually when the organs, tissues, and systems of the body are not working well, and we become concerned with our health. Chapter 9 explores the intellectual pattern of experience, in which we are concerned with our whole energies toward elucidating insights in a technically precise manner. In the dramatic pattern of ex-perience, our concern focuses on the drama of living with others. In the practical pattern, our concern focuses on getting things done. In the ar-tistic/aesthetic pattern of experience, our concern focuses on the beauty of things and the manner of symbolizing beauty in works of art. Chapter 3 will speak to a religious/mystical pattern more thoroughly.

---

4. Lonergan, *Insight*, 204–212.

5. Byrne, "*Ressentiment*," 231.

6. Byrne, "*Ressentiment*," 231.

7. Byrne, "*Ressentiment*," 232.

8. Lonergan, *Insight*, 410–11.

From these insights into the flow of experience within consciousness, we can appreciate the diminishment of a restricted concern that attends to mostly a single pattern. We can also understand the needed transformation to our concern so that our orientation is toward various patterns so that we do not contract as humans. While these patterns may be differentiated, we operate as a unity. The opposite of living as a unity is to be compartmentalized and fragmented in various aspects of our lives. It means that different moral criteria apply to different contexts of living. Fragmentation precludes the possible truth and value of one pattern being of service to the truth and value of another

To expand our patterns means that we can be engaged in practical matters and not have to be any less loving towards others or any less involved in intellectual issues or any less able to put aside practical things to pray. Whatever pattern we inhabit, we should remember that we are building or making the world through each one of these patterns. There is no mileage in exalting the practical over the intellectual or the dramatic over the religious. Though the world of the factory worker is different to the world of the university researcher and both of these are different to the world of the housewife and mother, each in his or her way is constituting the world and the more patterns of experience we allow into awareness, potentially the more insightful and precious our lives will be.

Horizon and Insight

As one's interests extend, there exists a greater possibility for the emergence of different correct insights. There are all kinds of insights that can expand one's horizon and therefore enable us to act with greater integrity. These include direct insights, inverse insights, reflective and cognitive insights, deliberative and moral insights, practical, theoretical, philosophic, and scientific insights, religious insights, and insights about our identity and affectivity, society and culture. Insight is what arises when the tension of inquiry ends and we can say, "that is it, now I understand." When we act from insight, we move from the realm of stimulus-response to action informed by reflection and purpose. Therefore, our life is not a series of behaviors merely reacting to some stimulus. Insight transforms our lives into a story of action. Through insight building on other insights, we increase the likelihood of freely creating the authentic story of our life. Personally, the expansion of our horizon, from insight building on insight, is crucial.

Our horizon can be closed off to questions through a distorted heritage, an incomplete development, biases, and personal unwillingness. We can become locked into a distorted horizon. If this is the case, we become disabled from needed insights and the process of transformation. We can repress inspiration. We can chill the heart even though love invites us to come into the warmth. We say of such people that they are living in a closed world, living a half-life, imprisoned in a state of ambivalence, indolent complacency, and self-deception. In as much as we refuse to allow insight, there is a contraction in our horizon and we become used to the irritation of this contraction. For example, Charles Taylor uses the expression the "buffered self" to describe a form of modern secular thinking and living that avoids vulnerability to external factors in favor of self-sufficiency, and preferences above all else the possession of a full set of practical tools for survival.[9] This self sees itself as invulnerable and the master of its meaning and destiny. This self can be prone to the temptation of refusing to ask important questions that might expand its horizon.

How we move from one horizon to another is the story of transformation. Any "closed" world is not the final story. We renew the journey of self-discovery and growth. We can be open to wonder and new questions. We can affirm through insight and judgments, whatever is better for ourselves and others, and be open to engaging the mysteries of life, death, love, and ultimate meaning. Our horizon may be blessed to expand through influences on us which encourage growth: the love of parents and communities grounding a feeling that we worthwhile and founding a hope and confidence that God will look after everything despite the setbacks of life.

Horizon and Values

Within our horizon, we can recognize a fundamental principle which structures and gives shape to it. The basic principle is a set of values or deliberative insights. What we value sums up our existential truth and is an integral part of our identity. We are evaluating things all the time: weather, food, other people, and their behaviors. We value institutions such as governments or schools or churches. When we use words such as

9. Taylor, *Secular Age*, 38.

better, best, worthwhile, good, worse, and evil, we are using the language of evaluation. We ask: What is the worth of this truth? What do I need to do in the light of this truth? Intelligence is involved in working out what is valuable or worthwhile. Beginning with questions, we engage in the process of deliberating, evaluating, and making a judgment of value. If reflective insights are essential for knowing the truth, deliberative insights are essential for understanding what is worthwhile.[10] What we value will shape and influence what we assess to be a better way to live and what could be a possible path of decisive action in different settings. I will speak more on this existential dimension in the section on responsibility.

Neil Ormerod takes the image of the horizon to explore our limitations and their relationship to our freedom.[11] We all live within the constraints of limitation: the kind of geography and climate we endure; the limits of our human embodiment; the restrictions of our developmental stages; and the type of family we grew up in, where we went to school, and neighborhood that shaped our friendships. There also exists the moral limits of a closed mind and a narrow set of concerns informed by false values or values simply based on our feeling preferences alone. All these limitations have the potential to curtail effective freedom. The critical truth to keep in mind is this: "I make myself who I am. If I act in such a way to undermine my effective freedom, I remain responsible."[12] The path of self-discovery toward authenticity begins with an honest self-understanding. By examining our felt concerns, understanding the influences and conditions impacting on us, and recognizing those conditions that have led to valuable deliberative insights, we will be better able to transform and grow.

Horizon and Feelings

There is also a link between feelings and values. Feelings emerge in our relationships with people, family, peer groups, and communities. Feelings are an essential aspect of the sensitive flow within our consciousness, providing momentum for what focuses our care. Our feelings change in tone and character as we question, seek understanding, come to insights, make decisions, and take direction in our lives. We look to the clarity of

10. Cronin, *Phenomenology*, 165–170.
11. Ormerod, *Grace and Disgrace*, 23–24.
12. Ormerod, *Grace and Disgrace*, 18.

insight, the assurance of judgment, the peace of a good conscience and the joy of being in love.

For Lonergan, there is a difference between intentional feelings and non-intentional feelings.[13] Feelings are an initial indicator that we value or disvalue something: whether some material object or another person. Therefore, if we are not aware of our feelings, we may not be able to respond in the best way to a situation. These are called intentional feelings or feelings that arise in response to something before us or within us pulling us in its specific direction. Non-intentional feelings are more like states or trends within us, such as the general state of hunger or thirst or sexual desire. What we believe and accept in the world is filtered through the feeling responses we have to everything that comes our way. If the feeling response is one of displeasure or anxiety or fear or hate, we might try to avoid that direction. Alternatively, if the feeling response is one of joy or love or desire, we try to cultivate that direction. The point is that through our feelings, each of us responds to whatever good comes our way. The value of something resonates in us by way of feelings. Without feeling, our thinking, valuing, and acting is paper thin.

Victor Capon offers many insights into the importance of feelings. First, feelings attach themselves to images, thoughts, and actions.[14] Within consciousness, there exist many images and thoughts. Images and thoughts come into consciousness accompanied by feelings. Therefore, recalling a memory from the past also recalls the feeling attached to that memory. When memory is traumatic and hurtful, the image associated will carry the attached distressing feeling. Ordinarily, the link between helpful feelings and images can be a mechanism for practicing the attitude of gratitude. There exists a reciprocal relationship between feelings and thoughts where feelings feed off our thoughts and specific thoughts sharpening feeling states. In the case of the link between feeling and thought, we can deal with overwhelming negative feelings by reframing our negative thinking. However, we are also capable of repressing our felt memories. Sometimes repression is so great that the negative feeling attached to the memory transfers to some other memory or image within consciousness which can easily confuse us.

13. Lonergan, *Method*, 30–31.
14. Capon, *Changing the Mind*, 182.

Second, we learn feelings through imitating other people.[15] Later in this chapter, the mimetic nature of desire will reveal insights into living together. We train ourselves to feel a certain way by observing and imitating the way people feel, think, and act in certain situations, toward people and specific objects. This observation of others and their desiring is the first way we learn to appreciate our feelings. In time, these learned feelings are assessed intelligently and chosen or rejected on their terms according to the best way to respond to people and events.

Third, feelings are complicated and sometimes tricky to work out.[16] There may be several factors that contribute to not recognizing feelings. We might not have the time, space, or an accepting environment to work out what we are feeling. We might not be mature enough to understand our feelings. We might not notice the physical changes to the body that may give rise to emotions. Other feeling states may be a complete mystery to us, spontaneously arising and departing quickly. For all these reasons, some feeling states will require the person to stick at it until the feeling is understood.

Fourth, feelings that remain over the long haul need our attention.[17] Such feelings may be indicating that something is very wrong or right for us physically, emotionally or spiritually. If we ignore our emotions in the same way we might overlook a friend who is shouting to us about the danger that lies ahead, then we will never know what has the potential to knock us off kilter. Chapter 10 will investigate more broadly the importance of being attentive to our feelings particularly those that can form neurotic complexes and adversely affect our ability to deal with people and life situations creatively.

Fifth, feelings have an influence on us bodily employing chemical pathways and electrochemical signals working through our neural networks and manifolds.[18] Negative thinking can cause stress to the body by aiding the release of certain chemicals such as cortisol which can adversely affect our immune system. The longer we think over specific negative thoughts, the more we create stress and the more permanent the imprint on our nervous system.

15. Capon, *Changing the Mind*, 183.

16. Capon, *Changing the Mind*, 183–84.

17. Capon, *Changing the Mind*, 184–85.

18. Capon, *Changing the Mind*, 185–86.

Sixth, overall, we must accept the fact that feelings are quite spontaneous and we cannot control them completely, yet healthy living requires strategies for recognizing and addressing the intentional flow of feelings.[19] The more control we exercise toward our feelings, especially through such mechanisms as avoidance, rationalizations, and denial, the more we will be stuck in unhealthy patterns of living and feeling. Further, we need to acknowledge that merely having some feeling does not mean we act on it. In such moments, we might have to recall the kinds of emotions and thoughts that produce a worthwhile life. Much of this approach comes from a developing understanding as to the difference between ordered and disordered desires which will be spoken about later in this chapter.

Horizon and Self-Esteem

One of the most important feelings is the feeling we have of ourselves. Self-esteem is central to transformation. Such a feeling is a product both of our response to any given interaction and the power of the event to elicit feeling from us. The resonance or response within to the things that impact our lives is not merely a passive reaction, as if we have no input over what resonates and what does not. If passivity were the only possible response, then this would be a sign of massive manipulation, possibly the product of a very abusive childhood or some other trauma. The resonance is an active feeling response to the events of life whether of people or events that come our way. This resonance depends not only on the circumstances acting upon us but, more profoundly, how we feel about ourselves.

Sebastian Moore highlights the importance of personal significance very succinctly. He states that if we could name a feeling that we all need then "that feeling is, I think, the feeling that whatever happens to me I am significant, I have worth, value, I *am* someone."[20] This feeling of significance is more expressive of our humanity than self-preservation, propagation, and sociality since our sense of personal importance takes a distinct human form in feeling worthy of surviving, reproducing, and socializing. Self-esteem arises out of the insight that our self-evaluation, self-feeling, or self-esteem is an active response by us to the events we

19. Capon, *Changing the Mind*, 187–88.
20. Moore, *Fire and the Rose*, 6.

experience. It is the prism through which the world's values refract. We feel differently meeting people, situations, and opportunities while imbued by positive self-esteem. While values may structure our horizon, self-esteem is a basic determining principle of our valuing horizon. Now, this self-esteem is mediated to us historically in part by parents, personal history, and personal encounters. We feel good when esteemed by another. We feel damaged when another disesteems us. Alternatively, we shape self-esteem by our own decisions. Self-esteem is a response to a fundamental question addressed by each of us to ourselves: Are we worthwhile? Are we of significance? Do we matter in the scheme of things? Do we have a contribution to make to life? We are asking this question and forming an answer to it in and through our values and decisions. In this way, we are the author of our own lives.

If we are living in the horizon of genuine self-esteem, then we are convinced that to be is to be good, to be desirable, desire-able, and desiring. Religiously, we believe that God made us good and in the words of Psalms: "For it was you who formed my inward parts; you knit me together in my mother's womb. I praise you, for I am fearfully and wonderfully made" (Ps 139:13–14). God desires us without limit. This knowledge makes us feel good about ourselves. At one point in the film *Chariots of Fire* (1981), Eric Liddell, an accomplished runner, and an Olympic Games prospect is challenged by his anxious sister. She convinces herself that Eric's focus on training and running in competitions is taking him away from the main game, being a Christian missionary in China. In an outburst of deep anguish, she tells him that she fears he is losing his vocation and possibly his religious faith to the vagaries of athletics. In a line full of passion, Eric describes to his sister the reason why he runs. He says, "God made me fast, and when I run, I give God pleasure." His statement implies that if his running gives God pleasure why should he not feel pleasure in doing it and feel the esteem of making God happy at the same time.

Horizon and Sublation

To better appreciate the transformation of our horizon, the notion of sublation helps us to understand how horizons transform. Lonergan's notion will need some unpacking, but it is worth the effort. Lonergan states that sublation "goes beyond what is sublated, introduces something new and distinct, puts everything on a new basis, yet so far from interfering with the sublated or destroying it, on the contrary needs it, includes it, preserves all its proper features and properties, and carriers them forward to a fuller realisation within a richer context."[21] Michael H. McCarthy, following Lonergan, states that "the higher forms preserve and respect the integrity of the lower while transcending their limited and intentional scope. The lower, in turn, serve as concrete enabling conditions of the higher's possibility and emergence."[22] The acts of feeling, thinking, valuing, and loving within any person's horizon bear a relationship to one another in the process of transformation. Any lower reality can be incorporated into a new or higher reality, de-centering the former but at the same time making it more itself through lifting it to a higher level. Through sublation, Lonergan describes the interdependence of lower and higher forms in life. The lower forms are the condition for the emergence of higher forms, while the higher take the lower forms to a new integration. The process of sublation takes the lower into a richer horizon expanding our concern for creation.

Horizon and Dialectic

To help better understand how horizons change, Lonergan employs the notion of dialectic. Lonergan uses the notion in two ways. First, dialectic as a general term indicates the existence of two or even three opposed yet linked principles or drivers of change in creative tension with each other within the same identity.[23] These opposed drivers mutually condition one another when they operate and take into account the existence and relevance of each other. In terms of the transformation to a person's horizon, dialectic can inform a more general notion of development which involves a tension between limitation and transcendence within different things.[24] The principle or pole of limitation is the integrator in the dynamic.[25] The principle or pole of transcendence is the operator in the dynamic.[26] The function of the integrator is to bring harmony and stabil-

---

21. Lonergan, *Method*, 241.
22. McCarthy, *Authenticity*, 141–42.
23. Lonergan, *Insight*, 242; *Method*, 236–37.
24. Lonergan, *Insight*, 497.
25. Lonergan, *Insight*, 496–97.
26. Lonergan, *Insight*, 490–91.

ity to the thing and a base from which change can happen. The function of the operator is to transform the current situation in the direction of authentic transcendence. The operator is ceaselessly transforming the integrator. Authentic development always respects this creative tension. When the tension between the two poles is broken and one becomes dominant, resulting in either too much limitation or too much transcendence, we have a dialectic of contradictories. When the tension is held in a creative tension and both poles are recognized for their respective contribution, we have a dialectic of contraries. Dunne notes that a triple differentiation within consciousness characterizes the experience of desire: spontaneously felt priorities, intellectual inquiry, and responsible assessment. All three principles are ongoing drivers of moral change. Dunne also asserts that each "person and every community is peculiar because the dominance of each driver rises or falls at every choice of every individual."[27]

Second, dialectic functions to help understand radically difference stances taken by persons where there exists an opposition between one position against the counterposition. Following Lonergan, Dunne notes that the dialectical nature of moral living is between authenticity and inauthenticity. One person's position may be intelligent and responsible while another person's position may be unintelligent and irresponsible. To understand our horizon is to appreciate the difference between the relative merits of positions or stances taken, realizing that some attitudes fall short of full human living. Later in this chapter, we will examine the dialectical nature of desire as ordered and disordered, centrifugal and centripetal.

Horizon and Conversion

While it is important to work out what stance people may be taking and why, each of us must take our stance around certain issues. Conversion is the process of taking a stance on how and why we will conduct our lives. Broadly, Lonergan describes conversion as "a change in direction and, indeed, a change for the better. One frees oneself from the unauthentic. One grows in authenticity. We drop our harmful, dangerous, misleading satisfactions. Fears of discomfort, pain, privation have less power to deflect one from one's course. Values are apprehended whereas before

27. Dunne, *Doing Better*, 174.

we overlooked them. Scales of preference shift. Errors, rationalizations, ideologies fall and shatter to leave one open to things as they are and to man as he should be."[28] This passage is worth unpacking.

First, Lonergan's notion of conversion requires a whole re-evaluation of the feelings, thinking, valuing, and acting that constitutes one's horizon. Often, in ordinary conversation, any mention of conversion is explicitly linked to religious conversion. Literally, in its Latin roots, conversion means "to turn around." In a religious context, the Latin is a translation of the word from the Greek Biblical text *metanoia* meaning "to change one's mind." We often use the religious word "repent" in faith communities to capture turning away from something that might be harmful to our relationship with God toward religiously healthy living. *Metanoia* is both turning away and turning towards, a conversion from and a conversion to something. This understanding of metanoia means a radical change of life away from inauthenticity toward authenticity. Authenticity is the goal of human transformation. Any radical change to the way that we feel, think, value, and act sets right our whole being so that we might become better persons for each other. Conversion helps to bring us back to the natural way that God created us to be.

Second, conversion can have a traumatic effect on our person. We ask fundamental questions, we discover new illuminating insights, and we make responsible decisions, such that not to act would then leave us with a narrow view of life. Each of us is left to either reject these new insights or to consent to them. To reject them is to settle for the routines that keep us comfortable and in control. To agree to conversion is to enlarge our horizon, creating a greater openness to truth, goodness, and love. If we consent to this change, then we move forward by way of "suffering," that is, letting whatever disrupts and prompts questions to be and allowing suffering to have its way.

Third, this notion of conversion takes into account that people have very different kinds of horizons of attention, understanding, judging, valuing, and loving. Some of these horizons differ developmentally, others are complementary, and others are radically opposed to one another.[29] Developmental differences mean that people are at different stages of growth, for example, the difference between the boy and the man, the girl, and the woman. We would expect that given enough time and the

---

28. Lonergan, *Method*, 52.
29. Lonergan, *Method*, 236.

right condition, the girl would mature into a woman. Complementary differences acknowledge that each person has unique contributions to make to life. Though people may come from different cultural and social backgrounds their attitudes toward such things as a family and human society might be very similar though often expressed in different ways and with various nuances. Radical differences show how the horizon of one may be radically opposed to the horizon of another. Conversion pertains to a radical stance.

THE EXPERIENCE OF DESIRE[30]

The turn to the subject and the importance of subjectivity grounds our investigations into the experience of desire. To accurately appreciate our story, we must thoroughly attune ourselves to our desires. We are creatures of desire. We were created to always "stretch" ourselves through desiring toward becoming a more authentic person. Our particular desires reveal to us what is important to us and what stirs us passionately. At a psychological level, desire is a natural attraction or wanting, directed toward something or someone. Even when we engage in an aversion or a withdrawal from something, this too is desire. As each of us happens upon a specific object, we feel inner goodness as we reach out to it since desire flows from an overabundance of goodness within, and not from some emptiness in us wanting to be filled. Desiring is transforming when it puts us on the path of wondering, prompting us to ask fundamental new questions, waiting to be illuminated by insight, and giving our heart to realizations that may bring about integral growth in our life. Desiring is illusory when it devolves into merely taking possession of a pleasurable object with the consequence that we lose all awareness of others and remain trapped in self-satisfied indolence.

Sebastian Moore presents a useful distinction to help unpack the psychological structure of desire. His fundamental distinction is between

---

30. I am staying with the word "desire," even though there is some debate as to whether it is the best term to use. For Jerome Miller, we too closely align the term desire with taking possession of someone or something else. He prefers the word "passion," which carries a greater sense of letting go of control and possessiveness in favor of self-surrender. I agree with him that we must be careful to make sure that the will to control and dominate does not power our desiring. See Miller, "All Love Is Self-Surrender," 65–68.

particular desires and general desire.[31] First, particular desire is wanting or having an appetite for some specific thing. Particular desires implicitly prescind from an assessment of what counts in our lives. What counts is what comes first. Patrick Byrne assesses that each person possesses a core desire out of which we judge what counts and what is real.[32] Everything else is measured and chosen according to this core desire. Our core desire might be the desire for some kind of material comfort, mental and physical health, the lifting of oppression, the importance of work, a set of relationships, or the prestige of power. Whatever it is, this desire becomes our measure for reality and guides everything else we do. We say of this desire: this is our reality, and this is the ground from which we make sense of life. We usually acquire this core desire from people, society, and culture that steer us toward this measure.

Second, there is another measure of reality that we do not pick up from others. Moore calls this desire general desire. This measure for reality is innate. At times, Lonergan calls it our innate natural desire, the "pure detached disinterested desire to know," and the "eros of the human spirit," permeating us and makes us human.[33] Using the metaphor of light, Moore states that this innate desire is the light that allows us to see other objects. For Moore, if we consciously exist before we can say this or that about ourselves, then it is also the case that we consciously desire long before we can say that we want this or that object.[34] The relationship between these two very different kinds of desire is such that wanting this or that object is "preceded by a continuous condition of myself in my environment, a continuous wanting-I-know-not what, a "just wanting.""[35] Through reflection, we move from an awareness of our particular desires back to "just wanting" and the more that this latter desire is satisfied, the more it increases.

---

31. Moore, Let This Mind, 26.
32. Byrne, "Passionateness of Being," 38.
33. Lonergan, Method, 13.
34. Moore, Let this Mind, 10–12.
35. Moore, Let this Mind, 5.

Natural Desire

To add even further depth to the language of desire and subjectivity, let us explore the difference between innate natural desire and elicited desire.[36] First, there is an innate natural desire to know, to value, and to love. Following Lonergan, Vernon Gregson states that "the desires and longings we have for what is beautiful, for what makes sense, for what is true, for what has value and for what has ultimate value are at the heart of what it means to be human."[37] Lonergan, primarily through his magisterial work, *Insight*, communicates a thorough understanding of our innate natural desire to know and in *Method in Theology* builds upon the desire to know with the desire to value and love.

Speaking of the innate desire to know, Lonergan asserts that "by the desire to know is meant the dynamic orientation manifested in questions for intelligence and for reflection. It is not the verbal utterance of questions. It is not the conceptual formulation of questions. It is not any insight or thought. It is not any reflective grasp or judgment. It is the prior and enveloping drive that carries the cognitional process from sense and imagination to understanding, from understanding to judgment, from judgment to the complete context of correct judgments that is named knowledge."[38] The distinctive touchstone of this desire is asking and answering questions.[39] We are asking and answering questions all the time whether we are plumbers or electricians, teachers or researchers, wives or husbands, mothers or fathers, philosophers or scientists. The point is that we do not always pay attention to this paradigm for reality since we are stuck in our own practical and particular world of desires. This desire points to the capacity to question in an unlimited and unrestricted manner, unless restricted or mutilated by the debilitating influences within a culture, society, and personal circumstances.

Therefore, the objective of innate desire is all reality, truth, and existence. We are continually asking different kinds of questions: questions for intelligence, for judgment, and for deliberation as to what is worthwhile. While there is a primordial element of spontaneity to this innate desire, it is often referred to as the "pure" question or the root and fundamental question, since its ultimate objective is the whole of

36. Ormerod, "Desire and the Origins," 784–94; "Questioning Desire," 356–71.

37. Gregson, "Desire to Know," 16–17.

38. Lonergan, *Insight*, 372.

39. Byrne, "Passionateness of Being," 39–40.

reality or the whole of existence, human and divine. Our questions find fulfillment in actual answers about anything and everything, even though these answers happen incrementally and sometimes only after considerable effort and persistence.

Following Lonergan, Byrne asserts that this second paradigm for reality "is rather a mysterious sense of reality because we don't yet know what the totality of being is. We don't yet know everything about everything there is. But we do have a sense about the totality because our questioning spirit keeps pointing us toward it by raising more and more questions about everything. The reality that we wonder about and that we desire to know provides us with an alternative, strange but even more basic, paradigm of reality."[40] We are drawn by an innate commitment to the notion of meaning, knowledge, objectivity, value, and love. A notion is not an idea or concept. It is an anticipation of something already at work in us, just like when we say that we have a notion of where we are headed in life but without any clear idea.[41]

Experience and Noticing

Our natural desire reveals itself by acts or operations or levels within consciousness that cannot be imagined but happen within time.[42] We experience them only when we are performing them for the sake of understanding, judging, and valuing something else.[43] Our natural desire is not a passive process. It is an active process or intentionality that is "heading toward" something. The first level or act or operation within consciousness is noticing something or experiencing. The level of experience presents the mind with something upon which we can ask questions. Reality is not given or known to us immediately. To understand reality, we must begin by responding to the imperative in consciousness to be attentive to what is before us, whether to the data of sense or the data of consciousness. Chapter 9 will give a more thorough understanding of these operations.

Being attentive is not easy. There are many reasons why we do not practice attentiveness. We can be distracted, which is easy to do in an age

40. Byrne, "Passionateness of Being," 40.

41. Morelli, *Self-Possession*, 18.

42. Morelli, *Self-Possession*, 26–27.

43. Morelli, *Self-Possession*, 33–34.

of distractions. We can be socially influenced not to attend to specific data. We can exercise the psychological practices of denial, suppression, or even repression. Our character can be egotistic and so anything that does not gain for us the goal of getting ahead of the pack is beyond our attention. We deem the desire to compete against others or to impress others to be more critical and energetic than paying attention.

The habit of being attentive is at the heart of any act of self-awareness or being in the present. The act of being attentive makes us more of who we are and moves us along the path of actualization than when we are asleep. The act of attentiveness sublates the multiple spontaneities of the psyche by recognizing their potential in dreams and waking states. No genuine effort on our part to pay attention is wasted. Even if the act of paying attention does not yield the fruits we were seeking; still, the very act of paying attention helps us to grow. As noted earlier, experience occurs in patterns, and our selective noticing of the data of experience depends upon the interests and concerns that structure our horizon. As our interests widen, so does the range of attentiveness to other patterns of experience.

Understanding and Intelligence

The second level or act or operation within consciousness is the level of understanding. The level of understanding sublates the previous level. This level means that the data of experience is drawn into a broader horizon and transformed. Here begins the process of questioning, wondering, and searching for insight in earnest. Questions for understanding the data of experience and seeking what is intelligible in the data are precise. We might ask: What is it? How is it? When is it? Why is it? Where is it? How is it related to other things? These questions help us make sense of what we experience. At this level, we are responding to the imperative to be intelligent. This response makes us more of who we are in comparison to noticing. Again, there is a transformation at work in each of us. It presumes that reality is mediated by meaning. Our goal is intelligent insights. We wait for insights or acts of understanding to emerge. We move towards insights which are then formulated into ideas, concepts, and hypotheses through the mediation of language. To form concepts, we need to focus on what is essential and let go of what is irrelevant or incidental to understanding. Chapter 9 will ponder the nature of insight more deeply.

Judgment and Reasonableness

The third level or act within consciousness is the level of judgment. The level of judgment sublates the previous level. Again, through judgment, we draw our insights into a broader horizon. There is a different kind of question asked at this level. Questions for judgment are seeking to weight up the appropriateness of our insights, responding to the imperative to be reasonable. We ask: Is it true? Is it so? Is this the way things are? This question looks for evidence to substantiate whether the insights that have emerged are true or false, probable or certain. In as much as we give scope to these questions, we arrive at judgments of truth. Judgments cannot happen without experiencing and understanding. Such questions from understanding to judgments drive all branches of knowledge. The act of judgment makes us more of who we are in comparison to noticing and understanding. Again, we transform through an act of judgment. We arrive at reflective insights.

Lonergan names this advance along these successive stages of consciousness, the unrestricted desire to know, for unlike other desires, this unrestricted desire will not be satisfied with this answer about this object alone but could potentially raise an infinite number of new questions and seek an endless number of answers. The objective of the natural desire is being in all its fullness or the whole of reality or reality as intelligible. Being is therefore not only the objective of the pure desire to know but also the objective of well-formulated questions, the objective of accurate insights, and the objective of correct judgments.[44]

Responsibility and Doing the Good

There is a fourth level or operation or act within consciousness, the level of deliberation and responsibility. The level of responsibility sublates the previous level of judgment. The level of responsibility is a richer horizon. We ask a different set of questions. We ask: Is the reality we have established truly worthwhile or only apparently worthwhile? At this level, the questioning is concerned not only with knowing and knowledge but with

44. Tekippe, *Bernard Lonergan*, 96.

implementing a course of action intelligently and reasonably through aspiring to and applying values. Values are involved in questions about what is indeed worthwhile to achieve some purpose. The act of being responsible makes us more of who we are than does noticing, understanding, and judging what is real. A new transformation is happening. We arrive at deliberative insights. A further desire is emerging: the desire to know the truth leading to the desire to do the truth.

At this level, questioning has an even higher level or register in human consciousness, reaching up to the best way we can live together. We ask: Is this system truly good or only seemingly good? When thinking about communities, Lonergan speaks about the good of order, that is, practical arrangements of living together which make possible the recurrence of particular desires towards a truly valuable purpose.[45] The good of order practically has us finding a system that might help us live together in society with all individual needs met cooperatively.

Again, this natural desire is not satisfied with this or that discovery of truth or value or action. It is not satisfied just with a handful of occurrences of meaning, truth, or goodness but is open to an unlimited and unrestricted horizon of the real and the valuable. Natural desire is built into what it means to be a human being. We do not need to learn it from others. We only need help in recognizing its presence in human consciousness. This natural desire is verifiable through noticing our interior acts when we are seeking knowledge and trying to implement some concrete good. Without some consistent attunement to this natural desire, we are more likely to practice an avoidance of new questions, rationalize our inconsistencies, fall into moral renunciation, and never fulfill our potential to love. However, such attunement is a long and challenging task.

Elicited Desire

Secondly, apart from the natural desire, there is another kind of desire: elicited desire. For Rene Girard, much of what we desire comes to us since relationships embed our lives. Elicited or evoked desire highlights the intersubjective character of transformation and its impact on us psychically to orient our lives toward particular desires. In the order of chronology, it is before the blooming of the innate natural desire. We are not first and exclusively individual but, for Girard, we are inter-dividual before

45. Lonergan, *Insight*, 237–39.

an individual.[46] Since each of us is born into webs of interrelationships, long before we can ask questions, we have been formed by inspirations, feelings, rules, insights, practices, ways of thinking, valuing, and acting, some helpful to human living and some not so helpful. Our spontaneous concerns and desires have already been shaped before the maturity to develop our innate natural desire occurs.

To express the intersubjective nature of desire, Girard asserts that we desire according to the desire of another. In other words, Girard is stating that we should not be mistaken in thinking that we are attracted to some object because it has some inherent property that draws us directly and explicitly. Girard's body of work points to the triangular dynamic of elicited desire within a context of relationships: mentor, respondent, and an object. He calls this dynamic of desire, mimetic desire. The mentor is the one in possession of the desired object. The respondent is the one who wants what the mentor possesses. The object is the desired possession. The desire for this or that object is conditioned and shaped by the desire of others for objects, and this conditioning affects our psychic life. Our desires do not happen because an object has some quality that we immediately see as worthwhile and desirous. Instead, we attach worthiness to an object because someone else has shown us that it is worthy through their wanting it.

Girard uses the word mimetic and not imitation since he is communicating that the quality of our desiring is unknown to the respondent or the mentor until we start to reflect on our lives. This mimesis also applies to the "behavior, attitudes, [and] things learned, prejudices and preferences" in our lives.[47] There is the element of choice tied up with mimetic desire, and it is this choice that sets it apart from instinct and the animal realm.[48] Mimesis is mostly neutral, and it comes in many forms. We may choose to desire particular material objects or we may want something more immaterial such as justice so as to deal more fairly with our neighbor. We may choose to pray in order to build a relationship with God based on what we have seen others doing and the way it has helped them practically in their lives.

However, negatively, Girard postulates that violence is a byproduct of rivalistic desire, that is, we seek to desire objects violently merely

46. Webb, *Self Between*, 6–7.

47. Girard, *I See Satan Fall*, 15.

48. Girard, *I See Satan Fall*, 15–16.

because others want them and all are willing to harm each other in the process of possessing them.[49] Here, we are dealing with acquisitive mimesis either covertly or overtly. This violence can reach such a fever pitch of obsession that two rivals locked into the desire to possess an object end up forgetting the object itself and become fascinated in each other as rivals. We convince ourselves that by having such objects, we will not only have more but be more, be somebody, feel more powerful, and act with greater self-sufficiency as the mentor we are emulating.[50] This kind of mimesis is contagious and can end up infecting whole communities, political and religious.

There are three points worth mentioning upon which Lonergan and Girard agree. First, Lonergan and Girard share a common concern when it comes to desire that leads to violence. While Girard seeks to establish the origins of violence in rivalistic desire, Lonergan acknowledges that the spontaneity of desire does not always display intelligence and responsibility. There is a tension between the spontaneity of desire, on the one hand, and intelligent thinking and responsible acting, on the other hand. Unless freed from and healed of this rivalry, people will not be able to reach up to the kind of intelligent thinking required in complex living. Such rivalry can distort the innate tendency to know, value, and love.

Second, for Lonergan, human nature is malleable. The person each of us becomes is not the outcome of some determinism, whether genetic or social. However, he would also say that we are not simply the product of our choices. We are the product of the combined influences of others and our choices. Long before we can make decisions for ourselves the drama of human living shapes our affectivity with fears, joys, sorrows, delights, hopes, hates, and disappointments. We emerge with a set of feelings and values, some helpful and others not so beneficial which we are compelled to work with and shift through during our lives. Transformation is an ongoing process.

Third, it would be a mistake to separate natural and elicited desire.[51] The desires formed from the intersubjective bonds of our life give positive movement and momentum to the desire to know, value, and love. Elicited desires can create within us a state of mind, a mood, and disposition that shapes and accompanies the human spirit and its quest

---

49. Girard, *Violence and the Sacred*, 145.

50. Girard, *Deceit, Desire*, 282.

51. Rosenberg, *Givenness of Desire*, 141.

for meaning, truth, value, and love. Where unhealthy desires have shaped us in such a way to distort our lives, the innate desire to know and love also distorts, and therefore healing is essential for the restoration of meaning, truth, and love. For both Lonergan and Girard, positive models have the power to elicit a new, life-affirming, and transforming orientation of desire.

Desire and Others

The highest level of transformation is to become a person of love. Love changes the whole inner disposition of the person and delivers a new kind of knowledge into our lives. It creates a new "we" to the dimension of personal and social responsibility, a new desire for truth, and a new attentiveness to all that we experience. Love sublates all the other levels of consciousness, and they are sublated by love. Since love is an interpersonal reality, Moore states that love "is the form or level of consciousness at which I am, consciously created. Love is the point of contact with the one who causes me to be."[52] We are no more fully alive than when we are a person of love and in love. If this is the case, then desire can have nothing to do with the will to control others or be content to cope with others or be powered by an ethos of self-fulfillment alone. Nor can love be determined by an attitude that makes ourselves self-sufficient, impenetrable to wondering, and the challenges these may pose for us.

As mentioned earlier, Moore asserts that the most fundamental need that any human person has at the start of their life is the need to feel *significant* so that whatever happens, each of us feels our worth, meaning, and value.[53] This human need cries out for acceptance in another person and only through such recognition from another is the need for significance fulfilled. There is a relationship between this need for significant and our love of others. When we mature, the need to feel significant changes so that the emphasis is on our importance *for another*.[54] Therefore, our significance is other-dependent at the beginning of life and other-fulfilling as we mature. Building on this understanding, Moore states that "desire is love trying to happen."[55] Surprisingly, he asserts that

52. Moore, "New Life," 152.
53. Moore, *Fire and the Rose*, 40.
54. Moore, *Fire and the Rose*, 40.
55. Moore, *Jesus the Liberator*, 93.

what adult people most need is not to know that someone loves them since such an affirmation helps and is wonderful when this person is someone we love. Moore states that our emotional design heads toward loving and we only flourish since our most ambitious desire "is to be the cause of joy in another."[56] Desire that begins in a quest for significance, worthiness, and meaning reaches up to the love of others, transforming the other and transforming ourselves.

Getting to the stage of being significant for another is a challenging process. In our early formative years, Moore posits that psychological growth requires a creative negotiation between the two poles of oneness or wholeness and separateness.[57] This tension is an instance of dialectic in the drama of living. To be authentic requires reconciling these polarities. He turns to Freud's oedipal stage in human development, an early ego form of human evolution. Before this early stage, we live in a state of symbiosis with our mother. Progressively, we begin to struggle with the tension between the primary desire of oneness with our mother and separation from her. Through a healthy separation, we embark on a path of discovering our ego or sense of our self. Sadly, through an unhealthy separation, psychic difficulties begin to embed in us. Throughout adolescence and into adult life, the demand for a new self is made on us when we struggle with desire moving us toward others. Whether we go through the crisis of falling in love or grief, we see desire powerfully pulling us toward another. In this way, "the development of desire is a progressive changing of what is desired and who is desiring."[58]

Desire always calls us back into oneness. The pull of desire invites us to let go of a previous ego-form of individuality and grow into a new self that become significant for another. Desire asks us to let go of any idea that we are meant to be alone, solitary, and self-sufficient. As Moore asserts, desire "is for the actualizing of my relatedness."[59] Each point of crisis feels like some part of us has died as we grow into fuller selfhood. Growth requires trust and acceptance of any uncomfortable suffering, as we move toward a new integration of the self. While claiming an autonomous individuality may feel powerful and ego-fixation may feel comfortable and secure, liberated desire moves us beyond ourselves. If we do not

56. Moore, *Contagion of Jesus*, 128.

57. Moore, *Jesus the Liberator*, 15.

58. Moore, *Jesus the Liberator*, 19.

59. Moore, *Jesus the Liberator*, 120.

trustingly give ourselves to the process of moving beyond our ego-state, then there is a danger that we will become self-absorbed and egocentric.

Desire and God

Since desire is love trying to happen, then all desire when rigthy pursued brings us to the ultimate cause of our desire, God.[60] More broadly, Lonergan draws insight from the writings of St. Thomas Aquinas to affirm that all human desire is a desire for God since to desire some good is to desire the source and terminus of goodness which is God. God is the deepest desire of our heart. Whenever we direct our will toward some good, we are implicitly willing God into our lives. God's will for us is to bring to fulfillment the work of creation.

God is not just another object among many that we can know, value, and love. The self is invited into an encounter with God and surrender to God, transforming the person so that the self reflects more fully the image of God. Lonergan states that being-in-love in an unrestricted manner is "the first principle. From it flows one's desires and fears, one's joys and sorrows, one's discernment of values, one's decisions and choices."[61] In other words, we may have structured our lives along diverse different ways of thinking about what counts and what is relevant or real. These other ways can only be secondary. The first principle to structuring our lives is being-in-love with God.

The love of God is a creative act towards us. We are created to be in love with God, we are sustained in existence moment by moment by the love of God, and we are urged to seek communion with God. God providentially guides the process of transformation within us, and we become who we are only to the extent that the mystery of God's creativity is at work in us. Doing the truth finds its fulfillment not only in the development of loving relationships with others but, ultimately, in the love of God and the experience of unlimited and unrestricted love. Our being becomes a being-in-love with God and all that God loves. For Lonergan, being-in-love with God in an unrestricted manner is the fruit of religious conversion, which will be examined more extensively in chapter 3 to 5.

God is the ultimate fulfillment of all knowing and valuing. We possess a natural desire for God. The radical spiritual dynamism of the

---

60. Lonergan, *Method*, 283.

61. Lonergan, *Method*, 105.

human spirit is directed to all understanding and absolute knowledge. If we were able to follow this orientation unimpeded, it would bring us to the question of God. However, since God is wholly transcendent, Other, eternal, and timeless, we cannot know God. While we can assert the existence of God and know about God through our natural resources, we cannot know God personally without God's self-communication. The fulfilment of the natural desire requires the grace of God. Miller, interpreting Lonergan, declares:

> Eternal rest in loving relationship with God is the ultimate aim of human self-transcendence. In this life, however, God has given human beings not rest, but a restlessness caused by an unrestricted desire. This desire is a natural longing for a supernatural fulfillment, a human yearning for perfect unrestricted love, good, truth, being, intelligibility, and beauty. This unified transcendent desire underlies all human activities. It underlies the going beyond that begins when one opens one's eyes, when one attends to one's feelings, and when one is moved to a spontaneous sense of wonder. It is the source of a rushing stream of questions, of an earnest search for satisfying answers, and of a moral exigence towards conscientious action in society.[62]

However, this natural orientation of the human spirit is difficult to realise due to the personal and cultural distortions of sin. Lonergan states that "human authenticity is not some pure quality, some serene freedom from all oversights, all misunderstandings, all mistakes, all sin."[63] A human person never fully possesses authenticity. The need to move beyond egoism urges us to seek redemption, recovery, and healing. Even though we can talk about becoming the person God created us to be, there will be choices in our lives leading in the opposite direction. We can be inattentive, unintelligent, unreasonable, irresponsible and unloving. The Christian tradition speaks about inordinate desires and inordinate attachments, just as the great Buddha speaks about acquisitive desire which only brings suffering to people's lives. Despite these inordinate desires, God is always seeking to draw us into a new direction through the power of God's love.

Moore outlines the two ways of being awakened to God through desire. First, we are awakened indirectly. When we are drawn to another person, this pull is our "sense of your goodness expanding. There is

62. Miller, *Quest for God*, 70–71.

63. Lonergan, *Method*, 252.

always in the attraction of another, the feeling of a larger life opening up in myself. I *am* more in being drawn to another. And the reason why I want that other to be drawn to me is that my awakening sense of being desirable wants to be completed by my *being* desired."[64] The "I *am* more" is the process of transformation. We have moved from a point of isolation to a realization that "people's essential power over each other, which is the power of their beauty and goodness, cannot be thought of as a possession of each, but has to be thought of as a life-force whose interest is to unite them. My power is my partnership in the energy that unities persons in love. The essential human power is not solitary but unifying."[65]

Real desire is intended for a shared life. We feel our best self when working within a relationship of interdependence. This dynamic indicates that there is a double aspect to being human that goes hand in hand: personal fulfillment and being for another. The "I am" that exists thanks to those who love us into life is the same "I am" that now reaches out to others in love. Moore argues that this is what we mean by life in God or "Spirit, inter-life, the mysterious energy that flows between persons, is what opens us to God. It is at once the opening of our *desire* to God and God's *point of entry* into us; our way of opening, God's way of entry."[66] Moore is asserting that true human love implicitly carries, at its center, divine love.

Second, we are awakened directly to God when our desire breaks the rules and reaches out to nothing or nobody-in-particular. This kind of awakening happens through centering prayer and contemplation. Without any object in mind, we learn the practice of just being and resting in our existence or what we might call the "I am" experience. In the mystery of God, to be significant is to be. This attentive presence to "nothing-in-particular" in centering prayer, concurrent with the feeling of a new and intense sense of self, is God.[67] Moore states that the "condition of being suddenly alive and wanting I know not what cannot be induced. It simply happens. But from time immemorial, in different cultures and different religious climates, people have used a method for quieting or simplifying consciousness so that a person may be better *disposed* of for the moment of awakening. Thus, while the moment of awakening consists in

---

64. Moore, *Let This Mind*, 14.

65. Moore, *Let This Mind*, 20.

66. Moore, *Let This Mind*, 25.

67. Moore, *Let This Mind*, 55.

wanting nothing in particular, the method consists in *thinking* of nothing in particular."[68]

Through this form of awakening, we come to our core-selfhood or desirability not through some object before us desiring us, but through feeling it simply and directly. While this desirability has no object, Moore asserts that all desirability reaches out for intimacy. The mysterious reality, which seeks affection with us and with whom we seek and find intimacy, is the mystery of God. This intimacy leads to a desire to surrender entirely to God. In the words of St. Ignatius, we can pray: "Take, Lord, and receive all my liberty, my memory, my understanding, and my entire will, All I have and call my own. You have given all to me. To you, Lord, I return it. Everything is yours; do with it what you will. Give me only your love and your grace that is enough for me." Only, in this case, it is not we who desire some object but God who first desires us. God's loving of us causes us to notice our desirability and to respond.

Moore suggests that God causes in us a form of desire which he calls "we know-not-what" while at the same time making our lives sure in its meaningfulness and ultimate significance. Our oneness with God as the cause of desire is like a river overflowing its banks pressured by the waters that have flowed down from some source high in the mountains. According to Moore, the heart of religion is reaching toward the source or the cause of our desirability, our being, and goodness.[69] This breakthrough into a sense of oneself grounds any other image we might like to use to communicate the quality of the relationship between ourselves and God.[70] Moore sums up his thoughts in this Coda: "God desires us before we desire God because God's desire makes us desirable which we must be in order to desire anything at all. In the new creation, we feel the creative touch of God's desire stirring us in our desirableness to desire nothing that can be named until this nothing is named as the cause of our desire, which being the cause of desire, is desirable."[71]

68. Moore, *Let This Mind*, 65.
69. Moore, *Let This Mind*, 43.
70. Moore, *Let This Mind*, 39.
71. Moore, *Let This Mind*, 47.

The Tasks of Desire

According to Dunne, the challenges of living invite us to consider three fundamental tasks toward desires.[72] First, there is the intellectual task of understanding our desires and our aversions, clarifying whether our feelings are actual desires that might accompany the choosing of values for the sake of loving. Margaret Silf invites us to think about root desires and branch desires.[73] She ponders on the image of a great tree with its roots and branches. If there is a thrust or vital energy to our desiring, then some desires plant us into the ground, and other desires make us reach out. Both kinds of desires are essential to human living. This tension is another instance of a positive dialectic in the development of desire. In one direction, there are root desires. Among the root desires, there are such desires as the desire for sociality (acceptance and belonging within a group), the desire for self-preservation (security and nourishment), and the desire for the propagation of the species (intimacy and oneness). These root desires integrate our lives. In the other direction, there are branch desires. The branch desires draw us outward crossing over into different societies and cultures into the world of self-expression, creativity, healing, caring, generous love, commitment to others, and generativity.[74] We note that root and branch desires while being contraries do not work against each other. They work best in our lives when there is a creative tension between root and branch, giving rise to a spirit of genuineness within us and a directedness toward others.

Second, there is the moral task of knowing the desire precisely and the object of desire so that we might more fruitfully discern whether to allow or suppress it. Values motivate this task and require a healthy development of feelings that help us to choose what is truly worthwhile in various situations. The movement of desire is always precarious since there is still the possibility of personal derailment into inauthenticity. Lonergan warns against engaging in a flight from understanding that stifles practical solutions, theoretical insights, and the development of our true self toward love.[75] There remains the possibility of evil that displays itself in broken promises, broken families, broken economies, and destroyed civilizations.

72. Dunne, "Desire," 4–7.

73. Silf, *Landmarks*, 116.

74. Silf, *Landmarks*, 113–114,

75. Lonergan, *Insight*, 8.

Through this moral task, we discover the distinction between ordered and disordered desires. Miller notes that ordered desires have a centrifugal effect on us while disordered desires have a centripetal effect.[76] Miller asserts these two contrasting effects are "the difference between choosing receptivity or closure, self-donation or self-protection, centrifugal movement towards the drama of the future or centripetal repression of possibility."[77] Ordered desires or giving desires and the centrifugal force created in us, lets the other be themselves. Ordered desires allow the other to be. Even though ordered desires draw us out of ourselves in care toward another, we find that this specific drawing does not diminish us. Ordered desire, in the language of Moore, is the real feeling of ourselves as good, going out to be good for others. It is to experience ourselves as the desired of God.[78]

Disordered desires or taking desires and the centripetal force created in us by such desires are concerned with expending energy to possess or control another or to engage in narcissistic self-protection. We can never control or be possessive since to be possessive of another would be to harm ourselves and the other. These are the desires fixated on an immature ego state. Initially, according to Moore, this disorder comes from doubting our desirability. This doubt has a voice. The voice centers on a lack of trust in ourselves and a lack of feeling good about ourselves or our convictions. We recoil in terror from our felt vulnerability and react by seeking to take control of another in what turns out to be a dead-end strategy to regain power.

The warning to guard against disordered desire does carry an insight. When our desires are grounded in self-satisfaction alone such as the satisfactions of excessive food, drugs, material goods, or sexual pleasure, then effectively we close ourselves off from the discovery of other realities, and we cannot grow. We are clinging to a state of homeostasis rather than living in the tension that genuineness requires of us for transformation to occur. A homeostatic context is a form of mental paralysis that can quickly act as an insulation from the challenges of growth and its upsetting character. The way of homeostasis is a return to the womb-like state we enjoyed with our mother, where we were untroubled by questioning. In that place, we were not required to suffer through finding what was truthful and valuable. In such a homeostatic state, other

76. Miller, "Desire, Passion," 1–11.

77. Miller, "Desire, Passion," 9.

78. Silf, *Landmarks*, 80.

persons cease to be of concern to us except for what they can do for us so that we remain undisturbed.

Third, there is the task of healing our desires from the debilitating effects of blindness, impotence, unwillingness, and despair. This third task brings into play the importance of the healing power of God. Our desires can become disordered, yet the awareness that our efforts alone will not make them ordered again opens the way to God and a surrender to the gift of God's grace.

3

Religious Experience
and Religious Conversion

CHAPTER 2 BEGAN TO build a framework for understanding transformation especially by exploring the notion of desire and how the unrestricted desire to know, to value, and love is our first paradigm for reality, reaching up into our passion for God. It is clear from this approach that, as we intend meaning, truth, and the good, desire transforms. It is also clear that transformation occurs when our horizon of concern undergoes conversion. Lonergan speaks directly to this transformation by naming three kinds of conversion: religious conversion, moral conversion, and intellectual conversion.[1] He also intimates strongly to a fourth conversion: affective conversion.[2] Lonergan appreciated the insights of Sigmund Freud and acknowledged the blindness of scotosis.[3] In the light of this acknowledgment, Robert Doran and Bernard Tyrrell pondered a fifth form of conversion, the conversion of the psyche. The following chapters will seek to explain the meaning of these conversions and their part in the process of transformation, beginning with religious conversion.

1. Lonergan, *Method*, 237–44.

2. Lonergan, *Method*, 105; *Third Collection*, 168–70.

3. Lonergan, *Insight*, 215–17. Lonergan describes scotosis as an unconscious process that prevents psychic content from emerging into the first level of consciousness. The result is that we do not ask the right questions and we miss needed insights.

Religious Experience and the Shift
to Religious Interiority

Any talk about religious transformation must move beyond the critical but dry language of dogmatic truth, which we find in religious creedal statements. When we come to experience the presence of God, religious faith invites us into an interior approach to transformation. The feeling of continuous desiring brings us to the threshold of divine love.[4] A sense of human worthlessness has the effect of distancing us from God. Distanced from God, we need another unimaginable fullness greater than ourselves to meet us in our alienation and blindness.

Before elucidating the meaning of religious conversion as a gift, this chapter will explore the meaning and centrality of religious experience to the process of transformation. What is the meaning of the term, religious experience? According to Louis Roy, the term religious experience did not assume a center stage in thinking about religion until quite late in western history.[5] From a western perspective, we can speak about the differences between pre-modern times and modern times. In pre-modern times, to experience something had nothing to do with religious phenomena. There are certain intimations of interiorly felt religious experience spoken about in the Sacred Scriptures. In Ezekiel 36:26, the prophet places these words into God's mouth: "I will give you a new heart and a new spirit I will put within you, and I will remove from your body the heart of stone and give you a heart of flesh." In the New Testament, St. Paul the apostle focuses on an interior knowledge of God. In Ephesians 1:18, he prays that God the Father will give Christians the wisdom and revelation of God's glory by means of "with the eyes of your heart enlightened, so that you may know the hope to which he has called you." Again, in Ephesians 3:16, Paul prays that the faithful "may be strengthened in your inner being with power through His Spirit and that Christ may dwell in your hearts through faith, as you are being rooted and grounded in love."

For the first fifteen centuries of the church's life, the main focus of religious writings was the meaning of salvation for human history, primarily through the writings of the Fathers and Mothers of the church. From their allegorical reflections on faith, they provided an exposition of the Christian faith that would bring people to Christ, by announcing what God had done in the missions of Christ and the Spirit. With

4. Moore, *Let This Mind*, 25.
5. Roy, *Engaging the Thought*, 48–49.

scholars such as St. Thomas Aquinas, a more systematic and theoretical account of faith was written to explain the reasonableness of religious belief and the compatibility of faith and reason. Within this systematic approach, Aquinas distinguished between speculative knowledge and affective or experiential knowledge.[6] Yet, while this systematic emphasis was couched in technical terms, holy men and women still spoke of their interior experiences of God using symbols, metaphors, and images including mentors such as Augustine, Benedict, Francis of Assisi, John of the Cross, Teresa of Avila, Therese of Lisieux, and many others.

In modern times, the conceptualization of religious experience has come into its own. It was the rise of humanism and modern science in Renaissance Europe that propelled a philosophic turn toward the individual. The religious, philosophical, and artistic focus shifted to the importance of the individual and interiority helped by the technological impact of the printing press. There began a revolution not just in what we know but in our grasp of how we knew it. Cynthia Crysdale sums up this momentous shift by stating: "It is not that previously people knew things in different ways; it was our understanding of understanding that gradually shifted. Truth is not merely what is handed down from on high but something that can be earthed from below upward, so to speak."[7]

Three European philosophers, Rene Descartes (1596–1650), David Hume (1717–1776) and Immanuel Kant (1724–1804) stand as the earliest representatives of the "turn to the subject" and the importance of interiority for philosophical thinking. Philosophers were now concerned not with the content of knowledge alone but with the question of knowing itself. The problem is: How do we come to know? In other words, what goes on inside the mind when we affirm some conclusion as a correct worldview or position on reality.[8] For Lonergan, if common sense knowledge with its practical orientation represented the first stage of meaning and theoretic knowledge with its technically precise orientation represented the second stage of meaning, then, the shift to interiority represents the third stage of meaning.[9] This shift to the interiority of the person set in motion the recognition that there is a difference between concrete knowledge and the knowing, valuing, and loving activities of the

6. Roy, *Engaging the Thought*, 49.

7. Crysdale, *Transformed Lives*, 98.

8. Crysdale *Transformed Lives*, 106.

9. Lonergan, *Method*, 93–96.

mind and heart. The active agent stands behind all truth claims including claims about God, self, others, and the world. It is in this context that the importance of personal experience gained a strong foothold.

The Meaning of Religious Experience

Chapter 2 noted that an intentional consciousness constitutes the human mind; that is, there is a tension in the human mind towards reality and the good that constitutes the person. The unrestricted desire to know and value reaches up to the question of God who understands all there is to understand with unrestricted insight and values all there is to value with an absolute goodness. The imperatives of consciousness reach their actualization when we fall in love. Falling in love is the highest level of consciousness that influences one's whole being. Lonergan positions religious experience on the fourth level of consciousness where the focus is specifically on infinite value.

Here are a few observations. First, religious experience is a unique state that forms consciousness into a being-in-love with the divine in an unrestricted manner. Responding to the love of the divine, the person loves the divine with their whole heart and mind.[10] Second, this experience is not primarily rational but one that *affectively* permeates one's whole being. Third, this experience, in the first place, is conscious but not known. It is an immediate affective undifferentiated awareness that precedes knowing. The awareness of the divine is at the level of love, self-surrender, and commitment.[11] Fourth, this awareness is an experience that is felt but not yet formulated into words. As such, we rely on the judgments, evaluations, and language of religious traditions to identify its authenticity. Fifth, the origin of this experience is not of the natural order but the supernatural order. What is supernatural sublates what is natural. The supernatural does not contradict or undermine the natural. It takes the natural into a higher context making the natural more profound. There exists a common reticence among many western people to speak about the supernatural and often the word is associated more popularly with paranormal phenomena. Notwithstanding this confusion, an experience of the supernatural represents a passage from one way of being to another higher and more authentic way of being. The

10. Lonergan, *Method*, 105–6.
11. Lonergan, *Method*, 106–7.

experience of the supernatural is transformative. Sixth, since the origin of this experience is supernatural, it is a pure gift of transcendent love coming from the free initiative of the divine.[12] Seventh, this experience brings to fulfillment everything else in our lives, brings peace and purpose, and turns us away from a trivialization of life.[13]

Eighth, this awareness is an experience of mystery, holiness, awe, and may even elicit feelings of fear.[14] Mystery does not denote a lack of understanding. We can understand mystery through reflective insight; however, knowledge of the divine is always proportionate to our human capacities and so our understanding of the divine can never be exhausted.[15] Ninth, religious experience leads the person into a prayer life, and the experience is mediated in the life of prayer. This life of prayer may find the person content to rest in the presence of the divine without needing to use words or form images.[16] Tenth, while the experience is immediate and effects an affective unity between the divine and the person, filling the whole being of the person, nevertheless, the person does not become divine but instead participates in the life of the divine. Eleventh, through this experience, the person is urged to deepen their awareness of the divine in all things.

Religious Experience and Human Development

Lonergan also invites people to verify that we develop in two ways.[17] Development happens through two vectors within consciousness. Lonergan calls these vectors healing and creative. The development from above downward is called the healing vector. Dunne calls it the healing helix.[18] This vector operates out of a felt sense of being-in-love that "commands commitment and joyfully carries it out, no matter what the sacrifice involved. When hatred reinforces bias, love dissolves, whether it be the bias of unconscious motivation, the bias of individual or group egoism, or the bias of omnicompetent, short-sighted common sense. When hatred

12. Lonergan, *Method*, 107.

13. Lonergan, *Method*, 106.

14. Lonergan, *Method*, 106.

15. Lonergan, *Method*, 110.

16. Lonergan, *Method*, 77.

17. Lonergan, *Third Collection*, 94–103.

18. Dunne, *Doing Better*, 91–94.

plods around in ever narrower vicious circles, love breaks the bonds of psychological and social determinism with the conviction of faith and the power of hope."[19] This vector touches the core of our spirit with love, moves us outward in love to others, and heals biases. This movement releases consciousness from anything that may cripple the proper working of the human spirit: inauthenticity, alienation, absurdity, and bias.

Love is the key to healing. Specifically, the love of God initiates a process of healing. The love of God is an experience of mystery which, in the first place, inspires our valuing of God, ourselves, others, and the world. It encourages us to seek the good in all its shapes. Lonergan places this falling in love at an even higher level than responsibility, asserting that "the gift of God's love occupies the ground and root of the fourth and highest level of man's intentional consciousness. It takes over the peak of the soul, the *apex animae*."[20] We learn that what is best begins beyond human love and leads us to love more vibrantly. Lonergan states:

> To be in love is to be in love with someone. To be in love without qualification or conditions or reservations or limits is to be in love with someone transcendent. When someone transcendent is my beloved, he is in my heart, real to me from within me. When that love is the fulfillment of my unrestricted thrust of self-transcendence through intelligence and truth and responsibility, the one that fulfills that thrust must be supreme in intelligence, truth, goodness. Since he chooses to come to me by a gift of love for him, he himself must be love. Since loving him is my transcending self, it is also my denial of the self to be transcended. Since loving of him means loving attention to him, it is prayer, meditation, contemplation. Since love of him is fruitful, it overflows into love of all those that he loves or might love.[21]

The other vector of development works from below upwards. Tad Dunne calls this movement the creative helix.[22] This vector operates out of questioning. Lonergan states that the creative vector proceeds "from experience to growing understanding, from growing understanding to balanced judgment, from balanced judgment to fruitful actions, and from fruitful action to new situations that call forth further understanding,

19. Lonergan, *Third Collection*, 101.

20. Lonergan, *Method*, 107. *Apex Animae* means the peak or top of the soul.

21. Lonergan, *Method*, 109.

22. Dunne, *Doing Better*, 87–88.

[profound] judgment, richer courses of action."[23] Usually, the word "creativity" is used commonly in our wider social discourse to speak about "creative types" and points toward artists, actors, and dramatists. Here, the word has a very technical meaning. It is the integrating spiral in our lives.

As soon as we pay attention to a numinous experience, we feel the need to understand. What are we experiencing? From where does it originate? What is happening to us? What is its implication for our life? How do we know that it is authentic? Understanding sublates and integrates the data of experience into a new level. We are seeking exact knowledge of this numinous experience. In the past, the formulations for understanding this religious experience have found expression in art, symbol, myth, and language. More significantly still, when we understand, we sense the normative drive to verify and check out that we have not misunderstood; therefore, judgment raises religious understanding to a new level. We might symbolize our experience through various mediations, yet through judgment we desire to verify whether such interpretations are correct understandings. Alternatively, our understandings might have been clouded by cultural and social distortions that conspire to serve up an aberration of religion.

The step of judgments of fact and value is critical since it helps protect us from the possibility of distorted mimesis postulated in the work of Rene Girard. In his investigation of the scapegoat mechanism, Girard found a brutal and violent outworking in the name of religion through archaic societies. He discovered that people worshipped the gods through human sacrifice, thinking that such sacrifices could bring peace to communities torn by violence and division. This assessment alone leads us to the conclusion that not all religious practices are authentic or helpful for human living and that we must learn to distinguish genuine and false religion. Nor should we rely solely on religious experience. We must subject such experience to the understanding and judgment of the religious community. There is a danger in thinking that religious experience is the only and sufficient source of religious objectivity. Roy states we are prone to "the age-old temptation of illuminism, that is, of relying only on one's own inner light" especially when we segregate such experiences from the levels of understanding, judgment, and responsibility.[24]

---

23. Lonergan, *Third Collection*, 101.
24. Roy, *Engaging the Thought*, 59.

Religious Experience and Realms of Meaning

It is helpful to also explore religious experience through Lonergan's notion of realms of meaning. This notion enables us to understand transformation in a more precise way. First, what does Lonergan mean by realms
of meaning?[25] The term realm of meaning points to the fact that we come
to meaning via various paths, with their own goals, procedures, and purposes. Chapter 2 spoke about human consciousness and its operations
which can be empirically verifiable through self-appropriation. There are
different kinds of desires and each is attained by a different path. We may
want to know some practical solution to a problem or some technical
explanation as to the way something works. Some questions concern the
external world, and some are special concerns about the interior world.
Each of these different desires evoke a different intentionality in human
consciousness. Lonergan states that any field of knowing inhabits a realm
of meaning and each realm is distinguished from the other since "any
realm becomes differentiated from the others when it develops its own
language, its own distinct mode of apprehension and its own cultural,
social, or professional group speaking in that fashion and apprehending
in that manner."[26] Each realm mediates meaning in a very different way.

Lonergan identifies several realms: common sense, theory, interiority, art, scholarship, and transcendence. Lonergan opens the possibility
for other realms to exist and it is possible to live within many realms of
meaning at the same time. Each of us can set about the task of mastering
each realm of meaning through appropriating or noticing our operations
in human consciousness and becoming familiar with the language, the
ideas, and modes of dwelling in each realm. However, to try to inhabit
one realm of meaning using the canons and procedures of a different
realm of meaning will not bear fruit. For example, we are not going to be
able to reach up to the mystery of God in an interpersonal and relational
manner simply by being artistic or by being intellectual. We will need to
engage in the practice of prayerfulness and become mystical.

The realm of common sense mediates meaning through working
out the most practical way to do something. Its goal is concrete outcomes.
The principal intention is practical living. The realm of theory especially
prevalent in the sciences mediates meaning through precise terms and
the relations between terms to answer questions that common sense

25. Lonergan, *Method*, 81–85.
26. Lonergan, *Method*, 272.

cannot answer. The realm of interiority focuses on the acts or operations of human consciousness that accompanies our desire to know, value, and love. The important question for this realm is: who is this person, this knower, this discoverer, this symbolizer, or this believer?

Specifically, religious experience belongs to the realm of meaning called transcendence. The realm of transcendence has both an inner and an outer dimension. Interiorly, it is the realm of encountering the divine, adoration, prayer, mysticism, and prostration in silence before the mystery of God. Outwardly, it is also the realm of sacred objects together with holy places, times, and actions, where priests, shamans, monks, and spiritual teachers often take on the role of mediator of divine reality. Throughout ancient cultures, it finds its expression first in the language of myth and magic and then, progressively in the language of ascetics and mystics.[27] When we read the Bible, we discern the divine message through an agreement about common sense idioms of language drawn from everyday life. Now and again, we come across occasions when the divine word affected people interiorly. When we abide in the realm of transcendence, all the activities of human consciousness are influenced, that is, our feeling, understanding, and reasoning, deliberating, and choosing as well as our action.

This realm of meaning is the kind of experiential flow out of which we create sacred institutional expressions and so is fundamental to the development of religious communities and their doctrines. Mark Morelli speaks to the mystical interest or concern that recognizes this experimental flow:

> The mystical interest is an interest in the Ultimate, the All, the One, the mysterious Beginning, the mysterious End, and the mysterious Ground and the Point of our existence. It emerges to pattern the flow of experience from *the combination of our presence to ourselves as inescapably limited being with an inescapable and unlimited aspiration* for meaning, objectivity, knowledge, truth, reality, and value. Our presence to ourselves in our basic commitment is at once presence to ourselves as unfinished, striving, and incomplete and presence to ourselves as radically dissatisfied with anything less than meaning, objectivity, knowledge, truth, reality, and value *in their absoluteness*.[28] Our operations of consciousness are configured in such a way by

27. Lonergan, *Method*, 266.
28. Morelli, *Self-Possession*, 238.

this mystical concern that we anticipate absolute truth, absolute value, and complete fulfillment.[29]

Love is the supreme testimony for the experience of absolute truth. Morelli states that between an unknown beginning and an unknown end in which each of us finds ourselves, no one can bring us absolute fulfillment since the human love we hold for one another is conditional and restricted. By contrast, Morelli asserts "the object of our mystical being-in-love is mysterious. The love we feel is a love that has no bounds. The acceptance we feel is an acceptance that has no conditions. It is unconditional and unrestricted love that sustains us and enables us to persist in our basic commitment to the pursuit of meaning, objectivity, knowledge, truth, reality, and value despite our dramatic failures and psychological suffering, our intellectual confusion, our aesthetic numbness, our practical obstacles and debacles, our physical pain, our distracting, derailing, and debilitating desires and fears, and undermining victimization by others."[30]

Within the realm of transcendence, we feel the presence of the divine as a "deep-seated joy, awe, fascination, peace, a feeling of union with the mysterious Ground. It is a spontaneous inclination to kindness, faithfulness, gentleness, self-control, gratitude, and a readiness to forgive and be forgiven. Because it is an affective or felt apprehension of *absolute value*, it can be as terrifying as it is fulfilling, as humbling as it is uplifting."[31] To this end, Morelli sums up the influence of religious experience on the other realms of meaning:

> Our practical preoccupations are disrupted by the reluctant recognition of the mysterious inefficiency and pointlessness of our life-persevering practicality. Our intellectual preoccupations are disrupted by the recognition of the mysterious restrictedness of our questioning. Our artistic preoccupations are disrupted by the recognition of the mysterious possibilities of our creativity. Our dramatic preoccupations are disrupted by the mysterious interventions that change the course of our lives and the mysterious turns our stories take independently of our deliberate dramatic decisions. Ultimately, we ask what our deliberate response

29. Morelli, *Self-Possession*, 239.
30. Morelli, *Self-Possession*, 240.
31. Morelli, *Self-Possession*, 241.

to this experienced apprehension of mysterious absolute value will be.[32]

Religious Conversion

With the scaffolding offered in chapter 2, an understanding of religious experience, and the transcendent realm of meaning we are now better able to understand religious conversion. Religious conversion is the core of religion, *the light* of faith, a light capable of healing people so that their wounded creativity and derailed capacity for responsibility might be released once again. An explicitly Christian horizon speaks to this event as the gift of the love of God poured into our hearts by the gift of the Holy Spirit (Rom 5:5). It is wholly intersubjective, interpersonal, unitive, and a gift long before it becomes an achievement in our lives. It is a gift that requires openness on our part to receive it. Although God creates us with a natural desire to know God, the grace of God heals our alienation from God and ourselves. Through grace, God restores us to the creation God intended us to be. The gift of grace given in religious conversion differs from simple self-esteem. In self-esteem, one may be able to affirm the goodness in oneself as having been made good by God. However, the experience of religious conversion grounded in religious love takes this a step further and asserts that one feels and understands one's value and the value of others as God values us, an existence bathed in the light of being loved by God.

In one of his most poetic moments, Lonergan describes religious conversion through the metaphor of music: "It is as though a room were filled with music though one can have no sure knowledge of its source. There is in the world, as it were, a changed field of love and meaning; here and there it reaches notable intensity; but it is very unobtrusive, hidden, inviting each of us to join. And join we must if we are to perceive it, for our perceiving is through our own loving."[33] Lonergan is inviting us to reflect on our response of self-surrender to a process that begins in a gift. Some people experience the first moment of religious conversion as overwhelming power. These people usually emphasize the awesome power of God. Others speak about a patient yet gentle power working steadily to make the world right. These people emphasize that conversion in the

32. Morelli, *Self-Possession*, 241.
33. Lonergan, *Method*, 290.

very act of being drawn to love God and the things of God slowly, quietly, and without great fanfare. Being-in-love with God conditions what we consider to be meaningful, truthful, and valuable and the social processes to build a better society. It facilitates the emergence of new insights and a new willingness to put them into practice.

When there is a transformation of our mind and heart through falling in love with God unreservedly, religious faith is born. Faith is a knowledge born of religious love. While we usually come to love something by first knowing that thing, in this case, we come to know God by first being-in-love. According to Roy, Lonergan seems to locate religious faith between two fundamental components.[34] The first component is our awareness of being-in-love unconditionally. This being-in-love awareness speaks to us through an affective knowledge; that is, we feel it transforming us. The second component is just as important. It is the component of the community of faith. Lonergan describes the word of the community as "the word of religious tradition that has accumulated religious wisdom, the word of fellowship that unites those that share the gift of God's love, the word of the Gospel that announces that God has loved us first and, in the fullness of time, has revealed that love in Christ crucified, dead, and risen."[35] Without the community of faith, there is a high possibility that we will not be able to understand the meaning of the experience of grace. There is always the possibility of distortion when affectivity alone is involved.

For any religious tradition which speaks of divine revelation, the revelation of God comes out of the interrelationship between people, tradition, and our falling-in-love with God. Religious conversion leads to a sense of the "we" between God and us. It is a "we" that takes shape by belonging and taking part in the life of a religious community such as the church, the mosque, or the synagogue. It will prompt individuals committed to each other to make a courageous stance, choose a different vocational path, or engage in the task of working through complex problems in the knowledge that God loves them personally and unconditionally. Religious conversion brings a specific completion into our lives and becomes a powerful undertow first to our deciding and, then, to our knowing, understanding and feeling. As such religious conversion sublates all other forms of transformation.

34. Roy, *Engaging the Thought*, 83–84.
35. Lonergan, *Method*, 113.

Religious Conversion and the Sinner

To say that religious conversion means turning toward God in a dynamic state of being-in-love also suggests turning away from something. It implies that any understanding of religious conversion takes note of the reality of sin and breakdown. Lonergan's understanding of sin proceeds from his first paradigm for reality, the innate desire to know, to value, and to love. Sin is a disregard for the five imperatives of human consciousness. For Lonergan, sin is not so much this or that external act that is against the will of God. It is the prior failure on our part not to choose what we ought to choose, the failure of the creature who dissents from the Creator's governing wisdom and rejects the first paradigm for reality.

Sin makes an idol of the ego stuck in its current fixated state. In that state, we negate the need to change, we deny the call to be more, and we become fixed in the error of thinking that who we are currently is enough. Sin is some form of self-assertion of the status quo coupled to the vulgarity and banality of the fixated ego state. Sin makes the fixated immature ego state so absolute as to put the possibility of our true selves beyond the reach of the suffering required for the ego's transformation. The sinner may engage in minimization or rationalization, arguing that the evil done was not so bad after all. Guilt outwits rationalizations and avoidances by taking one back to the single time and place when the sinner did the evil act. In doing the heinous act, the sinner has introduced something unlovable into the very being of the victim. The sinner's hell is recognizing the wound of the victim whom the sinner has offended.

From the perspective of our relationship with God, sin is the shrinking of divine meaning in our lives. The mystery of iniquity goes hand in hand with the revelation of God's love and only in the light of God's love can we truly appreciate sin. There are three words from the Old Testament that try to get at the heart of sin from a practical perspective: *pesha*, *awon*, and *hattah*. *Pesha* is an act of rebellion or unfaithfulness between two parties who are bound by a covenant, see 1 Kings 12:19. This rebellion against an alliance creates enmity and hostility between the parties.[36] *Awon* is the word for iniquity or guilt or the state of the sinner resulting from some transgression. It points to an image of something that has been distorted and bent out of shape by a heavy object. The weight of this distortion brings on feelings of punishment, and so guilt and punishment

36. Tierney, *Sacrament of Penance*, 14–16.

are indistinguishable.[37] *Hattah* is a word that means to miss the mark or the target. By our evil actions, we think that we may have achieved something, but all we have done is miss the true mark or deviated from our true north. The sinner is trapped in self-deception and lost in a wasteland of guilt. God also feels the delusion of the sinner since God expected one thing and got another, and so God responds with healing (Isa 5:1–13).[38]

We use several terms to name the sinner: perpetrator, victimizer, violator, or evil-doer. The human person is flawed by sin and so inclined to moral evil. As a personal reality, sin has both a religious and moral dimension.[39] Sin is a rejection of our real value as gifted by God, of that special divine intimacy made possible by the grace of God. It can cause a fundamental break in our relationship with God, which has been established by God's freedom toward us. Sin curtails our ability to be free. As a distortion of God's creation, it becomes a distortion of our freedom, so that we turn away from God and God's design. We can fail through doing too much, and wanting too much. We can all suffer from the overreaching of pride and end up with compulsions of one sort or another. Conversely, we can also fail through becoming trapped in our physical cravings and fears and refuse to go forward into the unknown. To the addict, nothing is more important than the object of his addiction. The desire of the human heart that is meant to find its fulfillment in God focuses all its energies on the finite object of obsession.[40] The Bible identifies this kind of sin as a form of personal idolatry or the worship of a false god. Ormerod states that each of us "can witness the compulsive addictive power of sin in the multiple addictions that plague our society. Drugs, pornography, power, violence, greed, sexual promiscuity, and alcohol are the most obvious examples; subtler are the distorted attachments to consumer products, shopping, entertainment, computer games, mobile phones, and automobiles! Much of modern consumer society is based on the compulsive power of shopping and our attachment to the products that fill our marketplaces!"[41]

37. Tierney, *Sacrament of Penance*, 16–17.

38. Tierney, *Sacrament of Penance*, 17–20.

39. Ormerod, *Grace and Disgrace*, 74–78.

40. Ormerod, *Grace and Disgrace*, 80.

41. Ormerod, *Creation, Grace*, 49.

Not only is sin personal and individual, but sin is also social.[42] Each of us cannot be responsible for the situation of our birth or what kind of community we are born into yet, as we grow, we are socialized into both the evil and good of society. Social sin can affect whole communities through moral crimes such as corruption and inequality, massive poverty, and marginalization. Social sin can destroy entire communities, and social structures can be debilitated and debilitating in their potential to deliver needed goods to society.

Evil and sin are not only personal and social but also cultural and historical realities. Sin entrenches cultural depravity through historical acts. The near extinction of the Australian Aboriginals was justified based on a social understanding of cultural superiority which underpinned the idea of the survival of the fittest. Human decisions, intentions, and actions bounce off one another, creating a trajectory. These are the stuff of history. Ormerod concludes that "as societies are prolonged through history, so to sin has its own historical dimension. Sinful institutions develop a momentum, a drive to expand, to crush opposition, to find scapegoats. Evil people flourish and attain power while the good remain silent trapped in their powerlessness."[43]

Any discussion of sin must distinguish between suffering and evil. Not all suffering is evil and not all evil brings about immediate human suffering. On the one hand, suffering connects to our finiteness or limitations often felt in our sense of vulnerability. However, there is also a kind of suffering that amounts to evil. Ormerod describes suffering that follows upon evil as "without any apparent meaning, suffering that is caused by callous indifference, or malicious intent, suffering that is caused for no good reason. This is meaningless suffering. This is where we find an overlap with the problem of evil."[44] Suffering as evil has the potential always to cast a blanket of meaninglessness over God's meaningful creation. It can even create doubt within regarding the very existence of God. The experiences of brute suffering and death can take on a different and distorted meaning through the lens of sin and evil. The plight of this evil inhibits growth.

42. Ormerod, *Grace and Disgrace*, 79–80.

43. Ormerod, *Grace and Disgrace*, 80.

44. Ormerod, *Creation, Grace*, 15.

Lonergan speaks of sin in several terms: inauthenticity, decline and alienation, absurdity, and bias.[45] First, inauthenticity comes about when we do not follow our natural desire to know, to value and to love. Instead of being attentive, intelligent, reasonable, and responsible and in love we are in fact inattentive, unintelligent, unreasonable, irresponsible and unloving. We restrict our horizon. We lose what we naturally could be and could do. Since God is the highest good in our lives, we lose authentic relations with God. Second, alienation goes to the heart of being estranged from our very self. Alienated from the self, we become alienated from others and God. Third, through inauthenticity and alienation, our lives can become more and more characterized as living absurdly. A thing is absurd when it has no intelligibility about it or it does not make sense when subjected to all the relevant questions. Within historical circumstances, we find that this absurdity accumulates and impedes our ability to discover desire's natural direction toward reality and the good. Notwithstanding this blanket of meaninglessness caused by evil, we look for meaning and a practical solution to the problem of evil. Ormerod describes it as a solution that will require us to suffer. He states:

> Such a process is likely to be a form of suffering. Evil may be a cause of suffering, as noted above, but there is another form of suffering that is not found in a lack of meaning, *but in giving birth to new meaning*. It is the suffering that absorbs evil, freely and willingly, making of it an opportunity for a gift of reconciliation and compassion for the sinner, who in the end is not just damaging the victims of sin, but mutilating the sinner's own humanity. Such a willingness to suffer can both expose evil for what it really is in all its banality and disarm it of its own power over us. For the power of evil lies in its ability to evoke, like for like, to respond to evil with further evil, an eye for an eye or worse, and so build a spiral of violence and evil spinning out of control, destroying all who cross its path.[46]

Fourth, Lonergan uses the category of bias to understand the ways that our sin derails our practical living. Bias fundamentally is anything within human consciousness which can stop the full flourishing of intelligence, reasonableness, and responsibility when searching for possible solutions. There are four biases: dramatic, individual, group, and general.

---

45. Lonergan, *Method*, 53–55.
46. Ormerod, *Public God*, 170.

Dramatic bias, or what Dunne calls neurosis,[47] means that we do not allow all memories, feelings, and images to emerge from our psyche into consciousness through a form of repression or suppression.[48] Dramatic bias is played out in our psychic lives. It acknowledges the power of fear and anxiety to dominate our practical search for solutions to living. Our ability to ask questions is dependent on images associated with feelings. Dramatic bias blocks relevant images coming into conscious experience. Lack of relevant images means a lack of insights which reduces the possibility of changing unhealthy ways of behaving. The result is a self-alienation which may flow into self-destructive behavior. Through repression, we block unknowingly the data that is distasteful, revolting, or dreadful to us. Through suppression, we prevent data knowingly.

Individual bias, or what Dunne calls egotism,[49] means that we are more attentive to what will benefit our desires and needs than those of other people and so, we intentionally avoid correct understanding.[50] Individual bias, often called self-centeredness, occurs when an individual, overcome by their fixated egocentric desires, suppresses a full use of intelligence for a cooperative living to look after their interest. This person is smart enough to design and implement courses of action that will enable him to outsmart others through exploitative behavior. He may also engage in enough suppression so as not to allow questions to emerge that might steer him towards a better course of action.

Group bias, or what Dunne calls loyalism,[51] means that we are more protective of the interests of a group over the common good, that is, the nation, class, race or gender, focusing on attaining stronger social and cultural ties.[52] Social or group bias solidifies by a group's increasing desire for self-preservation and power over other groups or individuals. Such groups rationalize their short-sighted position and argue that they have no other choice but to act in such a manner as to maximize the existence and perpetuation of their group. Depending on the character of the group, actions taken can either be reforming or revolutionary. In the latter, social conditions break down to such a point, that one group

47. Dunne, *Doing Better*, 77.
48. Lonergan, *Insight*, 214.
49. Dunne, *Doing Better*, 77.
50. Lonergan, *Insight*, 244–47.
51. Dunne, *Doing Better*, 77.
52. Lonergan, *Insight*, 247–50.

overpowers another group and, in the case of escalating violence, often the oppressed easily become the oppressors. Thus, group bias solidifies in societies where social conditions that may prove oppressive toward groups. This solidification invites reversal but without the guarantees that the new arrangement will be free of physical violence or oppression. Group bias is a good description of what we find in totalitarian regimes.

General bias, or what Dunne calls commonsensism,[53] is a lack of willingness in seeking answers to problems with a long-term view, or to exploring an in-depth investigation of the issues. This bias does not take into account the full use of intelligence.[54] Long-term solutions require giving full reign to thinking often across other creative and collaborative frameworks. Without critical thinking, fear, manipulation, and violence become distorted pathways for keeping people subdued, suppressing change. The ramifications of general bias are massive. We end up not being able to distinguish between what makes sense for living genuinely and what does not make sense. There is no criterion or authority for discerning the truth. What people judge as progress in one generation is seen by people in the next generation not to be progressive at all. The consequence is the brushing aside of relevant and challenging questions. The disinterested desire for truth and value is abandoned and, in its place, a single-minded and simplistic practicality becomes the dominant paradigm for reality. We fool ourselves into believing that every challenge or problem merely requires that we practically do something. Instead, the solution is to operate from a liberated intelligence and for wonder and questioning to become the dominant concern in our consciousness, requiring intellectual detachment and impartiality.

The last of our biases, especially within our western societies, is the bias of secularism. Secularism is a bias toward thinking only about the space-time world of our experience and against thinking about our ultimate significance in the eyes of God. It results in the evasion of thinking about our ultimate origins, ongoing purpose, and our final destiny. The truth of the matter is that to be human is to feel inner desires for beauty, understanding, reality, goodness, friendship, and to experience them in such a way that our desire becomes unrestricted. As we pursue these orientations, we go beyond ourselves as we are to something more and so

---

53. Dunne, *Doing Better*, 81–82.

54. Lonergan, *Insight*, 250–51.

become more artistic, insightful, creative, caring to others, and open to a relationship of love with God.

Religious Conversion and the Victim

While disregarding the design of God and rejecting our true selves, the sinner also creates victims and leaves behind the violated in their wake. The victim is the one who has been objectively wounded, harmed, or injured and yet remains innocent and undeserving of this action against them. When we speak about conversion in a religious context, then we must reflect on how the grace of conversion helps the victimized to overcome the effects of sin and evil done against them. Jerome Miller states that when a gravely evil act happens against a victim, the event is not something that happens *in* their world. It is something that happens *to* their world.[55] Sin ruptures the life of the victim as a whole such that the victim finds it difficult to assimilate the evil easily. It taints the past and can ruin the future. It insults, injures, and violates the person as a child of God and the one God has loved into being.

The Ancient Greeks pondered on how the victim bears this darkness in their lives. They may lose their social standing, worldly possessions, and even physical well-being. What the ancients did not see was the ongoing impact of evil. Despite the harm done against them, the ancients thought the victim as innocent remaining untroubled and at peace in the knowledge that they were not the source of evil. This innocence and moral untroubledness were thought to help the victim move on. All these insights fail to come to grips with the world-shattering character of trauma. To allow to go unnoticed the traumatic nature of evil is akin to accepting evil as a fact of life and normalizing it, and any attempt to do such a thing becomes morally horrifying.

When we delve into the concrete experience of the victim, we realize that the evil done to them enters their history, their very being, and their web of relationships. The victim finds it very hard to separate this evil from their person. They feel horrifyingly awful and, therefore, think that there must be something wrong with them in their very self. The victim is made to live with and bear this horrifying thing in such a way that surviving this evil and integrating this episode into their life becomes very difficult. Since the goodness of their being recoils from this evil, moving

55. Miller, "Wound Made Fountain," 534.

past it, assimilating it, living with it, and not allowing it to affect one's future becomes effectively impossible. Evil forces the victim into a dead end: a set of evil memories impossible to erase and excruciating to bear. Such experiences are witnessed today in the lives of children who are victims of abuse. Many years later into their adult lives, they still suffer from the impact of the abuse. Even when the courts have assuaged some of the reactive anger built up against the abuser, the suffering remains. Also, when counseling has helped the victim or, even when the victim has raised a family of their own, still the wound of the evil committed against them continues to cause suffering in their relationships.

Depending on the intensity and duration of the victimization process, psychic wounding, especially when inflicted at an early age, can have a devastating effect on the life of the person and their ability to be attentive, intelligent, reasonable, responsible, and in love. Victims still have the psychological responsibility to find the truth and do the truth, yet the victimization of our psyche can be such that we end up being self-victimizing as well as other-victimizing. The victim can become the perpetrator. Such victimization can also turn into neurotic obsessive-compulsive attention to a specific matter, a habit that forms in our psyche or our subconscious, taking possession of our focus instead of us learning to be attentive. The neurotic tendency to fixate on specific memories, fears, anxieties, and projects accompanies a lack of attention toward being fixated. In the end, we drive away from our minds questions that are important to healthy living.

Lastly, since we are dealing with victimization, often at an early age, it is important to explore what victimization can do to self-esteem. Again, Sebastian Moore maps this territory with poise and subtlety. From our beginning, real desire is feeling good within ourselves, and this feeling goes out to others in creative relationships. This feeling good is our true self or the true feeling about ourselves.[56] By contrast, he concludes that "the only way not to want to *go* to others is to go against, to *deny*, to try to strangle, my feeling of myself as good."[57] Saying no to "myself as good" is what Moore calls sin. Sin stifles real desire. Sin is the refusal to die into a fuller self. It is often at the basis of our hatred of others and our self-hatred. Why do we deny ourselves this goodness? We deny ourselves this good because we have become convinced that our desires cannot be

56. Moore, *Let This Mind*, 81.

57. Moore, *Let This Mind*, 81.

trusted, and if desires cannot be trusted then we cannot be trusted, and we doubt our desirability. Since we cannot feel right about any of our convictions, then we do not do what is right.

This situation of diminished goodness is especially tested at the crisis points of growth. According to Lawrence Kohlberg and Erik Erickson respectively, both moral and affective development bring us to points of crises in the process of becoming individuals. Crises bring discomfort to our psychic life. The separation from our parents is a force of nature and one such crisis impacting powerfully on us. Since this separation is not a trouble-free state. Suffering causes us to doubt ourselves. We cry inwardly "there is something wrong with me."[58] Each point of crisis may even be exacerbated by feelings of guilt, primarily when the parent communicates the message: "either you are a part of me, or you are totally on your own."[59] We feel a rejection of ourselves and what we have become. The child then begrudges their desire to be separate, and this reaction brings about a denial of a part of themselves and a resistance to growth. Ormerod states that in the child "it is displayed in an inability to trust the world, an anxiety that seeks to control the world, a fear in breaking out of familiar patterns."[60] We become lazy, scared to change, and unable to see the world as it is.[61] There emerges a radical disvaluing of our felt nature which becomes a pre-condition to sinful acts.[62] Since we are "beings in time" sin is the refusal to allow new questions and take on new-ego states.[63]

There exists a healing promise in religious conversion especially when nurtured within a community of faith. It addresses the person at the point of their breakdown. Moore asserts that the cure for the sickness of desire is *"to experience myself as I am, as the desired of God."*[64] For these reasons, healing for the victimized is never enabled through harsh judgment. It flows from the persuasion of love. A psyche that recovers through the persuasion of love is a psyche becoming more capable of

---

58. Ormerod, *Grace and Disgrace*, 154.

59. Roy, "Human Desires," 57.

60. Ormerod, *Grace and Disgrace*, 156.

61. Moore, *Let This Mind*, 85.

62. Ormerod, *Grace and Disgrace*, 156. Ormerod argues that this original disesteem is what has been called original sin.

63. Moore, *Let This Mind*, 100.

64. Moore, *Let This Mind*, 82.

spontaneously desiring the objectives of the human spirit and bringing the fruit of this desiring to bear on an actual human good within society.

Religious Conversion and *Babette's Feast*

Religious conversion transforms us through the gift of unconditional love and also changes our interpersonal love. To illustrate this insight, the film *Babette's Feast* (1987) has a storyline that suggests religious conversion. The storyline of the film is set in the barren, windswept terrain of Jutland, Denmark. There, we encounter a group of people belonging to a strict religious sect now dying out. Two central protagonists of the film are the sisters, Phillipa and Martina, whose father had been the founder of this austere community of faith. At the beginning of the film, we learn of their past relationships of love and loss. One sister gave up the possibility of being an opera singer and, the other, a proposal of marriage by a young lieutenant. Asceticism and self-denial have been the rule for their lives primarily in the way they eat and dress so that they may be worthy of heaven. As a condition for living the community way, they have accepted the imposition of celibacy.

In time, through a series of circumstances, Babette Hersant comes to live among the sisters as their housekeeper. After fourteen years among them, Babette wins a French lottery to the value of 10,000 francs, but instead of returning to Paris, she gets permission from her employers to spend the money on a French meal for them and their guests. Twelve people agree to attend the meal including Martina's lieutenant suitor from her youth, now holding the rank of general. The sisters decide to eat the meal but with their minds on their founder and not on the food.

However, as the meal unfolds, something surprising occurs. The participants cannot sustain their negating asceticism. Everyone begins to enjoy and take pleasure in the food. There is a pronounced transformation of desire. Martina and her friend renew their friendship. The parishioners gather outside holding hands and singing songs. Babette is proud to tell the sisters of her chef background, and she glows through being creative. The meal has a liberating effect on the participants who begin to share as never before. Her delicacies become an affirmation of the goodness of life and an act of gratitude by Babette toward the sisters for taking her in as their housekeeper. Babette is full of love and through her actions demonstrates that God is an abundant giver. We witness an indirect awakening to the true God. There is a degree of foolishness initially in Babette's action, given that the participants are reticent to enjoy the meal entirely. However, Babette's choice reveals a profound insight, namely, that all humans find their fulfillment in acts of love and care. We are "hardwired" for the love of others. We remain strangers to ourselves without the gift of love. Real self-esteem comes about when we are radically open to others and life. Indeed, the gift of human love which motivates us toward seeking the good wherever we may find it, implicitly carries, at its core, the divine love of God.

4

Religious Conversion, Mentors, and Cinema

LONERGAN DEFINES RELIGIOUS CONVERSION as the experience of falling in love with God, a surrender of ourselves to God without the loss of self, a transformation of our horizon through the power of unconditional love, and the fulfillment of our whole person.[1] It brings peace and joy, self-control, humility, patience, love of neighbor and self (Gal 5:22–23; Mark 5:30). Since this fulfillment impacts our feelings, it also impacts our values and the drama of our lives. By contrast, a lack of fulfillment may result in forms of self-centeredness, cynicism, the urge to dominate and control, despair, and violence. Religious conversion has also been called transcendent affective conversion.[2] This conversion is *transcendent* since it is a kind of conversion that we do not produce from our efforts but comes from the power of the divine operating in our lives. It is *affective* since it shapes our feelings towards wanting to know God and draws us to do what God desires. This chapter will examine religious conversion through the lives of mentors and in cinema.

RELIGIOUS CONVERSION AND ST. AUGUSTINE

St. Augustine (354–430 CE), Bishop of Hippo in Roman North Africa, is a very significant Christian mentor. He is best known for his work titled the *Confessions*, a classic autobiographical Christian text. The *Confessions*

1. Lonergan, *Method*, 105, 240.
2. Dunne, *Doing Better*, 139–40.

is a spiritual text written as a prayer to God and from an interior perspective, yet it has become a public piece of religious literature. The image is of a man praying to God with a quill in his hand. Through critical texts in the *Confessions*, we gain insight into shape of his conversion experience. The title *Confessions* means telling one's sins while calling out prayerfully to God in praise of God's mercy. This text is Augustine in his voice. All through the *Confessions*, a constant theme emerges based on personal experience; namely, we can only really know ourselves when we know God. Augustine's interior account becomes a work of faith seeking understanding about creation and God through the personal history of a man struggling to understand himself and God, while couching his narrative in the form of a prayer addressed to God.

Augustine's focus is on the inner self. His writing is scripturally informed as he relates the highs and lows of his life. Therefore, Augustine moves between the realms of interiority, common sense, and transcendence. In the realm of interiority, he is working from the assumption that we are likely to find the divine more "in" ourselves than in creation. He is thoughtfully attending to himself especially his feelings and evaluating. In the realm of common sense, he makes full use of Scripture, demonstrating a process of learning from the wisdom of the sacred text. In the realm of transcendence, he mediates the experience of grace through a prayerful writing addressed to God in whom all human restlessness finds peace. God is not only the One who keeps all created things in existence, but God is also the inner light powering our ability to notice, to know, and to value.[3]

As he tells the story of his soul from his birth to his ministry as the bishop of Hippo, we sense a man who remains troubled and anxious, yet quietly confident in the power of God's love to guide him. His deep and abiding faith in God does not take away his vulnerability and frailty but serves only to highlight even more just how much he is dependent on God. It is a story about the way God and the human soul are intimately related. It is also the story of a soul separated from God by sin and struggling to move beyond the false self in order ultimately to find peace.

How did Aurelius Augustine become St. Augustine of Hippo? Augustine's conversion ultimately moves him towards intelligent thinking and responsible living, illuminated by a graced faith in God and love for God. It requires him to think differently about reality as much as it urges

3. In chapter 6, I will examine the transformation to Augustine's moral life, and in chapter 8, I will examine his renewed intellectual orientation.

him to seek God. Some of this transformation to his thinking came when he was at Carthage, at about the age of 18, at a time when his father had died two years before. Carthage was the capital of Roman North Africa, a seaport and university city. At Carthage, he experiments with his sexuality, his feelings, and his intellect. He is the star of the university, praised and followed by other young men.[4] Augustine states of this time "My hunger was internal, deprived of inward food that is of you yourself, my God. But that was not the kind of food I felt. I was without my desire for incorruptible nourishment, not because I was replete with it, but the emptier I was, the more unappetizing such food became. So, my soul was in rotten health. In an ulcerous condition it thrust itself to outward things."[5] In these early years, his focus is on being great with words, style, and rhetoric to be able to persuade by the sheer force of his phrases and speech. However, a whole new set of desires emerge within him especially the desire to know the truth of things.

His first step toward God is to change the way he prays and the kinds of values he believes to be worthwhile. After reading *Hortensis* by Cicero, he asserts that the meaning of the text altered his feelings, gave him different values and priorities, and "suddenly every vein of hope became empty" and he "longed for the immortality of wisdom with an incredible ardor."[6] Through reading Cicero, Augustine's mind is enabled to transform, from acknowledging the existence of only visible and material things to accepting the existence of invisible reality or immateriality. Augustine is able then to discover the soul and the light of faith that powers it. He shifts his perspective from a dead-end way of thinking that equated reality only with what we see. In this former worldview God could not be seen, so, God must not be real. This shift in thinking comes as an enormous trauma for Augustine. It begins into focus a search not only for the wisdom found in Cicero, but wisdom itself and this search leads him to God. Augustine equates this event with the journey of the Prodigal Son, yet he did not know at that time precisely what God was doing with him. God works on him providentially and interiorly through someone else, the non-Christian philosopher, Cicero.

Apart from Cicero, many other significant people shape Augustine's religious, moral, and intellectual horizon. These include the charismatic

---

4. Haughton, *Love*, 129.

5. Augustine, *Confessions* III.i.1 (35).

6. Augustine, *Confessions* III.iv.7 (39).

Bishop of Milan, Ambrose. The translated works of Marcus Victorinus who, distinguished practitioner of rhetoric and philosophy who eventually becomes a Christian, impress Augustine with their insights. The host of significant people includes Simplicianus who succeeds Ambrose as Bishop of Milan. There were also closer friends such as Alypius, baptized with Augustine and another friend, who dies in his prime, and whose name we do not know from the *Confessions*. Lastly, there is his common-law wife of fifteen years who loves him deeply and who demonstrates a quality of love when she is sent away by Augustine, and where without bitterness she vows celibacy.[7]

Most importantly, there was the influence of Monica, his mother, who remained a key person in his life. Rosemary Haughton surmises that in her youth Monica was brought up in a strict though well-off household. She surmises that Monica's strict upbringing

> required the girls to be beaten and cowed into total submission, as the woman's role was that they should make a 'good marriage.' This particular girl was married young to a comfortably-off, good-natured irreligious, bad-tempered, unfaithful man of middle age called Patricius, whose mother ran his household and intended to keep on doing so. He was fond of his wife in a way and she avoided too many beatings by giving in to him over everything. Later the couple became much closer and before he died, he joined the Christian religion of his wife Monica.[8]

Haughton also adds that though she had given birth to three children, Augustine is the one most remembered. In her way, Monica tries to impart some understanding of Christ in Augustine, when he was a child, by planting a seed of the love of God through her sharing of religious faith. Haughton states:

> It was on this highly intelligent boy that Monica concentrated her hopes, her ambitions, and her frustrated affections. He was spoilt, and indulged, but obliged to go to school because that was the road to success. There he was beaten constantly like everyone else learned a great deal about sex, money, and how to get on in life and nothing whatever about love. His mother's fear of alienating him and losing his affection led her to avoid making any demands on him or trying to show him any good in life beyond the satisfaction of his desires. With her inbred

7. O'Donnell, *Augustine*, 56.
8. Haughton, *Love*, 128–29.

fear of and submission of the male this was natural enough. But there was at least a little real love. Augustine knew how much his mother centered on him and he seems to have tolerated this and even responded to some extent, though he found her Christian beliefs superstitious and feeble . . . and her moral exhortations ridiculous.[9]

After his schooling in Carthage, and despite Monica's prayers that he would come to Christian baptism and stay in Africa with her, Augustine remains unbaptized and leaves for Milan. Some ten years later, Monica follows her son to Milan, though by this stage she had matured and had become less possessive. She is still determined to make her son Christian and respectable through a good marriage. Haughton offers this assessment, "There was real love in Monica, in spite of all the distortions imposed on her by her upbringing and her marriage. She was wounded and she wounded her son, but neither of them was completely spoiled and in both the capacity for love, which had never been completely crushed, finally came out on top. In some ways it is an appalling story of distorted emotions; from another point of view it shows how love can survive even such conditions."[10] By this stage, Augustine had shifted spiritually in his life. He has come to the belief that sexual renunciation must be a condition for the religious and moral transformation of his life. He leaves his partner and common-law wife to whom he bore a son, Adeodatus, and becomes a Christian, resolving himself to celibacy.

The text most often referred to as central to his religious conversion is found in Book 8 of the *Confessions*. The scene is a garden in Milan. There is a fig tree, the voice of a child, and the uncontrollable outpouring of tears. Many other events precede this event and all these events accumulate in significance for Augustine: the story relating to Victorinus's conversion to the Christian faith; the example of Anthony of Egypt who gives away all he possesses and goes to live as a Christian hermit in the Egyptian wilderness. All the while, Augustine has been struggling inwardly with anxiety, terror, panic, trembling, quivering, and horror. Augustine feels the pull of waking up to the light rather than remaining in sleep. His response is to delay. He knows that he should give up those pleasures that kept him away from God, yet he cannot bring himself to make the final step. Finally, Augustine states:

9. Haughton, *Love*, 129.
10. Haughton, *Love*, 131.

I had no answer to make to you when you said to me. "Arise
you who are asleep, arise from the dead and Christ shall give
you light" (Eph 5:14). Though at every point you showed that
what you were saying was true, yet I was convinced by that truth
and had no answer to give you except slow and sleepy words:
"At once"—"but presently"—"just a little longer please." But "at
once" never came to the point of decision, and "just a little while
longer please" went on and on for a long time.[11]

Then, under the fig tree and in the garden, drowning in a flood of
tears, Augustine hears a voice "Take up and read; Take up and read." Remembering what he has heard of Anthony of Egypt and his chance meeting with the words of the Gospel to sell all and follow Christ, Augustine
goes back to his friend Alypius and takes up the writings of St. Paul. He
begins to read the first words that he sees. He writes "I seized it, opened
it and in silence read the first passage on which my eyes lit: 'Not in riots
and drunken parties, not in eroticism and indecencies, not in strike and
rivalry, but put on the Lord Jesus Christ and make no provision for the
flesh in its lusts' (Rom 13:13–14)."[12] Shortly after, Augustine resigns from
his teaching duties and retires to Cassiciacum where he notes that he laid
awake and prayed all night in tears. Finally, he and Alypius come back
to Milan, and a priest baptizes them. At that point and perhaps for the
first time, Monica and Augustine understand one another. Later, at his
mother's death, he is granted another instance of the same embrace of
love and understanding.

We find moments of joy and transformation in his life yet they do
not bring about a cessation to the restlessness verbalized at the beginning
of the *Confessions*. Conversion is a long step by step process and not all
at once. Although he finds in the garden a reversal of what Adam and
Eve found in their garden, still all of life's problems are not from that moment worked out for him. What he discovers is the centrality of love and
its importance if he is to journey onward. God heals him of his egoism
and his desire to be in the limelight, yet more challenges awaited him in
Africa where he returns hoping to find time for solitary prayer and study.
In Africa, he is forced to attend to the needs of others in a community
of faith strongly divided by the controversies of doctrine. He becomes
the Bishop of Hippo at a time when the Roman Empire is in collapse,
and the barbarians of the north are rapidly crumbling the borders. Thus,

11. Augustine, *Confessions* VIII.vi.12 (141).

12. Augustine, *Confessions* VIII.xii.29 (153).

Augustine becomes a champion for his community of faith against the enemies of the church both internally and externally.

In Book 7 of the *Confessions*, we read that the centrality of God's love sustains him through his trails. Augustine writes:

> Late have I loved you, beauty so old and so new; late have I loved you! And see you were within me and I was in the external world and sought you there and in my unlovely state I plunged into those lovely created things which you made. You were with me and I was not with you. The lovely things kept me far from you, though if they did not have their existence in you, they had no existence at all. You called me and cried out loud and shattered my deafness. You were radiant and resplendent, you to put to flight my blindness. You were fragrant and I drew in my breath and now pant after you. I tasted you and I feel but hunger and thirst for you. You touched me and I am set on fire to attain the peace which is yours.[13]

In this passage, Augustine feels the healing of grace to overcome blindness, implant a desire for beauty, and receive the deep need for peace. The power of love enabled Augustine to live morally, to have courage, and to think about reality and truth in a different way. The love of God gives him the stability for which he longs.[14] This stability enables him to push forward to embrace the truths of faith, to endure purification in his own life, and to be a public servant of God. It is the gift of God's love as a dynamic process within him that brings Augustine to various milestones in his journey.

Finally, Augustine acknowledges the importance of desire. Upon retreating to the country home at Cassiciacum owned by his good friend Verecundus, he writes his first texts following his conversion which have come to be known as the Cassiciacum Dialogues. These writings include *Against the Academics, On the Happy Life, On Order*, and *Soliloquies*. They map out Augustine's experiences and thoughts around desire and its relationship to contentment and happiness. Over a long period, Augustine has pondered on the difference between the sinful person's disordered desire and the desire of a believer touched by God's grace. Augustine approaches desire via a medical analogy: "Observation of symptoms, diagnosis of the underlying problem, a therapy for the curing

---

13. Augustine, *Confessions* X.xxvii.38 (201).
14. Augustine, *Confessions* VII.v.7 (115–16).

of the pathology, and an ideal of spiritual health."[15] At this stage, Augustine is still under the influence of the philosophy of Neoplatonism. The Neoplatonists diagnosed that all desire was for physical things, and so the root of all spiritual pathology. Accordingly, we should not be seeking after the things of this world since the right object of desire was spiritual and immaterial. Therapy of the soul alone would help the individual refocus on religious matters.

After his conversion, Augustine, though finding some sympathy with his preferred philosophical direction, chooses Christianity as his chief inspiration. Through listening and meditating on the Gospels, he begins to understand the essential inspiration of Christianity: a relationship with Christ Jesus as Lord. Now, seeking to be a devout Christian, he believes that divine revelation and the sacred words of the Christian Scriptures within the community of the church holds the best account of a good life and the proper end of real desire. Through the lens of these texts, Augustine accepts and recognizes many forms of spiritual pathology including "anxiety and the fear of losing what we love; misery in the face of misfortune; frenzied pursuits of money and power, and physical pleasure; the near ubiquitous fear of death; and the desire to be glorified in the eyes of others."[16]

Augustine arrives at these conclusions concerning desire. First, people ought to desire above all to love God and dwell in a right relationship with God and his fellow humans. Second, we love each other for God's sake and not for each other's sake. Third, desires go wrong when we seek to be satisfied only in the material things of this world and so for this reason, grace is essential. Fourth, we need God's help through, with, and in Jesus the Lord coming into our hearts. Sixth, self-surrender to Christ is, therefore, the key to the restoration of our desire made possible by the grace of religious conversion.[17] The theological virtues of faith, hope, and charity are also fundamental. For Augustine, conversion is not merely a change from one perspective to another but a radical reordering of our horizon so that Christ is at its center. Certain philosophies and psychologies may be helpful as therapies for our desires and even in redirecting our soul to God. However, it is the power of Christ, following him, and

---

15. Boone, *Conversion and Therapy of Desire*, 23.

16. Boone, *Conversion and Therapy of Desire*, 25.

17. Boone, *Conversion and Therapy of Desire*, 27.

joining to others in Christ's Body, which alone can fully heal our desires and sustain us as humans.

THE VOCATION OF DAG HAMMARSKJÖLD

Dag Hammarskjöld was born in 1905 in the city of Jonkoping, Sweden. He was raised in a Christian Lutheran home and into a family that was used to public life. His father, Hjalmar, was a very distinguished professor of law with an intimate connection to both politicians and churchmen over his lifetime. Dag studied law and humanities, earning a doctorate in economics and worked in the Central Bank of Sweden. After the Second World War, he worked in the Ministry of Finance and became Sweden's representative at the Organization for European Economic Cooperation.

He was recognized for his intellect and negotiation skills and finally became the second Secretary-General of the United Nations in 1953. In this role, he handled many crises at an international level. These included his successful efforts at mediation between America and China when fifteen American soldiers were captured and imprisoned by the Chinese government during the Korean War in 1955. He was also involved in efforts of mediation to avert a war between France and Britain, on one side, and the Egyptian government, on the other, during the crisis of the Suez Canal in 1956. There was also crisis in the Congo. Upon independence in 1960, the Congolese soldiers refused to take orders from Belgian officers. The subsequent eruption of violence and the secession of a mineral-rich area of the Congo by pro-Belgium actors, threatened violence, and he involved himself. It was in this latter assignment that Hammarskjöld intervened personally attending mediation talks. During these talks on the night between the 17th and 18th of September, his plane crashed about fifteen kilometers from the airport of Ndola, and he died.

After his death, Hammarskjöld's private diaries were published under the title *Markings*.[18] Leif Belfrage, the Swedish Permanent Under Secretary for Foreign Affairs, found a letter in his house with an undated letter addressed to him. In the letter, Hammarskjöld explained to Leif how he had kept a diary with no other purpose than for it to be private and personal; however, he goes on to state that "with my later history and

---

18. There remains a division of opinion as to the exact meaning of the Swedish word, and many people have variously translated it as road marks, guideposts, waymarks, and lastly, cairns (the objects used by mountaineers to chart for other uncharted steps across mountain terrain).

all that has been said and written about me, the situation has changed. These entries provide the only true 'profile' that can be drawn. That is why, during recent years, I have reckoned with the possibility of publication, though I have continued to write for myself, not the public. If you find them worth publishing, you have my permission to do so—as a sort of 'White Book'—concerning my negotiations with myself—and with God."[19] These words signal the importance of religious conversion which he calls a negotiation with self and with God. The word negotiation suggests dialogue, insight, facing obstacles, and hopefully moving beyond them to new horizons. The words of his diary, *Markings*, point to a man who wanted to address the demands of life through self-discovery, self-scrutiny, and openness to God.

In the entries from 1925 to 1930, we hear the voice of a man who realizes that there is more than his horizon of awareness. In a theme reminiscent of the mystics, he senses an unknown and mysterious horizon that invites and drives him forward. He writes "I am being driven forward; into an unknown land, the pass grows steeper, the air cooler and sharper, a wind from my unknown goal stirs the strings of expectation. Still the question: Shall I ever get there? There where life resounds, a clear pure note in the silence."[20] His conviction is that we will find hope and new insights will come from a meditative listening.

Later, in 1951, he speaks again of this strange and unknown territory:

> Now. When I have overcome my fears—of others, of myself, of the underlying darkness: at the frontiers of the unheard—of. Here ends the known. But, from a source beyond it, something fills my being with its possibilities. Here desire is purified and made lucid; each action is a preparation for, each choice an assent to the unknown. Prevented by the duties of life on the surface from looking down into the depth, yet all the while being slowly trained and molded by them to take the plunge into the deep from which arises the fragrance of a forest star, bearing the promise of a new affection.[21]

Hammarskjöld feels himself at the edge of his known horizon, breaking into the unknown, and led forward by "something that fills my being with its possibilities." In a Christian context, this moment of grace brings

19. Hammarskjöld, *Markings*, 7.

20. Hammarskjöld, *Markings*, 31.

21. Hammarskjöld, *Markings*, 78

about a completely transformed horizon, where crossing over symbolizes a leap of religious faith that in turn re-organizes the way we feel, think, and act. The loneliness of his younger years transforms through an awareness of a more in-depth resource. The self-centeredness of the earlier years is replaced by a journey inward to discover God. The sense of meaninglessness gives way to the conviction that God has a use for him and that his life is meaningful and significant in human matters and in the heart of God.[22]

Throughout his life and career as an international civil servant, we hear how it is essential for Hammarskjöld to say yes to God and affirm the gift of human existence. To experience the presence of God leads to the desire to be in a good relationship between oneself and others. The path of life may be quite difficult but the affirmation of faith helps him find meaning and to know what to do. He states, "when the morning's freshness has been replaced by the weariness of midday, when the leg muscles quiver under the strain, the climb seems endless and suddenly, nothing will go quite as you wish, it is then that you must not hesitate."[23] Personal significance and saying yes to God are intertwined. He asserts "You make your Yes—and experience has meaning. You repeat your Yes—and all things require meaning. When everything has a meaning, how can you have anything but a Yes."[24] All the while, any yes to the gift of existence is, for Hammarskjöld, a yes to God and "the best and most wonderful thing that can happen to you in this life, is that you should be silent and let God work and speak. Long ago you gripped me Slinger. Now into the storm. Now towards the target."[25]

Such religious faith cannot be merely a sacred formula or paraphrased dogma. It is a definite surrender to God and the desire to become the instrument of God.[26] Too often, we reduce our knowledge of God to reflecting on the idea of God and not loving God. Hammarskjöld has a warning about such a position: "On the bookshelf of life, God is a useful work of reference, always at hand but seldom consulted. In the whitewashed hour of birth, He is a jubilation and a refreshing wind, too immediate for memory to catch. But when we are compelled to look

22. McClendon Jr., *Biography as Theology*, 53.

23. Hammarskjöld, *Markings*, 109.

24. Hammarskjöld, *Markings*, 110.

25. Hammarskjöld, *Markings*, 134.

26. Hammarskjöld, *Markings*, 91.

ourselves in the face—then he rises above us in terrifying reality, beyond all argument and 'feeling,' stronger than all self-defensive forgetfulness."[27] In these lines, Hammarskjöld highlights something of the trauma and suffering of conversion.

Finally, there is a well-known text written on the feast of Whitsunday or Pentecost, 1961, and near to his death. The years from 1960 to 1961 were extraordinarily challenging for Hammarskjöld. The circumstances were around the movement for independence in the Congo after a long colonial reign by Belgium over the African country. This event triggered enormous violence, heading at breakneck speed towards civil war. The UN received a request from the Congolese government to act. What made the situation even more complicated was the secession of the territory of Katanga, a mineral-rich area that remained under the control of the Belgian mining company, Union Miniere, with Belgian troops and mercenaries guarding the borders. The situation worsened when the head of the Congolese government Patrice Lumumba was kidnapped, tortured, and executed with the direct involvement of the CIA.

Throughout this whole crisis, people besiege Hammarskjöld on all sides. On the one hand, he is accused by the Soviet leader Khrushchev of partiality toward Belgium and the West. On the other hand, the Belgian, French, and British governments cry out for his resignation from the UN, as they feared for their economic interests. Henning Melber notes that amid so many stakeholders and diverse loyalties, ideologies, and interests, Hammarskjöld would have found it very difficult to bring about a peaceful settlement.[28] In an entry written a few months before his death, Hammarskjöld tells about his life commitment to the peace work of the UN and what this had meant for him. He writes:

> I don't know who—or what—put the question, I don't know when it was put. I don't even remember answering. But at some moment I did answer Yes to Someone—or Something—and from that hour I was certain that existence is meaningful and that, therefore, my life, in self-surrender, had a goal. From that moment I had known what it means "not to look back" and "to take no thought for the morrow." Led by the Ariadne's thread of my answer through the labyrinth of Life, I came to a time and place where I realized that the Way leads to a triumph which is a catastrophe, and to a catastrophe which is a triumph, that the

27. Hammarskjöld, *Markings*, 37.

28. Melber, *Dag Hammarskjöld and Conflict Mediation*, 5–10.

price for committing one's life would be reproach, and that the only elevation possible to man lies in the death of humiliation. After that the word "courage" lost its meaning, since nothing could be taken from me.[29]

Hammarskjöld remains humble about his religious experiences. He admits to not knowing who or what posed the question, but he did give a yes to human existence and someone or something not of the created order. This yes was a growing affirmation of what his life was about and an affirmation only gradually understood. He considers that life is meaningful and that one reaches the goal of a meaningful life through self-surrender to God and an acceptance of one's circumstances. In this passage, many religious themes come together: divine presence, the cross of Jesus, invitation and response, responsibility, humiliation, and triumph. The Ariadne-thread that leads him out of the labyrinth references Theseus in the Greek myth and the thread is Jesus. Bernhard Erling states:

> Though he can speak of God in both personal and impersonal terms (who or what, someone or something), his commitment is related to Jesus. Since making (the diary) he has understood the meaning of Jesus' teaching, "No one who puts his hand to the plow and looks back is fit for the kingdom of God" (Luke 9:62), as well as, "So do not worry about tomorrow, for tomorrow will bring worries of its own. Today's trouble is enough for today" (Matt 6:34) . . . his understanding of victory does not come from Greek mythology, for the way that he is following is one in which triumph and catastrophe, exaltation and humiliation, are strangely linked. His guide along this way has been Jesus, especially Jesus' words in the Garden of Gethsemane and from the cross.[30]

Catastrophe and humiliation often draw us into the experience of our vulnerability. It is possible that at our darkest hour, we can realize that we must let go of the will to control, allow crisis to occur, suffer it, be open to the unknown, and let insight emerge, trusting that God will show the path. At that point we are indeed vulnerable, clutching the hand of God with hope. This transforming process happens when religion is not a means to an end, that is, using the divine for future benefits or therapeutic purposes. It happens when religion is a call to transformation. When we reach the point of humiliation and vulnerability, we can only bow in

29. Hammarskjöld, *Markings*, 169.
30. Erling, *Reader's Guide*, 267.

prostration to God and know God, not as an idea worth having, but know God by letting God be God.[31]

Vaclav Havel and the Horizon of the Infinite

Vaclav Havel is best known for the 1989 "Velvet Revolution" of Czechoslovakia and his claim that the moral authority of the politician above all else inspires the formation of a good society. The country of Czechoslovakia fell into the hands of the Soviets after the fall of Nazi Germany in 1945 and remained in the hands of the Communist Party system from 1948 until 1989. Havel was a playwright and wrote plays in the style of Ionesco and Beckett, to draw peoples' attention to subjects such as the meaning of identity and moral duty that became confronting issues during the Soviet communist era. He was politically active through the Prague Spring of 1968 which came to an end when Soviet tanks rumbled into Wenceslaus Square and crushed any rebellion in August of that year. On January 19, 1969, in that same square, an ordinary citizen, Jan Palach, set fire to himself in protest against Soviet repression. At that time Havel was already well known as a superb essayist, public intellectual, playwright, and dramatist who loved philosophy and thought much about responsible politics. He was not a religious thinker nor was he enthusiastic in confessing faith in God, always conscious that the term "God is" was too vague and too personal an experience to be projected into the public space.

The writings of the philosopher and president of the first Czechoslovakian Republic, Garrigue Masaryk, who held office from 1919 to 1938, after the fall of the Austro-Hungarian Empire, influenced Havel. The philosophy of earlier thinkers such as Edmund Husserl and Franz von Brentano influenced Masaryk, and they asserted that scientific progress on its own could not help people discern the difference between good and evil. Jan Patocka (1907–1977) also mentored Havel. Patocka was instrumental in setting up Charter 77, an initiative that sought to address human rights and fundamental liberties in a more liberal society. He eventually died of a brain hemorrhage after constant arrests, interrogations, and beatings by the Soviet authorities. Havel also felt the iron fist of the communist government, especially in the years when he became part of Charter 77. He went to jail on two occasions and on the second of these for an extended period from 1979 to 1983. It was within his prison cell that he wrote some

---

31. Miller, *Way of Suffering*, 167.

of his most important works. Finally, Havel took office in 1989 as the first president of post-communist Czechoslovakia and was re-elected twice.

One of the barriers or biases to religious conversion is the barrier of a distorted cultural and social milieu. The culture of the broader society and even within the church is far from neutral. Distorted cultures can cause us to suffer from a narrowness of horizon through a stifled imagination concerning God and human living. For such a narrow vision to be challenged and changed, another more dominant imagination must come forward, since we are all people of imagination and live within social institutions. A mistaken assumption about knowledge that causes a narrowness in thinking is this: what cannot be measured is not real or what we cannot see cannot be real. It is the basis of a materialist view of life. Soviet based communism is grounded in this materialist philosophy, asserting that matter is the underlying constant within the universe. The materialism of communism and its reliance on technological progress was the cultural and social milieu that surrounded Havel's upbringing.

Though Havel was a part of this milieu, he knew that communism suppressed an imagination of hope and the responsibility to be fully human. Through Havel, we encounter a man who pierces through the distorted vision of communism to something more. His concern is that if an integral democracy did form, it would appear as "a multileveled and multicultural reflection, with a new political ethos, spirit, or style and will ultimately give rise to new civic behavior and one that understands how unbelievably short-sighted a human being can be who has forgotten that he is not God."[32]

In his *Letters to Olga*, addressed to his wife and his fellow philosophical thinkers who met regularly at Havel's cottage in Hradecek, Havel recalls one his most profound experiences while in prison. He writes of what Charles Taylor calls a "self-authenticating, one might say 'epiphanic' experience."[33] In other words, it is the kind of experience that only the person who has had the experience can say is genuinely authentic by the way he lives after having been through it. It is genuinely epiphanic since, within the experience, light manifests itself in a manner that changes the way one understands and one becomes committed to everything else. Havel recounts:

32. Havel, "Forgetting We Are Not God."
33. Taylor, *Secular Age*, 729.

Again, I call to mind the distant moment in Hermanice when on a hot, cloudless summer day, I sat on a pile of rusty iron and gazed into the crown of an enormous tree that stretched, with dignified repose, up and over all the fences, wires, bars and watchtowers that separated me from it. As I watched the imperceptible trembling of its leaves against an endless sky, I was overcome by the sensation that is difficult to describe: all at once I seemed to rise above all the coordinates of my momentary existence in the world into a kind of state outside time in which all the beautiful things I have ever seen and experienced existed in a total "co-present"; I felt a sense of reconciliation, indeed of an almost gentle assent to the inevitable course of events as revealed to me now, and this combined with a carefree determination to face what had to be faced. A profound amazement at the sovereignty of Being became a dizzy sensation of tumbling endlessly into the abyss of the mystery; an unbounded joy at being alive, at having been given the chance to live through all that I had lived through, and at the fact that everything has a deep and obvious meaning—this joy formed a strong alliance in me with a vague horror at the incomprehensibility and unattainability of everything I was so close to in that moment, standing at the very "edge of the infinite"; I was flooded with a sense of ultimate happiness and harmony with the world and with myself, with that moment, and with all the moments I could call up, and with everything invisible that lies behind it and has meaning. I would even say that I was somehow "struck by love," though I didn't know precisely for whom or what.[34]

This very memorable recollection indicates a moment of religious experience. First, there is the unitive experience or sense of co-presence and reconciliation with events and things, past and present. For Havel, it is a moment when he feels that everything thus far in his life is meant for this moment. The experience fills him with the joy of being alive and united to an all-encompassing reality. Second, Havel also feels in this experience "a vague horror at the incomprehensibility and unattainability of everything." The felt sense of awe or "incomprehensibility" evokes in him an awareness of how small and vulnerable we all are.[35] He feels a sense of horror at his nothingness. He feels his mortality and vulnerability. Jerome Miller asserts:

34. Havel, *Letters to Olga*, 331–32.
35. Miller, *In the Throe of Wonder*, 188.

> Awe in the face of the sublime can become astonishment that
> being is the Wholly Other; our awareness of our poverty can
> become our confession that, in and of ourselves, we are nothing.
> But whether its ontological import is consciously appreciated
> or not, awe always exposes us, as do wonder and horror, to the
> unknown in its very character as unknown and beyond us. If
> the sublime were so far in front of us that we were incapable of
> being aware of it, it would not be able to overwhelm us; if we
> could understand it, it would by virtue of that very fact lack the
> superior stature it must have to make us aware of our inferiority.
> Awe is possible only because we can be aware of what is beyond
> us *as* beyond us.[36]

Again, comparing awe to wonder and horror, Miller suggests that
we are capable of being humbled in the various limit experiences of life
such as wonder, love, suffering, and death. He asserts that awe "gives us
an intimation of being, but radically differentiates being from beings and
it does so by requiring of us a confession of our nothingness which even
the experience of horror does not ask of us. Wonder inspires us; horror
devastates us, but only awe can humble us. And while humility is the
attitude toward oneself which is developed from a confession of one's
nothingness, worship is the attitude toward the Other which develops
from the affirmation of its transcendent Otherness."[37]

These experiences help transform Havel's horizon of values, and his
new values sublate his understanding of politics. Havel ponders about the
source for his understanding of responsibility in politics. He asserts that
the source is:

> Someone who "knows everything" [and is therefore omniscient],
> is everywhere [and therefore omnipresent] and "remembers
> everything," someone who, though infinitely understanding,
> is entirely incorruptible, who is for me, the highest and utterly
> unequivocal authority in all moral questions and who is thus
> Law itself; someone eternal, who, through himself makes me
> eternal as well, so that I cannot imagine the arrival of a moment
> when everything will come to an end, thus terminating my de-
> pendence on him as well; someone to whom I relate entirely and
> for whom, ultimately, I would do everything. At the same time
> this "someone" addresses me directly and personally.[38]

36. Miller, *In the Throe of Wonder*, 188.

37. Miller, *In the Throe of Wonder*, 189–90.

38. Havel, *Letters to Olga*, 345–46.

During the historic visit of St. John Paul II to Prague shortly after the revolution, while Havel is president of Czechoslovakia, his welcome speech for the Pope reveals his spiritual orientation. He states: "Your visit will remind us all of the genuine source of real responsibility, the metaphysical source . . . of the absolute horizon to which we must refer, that mysterious memory of being in which each of our acts is recorded and in which and through which they finally acquire their true value."[39] We glimpse Havel's horizon as complementary to the religious horizon of the monotheistic religions. He is trying to make sense of what he has experienced in terms beyond the created and historical order. His religious experience within the prison walls and his subsequent moral views on political responsibility are answerable to a higher power, making him a person with whom the religious convert might find much common ground. Within that experience, he receives the gift of determination to face what needed facing.

At that point, Havel finds the strength to carry forward a political responsibility. He names that moral vision as the best of democracy—human rights, civil society and the free market in the best sense of these touchstones. Havel is also always conscious of the worst aspects of a decadent form of democracy. He writes of this decadence as moral relativism and materialism. Its ideologies assert the denial of any spirituality, the proud disdain for everything supra-personal, and an absence of religious faith in a higher order of things. The results are a crisis of authority and general decay, a frenzied consumerism and a lack of solidarity. Consumerism strengthens a selfish cult of material success and a mentality that contemptuously resists any questions or problems to do with globalism and the rationalism of technical civilization.[40]

This commitment to moral responsibility is grounded in an experience of mystery expressed in language more in line with philosophical notions such as the sovereignty of Being, the edge of the infinite, the absolute horizon, the higher authority of conscience, the abyss of mystery, and the memory of Being. These terms point to a reality that knows everything, is everywhere, and remembers everything. What might be the meaning of these terms and how could they help us understand what transformation means for Havel? First, one way of understanding Havel's vision is to affirm that the abyss of mystery points to an eternal truth beyond history.

39. Zantovsky, *Havel*, 385.
40. Havel, "Speech Delivered at Stanford University."

Historical symbols may change and be contextually shaped, but beyond these, there is a constant ground to all our knowing, valuing, and acting. Our paradigm for reality is the whole of being. Through the experience of awe, wondering, and questions, we are guided to a new horizon, and a new world mediated not only by the meaning of this world but also by ultimate purpose. Since for each of us, "the new belongs somewhere else,"[41] we are potentially enabled as seekers to move beyond our current horizon. The rule for any seeker is to allow themselves to be surprised by the new world they may discover. Havel, the playwright, understands all too well the importance of words as sacramental carriers of experiences and the gift of wonder, acting as a hinge, and opening the door to a new world. As a playwright, Havel knows that words make reality accessible for the first time to a larger community and thus have the capacity to free people from the suppression of technical rationality.

When a person is caught in wonder and open to new questions, there is a profound effect on their desiring and orientation. Our desire to know and to value move us forward, through wondering and questioning. Then, we are like children standing at a door and perhaps subsequently many doors, in an experience of play, open to a new and infinite horizon. To cross the threshold of these doorways time and time again is to surrender to a process of conversion. Equally to deform wonder with stagnation, to narrow our experiences through avoidance, and to allow questioning to dry up is to lurch towards despair and to be trapped by fear. Those steps that wonder and questioning urge us to take can feel daunting and horrifying for us. We are reluctant to leave the familiar and comfortable, even if the place we are leaving may provide little freedom and the suppression of truthfulness. When this kind of fear becomes overwhelming, we would instead turn away from an unknown future that might prove to be upsetting for us. Authentic religious experience and intimations of the Sacred have always felt fascinating, awesome, and terrifying, while at the same time inviting us to a more responsible way of living.

Second, Havel is more a playwright and statesman than a philosopher using terms that suggest diverse worlds of meaning which each of us can discover. He discovers that Soviet communism suffers from a lack of openness to new questions as a means to controlling the population. Wonder and questioning open us to the universe of being and to a wiser

41. Arbuckle, *Health Ministry*, 215.

more responsible way of living. The capacity to wonder and question opens us to the mystery of infinite worlds of meaning and fuller horizons. By contrast, in Soviet communism, there was only one world of meaning. This ideology professed the infinite to be merely an illusion and held up its system as absolute. It declared a worldly interpretation of human existence and history. It asserted that the goal of human history was known absolutely and depended for its realization on the party system. As long as one adhered to the doctrines of the party, one achieves the goal of history.

The totality of the fail-safe system that was Soviet communism offered a measure of protection to its adherents. At best, we can say that the Soviet State put boundaries around its citizens out of a desire to protect what was best in communism. At worst, the controllers of the State apparatus were fearful of losing their power and prestige, forcefully stating and coercively make sure that their world was the only world. Havel diagnosed the oversights in such a system. Miller states that "none of the worlds that fascinate us are closed systems, all-consuming totalities" and that "precisely what makes it radiant is the fact that, at its very center, it opens out into a multiplicity of different directions, each of which has the possibility of leading us to another world."[42] In this regard, Havel and Miller are of the same mind when evaluating total systems.

Third, implicitly Havel also advocates that we should not be free floating or drifters through life. Nor should we be stuck in the world of practicality alone, promoting that nothing has meaning apart from living a practically efficient existence. Nor ought we purport that there are no matters of life or death worth striving for or nothing that should mean the world to us. When nothing has intrinsic meaning, a person's attitudes default to the pragmatic, treating each world as a stratagem directed by one question—what can we get out of this world before we move on? Miller asserts that the act of choosing to accept new insights or refuse them may at times amount to a matter of life and death. He affirms that each of us needs to be open to the possibility of love, suffering, and the new world they invite in.[43] Narrowed by pragmatic concerns alone prevents us from enjoying the captivating effect that insights out of different experiences offer. We end up looking for practical insights alone, dealing with them, coping with them, and subordinating them to our practical

42. Miller, *In the Throe of Wonder*, 95.
43. Miller, *In the Throe of Wonder*, 100.

requirements. We approach life with a will to control. Our everyday world assumes a state where nothing in it matters except practicality. In the end, the psychic work of repression dominates since the questions that other worlds or horizons might inspire can always be pushed aside by denials and avoidances. To break out of this world into a universe of meaning and to find ourselves at the edge of the infinite would be like dying and being born, an apt description for the process of transformation.

Religious Conversion and *As It Is in Heaven*

By way of demonstrating religious conversion in cinema, I invite you to watch the film *As It Is in Heaven*. As you watch the movie, ask yourself: What kind of openness needs to be present in the individual or the community for the presence of God to be felt? Daniel Dareus, a well-known and internationally recognized composer and conductor, returns to the town in which he grew up until he was five years old. He is suffering from mental and physical exhaustion. It would appear that his commitments to the world of music have brought him to this challenging period. When he arrives in the town, Daniel accepts the task of developing the church choir. It becomes a commitment that brings with it many highs and progressively reveals the vulnerability of people.

At one point in the movie in the final scenes, the members of the choir decide, at Arne's insistence, to participate in a choir competition in the town of Innsbruck. At first, Daniel is against this idea since, for him, music was never meant to be competitive. It was the competitive instinct and the desire to be better than others that drove the accomplished composer and conductor to physical and emotional exhaustion. However, since it is what they want, Daniel reluctantly relents.

On the day of the competition, the choir is ready to go on stage, but Daniel has left the building. Before this gathering and performance moment, Daniel and Lena, one of the choir members, have made love. Their love has been blossoming throughout the film's story. There are good signs that their love will blossom into marriage and children, a reality that fills Daniel with great joy. Basked in this joy, he goes out riding his bicycle. Happiness is evident on his face while his underlying physical weakness is unrecognized. He has lost track of time and only realizes very late that he should be back conducting the choir's rehearsed performance. However, he has another physical attack due to the physical strain of the bike riding. Daniel mounts the staircase to get to the auditorium, stumbles up the stairs, staggers into the restroom, and hits his head on a pipe below the wash basin, causing him to bleed severely. He lies helplessly on the tile floor, blood gushing from his head.

At this very moment, a most extraordinary thing happens in the auditorium. The choir has assembled, and the master of ceremonies has hurried them to their place and is pressuring them to do their performance. As much as possible they try to delay, waiting for Daniel to turn up. Finally, almost out of anxiety and stress, a sound emerges from the most disabled member among them, Tore. This sound seems meaningless at first but then gives rise to another sound, this time by Gabriella in harmony with Tore's first sound. Soon each choir member is joining in harmony to the sound of the other. At first, the assembled audience is perplexed at this sound presentation. Over the loudspeaker in the bathroom, Daniel listens to the choir harmonizing with each other. Then, the miracle happens. The audience, enchanted by the harmonies, start to sound their notes one by one in union with the choir until the whole assembled people are creating a beautiful sound in harmony with one another.

Daniel smiles and weeps to himself, fulfilled at reaching his life's goal and, in his heart of hearts has a vision of a boy, perhaps himself, with a violin, being picked up by a man in a wheat field ripe for the harvest. The symbols of the wheat field, a boy, and a father-like figure combine to elicit feelings of love and connection and are symbols of God's will, and echo the words of the Our Father, that God's will be done on earth as it is in heaven. The experience of the choir and audience is indeed heaven on earth: competition is no longer the standard for living and engaging one another. An attitude of compassion and solidarity replaces competition. We all receive new insight into human life through this transforming moment. This change of heart is a gift and the people in the auditorium feel this gift and respond in a collective voice and the harmonizing of differences. If people felt as if they were strangers to one another, now each is being accepted and welcomed as a stranger on their terms. The harmonizing voices of the choir are like a wave of love going out to the listening audience, and, in response, the harmonizing sounds of the responsive audience are like a message coming back to them, we are all desirable and desire-able. Between this wave of harmony and their response is the Spirit of God as a divine communion and communication. In some respects, it is a Christian Pentecost experience, a reversal of the separation between peoples that occurred with the Tower of Babel. Each person hears the praise of God in their sound. This event is a moment of religious experience, and in this experience, each person is moved emotionally, drawn by a gift toward greater compassion and solidarity.

5

Religious Conversion
and Christian Discipleship

THE PREVIOUS CHAPTER EXPLORED religious conversion. This chapter locates religious conversion even more specifically in the Christian tradition. The Christian Scriptures affirm God is love (1 John 4:8). God offers God's love without reservation and unconditionally. The language used by Christians to name God's sharing of life and love with humankind is the language of grace. Grace enables a personal and unitive relationship to the mystery of God. The key orientation is participation through grace in the life of God and communion with God and others. Grace is the gift of God's self-communication to human beings for the sake of establishing a trusting relationship with humankind. Before human beings ever become aware of this grace, grace is already at work in their hearts as the divine initiative of God. Love is always already there as a healing vector in human lives. Once we have recognized the presence of grace, we can pursue a relationship with the divine in a decisive manner. Therefore, religious faith has, on the one hand, God initiating and empowering and, on the other hand, the human person freely responding. If the person accepts the invitation, then, grace enters awareness, and the person becomes conscious of religious conversion. Again, no one can control grace, since grace belongs to the mystery of God and is a pure and unexpected gift.

RELIGIOUS CONVERSION AND JESUS CRUCIFIED
AND RISEN

For Christians, the person of Jesus Christ and the meaning of his cross and the resurrection grounds religious conversion. It is especially through these mysteries of the Lord's life that Christians recognize that God is love. Christian religious conversion then becomes centrally about the person of Christ and the dwelling of his Spirit in our hearts. St. Paul states "I have been crucified with Christ; and it is no longer I live, but it is Christ who lives in me" (Gal 2:20). In the whole Christian story, the resurrection of Jesus and the sending of the Spirit are central events of faith. While the death and resurrection have the characteristics of temporal continuity, still to base one's faith on this chronology is to miss the point. James Alison puts the matter well: "the resurrection was, *for the disciples*, the next step in the story: for them, first Jesus as dead, then he is alive. But *it was not so for Jesus*. For Jesus, the resurrection was the giving back of the whole of his human life, leading up to, and including his death. It was not simply the next stage in his human life."[1] Only in the light of the resurrection does Jesus' life and death make complete sense to the disciples. Jesus has done something completely new. The disciples are transformed, enabling them to understand for the first time who Jesus is and what Jesus has done. They understand the events of the Lord's life, his actions, and words as never before. Through the resurrection experience, their horizons of understanding shift dramatically.

The Awakening of Desire

Alternatively, we can capture the unique impact of the resurrection through an interior account of the disciples, as if the disciples are telling their story from an interior perspective. So, we can understand conversion by getting into the mind and heart of the disciples. Sebastian Moore gives an insightful account of the disciple's inner journey using the language of desire.[2] Our story starts when Jesus is walking among them. Initially, his words, deeds, and quality of relationship draw the disciples to him. The desiring of the disciples for Jesus is a response to his desire for them. This attraction toward Jesus can only be characterized inwardly

---

1. Alison, *Knowing Jesus*, 19.
2. Moore, *Fire and the Rose*, 80–89.

as a profound awakening of desire. Feeling differently toward Jesus, they feel differently towards themselves, people, and God. They are in touch with their most basic feeling, namely, the feeling that whatever happens, they are significant, worthwhile, and a meaningful human being. This feeling is like the nerve of a tooth: it is felt more when it is not operating well. We usually know the fact of it when our significance is not recognized, then we appreciate how important it is to us. We realize that it is a feeling that flourishes and grows in an atmosphere of love. This need which begins in the child crying in the corner of the room, inconsolable until it is picked up, reaches its full meaning as an act of love that creates happiness in another person.

An authentic feeling or real desire in the disciples is the felt discovery that they were desirable and this discovery enables them to be self-giving and ultimately, to desire God. Jesus' words and deeds made sense to the disciples. He lifts their hearts immediately to God, promises a renewed society, and causes to well up inside of them a desire to follow his example. They desire to join Jesus and witness to him. This period with Jesus was a time with him characterized by joy and bliss. During this time, they experience in and through being with him a new sense of self, unburdened by guilt and unworthiness, and a new sense of God's identity. The God of Jesus is not judgmental or jealous. God is a merciful and loving presence, revealed in the person of the human and earthly Jesus. However, their experience of Jesus causes a twofold response in them. It creates both attraction and repulsion. They are attracted to this authentic person. However, they are also repulsed by the guilt that they harbor at not being able to live up to the demands he asks of them, of falling short, or not living up to his example. So, this first phase of their personal story can be called an "awakening of desire."[3]

This feeling of significance comes out of a message which we call "the mind of Jesus." St. Paul states "Let each of you look not to your own interests, but to the interests of others. Let the same mind be in you that was in Christ Jesus" (Phil 2:4–5). Alternatively, Anthony Kelly prefers to name the words, deeds, and relationships of Jesus as a new and subversive imagination with the beatitudes at the heart of the reign of God. He states:

> The parables he told, in the meals he shared with his followers
> and with the sinners and outcasts, Jesus was in effect inviting
> all those to share his subversive imagination. He imagined the

3. Hunt, *Trinity*, 98.

world otherwise. The master symbol of his imagination was the Reign of God. The divine realm contrasted with the harsh, God—remote, segregated domains jealously defended by the religious and secular authorities of his day. That old world constantly reinforced the rules of exclusion. It expressed itself in the fierce etiquette of apartheid. The unworthy "nonperson" was no fitting companion to the worthy. He or she had no place at the table. Hospitality had defined limits. As Jesus proclaimed the Reign of God, he was the focus of wondrous new hopes. He made room for all those whom the cultural idols of his day—and throughout time-had excluded and demeaned. In his imagination, the murderous fantasies of the world are disarmed. To the poor in spirit belonged the great gift of the Kingdom of God. The meek, in their renunciation of violence and revenge, would be the decisive voice in history; they would inherit the earth. The merciful would find themselves in a universe of mercy. The pure of heart, surrendered to God's will and God's Reign, would see God—revealed in the love that Jesus embodied. Peacemakers would be called God's very children. In the same way, all who accepted the struggle of doing what is right and in witnessing to what is truly good would find themselves anew in God's Kingdom. No matter how they might be vilified, they would have reason for rejoicing in what was coming into being (Matt 5:3–11).[4]

The Desolation of Desire

Then, something quite dramatic changes through the events of Jesus' arrest, persecution, and death. What follows is a crucial period of crisis when the disciples fall into darkness. He is cruelly taken by force and executed as a common criminal, and this turn of events brings on the second state of desire, the "desolation of desire."[5] The awakening desire once felt for him undergoes a fatal rupture. Indeed, the disciples feel themselves to be as good as dead. Desolation is a profound sense of rootlessness, lack of direction, and the experience of one's world caving in and shattered at its core, with the sense that things cannot be the same. Severe depression, the struggle to survive, and a lapse into a coping mode of existence often follow desolation. Desolation often leads to the felt experience of

4. Kelly, *Eschatology and Hope*, 182–83

5. Hunt, *Trinity*, 99.

failure and worthlessness. The disciples also experience what seems like the death of God, for the sense of God awakened by Jesus dies with his death. God must be dead since they do not feel the same significance or worthiness as they felt when he lived. They experience despair which we find out later is the kind of despair that only God can dispel. Imagine first the terror, then the shame and guilt at not being able to measure up to Jesus, the confusion in the hours leading to Calvary, and utter desolation that comes after the execution. Imagine being huddled in a room in fear and dread at the prospect of one's arrest, torture, and execution. Imagine the shame and guilt at having left him to his plight and deserted him.

The Transformation of Desire

Then, something entirely new happens, not only to Jesus but to the disciples as well. We enter the third stage of their story of desire, "the transformation of desire."[6] Moore outlines the process in these words: "Still this desire, while feeling its infinity, was necessarily channeled into the finite Jesus, its awakener. At the climax of the story, the channel is destroyed, to produce a death of ego in which everything is lost. With the risen Jesus, desire infinite in its essence becomes infinite in its exercise. Desire is liberated, becomes itself. This is why the Risen One is invisible, partakes of the invisibility of God known as the Spirit. Resurrection is the liberation of desire."[7] Jesus is risen, meets them, and speaks to them. Everything changes to the way they feel and understand God; the way they see themselves; the way they view their world and their destiny; and the way they understand sin, guilt, death, and suffering. He awakes in them a liberation of their desire towards its end in God.

Kelly states, "The crucified Jesus, who had been known in the course of his earthly life and through the impact of his mission, is now glorified, and given back to them. In his return, from beyond the domain of death, he comes to "mean the world" to them in a new way."[8] The resurrection pulls the disciples beyond the limits of their life with him before the cross. The Risen Jesus meets the disciples in the place left empty by the death of God. As such, the resurrection is not some once-off transformation. It is an event that draws the believer into an on-going process of

6. Kelly, *Eschatology and Hope*, 99–100.
7. Moore, "Jesus the Liberator of Desire," 497.
8. Kelly, *Resurrection Effect*, 132.

transformation. They experience healing of their whole self and in a new way. They feel rescued from their sense of being nothing, from their guilt, and from the false image of God that is part of their shadow, both during Jesus' ministry and after his death.

Just as Jesus awakens a new feeling for and understanding of God during his time with them on earth, now he makes God alive to them in the resurrection with an aliveness never felt before. Moore asserts, "What did it mean to experience this dynamic oneness of God and Jesus? It meant that Jesus no longer appeared as an extension of God such that each who experienced him would be confined within himself as one who saw and wondered: Jesus was now experienced as the extension of God in celebrating which the disciples came into a single common consciousness."[9] The teaching of the earthly Jesus and his relationship with them awakened their desire, but the presence of the risen Lord psychologically brings about a "displacement of divinity"[10] away from the old and false god who led them more and more into feeling guilt, who was remote, and simply overpowering. It becomes a displacement of divinity toward Jesus. The presence of the risen Jesus causes that process of displacement to be complete; for now, God and divinity are fully alive in Jesus. These strictly monotheistic disciples are free to celebrate Jesus as an extension of God in the same breath.

CHRISTIAN CONVERSION AND FORGIVENESS

One of the essential elements of Jesus' death is his forgiveness. Chapter 3 spoke about the importance of religious conversion for both the sinner and the victim of sin. It is vital now to explore the place of forgiveness within Christian conversion. It was William Shakespeare who immortalized these words in the English world: to err is human, to forgive divine. If there is one action that we associate with Christian religious conversion, which is often beyond the power of our efforts alone, it is the act of forgiveness. Through a direct or indirect awakening of desire for God, God's grace brings us to the point of being able to forgive and to the point of accepting another's repentance in the right spirit.

Using a medical image, Carla Mae Streeter emphasizes the centrality of grace and prayerfulness to forgiveness. She likens forgiveness to a soul,

9. Moore, *Fire and the Rose*, 88–89.

10. Moore, *Fire and the Rose*, 89.

cleansed of substances that would make it otherwise very difficult to pray. She states that "prayer is coming before divine love, clothed in nothing but faith, drawn by hope's aching desire, and breathless on love's bare feet. Unforgiveness covers the ground with shards of broken glass."[11] Streeter describes the negative impact of unforgiveness in terms of rippling our attempts at prayer.[12] For Streeter, forgiveness is a mighty attitude and action as well as a barometer of our inner well-being since forgiveness "takes love's temperature. Low, the love is cool; high, the love is warm and real. Without forgiveness, love languishes in the never-never land of the lukewarm. With forgiveness, love holds no prisoners and as a result is itself free. We free our prisoners not because they are not guilty. We free them because to hold them poisons our own souls."[13] Streeter goes on to describe the heart open to the gift of forgiveness as a gate "likened in the Song of Songs to a lovely latticework. The gate of welcome and admittance swings freely in and out. There is no blockage, no barrier."[14]

Streeter also describes the interior damage and toxicity wrought by unforgiveness especially when the heart becomes like a jail cell. She describes unforgiveness as a "subtle form of revenge" and its toxicity through our being "leeches its way into the soil of our humanness, contaminating the groundwater from which our love seeks to draw. There is such satisfaction in getting even by keeping bound one who has hurt us. It feels so right, this getting even. Yet something is wrong with this picture. Shouldn't I feel elated? Then why am I depressed? Buried unforgiveness is like a toxic dump. Unsuspecting hikers travel in the location and wonder why they feel ill when they get home. The unsuspecting pilgrim needs to check often for the unfinished business of unforgiveness."[15] For Streeter, there is nothing more destructive to the human person than being trapped in unforgiveness. While victims need healing and sinners need forgiveness, there also exists the possibility of victims becoming perpetrators and sinners becoming victims.

Streeter explores the subtle action of grace probing its way into our jailed and jailing heart. It is the power of love, helping us to let go of control, revenge, and power over the other. She states that "the offender will

11. Streeter, *Foundations*, 106.

12. Streeter, *Foundations*, 106–7.

13. Streeter, *Foundations*, 107.

14. Streeter, *Foundations*, 107.

15. Streeter, *Foundations*, 107.

wield continuing power over the victim's memory, which rehashes the injury over and over. The risen one holds out a wounded hand, requesting not only the key but custody of the prisoner. The click of the key must be felt more than heard, the jail cell door swung open, and the prisoner released into this one's custody for truly just handling. Empty the cell reconfigures itself into agate of welcome, barring no one."[16]

Victims, Sinners, and Forgiveness in Christ

The saving death of Jesus or what Christian tradition calls the mystery of redemption will be experienced differently by both victimizers and victims. Many sermons listened to by Christians from Lent to Good Friday usually direct the divine purpose and meaning of redemption primarily towards the sinner, and reflect upon how the death of Jesus redeems the sinner. Often the victims of sin are passed over strangely in silence. By and large, church ministers overlook the victims and violated as needing redemption. Even when visited through pastoral solicitude, pastors think that the victim's heart remains innocent and untroubled morally by the horror they have experienced. This simple action reflects the conviction that it is the sinner who is more in need of redemption. This omission in pastoral practice and diminished understanding of redemption seems to forget something. Jesus himself was a victim of political murder. Many overlook this horrifying affirmation of the meaning of the death of Jesus since the focus is on what Jesus did for us on the cross, bearing it courageously and willingly, and not on what is done to Jesus before the water flows from his side.

If we are to understand the significance of the cross, we must take into account all the data of the sacred text. Jesus' response to his murder and his murderers is critical. We cannot appreciate the meaning of the crucifixion unless we see the death and murder of Jesus as an act of evil that no just God could have ever countenanced. How can the killing of the innocent relate to the victim? Jesus opens himself to being victimized for the sake of the empathy he has toward the victim. His death on the cross is an act of identification with all the victims of history. In this way, Jesus comes to set victims free from the evil done to them by entering into "solidarity with every historical individual who has been violated. As Jesus describes it, this solidarity is so intimate, so profound, [and]

16. Streeter, *Foundations*, 107.

so complete, that it is nothing less than identification. This [solidarity] suggests that [the Father's Word] responds to the historical reality of evil principally and primarily by becoming one with the violated."[17]

There is another element we cannot forget when we embrace the cross with religious faith. Miller suggests that Jesus directs all his love to the wound in his side which all the violated would typically recoil from in horror. For the violated to open their wound would be humanly impossible. The horror of taking on this evil and integrating it would be too alien and beyond the violated. To open our wound and allow the love flowing from the side of Christ to then flow through the wound of the victim requires a divine self-giving. This divinizing love "if it were to freely circulate in the victim, would do what would otherwise be not only impossible but unimaginable and inconceivable: flooding the wound with love, it would [in its very being] transform it into a fountain. What flows from this fountain would be precisely the divine love that is poured into it."[18] Miller asserts that if the victim experiences this divine empathy, they will let it flow through themselves to others, first to other victims, and, then finally, to those who have committed the evil. It would be salvific for the sinner or violator only because it has come to them through their victim's wound.

Redemptive love is a response to the shriek of unbearable horror suffered by the victim, reaching down to that place that generally the victim cannot bear and cannot escape. In this way, Jesus suffers sin by allowing it to affect him and by letting sin have its way with him.[19] Using the Johannine image of Jesus pierced on the cross by a lance (John 19:34–37, Miller sums up the unexpected and surprising nature of grace as divine madness flowing from the wound of Jesus to the wound of the victim. He states "You pour into the very wound of evil a love that enfolds this wound in Your divinity. This divinizing love, if it were to freely circulate in the victim, would do what would otherwise be not only impossible but unimaginable and inconceivable: flooding the wound with love, it would [in its being] transform it into a fountain. What flows from this fountain is precisely the divine life that is poured into it."[20]

17. Miller, "Wound Made Fountain," 545.

18. Miller, "Wound Made Fountain," 547.

19. Miller, "Wound Made Fountain," 546.

20. Miller, "Wound Made Fountain," 547.

As well, the redemption of Jesus frees violators from the evil done by them but not without the violator feeling loved despite their evil which brings a special kind of anguish upon them. To receive this grace from the victim would be no easy task, for to accept it would be to open themselves as violators to it, and to be open to it, would be to encounter the wound that the violator has inflicted. The flow of divine love would have to reach the sinner and violator who inflicted harm on the victim. The victim transforms the evil committed on and to them into an act of self-giving love. What makes divine love so salvific is that the divine love is offered to violator as a doer of evil or as a murderer, in other words, to the "unlovable *as* unlovable."[21] There is no sense of looking for the good in the violator and offering forgiveness based on finding this good. The violator is offered forgiveness as a violator. Miller poetically sums up what is at play in the exchange between Jesus, the violated, and violator: "You turn my murder of you into Your dying out of love for me *as* Your murderer."[22] Miller does not mince his words as to the impact and devastation of evil by the violator towards the victim.

Miller unpacks the dynamic impact between the victim and the violator. He states:

> The violator *as* violator, would be able to receive what flows towards him from the wound of the victim only by opening himself *to* this wound and allowing himself to be affected by it. But to open oneself to a wound is to become an open wound. Just as such forgiveness would not erase the wound of the victim or enable the retrieval of original wholeness, so it would not "wash away" evil from the violator or restore the violator's original integrity. Forgiveness would [in the being of the victim] transform the wound of the victim into a fountain; to receive it the violator must drink from this spring. The excruciating love that flows from it would not remove, diminish, or assuage the torment I experience when I realize that I am evil. It would transform the torment of being unlovable into the anguish of being loved. To be loved in this way is ex-cruc-iating because the very tenderness of this love tears my heart open and makes it a wound. There is nothing in the universe that could be as poignant as being forgiven-or as heart-wrenching. There is no human pain as traumatizing as the anguish of being loved *in*

21. Miller, "Wound Made Fountain," 549.
22. Miller, "Wound Made Fountain," 549.

one's evil—and no human joy that remotely approaches the ec-statis constitutive of it.[23]

Christian Conversion
and the Theological Virtues

St. Paul exhorts the followers of Jesus to be ambitious for the higher gifts in 1 Corinthians 12:31–13:13. He concludes his hymn to love by stating in verse 13, "and now faith, hope, and love abide; and the greatest of these is love." What can we say about the interior dimension of religious faith, hope, and love?[24] Religious faith is a knowledge coming out of a *judgment of value* born of religious love.[25] Our values change because of our experience of God's love. A new kind of knowing accompanies our being-in-love with God. We often say that faith is a "yes" to God and the things of God (2 Cor 1:18–20) and so any yes requires judgments of value, choices, and decisions. In the context of Jesus' faith, the presence of His *Abba* Father was crucial. If we are to say yes as he did, the Heavenly Father will become our Father as well.

The feeling that best captures the nature of religious faith is grateful appreciation.[26] We judge that what God has revealed is to be welcomed as valuable and this judgment fills us with delight and appreciation for the things of God. The first stance of religious faith is an appreciation for the revelation of God. These welcoming and appreciative feelings allow us to gaze in wonder, listen with an open heart to stories about God, and discern concrete proposals as worth doing in the light of God. If ordinary human loving helps us appreciate the other person as a value in themselves, faith motivates us toward an appreciation and affirmation of all reality as valuable in the eyes of God.

If religious faith allows us to live in an appreciation of where the divine mystery has penetrated the human arena, religious hope is desire born of religious love filled with confidence.[27] Hope cultivates in ordinary people heroism to fight the good fight even in the face of challenging evil,

---

23. Miller, "Wound Made Fountain," 549–50.

24. Arcamone, *Religion and Violence*, 75–76.

25. Lonergan, *Method*, 115.

26. Dunne, "Faith, Charity, Hope," 57

27. Dunne, "Faith, Charity, Hope," 60.

reinforcing an intelligent and responsible commitment to the good. Pope Francis states:

> Paul, before the fears and perplexity of the community, urges [the community] to wear firmly on the head like a helmet, 'the hope of salvation,' especially in the trials and most difficult times of our life. It is a helmet. This is what Christian hope is. When we speak about hope we can be led to interpret it according to the common meaning of the term, that is, in reference to something beautiful that we desire, but which may or may not be attained. We hope it will happen; it is as a desire.[28]

Hope longs and desires for the full good and all truth. It longs and desires for a great outcome to human history despite the frustrations, setbacks, and limitations of sin and bias. Hope's desire is confident because of faith. If faith gives a judgment of value concerning God, hope renders desire sure, enabling us to commit to a path despite difficulties and setbacks. There is no need to despair or to feel hopeless.

While Christian faith might gain its momentum from an act of appreciation, through meditating on the words of Jesus, hope is sustaining the desire for God with confidence and imaginatively caring that the things God will come about. Therefore, we support hope through art, dance, incense, ritual and symbol, intersubjective living, and architecture. Hope and faith reach for symbols that alone can represent the mysterious work of divine mystery. It is through such symbols that hope resists the immense pressure of social decay and the resolution of such collapse into nihilistic instincts. Hope promotes us to feel the same joy that God expects of his creation.

Finally, religious charity is an active love for persons and community (Matt 22:36–40).[29] Lonergan states that "if passions are to quiet down, if wrongs are not to be exacerbated, not ignored, not merely palliated, but acknowledged and removed, then human possessiveness and human pride have to be replaced by religious charity, by the charity of the suffering servant, by self-sacrificing love."[30] Each of us animated by the love of God falls in love with God and manifests this love by acts of benevolence and beneficence toward others. Ultimately, we come to understand and value such acts of love as an overflowing of God's love in us,

---

28. Francis, "Christian Hope."
29. Dunne, "Faith, Charity, Hope," 58.
30. Lonergan, *Method*, 117.

compelling us to act. Charity is thus the decision to act from judgments of value made in faith and confident desires made in hope. Religious love motivates us towards a response that our ordinary human living would not usually point to, for example, the spiritual imperative to overcome evil, love the enemy, and act well towards those who wish to persecute the believer.

In so far as we practice the supernatural gifts of faith, the divine mystery draws us in different ways. While each theological virtue has an impact on the way we are towards people, events, and human living generally, these graced virtues also shape the way we are towards God. Faith appreciates God as the source of our judgments of value and truth. Hope is the confident expectation of arriving at the end of our exploring in a way that will satisfy our heart's longing despite the difficulties encountered. Charity moves us towards God with thanksgiving and praise, and, through this personal encounter with God, compels us toward the service of others.

Christian Conversion and Belief

Religious conversion is centrally concerned about the "we" between the divine mystery and each other. This "we" is not isolated or solitary. It is creative of a community of faith. We achieve a full flowering of religious conversion through an ongoing receiving of the gifts of religious faith, hope, and love within a community of faith that helps us discern the value of believing. Believing implies that we are initiated into a religious tradition that Lonergan calls "the word of religion."[31] The traditions of the church, especially in the sacred texts, help us understand the meaning of the primordial experience of being-in-love. We would not be able to be fully attentive to this experience unless we had some set of values, symbols, beliefs, mentors, and religious communion, setting us on the path of appreciating the experience. Within communities of faith, the Christian heritage offers itself to us mediated through mentors and guides such as our teachers and parents, and, more distantly, in the example of martyrs and saints. Out of love, loyalty, trust, and commitment for our mentors and guides, we accept what they say as truthful. In this case, faith means valuing the truths of our faith and this valuing is born out of love or trust

31. Lonergan, *Method*, 118.

in our mentors. Faith moves forward through appreciating beliefs and creeds.

In contrast with those who would sharply distinguish and separate religious faith and collective belief, Lonergan differentiates and unites them as two sides of the one coin. The word of religion becomes historical through the entrance of Christ into human history.[32] The word of religious expression is first and foremost the person of Jesus Christ. The sacred texts and doctrines founded on judgments of value and truth summon us to a commitment to Christ through discipleship, prayer, a meditation on the holy texts, and lives of self-sacrificing love. Believing is valued as a good thing and since it is a good thing urges us to the point of obligation.

Discipleship does not mean that we stop growing. As we mature, we embark on a process of discovering religious truth for ourselves so that our expression and understanding of faith becomes more mature than it was previously. This process of discovery may mean letting go of aspects of an imparted heritage that no longer make sense and even re-discovering new elements of the tradition that have remained hidden, forgotten, or unexplored. This process usually requires ongoing religious conversion.

CHRISTIAN CONVERSION AND TRUST

More significantly, religious conversion gives rise to trust in God. Michael Paul Gallagher, reflecting on the work of the theologian Pierangelo Sequeri, states that the "act of trusting another person is by its nature relational, and therefore not lonely. It is rooted in the gradual recognition that the other person is worthy of our confidence. It is an act that unites thinking, deciding and feeling. In fact it is the universal characteristic shared by all humanity and where it is damaged or reduced, something tragic happens to people."[33] Trust is vital in all areas of human living. Perhaps this experience is best appreciated when trust is lost and, in its wake, comes disillusionment, despair, and hopelessness. Trust signifies that the other is worthy of our confidence, moving us away from the battleground of suspicion and hostility.[34]

32. Lonergan, *Method*, 119.
33. Gallagher, *Faith Maps*, 123.
34. Gallagher, *Faith Maps*, 124.

Any attempt to transform our images of God also require trust. Gallagher notes that the link between self-understanding and our understanding of Christ needs rebuilding through utilizing an attitude of trust.[35] In other words, we are to let go of all reductive images of ourselves that do not do justice to our potential and, similarly, all reductive images of God that do not do justice to the true God. In terms of reductive images of ourselves, we cannot separate truth from the act of trust. If something is truthful, it summons us to commit trustfully with all our being. Appropriating religious truth is not just a rational reality. Religious truth begins in the act of trust and invites us to surrender ourselves to a Person. Beyond reductive and immature images of God, our relationship to Jesus, founded on trust, draws us into His Abba experience. For Jesus, the Heavenly Father is the source and end of his life. In and through Jesus, we discover a relationship with God as the Father of Jesus and the conviction that he came from God to inaugurate a new way of living by transforming humanity.[36]

CHRISTIAN CONVERSION AND BEAUTY

Lonergan speaks to the possibility of experiences of beauty orienting consciousness toward God, whether through the natural world or artistic creativity.[37] Artists express meaning through a multiplicity of mediums: paintings, sculptures, symphonies, folk songs, poems, plays, novels, photographs, or films. This concern or orientation is two-sided: the aesthetic pattern of experience that focuses on experiences of beauty and the artistic pattern of experience that explores ways to "unfold artistic wonder, artistic understanding, artistic evaluation and creative artistic production and expression."[38] Following Lonergan, Morelli states that beauty "is manifested in celebratory, spontaneous joie de vivre, rather than in the sober, business-like desire to survive. Like the intellectual interest it's related to our concern for meaning and value. But its relation to our desire for meaning and value is manifested, not in detached, rigorous pursuit of explanatory, universal knowledge regarded as the highest value, but

---

35. Gallagher, *Faith Maps*, 124.

36. Gallagher, *Free to Believe*, 89.

37. Lonergan, *Insight*, 207–9.

38. Morelli, *Self-Possession*, 223.

in joyful, creative expression of the open-endedness of our orientation toward meaning and value."[39]

For Lonergan, beauty is encountered "in the untiring play of children, in the strenuous games of youth, in the exhilaration of sunlit morning air, in the sweep of a broad perspective, in the swing of a melody."[40] The central aspect of the aesthetic experience is the sheer joy and delight one finds in living and the contentment of freedom and leisure that takes us out of the word of hard work. Glenn Hughes notes that art is created to question and explore human possibilities: "The possibilities of experience and feeling and perception, possibilities of comportment and decision, possibilities of living."[41] These possibilities are presented to us by way of emotionally powerful and symbolic images so that "such possibilities are felt before they are carefully reflected upon, and thus they first enter our horizon of concern as existentially *participated in*, rather than intellectually *cognized about*."[42] Art can cause us to be transformed, freeing us from a "general insensitivity due to habit and routine; from the practicalities of getting and spending; and from the constraining disciplines of scientific or systematic or logical thinking."[43]

More importantly, Lonergan's emphasis on persons making their lives into work of art has relevance to the appreciation of beauty. He states that each person is "capable of aesthetic liberation and artistic creativity: but his first work of art is his own living. The fair, the beautiful, the admirable is embodied by man in his own body and actions before it is given a freer realization in painting and sculpture, in music and poetry. Style is the man before it appears in the artistic product."[44] Here the aesthetic and the dramatic patterns of experience blend with each other.[45] While the aesthetic is concerned for an experiential flow of beauty, the dramatic pattern focuses our attention on all those experiences that have to do with living with others including our feelings toward them, how we manage our relationships and the way we live the drama of everyday existence. Morelli states that the content of experiences that pertain to the dramatic

39. Morelli, *Self-Possession*, 219–20.

40. Lonergan, *Insight*, 207.

41. Hughes, *More Beautiful Question*, 27.

42. Hughes, *More Beautiful Question*, 27.

43. Hughes, *More Beautiful Question*, 27.

44. Lonergan, *Insight*, 211.

45. Dadosky, *Eclipse and Recovery of Beauty*, 89–90.

pattern includes attending to experiences that relate to "my and others' sensible beauty, my and others' intellectual respectability, my and others' critical and moral authority, and my and others' worthiness to play the leading roles in the unfolding dramas of our lives."[46] The meaning sought is precisely personal and interpersonal, and is tied up with the success or failure of one's role as a "leading actor in the drama of my life."[47]

We discovered that Augustine's gift of religious conversion enables him to grasp the beauty of Christ whose birth, life, death, and resurrection are all beautiful. Taking the whole sweep of the Father's plan in Christ, and reminiscent of the prologue of John's gospel (John 1:1–18), Augustine states that Christ is "beautiful in heaven, beautiful on earth; beautiful in the womb, beautiful in his parents arms; beautiful in his miracles, beautiful under the scourge; beautiful when invited to life . . . beautiful in laying down his life; beautiful in taking it up again; beautiful on the cross; beautiful in his sepulcher; beautiful in heaven."[48] The beauty of Christ is revealed in the womb of Mary (Luke 1:41–44). The beauty shows itself when the joy and the praise of the shepherds witnesses to his beauty (Luke 2:25–38), in the lives of the Magi overwhelmed with joy (Matt 2:10–11), and in the glory of God filling the heavens at his birth (Luke 2:9). During his ministry, people search Jesus out to hear his words of wisdom. He heals them and forms a relationship with them. In the event of the Transfiguration, three apostles witness his face shining like light (Matt 9:2–8). More paradoxical, his crucifixion which starkly presents the horror of his suffering and death at the same time brings us to a new appreciation of his beauty. Joseph Ratzinger asserts that Christ "who is beauty itself let himself be slapped in the face, spat upon, crowned with thorns . . . in his face which is so disfigured, there appears the genuine, extreme beauty; the beauty of love that goes '*to the very end*'; for this reason, it is revealed as greater than falsehood and violence."[49] The beauty of Christ reveals itself in the resurrection and the coming of the Holy Spirit, evoking the author of the Book of Revelation to declare that the face of Risen Lord was "like the sun shining with full force" (Rev 1:16).

Our personal and individual encounter with the beauty of Christ enables us to become God's work of art: "So, if anyone is in Christ, there

---

46. Morelli, *Self-Possession*, 229.

47. Morelli, *Self-Possession*, 233.

48. Augustine quoted in O'Collins, "Beauty of Christ," 7.

49. Ratzinger, "Feeling of Things" par. 18.

is a new creation; everything old has passed away; see, everything has become new" (2 Cor 5:17). For this work of art to become a reality, we are to be "clothed in compassion, kindness, humility, meekness, and patience. Bear with one another, and if anyone has a complaint against another, forgive each other; just as the Lord has forgiven you, so you must also forgive. Above all clothe yourself with love which binds everything together in perfect harmony" (Col 3:12–14). God invites us to an intersubjectivity that reflects the beauty of God through friendship, love of spouse, family, and neighbor so that communally, our lives might become a work of art. In this endeavor, the dramatic and aesthetic blend together and religious conversion sublates all our moral, intellectual and affective directions. Religious love is the gift of God transforming us into a beautiful work of art while opening our eyes to witness the beauty of God in creation, in others, and the events of life. The grace of conversion leads Augustine and each of us to state "late have I loved you, beauty so old and so new."[50] Through divine love, we experience the joy and delight of the Creator for his creation and for his sons and daughters, long before we can express it in words with any clarity. This experience is transformative.[51]

A CONVERSATION: FRIEDRICH NIETZSCHE AND THERESE OF LISIEUX

To illustrate the drama of Christian religious conversion, Michael Paul Gallagher has constructed an imaginary conversation.[52] The conversation is between the atheistic philosopher Friedrich Nietzsche (1844–1900) and St. Therese of Lisieux (1873–1897), a Doctor of the Church and the Patron saint of Missions. Nietzsche and Saint Therese, though contemporaries, never met one another. Through Gallagher's imaginative conversation, companion spirits become alive. This dialogue elicits themes important to a western cultural milieu of unbelief. It takes creative liberties and goes beyond anything we know of the explicit statements of either Nietzsche or Therese. Gallagher's conversation divides into several sections: clash of yes and no; risking the darkness; moments

---

50. Augustine, *Confessions* X.xxvii.38 (201).

51. Dadosky, "Proof of Beauty," 9.

52. Gallagher, *Dive Deeper*, 70–76. Michael Gallagher died on November 6, 2015. His parting is a significant loss to the Christian community.

of breakthrough; and companions on the edge. It would be best to engage with the whole conversation.

Nietzsche was the only son of a Lutheran minister and part of a family that had given ministers to the Christian community for 250 years. In his early life, Nietzsche received influences by the devotion of his mother. At the age of thirteen in 1858, he writes this prayer;

> I have firmly resolved within me to dedicate myself forever to His service. May the dear Lord give me strength and power to carry out my intention and protect me on life's way. Like a child I trust in His grace: He will preserve us all, that no misfortune will befall us. But His holy will be done! All He gives I will joyfully accept; happiness and unhappiness, poverty and wealth, and boldly look even death in the face, which shall one day unite us all in eternal joy and bliss. Yes, dear Lord, let thy face shine upon us forever! Amen![53]

Nietzsche was born nearly thirty years earlier than Therese, and as a philosopher became the symbol for a radical rejection of God, in a spirit of alarm rather than of triumph. In January 1889, in the city of Turin, he tried to stop a horse from being whipped and following that event entered a period of mental illness that never left him until his death in 1900.

The Canadian philosopher, Charles Taylor, names Nietzsche's group as "the tragic set."[54] The tragic set is still secular in orientation, having taken on the pseudo-scientific beliefs of an age which viewed religious faith as the dangerous enemy of human freedom. The tragic set seems to be a revolt against the secular humanism of the time and its emphasis on the primacy of stability, prosperity, comfortable living, and security. Nietzsche is the quintessential, rebellious, and modern man with absolute confidence in reason as the only guide to life. He observes his society and attacks those who have grown rich and satisfied with the products of the capitalist venture. He rebels against the idea that the highest purpose of life is to relieve suffering, increase stability, and seek comfort.[55] By contrast, for him, the raw experience of life pushes to cruelty, domination, and exclusion in its most exuberant moments.

For Nietzsche, we are born to extract as much energy as we can out of life with the awareness that, without suffering and sacrifice, none could

---

53. Nietzsche quoted in Benson, "Friedrich Nietzsche," 174.
54. Taylor, "Spirituality of Life," 5.
55. Taylor, *Secular Age*, 664.

reach their true goal. Gallagher's conversation has Nietzsche stating: "My passion is to live a huge yes, but there is so much rubbish on the way. I hate cramped and small lives. My vocation is to disturb them."[56] We attain the highest ideal through attuning ourselves to the myriad of energies within the human soul and to "go with the flow" through self-assertion and the will to power.[57] Gallagher gives voice to Nietzsche: "I have only my own will to live from. We have to invent our lives ourselves."[58] Moreover, Charles Taylor asserts that "[the tragic set] chafes at the benevolence, the universalism, the harmony and the order. It wants to rehabilitate destruction and chaos, the infliction of suffering and exploitation, as part of the life to be affirmed. Life properly understood also affirms death and destruction. To pretend otherwise is to try to restrict it, tame it, hem it in and deprive it of its highest manifestations, precisely those manifestations that make it something you can say 'yes' to."[59]

The mindset of the tragic set dismisses religion by saying "religion cannot face the real hard facts about nature and human life; that we are imperfect beings, the products of evolution, with a lot of aggression and conflict built into our natures; that there is also much that is horrible and terrible in human life which cannot just be washed away. Religion tends to *bowdlerize*[60] reality."[61] For the tragic set, religion avoids the hard facts and the cruelty of nature, overlooking the demand to adhere to a survival of the fittest orientation in both the natural and human world.

Nietzsche tells the parable of the madman who appears in the marketplace confronting people with a lantern looking for God. Because they no longer believe in God, the people scoff at the madman and ask him where God might have gone. Nietzsche is stating that the God of nineteenth-century European religious culture, imagined as a remote God, divorced of any divine affectivity, who started creation like a big clock and left it to its own devices, is dead. With the death of God, western culture is undergoing a revolutionary transformation. He sees himself as the prophet of this new age. He is signaling the enormous and terrible

56. Gallagher, *Dive Deeper*, 70.

57. Taylor, *Secular Age*, 634–35.

58. Gallagher, *Dive Deeper*, 71.

59. Taylor, "Spirituality of Life," 5

60. "Bowdlerize" means to censor, edit, or cut out.

61. Taylor, *Secular Age*, 624.

responsibilities which fall on the human person when the transcendent ground of western values falls away.

Speaking through the madman's voice, Nietzsche states:

> "Where could God have gone?" shouts the madman, turning on them. "I will tell you. We have slain him—you and I. We are his murderers. . . . But how did we do it? How could we drink up the sea? Who gave us the sponge to wipe out the whole horizon? What did we do when we unchained this earth from the sun? . . . Do we not wander through an endless nothingness? Does empty space not breathe upon us? Is it not colder now? Is not night coming and even more night? Must we not light lanterns at noon? God is dead. God stays dead. And we have slain him.[62]

He often voices a hatred for Christianity as life-denying to the point of being an oppressor of humanity. Through Gallagher, Nietzsche speaks: "I despise in Christianity—its ascetical ideal, its disgust with life, its slavery mentality, its hatred of the senses, [and] its escape into eternity. I have been through the misuse of power in the name of religion. It is too sick to be believed by someone who has passed through my crucible of suspicion."[63] Despite this, Nietzsche retains a strange admiration for the person of Jesus: "Do not talk to me about him. His beauty haunts me in spite of my hatred for his followers."[64] He admires the anti-establishment stance of Jesus, his single-mindedness, and his commitment to his cause. The twin aspects of human will and passionate commitment are Nietzsche's touchstones. Through Gallagher, he asserts: "I can only believe in my own urge to create. The religious urge, set free from the old forms of 'god,' can give birth to great art."[65]

It is false to portray Nietzsche as simply cold-hearted and atheistic. He is more a harsh critic of complacent religion and the kind of grey thinking that lacks imagination and passionate commitment. Sadly, in his desire to live fully, Nietzsche becomes a believer in the power and strength of the human will alone to endure, leaving behind the importance of trust and love, which also potentially link us to the truth. For Nietzsche, Christianity draws to itself condemnation for its fear, denial, and avoidance toward the sensual pleasures of the body. In the conversation,

---

62. Nietzsche quoted in Thornhill, *Modernity*, 31–32.

63. Gallagher, *Dive Deeper*, 72.

64. Gallagher, *Dive Deeper*, 73.

65. Gallagher, *Dive Deeper*, 72.

he states: "Religion is sickness, born of fear and need."[66] For him, Christians follow a slave mentality. The ancient Greeks and Romans allowed their will to power to flourish, championing strength and honor, and did not deny the drive within life to establish oneself as more excellent than others. By contrast, the slave mentality represses the will to power. This mentality involves the weak turning around the values of the strong and asserting the way of humility to be a better way to live.[67] For Nietzsche, St. Paul devalues the wisdom of the world in favor of the wisdom of heaven as revealed in Christ (1 Cor 1:25).

Confronted by the death of God, Nietzsche goes in search of a new artistic orientation from which to live. He sees himself as trying to revive the untamed energies of life, holding up the noble pre-Christian warrior as an aristocratic or elite model for humanity.[68] In this aristocratic warrior, we are to appreciate the virtues of courage, elite excellence, and greatness. The aristocrat is someone who stands apart from the herd mentality and differs from the kind of person that the apostle Paul exhorts the followers of Jesus to be. Eventually, he begins to formulate a new faith that adopts Dionysius, the god of affectivity, as a mentor. One of the central themes of this Dionysian way is to accept all tragedy that comes along in life. He states: "My formula for greatness in a human being is *amor fati*: that one wants nothing to be different, not forward, not backward, not in eternity. Not merely bear what is necessary, still less conceal it—all idealism is mendaciousness in the face of what is necessary—but love it."[69] We must embrace the world as it is in all its complexity and suffering. Another element of the Dionysian way leads him to praise those who are free spirits. In *Thus Spake Zarathustra* he writes: "I love those whose souls are deep, even in being wounded. I love those whose souls are overflowing so that they forget themselves. I love those who have free spirits and free hearts."[70]

Frederick Lawrence concludes that Nietzsche's most important criterion for being an authentic person is passionate commitment.[71] In other words, Nietzsche's position is that we judge and evaluate what is

66. Gallagher, *Dive Deeper*, 73.

67. Benson, "Friedrich Nietzsche," 177–78.

68. Taylor, *Secular Age*, 642.

69. Nietzsche quoted in Benson, "Friedrich Nietzsche," 175.

70. Gallagher, *Dive Deeper*, 67.

71. Lawrence, "Ethics of Authenticity," 140–41.

truly worthwhile from our natural and intense feeling for a cause. On this reading, Nietzsche's position too quickly leads to the conclusion that values are the arbitrary positing of the willful self and, as such, values come from merely arbitrary choices held passionately, and not from judgments of truth based on weighing the evidence. To their credit, the tragic set sees through the anesthetized life of modern secular existence, which avoids passion and wholehearted commitment for the sake of comfort and security. For Nietzsche, this secular mindset reinforces a way of life that normalizes unchallenging social stability. In its place, he urges heroism, commitment, and challenge.[72] Toward those he opposes, he asserts the impossibility of filtering out "the tragedy, the wrenching choices between incompatibles, [and] the dilemmas, which are inseparable from the human life" and he opposes the illusion "that all things come together effortlessly."[73]

Despite his misgivings about religion, Gallagher has, at one point in the conversation, Nietzsche beginning to appreciate the authenticity of Therese's way of humility and love. He admits to her: "I cannot, simply cannot, trust that simplicity." Nevertheless he chooses not to destroy Therese's faith claiming: "I thought it was the usual weak and demeaning thing but it is not. It is real for you, deep and costly. Such *genuine faith does not deceive. It fulfills whatever the believer expects.* You have come from poverty into power."[74]

At this point, we link to the context surrounding Therese's life journey. Therese's father, Louis, had a desire to become a priest but chose instead to marry his wife, Zelie. When Therese was born in 1873, her parents had already lost four children. The five surviving children were all girls including Therese, the last in the line. Four years later Therese's mother Zelie also died with breast cancer and Louis moved the family to Lisieux. Her upbringing was French Catholic. In late 1888, Therese entered the Carmelite Convent. She was fifteen years old and was given special permission to enter the convent at such an early age. Therese had already seen three of her siblings leave home to join the Carmelite order. Seven years later came the chapter in her life that made her a possible dialogue partner for Nietzsche, her dramatic eighteen months of a crisis of faith. She died in 1897 of tuberculosis.

72. Taylor, *Secular Age*, 635.
73. Taylor, *Secular Age*, 635.
74. Gallagher, *Dive Deeper*, 75.

When it comes to St. Therese of Lisieux, it is vital to disavow ourselves of any sugar-coated images we may have about her. An unrestricted
falling-in-love with God marks her life. Therese loves the Father, Son, and
Holy Spirit and surrendering to the Trinity becomes the central concern
of her life. On Trinity Sunday, June 9, 1895, she feels strongly enough
to offer her whole life to God. She writes: "In order to live one single
act of perfect love, I offer myself as a victim of holocaust to your merciful love, asking you to consume me incessantly, allowing the waves of
infinite tenderness shut up within you to overflow into my soul, and that
thus I may become a martyr of your love, O my God."[75] Her surrender
recognizes love as the focal point of her experience. In Gallagher's conversation, Therese is also aware of the commitment to love. She states, "I
too have a mission. My small life wants to be a [wholehearted] yes." Then,
she qualifies this yes, saying, "My mission is to awaken the world to the
call of love" and "I am not afraid to love. And to me to love is to live. My
deepest fear is not to love—to waste this life, making everything revolve
around me."[76] This commitment to love flows out of her contemplative
experience. Through prayer, silence, listening to the Gospel, and meditating on the Word, she discovers the God of merciful tenderness: God who
suffers when love is "blocked, refused, [and] forgotten and hence a God
who seeks to pierce the lonely shields of indifference with the amazement
of relationship in love."[77]

What we know from the famous C-text addressed to Mother Mary
Gonzaga gives us a fresh insight into this important saint of our time.
During the Easter Triduum of 1896, the doctor gives Therese a diagnose
of tuberculosis and what follows are long periods of vomiting blood. At
first, she looks forward to death as a gateway to union with God. Then,
when death does not ensue, she transitions from a sense of joy at the
thought of dying and joining God to a dark period of darkness and
struggle, which remains with her for the following eighteen months until
her death. Again, Gallagher's conversation has Therese saying: "I hear
inner voices that mock me. They tell me that all is illusion, that there is no
God, no heaven, that I am wasting my little life in this impossible fantasy
of loving."[78] This period marks a crucial turning point in her spiritual

75. Therese of Lisieux, *Story of a Soul*, 82.

76. Gallagher, *Dive Deeper*, 70–71.

77. Gallagher, "St Therese and Atheism," 5.

78. Gallagher, *Dive Deeper*, 72.

maturity from a faith that desires only the things of heaven, releasing her from this earthly existence to a faith that trusts Jesus, even though such trust promises only a darker night, the night of nothingness. Her madness is to keep hoping for her Lord, despite the darkness. Gallagher shows her aware of the dangers of this nothingness: "You might go mad if you cannot receive in love. Darkness without trust is a danger zone."[79]

From that Easter until her death, Therese produces many poems and other imaginative writings, reflecting a strategy to resist the darkness utilizing a determined will-to-believe. During this time, the quickly fading flashes of joy give way to even more darkness. Did this faith in God reflect the childish clinging of a scared and insecure person toward an imaginary god? It would seem that this is not the case and that despite the darkness of faith, Therese is committed to loving God. Gallagher speaks through Therese: "Embracing the darkness of solitude is a form of love."[80] She affirms the beauty of Jesus revealed in his descent in darkness.[81]

Her commitment to love is no less the case when it comes to loving her fellow sisters, especially those she found it hard to get on with, and all others beyond the walls of the convent for whom she prayed. She is not afraid to be disturbed. She did not approach life with a will to control her spiritual transformation, nor to control the outcomes of her vocation, nor the circumstances around her. She remains open of heart, to fundamental questions, and disturbing new insights that might come through the gift of grace. The darkness of faith means enduring periods when she is plagued by voices and thoughts that suggest that her act of love is futile and empty. She even imagines suicide as a relief from the darkness. She comes to realize that her silences and solitude are possible places of encounter with God and that all she can do is wait and hope that God would meet her in that space.

Randall S. Rosenberg presents many insights into the ongoing religious conversion of Therese. Drawing on the theological work of Hans Urs von Balthasar and Bernard Lonergan, Rosenberg focuses on the relationship between Therese's life of contemplation and her action in the world.[82] People often criticize ascetics and contemplatives in the modern world, especially those ascetics who leave the world for a life of solitude,

---

79. Gallagher, *Dive Deeper*, 73.
80. Gallagher, *Dive Deeper*, 71.
81. Gallagher, *Dive Deeper*, 73.
82. Rosenberg, *Givenness of Desire*, 162–63.

accusing them of escapism. People question their choices and protest how easy their lives are. The cry goes out: after all, they do not have to raise and educate children; they do not have to be demeaned by the day to day humiliations of working life or think about the future. Examining Therese's life, we can say that it is through her being apart from the world of the broader society and through her experience of prayerfulness that Therese could join herself to everyone in the world and especially to the world of unbelievers who would not know how to turn to the consolation of God.

Therese appreciates that the loss of spiritual joy in her night of sorrows helps her unite herself to all unbelievers. From this night, she ponders on the dark loss that unbelievers are enduring by not knowing the unconditional love of God. She understands her trial of faith as a more profound invitation through a deep self-surrender to God, and she endures this trail by turning to Jesus. From this, Therese feels an even more urgent sense of mission within the convent walls, toward a world without faith, and toward people like Nietzsche. She desires to unite herself to all unbelievers who have never been open to the love of God. Bravely, she embraces the tremendous religious and cultural drama of her time, the deepening stance of unbelief and its assertion that God is nothing more than a source of projection, alienation, deception, and irresponsibility. Her symbols for the divine encounter are the tenderness of God, friendship with Jesus, and an ordinary life punctuated by daily acts of love.

Therese also believes that if the grace of charity could not help her to live peacefully with others in the convent, then she is not responding as God wanted. She writes:

> Not wishing to give in to the natural antipathy I was experiencing, I told myself that charity must not consist of feelings but in works; then, I set myself to doing for this sister what I would do for the person I loved the most. Each time I met her, I prayed to God for her, offering Him all her virtues and merits. I felt this was pleasing to Jesus, for there is no artist who doesn't love to receive praise for his works, and Jesus, the Artist of the souls, is happy when we don't stop at the exterior, but, penetrating into the inner sanctuary where He chooses to dwell, we admire its beauty. I wasn't content simply with praying very much for this Sister who gave me so many struggles, but I took care to render her all the service possible, and when I was tempted to answer her back in a disagreeable manner, I was content with giving

her my most friendly smile, and with changing the subject of conversation.[83]

Rosenberg also focuses on one of the most dominant images associated with Therese, her holiness through embracing her "littleness" thus becoming for many the "Little Flower." This way demolishes the focus on accomplishing great heroic deeds, or focusing one's efforts on personal greatness, and refocuses the person in becoming small and humble in the arms of God, acknowledging our vulnerability and weakness and trusting in divine providence.[84] If the conversion years before entering the convent meant leaving behind the sufferings of her childhood and embracing a renewed ownership of her life with child-like trust, the adult period of her life calls forth the same childlike spirit. This child-like humble way and this new strength of spirit cause her to renounce the desire for joy and pleasure that accompanied familial love and the goal of social status, preferring an attitude of thanksgiving and simple surrender instead.[85] Gallagher's Therese states:

> I had several turning points but perhaps two main ones. The first was before I entered Carmel. It happened at Christmas, a week before my fourteenth birthday. A small episode provoked a major change. I overhear my father comment that it was just as well this was the last time for the childhood custom of Christmas stockings. My first reaction was typical of me: I nearly burst into tears. But then I crossed a threshold in myself. I went downstairs as an adult, playing the old tradition with a new lightness. My father was delighted. In that *night of light, I rediscovered a strength of spirit that I had lost at four and a half* when mother died. I had taken my life into my own hands. I became strong. I stopped being a sensitive victim.[86]

Finally, Rosenberg speaks about the unity between sanctity and apostolic activity found in Therese's heart. There is a link between grace and action. Her surrender to God in contemplation does not take her to a place sealed off from everyday life. For her, there is no dichotomy between Mary and Martha in the Gospels. Instead, Therese devotes herself to sharing with everyone the gifts of God received in contemplation.[87]

83. Therese of Lisieux quoted in Rosenberg, *Givenness of Desire*, 168–69.

84. Rosenberg, *Givenness of Desire*, 164.

85. Rosenberg, *Givenness of Desire*, 165.

86. Gallagher, *Dive Deeper*, 74.

87. Rosenberg, *Givenness of Desire*, 167.

Though she has set her heart on heaven and the eternal vision of the Heavenly Father, this did not distract her from her human activity as a novice mistress.

6

Moral Conversion and Living for Values

THE PREVIOUS CHAPTER ASSERTED that Nietzsche's criterion for authenticity was measured against the intensity and passionateness of one's commitment. This horizon of understanding offered both insight and oversight. It contrasts somewhat with the criterion for human living underpinning Therese of Lisieux's horizon, namely, her commitment to Christ who suffered darkness out of love for us. For Therese, the central criterion for authenticity was her love of God and neighbor in and through Jesus. Love is the fulfillment of all values. Love transformed her consciousness. This chapter will continue to deepen the process of transformation through its existential and moral dimension by unpacking the meaning of moral conversion.

THE MEANING OF MORAL CONVERSION

Lonergan defines moral conversion as a change in the criterion by which we make commitments and choices in our life "from satisfactions to values."[1] What does he mean by satisfaction? By satisfaction, Lonergan not only means using pleasure or what makes us feel good to assess what is good or bad when making a decision. Satisfaction, for Lonergan, is closer to the paralysis of indolence or "a kind of apathetic complacency about oneself just as one presently is."[2] Satisfaction is the condition of the drifter. Following the path of what is merely satisfying or agreeable

1. Lonergan, *Method*, 240.
2. Byrne, "Moral Conversion," 18.

for us may not always be the right direction to take.[3] Byrne describes satisfaction as "a preference to remain as one is in order to avoid anything that would involve effort and that would challenge or stretch oneself toward fuller understanding, more critical knowledge, deeper and more refined feelings or a broader appreciation of values."[4] Moral conversion "overcomes the resistance of self-contentment."[5]

In chapter 3, we looked at our personal moral story and affirmed that behind all our deliberations and decisions stand a set of criteria for judging whether something is real and worth doing. We ask: What kind of criteria might guide our judgments of value? The most basic criteria that we share with the animal world are the desires for sociality, sexuality, and self-preservation. These are our most basic root desires. As we grow through childhood, we are taught to make moral choices according to the criterion of reward and punishment, associating good choices with pleasure and bad choices with pain, good choices with what is acceptable to our parents and bad choices with what is rejected by our parents. The value of belonging to a family is vitally important to us. Yet, we notice that this measure is self-regarding and still has a lot of personal comfort and security at its core.

Moral conversion moves us beyond the measure of self-satisfaction toward an authentic living based on values and grounded in reasonable choices. We go beyond our world to choices that affect the lives of others. Our choices and actions cannot be grounded only in sociality, propagation, or self-preservation. Reasonable choices must be subject to critical thinking. With reasonable choices, we must consider that no person is an isolated individual, but every person is part of a network of relationships. Many bonds connect us within society and the natural world. If we are interconnected, then feelings and the quality of our relationships become essential indicators of possible moral values.

Rarely do we find anyone for whom self-centered satisfaction and gratification are their sole criteria for moral decisions. Often, even the most immoral person has specific values in their lives which are generally considered important even in the minds of critically thinking people, for example, the value of family or the relationship of a spouse or partner.

---

3. Lonergan, *Method*, 104.

4. Byrne, "Moral Conversion," 18.

5. Byrne, "Moral Conversion," 18.

We have seen how St. Augustine was committed to a life of knowledge though he had not yet renewed himself morally.

Moral conversion becomes possible when we have grown sufficiently in self-knowledge and self-understanding. Only then will we be able to stop blaming anyone else for the disordered person we have become.[6] Byrne asserts that the first decision on our part in the process of moral conversion is not all encompassing. It is the beginning in "a succession of new questions, new feelings, new judgments and new decisions that work out the consequences of one's decision for moral conversion."[7] Moral conversion is a long process of "stripping away biases and self-delusions."[8] It asks of us to finally decide what kind of person we want to become. We cannot "blame physical or biological determinism, or one's given nature, or one's parents, or one's social and economic circumstances, or one's historical or cultural influences [or God or Satan or anything else]."[9] It is we who decide for or against moral conversion.

Moral Conversion and Katherine Ann Power

Byrne gives an insightful account of the life of Katherine Ann Power to demonstrate the process of moral conversion.[10] On September 20, 1970, five people robbed the National Guard Armory in Newburyport, Massachusetts. Three days later, the same group robbed the State Street Bank in Brighton, Massachusetts. One of the Boston Police officers who first responded to the robbery was Walter Schroeder, a decorated office. He died while trying to stop the robbery. His death left behind his wife Marie and nine children who had to move into public housing not too long after the tragic event. Within seven days, the police had apprehended four of the five criminals. Katherine Ann Power got away, changed her name, and remained in obscurity, finally moving to Oregon where she married, set herself up in business, and began to raise a family.

Twenty-three years after the death of Officer Schroeder, Power handed herself in to authorities and in September 1993 pleaded guilty to armed robbery and manslaughter. She surrendered because she did

6. Byrne, "Moral Conversion," 21.
7. Byrne, "Moral Conversion," 22.
8. Byrne, "Moral Conversion," 22.
9. Byrne, "Moral Conversion," 25.
10. Byrne, "Moral Conversion," 11–15.

not want to go through life unable to tell her son the true story of her life. She received as punishment for her part in the crime, a total of eight to twelve years for the manslaughter charge and five years to be served concurrently for the National Guard Armory Robbery. Five years later, Power was eligible for parole. She came before the parole board to answer questions put to her by the Board members and the surviving family of Officer Schroeder. While the family and Board could hear that Power had become a changed person, Power decided to withdraw from the parole hearing. She felt that while her remorse and statements of responsibility were tied to her request for release, then, her remorse could not be shown to the public. She felt that there was still self-interest in her plea for parole. In October 1999, Power was released from prison and placed on a fourteen-year good behavior bond.

In an interview some fifteen years later, Power reflected on her prison time as a period where the layers of defensiveness covering the real evil of the crime she had committed were, one by one, peeled back. It was in jail that she realized for the first time the grave harm done by her group toward Officer Schroeder and the devastating consequences of his death on the family. Indeed, she came to realize that the family still felt the suffering and pain so many years later. She stated that the whole event would be something horrifying that she would have to live with for the rest of her life.

Reflecting on Power's parole appeal, Byrne states that "the process of moral conversion is slowed down and spread before public view so that what is involved can be seen more clearly."[11] Clearly, over the time of her incarceration, Power was not a person devoid of all values. She valued family life and the value of truth-telling, especially toward her son. However, it was when she was able to value truth-telling surrounding the death of the police officer and the consequences following his death for his family that people witnessed the beginnings of moral conversion in her.

Moral Conversion and Feelings

What place do feelings have in the ongoing formation of our values? Feelings can point towards values and give us the momentum to search values out and the motivation to put them into practice. People may have

11. Byrne, "Moral Conversion," 15.

matured to the extent that when it comes time to deliberate, evaluate, and make decisions, their feelings point them in the direction of what is best to do. Further, Dunne suggests that specific feelings accompany our choices at different points along a continuum. Initial feelings emerge when we ask a question as to what is best or worst about a situation. Then, once we have made our choices, we experience feelings of confirmation from them.[12] These kinds of feelings are not the kind that immediately come and go. They are mental and spiritual habits. In other words, it is possible to develop our life of feelings to such an extent that we reach up to an affective self-transcendence or a life of constant authentic feelings where the right feelings point and move us toward responsible action.

Dunne suggests that one pedagogical technique for training our feelings involves the discernment of inspiration. Are our feelings leading us to become self-absorbed persons, always concerned to find ways of being in control of life? Alternatively, are our feelings tending to open us to ever-widening ways of learning, doing better, and loving without reserve?[13] Further, St. Paul speaks about peace, joy, patience, kindness, love, and humility (Gal 5:22–24) accompanying our better choices. Arriving and putting into practice such values may bring deep joy into our lives. Basing our lives on specific values may also mean that we will suffer because of the stance we take.

When it comes to feelings, the ascetics of the Christian tradition are also aware of how egocentrism gathers to itself feelings that contribute to maintaining dangerous illusions. The ascetics understand temptation as less to do with choosing evil and more to do with indolence, self-deception, and seduction. We could be lazy about moral transformation. We could deceive ourselves into thinking that something is good when it is not good for us. We could be seduced by the good concretely before us and not appreciate the overall good. Whenever we choose something, we see some good in it. For this reason, direct and unadulterated evil is a harder position to maintain.

Moral Conversion versus the Will to Control

There exists another dangerous illusion that can damage our desire to do good, giving birth to unhealthy feelings, and poor choices in life. Chapter

12. Dunne, *Doing Better*, 123–24.
13. Dunne, *Doing Better*, 234.

1 introduced the distortion of the will to control. First, what happens when the will to control becomes all pervasive? Miller states that "The practical person wills to impose boundaries on everything and to exclude from his life anything that proves to be uncontrollable. The paradox of this way of life lies in the fact that the very desire to control comes to dominate one's life completely."[14] Miller is warning us against the existential stance of taking control over everything. Miller elaborates on the outcome of a control centered horizon:

> Things serve this project by becoming goals, intelligence by submitting to the rules of technique, emotion by allowing itself to be confined to the habit of oscillation between comfort and complaint. To the degree that one manages everything, one feels like the master of one's situation. But this control has been achieved only by allowing my desire for control to govern my attitude toward everything including all aspects of my self. It is clear that there is one experience that [we] cannot handle: the experience of not being in control of whatever situation [we are] in.[15]

Second, the will to control shapes our psyche. Miller is alluding to a kind of attitude that insinuates itself into our psyche. If something comes along to disrupt our limited and closed horizon, we desire only to return as quickly as possible to a psychically homeostatic state, since it is there that control feels most at home. Something that starts as a desire for some order to remain safe and achieve some balance, turns into a trait that bolsters egocentrism and impedes moral conversion and needed transformation.

Third, Miller unpacks the terrible cost to our heart when we are stuck in the will to control. The heart symbolizes the very center of our being to which all other capacities such as intelligence and reason belong. The heart is the spring form which our passion for life flows. He asserts that we "might conclude that the heart must be a profoundly fragile thing if we take such pains to keep it concealed from even our own awareness. But in fact it is not its fragility that terrifies us but its power—the piercing truth of its deepest wounds, the unbearable weight of its regrets and longings, the terrible import of its darkness and silences. It is all of this

---

14. Miller, *Way of Suffering*, 13.
15. Miller, *Way of Suffering*, 13.

we want to be ignorant of, at almost any cost. We do not want the deepest truths within us known to us."[16]

Fourth, when naming events that can penetrate to the heart, Miller has in mind examples such as the act of falling in love or going through some trauma or grief. In other words, events that evoke strong feelings. These are the kinds of events that invite new questions about life and our direction. If a will to control dominates our lives, then it is possible that the feelings following upon such events will be unattended. We will not allow ourselves to be affected by their invitations. The potential for something beyond us to astonish us and to overwhelm us, will not find a root. Miller declares:

> We would like to mind our own business and have nothing to do with it. The wounds love has inflicted are too deep, the dread the heart harbors is too perilous, for us to want to think about what it might teach us. We know just enough about the heart's core to keep as much distance from it as possible. Its joy, just as much as its weeping, is too overwhelming for us to bear. That is why we do not often [talk to each other]. Perhaps twice or three times in our lives we break through and acknowledge to one another the truths we have kept hidden from even ourselves. Sometimes this happens on one's deathbed, sometimes not even there.[17]

Fifth, when we cannot bear learning from the heart, our vulnerability becomes a problem. Miller asserts that "vulnerability is the rub. It's precisely our weakness, our susceptibility to wounds that we are tempted to—and able to—flee. We are tempted to flee because wounds can be traumatizing. We're able to flee because we can refuse to suffer our vulnerability, even though it is constitutive of us."[18] He goes on to assess what happens to the human heart when the will to control takes center stage. When the will to control takes center stage, we do not listen to our heart and, therefore, do not know the wisdom that our hearts can offer. Questions are successfully suppressed or even repressed, and we return to a state of invulnerability. We may not be able to cause ourselves to fall in love but we can protect ourselves from the pain it might otherwise cause. The result of dissociating from our vulnerability is that we separate ourselves from our heart. The various operations of intentionality

16. Miller, "Way of Suffering," 23.
17. Miller, "Way of Suffering," 23.
18. Miller, "Addiction and Tears," 57

are divided and separated so that emotion, imagination, sensation, intelligence, and rationality are no longer acting in unison.

Religious Conversion and Moral Conversion

The temptation to overlook values holistically and instead pick and choose our values moved by the will to control invites us to consider the importance of grace and the relationship between religious conversion and moral conversion. They are distinct yet interrelated dimensions of transformation. Religious conversion is falling-in-love unreservedly with God who has first loved us. Religious value is higher, more fundamental, and more originating for human living than simply values. Byrne states that while living according to worthwhile values is one thing, religious value recognizes that the ultimate originating value is the light of God.[19] Religious conversion goes beyond moral conversion. If the final good of moral conversion is all human good, the final good of religious value is the whole universe. If moral conversion is a decision in favor of all human values, religious conversion is in favor of an unconditional love of "everything about everything."[20] There exists the added transformation of religious conversion to those who have already grown in some measure of moral conversion.

For Lonergan, there exists a profound relationship between religious conversion relationship to moral conversion. By the grace of God, we shift from existential moral subjects to subjects of love. Lonergan acknowledges this transformation as a "new basis for valuing and all doing of good. In no way are the fruits of intellectual or moral conversion negated or diminished. On the contrary, all human pursuit of the true and the good is included within and furthered by a cosmic context and purpose and as well, there now accrues to man the power of love to enable him to accept suffering involved in undoing the effects of decline."[21]

When the will to control becomes our center, what is the problem? Miller states what the problem is quite frankly, namely, "that for most of us, in our heart of hearts, God does not exist. Or, if God does exist there, it has little effect on us: we keep our hearts as buried as we can so that they will not interfere with the ordinary business of living. In the

19. Lonergan, *Method*, 23.
20. Lonergan, *Method*, 24.
21. McCarthy, *Authenticity*, 242.

one case, God has never become real for us, has never ceased to be an abstraction; God is something we talk about because we have learned the word."[22] The biblical equivalent to living from the will to control is the "heart of stone." By contrast, the "heart of flesh" denotes a way of being where authentic feelings have a prominent place in our deliberations. We allow ourselves to be affected by realities other than ourselves. These realities bring on suffering. To suffer is not a passive act since to suffer is to actively allow ourselves to feel vuln*erability*. Being affected we give ourselves to whatever has moved us. In short, we choose not to make control the main thrust of our lives. Previous chapters have argued that only the grace of God makes possible the heart of flesh.

If we are to grow morally as people, then we must be willing to endure and to suffer what might, at first sight, appear to us disagreeable for the sake of maturing. Miller names the "impassioned" life as one that releases a more authentic narrative into our story and our giving ourselves to that which moves us in our deepest vulnerability. In this way, Miller stands with both St. Therese and Friedrich Nietzsche, for whom wholehearted and passionate commitment toward an ideal is critically important.

Moral Conversion and the Virtues

One way of discerning the best choice is by developing a virtuous life and letting these virtues guide our decision making and form our affectivity. Moral conversion helps cultivate within us a set of virtues in relationship to others. Living these virtues gives rise to a cluster of moral feelings that progressively help us to find direction. The word virtue comes from a Latin word meaning strength. On this matter, two insights are worth exploring. First, the importance of a unified view of the virtues. Second, in the Catholic moral tradition, there are four cardinal virtues which potentially grow out of moral conversion: prudence and the practice of discernment, justice, temperance, and courage. Third, there is the practice of discernment.

22. Miller, "Way of Suffering," 22.

A Unified View of the Virtues

Without a unified view of the virtues, errors creep into our deliberations. Our efforts at self-sacrifice may disguise the distortion of a hidden
abandonment to disesteem. The outward movement of love may cause
us to deny the urgent need to care for ourselves. The emissaries of love
called to endure all things forget that they must also vehemently resist
what is harmful even to the point of self-sacrifice. People demand others
who have been harmed grievously to forgive without understanding the
trauma that such an appeal can visit on the victim.

The lack of a unified view of the virtues props up a lack of unity
among our moral deliberations. Alasdair MacIntyre attests to the phenomenon of compartmentalization. He states:

> The thesis of compartmentalization is this: that increasingly
> all our lives are compartmentalized, so that as we move from
> the home to the workplace, to the meeting of the trade union
> branch, to the sports club, to some religious service in the par-
> ish, whatever it is, we move into and out of areas each of which
> has its own autonomous sets of norms, each of which requires of
> us that we adapt to those norms if we are to be effective in that
> situation and in such a way that we have to exchange one set of
> attitudes and norms for the other as we move between them.
> So it comes about that a new virtue is added to the list of the
> virtues, adaptability; and a new vice is added to the list of the
> vices, inflexibility.[23]

Wendy Farley attests to the importance of a unified view of the
virtues:

> We distinguish courage, wisdom, serenity, love, patience,
> strength, anger, forgiveness, self-manifestation, humility,
> kenosis, mercy, forbearance, urgency, justice, and so on. These
> separated virtues are healthy when they are united and interde-
> pendent. When they are split apart, they can become distorted
> and damaging. [However,] it is primarily through isolated vir-
> tues or ideals that our desire for good comes to us. The formation
> in us of desire for good happens in particular families, societies,
> and historical epochs. But particular communities tend to sever
> these erotic powers, exaggerating the importance of some, vili-
> fying others. At the same time, each of us has a natural affinity
> for some powers for good more than others. We may be [active]

23. MacIntyre, "Culture of Choices."

and energetic, aflame with anger over injustice, but, when severed from mercy or wisdom, these erotic powers can themselves
become instruments of humiliation and violence. Our zeal for
justice can wear out, body and soul, in the absence of equanimity or nurturing companionship.[24]

The Cardinal Virtues

The first of the cardinal virtues is prudence. If love is the fulfillment of
self-transcendence, then prudence is love's discretion. Referring to prudence, Patricia Lamoureux asserts that "a virtuous person wants to do
the good: however, actually achieving the good in a particular situation
requires insight, thoughtfulness, a keen assessment of circumstances,
careful deliberation and reflection, and a moral imagination healthy
enough to enable us to judge different possibilities for appropriate action.
That is what prudence provides."[25] Prudence is more than meaning well
or having good intentions. The virtue of prudence is essential since each
person needs to know how to make thoughtful and wise decisions. There
is a measure of patience and humility in prudence. Patience teaches us to
slow down our decision-making process. Humility helps us to acknowledge that each of us is not the total font of wisdom and there will arise the
need to consult with others.

The virtue of justice turns our gaze outward towards others and
shows us that we have rights and responsibilities towards them. We need
to know how to live with others. Justice can direct our choices between
ourselves and another person (commutative justice) or between ourselves
and a community (distributive justice). Lamoureux states that "justice
helps us see that we depend on, and continually benefit from, the care,
generosity, and goodness of others, just as they continually depend on
and benefit from us."[26] Justice is love's fairness.[27] However, if we too rigidly equate justice with fairness regulated only by law, then, we may miss
the opportunity to exercise justice with generosity. The task of *generously*
living with others is the virtue of justice. Chapter 7 will explore the theme
of distributive justice in the film *Romero*.

24. Farley, *Wounding and Healing*, 77.
25. Lamoureux and Wadell, *Christian Moral Life*, 124.
26. Lamoureux and Wadell, *Christian Moral Life*, 127.
27. Streeter, *Foundations*, 87.

There is the virtue of temperance. We also need to know how rightly to balance and integrate competing desires and attractions in our lives. Temperance is love's moderation.[28] We are all creatures of powerful inclinations, and the prevailing social and cultural milieu strongly influences our desires. When these desires render us unreasonable, then we will be adversely affected.[29] The exercise of our intelligence tempers us. It is no wonder that most counselors suggest that people filled with rage take several deep breaths, calm themselves, and allow the brain to let go of certain chemicals associated with rage and so function more intelligently. Conversely, unrestrained pleasure and the neglect of beauty can have a detrimental effect on us. Neither fear of pleasure nor over-indulgence gets temperance right.

Lastly, there is the virtue of courage. We may also need to know how to confront and overcome our fears in times of danger for the sake of some higher good. This moral attitude is the virtue of courage or fortitude. Courage is love's strength.[30] More than any other, we associate the virtue of courage with the gift of hope. It is the virtue that we need when fears plague us, difficulties, setbacks, and dangers that almost challenge us to the point of defeat.[31]

The Practice of Discernment

The practice of discernment consists of three steps: deliberating on the worth of something, making judgments of value, and decisions. First, in order to deliberate on the worth of something, we begin by gathering all possible information and analyzing it critically. This analysis may mean checking the reliability of sources, distinguishing between opinion and evidence, truths, and half-truths. Across society, many groups broadly confuse fact and fiction. Many who do not take a critical approach to the media are susceptible to false messages and biases. This does not mean taking a cynical approach to life and thinking that there are only hidden agendas behind everything. Instead, we need to foster a healthy critical spirit in ourselves and others. A critical spirit starts in asking the right questions. If we can keep asking the right questions, at least we are on the

---

28. Streeter, *Foundations*, 88.

29. Lamoureux and Wadell, *Christian Moral Life*, 130–32.

30. Streeter, *Foundations*, 87.

31. Lamoureux and Wadell, *Christian Moral Life*, 132–34.

road to being critical. Lonergan states that the road to reality is long and bloody. He realizes that knowing reality involves significant effort and challenging action.

In short, it requires hard and patient work in a time poor world. To deliberate well means avoiding hasty conclusions. Jumping to conclusions means twisting the data to fit one's pre-conceived assumptions often for one's motives of satisfaction. There may be a need to put aside prejudices—prejudices spring from a lack of humility. Many of our prejudices come from our upbringing, group bias, and individual bias. It is the journey of a lifetime to keep the lens focused on ourselves by means of an examined life so that we might each identify what prejudices we hold, and then having found them, slowly, gently, and carefully uproot them. Lastly, we should try to foresee as many consequences to actions as possible and not shut ourselves off from possible consequences expressed by people who make life generally hard. Having insight into consequences and foreseeing them relies a lot on insights gained previously. Sometimes we have that experience, and sometimes we do not. Sometimes we must talk to others who have more insight than we do.

It can be challenging to understand a complicated situation, especially when much of the data relevant to decisions are hidden from our attention in other very complex processes. Take for example the cumulative decisions that preceded the global financial crisis. In any fair estimation, it was a combination of several complex elements with whole groups of people not knowing what others were doing in other financial institutions. However, importantly, they did not want to know because there was a group-think about how to do business; namely, make as much money as possible with minimal ethical reflection and let the next person deal with the consequences.

Second, having analyzed critically, we are ready to make a judgment of value and to choose. Feelings play a big part in this step. Do these judgments of value fill us with joy, peace, kindness, humility, patience, self-control? Do these judgments fill us with turmoil, anxiety, and fear? To judge is to weigh up the pros and cons and arrive at what is the most worthwhile thing to do. Sometimes the weighing up is very simple: one moral position is very wrong for a situation, and the other is very right. We can quickly make these sorts of judgments of values. The ones that are not made so easily are those where there are goods to be gained from taking either direction or where either direction may require a measure of courage.

Third, the final step is making a decision. This step is critical because of the problem of indecision or procrastination. A decision is about the exercise of the will. Sometimes our will is free, that is, able to flow with and be attuned to the truth and other times our will can be bound up by personally and socially conditioned knots. A decision is essential together with a proper communication strategy so that the people who are being affected by the decision will be able to act appropriately.

Fourth, there exists a four-fold alteration of mood within consciousness that will help us in the process of discernment. These moods were recognized by St. Ignatius through his own examination of consciousness. These moods are: consolation, desolation, false consolation, and consolation without a cause. These alterations of mood identify the action of grace in our decision making. We experience spiritual consolation when our hearts are drawn to God and connected to God. We feel the fruits of the Spirit within: love, peace, and joy. Consolation directs our focus outside and beyond ourselves, lifts our hearts so that we can see the joys and sorrows of other people, bonds us more closely to our human community, generates new inspiration and ideas, restores balance and refreshes our inner vision, shows us where God is active in our lives and where God is leading us, and releases new energy in us.[32] Alternatively, we experience spiritual desolation when our hearts are turned away from God. Desolation turns us in on ourselves, drives us down a spiral ever deeper into our own negative feelings, cuts us off from community, makes us want to give up on the things that used to be important to us, takes over our whole consciousness and crowds out our distant vision, and covers up all the signs of our journey with God so far while draining us of energy.[33] Our ability to recognize the difference between these two moods is the difference between an attunement to the true self over against the false self, the deeper self over against the imprisoning surface self.[34]

The recognition of these moods is essential since there also exist false consolations. Margaret Silf notes that mostly we think of false guides as external to us. These are moods that possess an apparent positive experience of encounter with God but upon further reflection turn out to be moods of desolation. The test of their helpfulness is whether they turn

32. Silf, *Landmarks*, 88.
33. Silf, *Landmarks*, 88.
34. Gallagher, *Free to Believe*, 17–18.

us away from God or toward God. Lastly, consolation without a prior cause is the experience of being moved by the grace of God when we least expect it even in the midst of a difficult period of decision-making.[35]

Moral Conversion and the Scale of Values

So far, this chapter has explored moral conversion from the perspective of the individual. It is individuals that change social situations. Commenting on Lonergan's understanding of moral conversion, Byrne states that the element making moral conversion ongoing is a shift "from life in pursuit of *some* values to a life in pursuit of *all* values."[36] We do not exercise all values all at once; instead, we grow in our awareness of values and the knowledge that there are higher and lower values connecting us to one another. To understand how higher and lower values connect us, Lonergan speaks to the idea of a hierarchy or scale of values.

Again, feelings respond to values according to a scale of preference, and since we are committed to all human values, this very decision shifts the horizon of our feelings. Lonergan proposes a scale of values that may serve to establish an ordered arrangement within society that can deliver goods and services recurrently in response to human need. After all, we are members of communities. The scale of values introduces a scale of preference or hierarchy where one level of value is more important than another. As we move from one level of value to another, a richer context of collective responsibility exists. Values at higher levels sublate values at lower levels. Again, whether we are convinced about this scale of values or not will depend somewhat on our living of these values, and our moral maturity to move from what is merely agreeable or satisfying to what is truly worthwhile.

Lonergan states:

> Not only do feelings respond to values. They do so in accord with some scale of preference. So, we may distinguish vital, social, cultural, personal and religious values in an ascending order. Vital values such as health and strength, grace and vigor, normally are preferred to avoiding the work, privations, pains involved in acquiring, maintaining, restoring them. Social values such as the good of order which conditions the vital values

35. Silf, *Landmarks*, 91.
36. Byrne, "Moral Conversion," 20.

of the whole community have to be preferred to the vital values of individual members of the community. Cultural values do not exist without the underpinning of vital and social values but nonetheless they rank higher. Not on bread alone doth man live. Over and above more living and operating, men have to find a meaning and value in their operating. It is the function of culture to discover, express, validate, criticize, correct, develop, and improve such meaning and value. Personal value is the person in his self-transcendence as loving and being loved as originator of values in himself and in his milieu, as an inspiration and invitation to others to do likewise. Religious values finally are at the heart of the meaning and value of man's living and man's world.[37]

The first level of this hierarchy of values deals with *vital values*. Sometimes people refer to the physical level of life. These are biologically based: vitality, health, physical prowess, self-preservation, sociality, and reproduction. Maintaining vital values will never be able to eliminate the inevitability and limitations of loss, aging, and death. While important to health, vital values are very self-regarding and self-preserving. To understand how vital values are to be provided in a recurrent and continuous manner we turn to social values. The second level deals with *social values*. The social level sublates the lower level of vital values. Social values are higher ends than simply vital values. These are the recurring schemes that achieve, through cooperation with others, the delivery of goods and services in society. Families become groups and groups become villages and their living together still requires goods and services. The primary connection that people have with one another through family grows in complexity and becomes a social structure called a society. A society contains a means of technology, an economy, and the political realm to achieve consensus around ways for delivering goods and services efficiently and effectively. The creative tension between bonds of connection and practical intelligence is another instance of dialectic. Social values are more critical than vital values and deliver goods today, tomorrow, and into the future.

We can ask of our social values: to what human end do we work and strive for in these social arrangements? This question prompts a definite shift to a higher level of thinking and acting. This third level deals with *cultural values*. Cultural values are still higher human ends. Cultural

37. Lonergan, *Method*, 31–32.

values sublate social and vital values. Our social ordering prompts us to ask the questions that will achieve full human flourishing. Cultural values require a greater sense of moral purpose than do vital values and social values. They come from enlightened people who think critically and evaluate responsibly. Where do these cultural values come from? The fourth level deals with *personal value*. In personal value, we focus on ourselves as individual subjects in the process of self-transcendence. The decisions and the choices we make, make us, and make the world. We are meaning-makers. There will come a time when we will have to choose the values we affirm, and the disvalues we discourage. Based on the development of our personal value, we can go beyond the context in which we are born. We realize that we must make something of our lives. Lastly, there is the level of *religious value*. Religious value sublates all the other values and transforms our horizon into a new setting such that the universe that God created becomes important to us. If we believe in God, then we believe that God is the source of all beauty, meaning, value, and love. Our relationship with God shapes the kind of person we become and the way we live with others and God's creation.

Not all values are equal in weight. We pursue lower values as a means of pursuing the higher values. Chapter 3 explored the insight that there are two movements of development within human living. As we move from lower values upward, there is a movement of creativity in response to new questions. However, creativity can be blocked, and bias can set in. When this occurs, there is also the possibility of a movement from above downward. Religious value unblocks creativity and bias. Our being-in-love with God heals and elevates a willingness to love all that God loves and to seek social justice for them.

7

Moral Conversion, Mentors, and Cinema

IN THE PREVIOUS CHAPTER, we examined the distinctiveness of moral conversion. There is a link between religious conversion and moral conversion. The process of moral transformation finds its embodiment in a life of virtue lived socially and individually. This chapter, using narrative and cinema, will explore the lives of various people who have integrated moral and religious conversion into their lives.

RELIGIOUS AND MORAL CONVERSION: ST. AUGUSTINE

Chapter 4 noted that the *Confessions* is a very personal account of how Augustine came to be guided in his whole being by the light of faith. From this point in his life, he looks back and makes no excuses. He is willing to strip away all self-delusion and allow God to reveal His glory acting in his life. In his earlier life, Augustine finds an attractiveness to things beautiful to the eyes, things agreeable to the touch, the honor of others, the friendship of a broad group of people, and sexual attractions. He is also attracted to ideas, philosophy, mathematics, music and rhetoric and the pleasure and pride coming from an incisive intellect. We look at this impressive list and could quite easily conclude that these are human goods and, therefore, valuable in themselves. However, for Augustine, these values hamper his ability to see the highest value of all, the value of the light of faith and divine love. All these goods are judged by him to be out of proportion and not adequately ordered according to a scale of values. Augustine comes to the conviction that each value is "valuable only in the context of the wholeness of value."[1] More would be required of Augustine before he could state that he has a commitment to all values.[2] This process of transformation was to be a long and arduous process.

Augustine's transformation comes about due to a new way of thinking critically. This way of thinking begins to germinate after Augustine had read Cicero's, *Hortensius*. He subsequently wrestled with "a spatially bound conception of reality but not yet a turning toward reality as manifested through truth."[3] His understanding of reality connects to the way he understands evil and his responsibility for evil. Coming to a different vision of reality helps him plot a course on how he is to be responsible.[4] For example, he subscribed to a view of life promulgated by Manicheism, in which there are two opposing drivers at work in the universe, one evil, and the other good, continually fighting each other for dominance of their own space and time. This view permitted him not to accept responsibility for his own moral failings. He could rightly say that his shortcomings are the fault of somebody else. However, what we find in the *Confessions* is the testimony of a man who, looking back on his life, is moving beyond self-delusion or blaming other people or circumstances for his moral failings. The path of moral conversion lay in deciding for himself what kind of person he would become.[5]

One final step is needed before Augustine could reach up and embrace all values. He needs to abandon his pride and his will to control his life through the power of his intellect alone. Augustine needs to realize that his decision for specific values is not as important as religious value and what God's love does in the soul. Though he loves God at this stage, still he has to surrender himself into the hands of God without reserve, allow the discomfort of being humble to exist, and let God work in him.[6] This enormous struggle is picked up in Book 8 in the garden scene. Here is an exceptionally talented intellectual who comes to terms with the realization that the grace of God is indispensable for making decisions so as "to embrace the whole of value"[7] and also for overcoming the existential

1. Byrne, "Moral Conversion," 28.
2. Byrne, "Moral Conversion," 28.
3. Byrne, "Moral Conversion," 29.
4. Byrne, "Moral Conversion," 30.
5. Byrne, "Moral Conversion," 31.
6. Byrne, "Moral Conversion," 33.
7. Byrne, "Moral Conversion," 34.

problem of evil in daily life. Only God as the highest value could help him
to place all the other values in his life in the right order.

Religious and Moral Conversion: Franz Jägerstätter

Let us briefly listen to the voice of another person who lived from religious values where divine love sublates moral values. It is easier to make
good choices when there is no pressure to do otherwise. The mark of
a person's authentic and courageous character is to make good choices
when so much conspires against them. If love means bearing our suffering patiently, then the life of the Austrian farmer Franz Jägerstätter
speaks to us of a man who lived from the heart of love while seeking
authentic human values in troubled times.

Franz Jägerstätter was born in Sankt Radegund, Upper Austria in
1907. He was the illegitimate child of Rosalia Huber, a chambermaid,
and Franz Bachmeier, a farmer. Franz was first cared for by his grand-
mother, Elisabeth Huber and when Franz's natural father died in World
War I, when he was still a child, his mother married in 1917, and her
husband, Heinrich Jägerstätter adopted Franz. In his youth, Franz gained
a reputation for being a rebel, but, in general, his daily life was like most
Austrian peasants. From 1913 to 1921, his education happened in a small
single room school, where one teacher taught all seven grades. He lived
in a very Catholic area of Austria. He worked as a farm hand and as a
miner until he inherited the farmstead of his foster father in 1933. In that
same year, he fathered an out-of-wedlock daughter, Hildegard to There-
sia Auer. Typically, marriage would follow but, in this case, it did not,
and on Maundy Thursday of 1936, he married Franziska Schwaninger
(1913–2013), a deeply religious woman. After the ceremony, the bridal
couple went on a pilgrimage to Rome. The marriage produced three
daughters: Rosalia, Maria, and Aloisia.

Both Franz and Franziska were abreast of Germany's politics since
1933. When German troops moved into Austria in 1938, Franz was the
only person in the village to vote against the *Anschluss*. The *Anschluss*
plebiscite of April 10, 1938, argued a proposed union between Austria
and Greater Germany initiated by Adolf Hitler and the Third Reich. It
was critical in the life of the Austrian people. After voted on, the local
authorities suppressed Franz's dissent and announced a unanimous

approval. After all, even the Catholic hierarchy advocated a yes vote. Although he was not involved with any political organization and did undergo one brief period of military training, Franz remained openly anti-Nazi. He joined the Third Order of Saint Francis in 1940 and worked as a sacristan at the local parish church, being deferred from military service several times. In 1940, aged 33, he was conscripted into the German army and completed basic training.

Returning home in 1941 under an exemption as a farmer, he thought more deeply upon the morality of the war and discussed this with his bishop. He emerged from the conversation saddened that the bishop seemed afraid to confront the issues. After many delays, Franz received the call to active duty on February 23, 1943. By this time, his eldest daughter from his marriage to Franziska was not quite six years old. He maintained his position against fighting for the Third Reich and, upon entering the Wehrmacht on March 1, declared his conscientious objection. The Third Reich ignored his offer to serve as a paramedic. He was immediately imprisoned, first at Linz, then at Berlin-Tegel. A priest from his village visited him in jail and tried to talk him into serving but failed. During a military trial, the court accused him of undermining military morale. He received a death sentence and was executed by guillotine at Brandenburg-Görden Prison on August 9, 1943, aged 36. In 1946, his ashes were buried in his hometown cemetery.

Just before his execution, Franz writes what has become known as "Text No. 85" to his wife on a stiff piece of paper which was later given to her. This passage highlights how important the commandment, love God and our neighbor is for Franz. He is enabled to live this commandment to the point of his execution only because of the forgiveness and mercy of God. He declares:

> My dear loved ones, the hour draws ever nearer when I shall give my soul back to God, the Lord. I could say many words of farewell to you, and it is hard to imagine saying no more goodbyes to you. I would have gladly spared you the pain and the suffering that you have borne on account of me. But you surely know that we must love God more than our family, and that we must be ready to let go of everything that we love on this earth and that is dear to us rather than to offend God in the least. And I would not dare to offend God on account of you. We know what suffering God could have sent you on account of me! It was surely hard for our dear Saviour to give his dear mother pain because of his death. [Moreover] what are our sufferings in

relation to those which those two innocent hearts suffered for us sinners? Moreover, what must a farewell [at death] be for those people who do not fully believe in eternal life and who, therefore, do not have much hope for a reunion? If I could not have trusted in God's mercy and forgiveness for all of my sins, then I would have hardly had peaceful days during my solitary time in prison. Although people have already accused me of criminal behavior and condemned me to death, be consoled, knowing in God's eyes not everything is criminal that the world perceives to be criminal. I hope that I do not have to be afraid of the eternal judge because of this [so-called] criminal behavior.

Franz goes on to explain to his wife the centrality of the commandments of God and the importance of restraining from the temptation to blame others for the decisions they may have made. He states "I have nothing more urgent to set before you than that you resolve to keep all the Commandments and to avoid every sin. You should love God, our Lord, and also your neighbor as yourself [see Mark 12:28–34]. On these two Commandments rest the entire law. keep these, and then we have reason to hope for an imminent reunion in heaven. One must not think poorly about others who act differently than I have. It is much better for everyone to pray for them than to pass judgment on others. God intends that everyone should become holy."[8]

There is profound inner freedom to his thoughts. Franz feels deep sadness for what his wife and children are enduring. He imagines the pain they will be going through in the future due to his decisions. Through a process of critical thinking, he seeks to discern the difference between a just and an unjust war. He feels at peace in his prison cell while awaiting his execution, in the knowledge that he is not living his life as "half a Christian." He begs his wife, together with his mother, who disagree with him over the whole issue, not to go on being bitter about the situation, or to worry about his physical survival. Franz writes in "Text No. 88":

Now I'll write down a few words as they come to me from my heart. Although I am writing them with my hands in chains, this is still much better than if my will were in chains. God sometimes shows his power, which he wishes to give to human beings, to those who love him and do not place earthly matters ahead of eternal ones. Not prison, not chains, and not even death [is] capable of separating people from the love of God of

8. Jägerstätter, *Letters and Writings from Prison*, 235–36.

robbing them of their faith and free will [see Rom 8: 31–39].
God's power is invincible.[9]

Franz judges the immorality of war prosecuted by the Nazi Party
from the perspective of a man guided in his moral deliberations by
prayer. On this inner conviction, Franz writes many words between the
periods of 1941 to 1943. In text 88, he writes:

> What can it benefit me if I obey and execute the evil orders of
> the Fuhrer and, in doing so, commit sin but also am not able
> to attain perfection? Moreover, if someone who chooses not to
> follow the Fuhrer's evil orders is alleged to be doing something
> seriously sinful, then it is impossible for someone today-amid
> the greatest persecution of Christians that has veer happened-to
> sacrifice his or her life for Christ and the Christian faith. Does
> it make then no difference today whether we are carrying out a
> just or an unjust war? Perhaps I would have come to a different
> answer to this question if I had not read so many Catholic books
> and journals. How can people today declare many men and
> women of earlier times to be holy—men and women who put
> their lives at risk—when most of these men and women have
> refused to carry out the evil orders that are now required of us?
> Is there anything [with a greater] evil than when I am required
> to murder and rob people who are defending their homeland
> only so that I might help an anti-religious power attain victory
> and then be able to establish a world empire with belief in God
> or, to be more accurate with no belief in God?[10]

From these texts, we can begin to understand Franz's process of
discernment. In the months leading up to his death, the central question
for Franz is around choosing rightly. To know this answer requires an
examination of his consciousness. Is his heart moving toward a set of
actions that are destructive of himself, closed to compassion, distrusting,
and disconnected from others? Alternatively, is his heart moving towards
God with the help of what St. Paul calls the fruits of the Spirit? To make
good moral decisions ordinarily requires freedom from outward pressures. Franz did not have control over the enormous outward pressures
on him. More importantly, he has inner freedom. He evaluates the moral
impasse that both Germany and Austria have come to and the part he
would play in the social and political forces at work. The words of his

9. Jägerstätter, *Franz Jagerstatter*, 243.
10. Jägerstätter, *Franz Jagerstatter*, 197.

letters portray his feelings, moral insights, and religious commitment through a heart searching for answers to questions, concretely inspired by the grace, peace, and love of God.

RELIGIOUS AND MORAL CONVERSION: *THE MISSION*

Many of these same religious and moral themes come to prominence in the film *The Mission* (1986). It would be helpful to watch the whole film to better appreciate the context for the decisions and actions taken by the protagonists. There are two main protagonists in the film: the mercenary soldier, Rodrigo Mendoza, and the Jesuit priest, Father Gabriel. Viewers may be familiar with the instrumental piece called *Gabriel's Oboe*, composed for the film by Ennio Morricone. There is a tension between the storyline of the film written for dramatic effect and the actual historical events that stand behind the storyline. Indeed, the emergence of the Guarani people and their relationship to the dominant European powers as early as the sixteenth century is a rich and complex history.[11] The life of the Guarani intersects with Spanish colonialism and the Jesuit operation to congregate these native people into mission areas, even as late as the end of the seventeenth century.

The episode which features most centrally in the film concerns the events that followed the signing of the Treaty of Madrid in 1750. This treaty sought to determine how Spain and Portugal would divide up the South American continent between them both. The Spanish king agreed to remove all natives who were in Spanish controlled territories but soon to become Portuguese territories. The Guarani, some 300,000, from seven Jesuit missions, were to be removed and resettled elsewhere. All their buildings, churches, and lands were to be taken by the Portuguese. The Guarani also feared being enslaved by the Portuguese. The Guarani leaders were constructive, cooperating with Spain in trying to find an alternative solution as a growing rage built among them fearing dispossession.

Sadly, the Spanish and Portuguese governing powers responded to their lack of compliance with violence, unleashing a war that took place from 1754 to 1756. Paradoxically, difficulties in implementing the treaty led to the annulment of the agreement and the lands were returned to Spain in utter ruin by 1761. While it is true that the Guarani displayed an anti-Portuguese bias, they also felt betrayed by the Spanish. By 1801, the

11. Herzog, "Bordering the Spanish," 1–5.

seven mission areas became Portuguese not by military means but by a more favorable approach by the Portuguese toward the Guarani.

The film is probably set in the 1740s with the storyline beginning when a Spanish Jesuit priest, Father Gabriel, enters the northeastern part of Argentina and the western Paraguayan jungle to build a mission station and convert the Indigenous Guarani to Christianity. The Guarani community is not initially receptive to Christianity or outsiders in general, shown by the opening scene where a priest, tied to a wooden cross, crashes to his death over the Falls. This act does not stop the courageous and forgiving Father Gabriel traveling to the Falls, climbing to the top, and playing his oboe to attract the attention of the Guarini. The Guarani warriors, captivated by the music, allow Gabriel to live, though they remain suspicious of the men in black.

Meanwhile, there is another central protagonist, the mercenary soldier and slave trader Rodrigo Mendoza, who makes his living kidnapping the Guarani and selling them to the nearby plantation owners. Slavery makes it possible for the plantation owners to make larger profit margins. After returning from another kidnapping trip, Mendoza is told by his legally recognized fiancée, Carlotta, that she loves Mendoza's younger half-brother Felipe. Mendoza later finds them in bed together, and in a fit of rage, Mendoza kills Felipe in a duel. Although the courts acquit him of the killing, Mendoza spirals into anger against himself, and a suicidal intent fills his being.

Upon his return to the settlement, Father Gabriel is asked to go and see Mendoza in jail. Gabriel finds him a broken man, intent on killing himself by starvation. He challenges Mendoza to undertake a suitable penance and come with him to the region above the Falls. Mendoza accompanies the Jesuits on their return to the Guaraní village, scaling a vertically uphill stretch of jungle, and a waterfall, while dragging a massive bundle containing his armor and weapons. Along the way, the members of the Jesuit fraternity beseech Gabriel to end his task of carrying this heavy load taken on by the broken Mendoza. Wisely, Gabriel instructs them that while he feels the same compassion for him as they do, it is Mendoza who must make the first step of unburdening himself. When they reach the camp of the Guarani, and immediately after being greeted, the Guarani men recognize him and threaten him with death. They know who he is and they are intent on killing him for his past crimes. Upon further inquiry, the chief gives the order not to kill him, and Mendoza's would-be executioner cuts the weight from his shoulders. Mendoza weeps without reserve.

What insights can we draw from this segment of the film regarding moral conversion? First, here are some insights on those tears shed by Mendoza on the cliff top. Jerome Miller suggests that there is a difference between crying and weeping. He states:

> When one cries, [there is] a rent in one's composure—a quivering lip, a slippage of breath, a trickle of tears; but one's self-possession remains [substantially] intact. [However,] when one weeps, one's being as a whole temporarily breaks down. The ego, the control center of the psyche that's usually so proficient at keeping emotion in check, collapses. The body shudders under a weight it [cannot] bear. Weeping is, as it were, the signature of man's vulnerability. It is the paradigmatic idiom of human suffering. It testifies more eloquently than speech to the depth of our affections.[12]

The will to control is the modality we adopt when we refuse to open ourselves to something beyond ourselves. By contrast, weeping is a sign that something beyond ourselves has affected our whole being. The once divided and partitioned psyche is open, made vulnerable, and receptive to moral truth. At this point, Mendoza receives insight coming from the deepest recesses of the heart. Our sense of vulnerability does not stop there. Miller continues: "When we're finally realizing what a mess we have made of our lives, all we can see is our impotence, our terminal failure [while] the fact of this very breakdown of our previously self-assured ego, this very inability to control our tears, is opening us to the influence of sublimities that transcend us."[13]

Second, these are the tears of a man who has come to know forgiveness from such an unexpected source, namely, the people he enslaved so brutally. Mendoza's tears come from one who has just received a gift of grace undeserved and unmerited. They are the tears of a man who has finally acknowledged and recognized his vulnerability. More instructively, we must understand these events through the lens of Mendoza's psychological state. When Gabriel first meets Mendoza in jail, he meets the self-hating hero. As one searching for the most heroic action to take, Mendoza is the broken soldier who considers killing himself as the only

---

12. Miller, "Addiction and Tears," 60.
13. Miller, "Addiction and Tears," 61.

heroic action to take following the murder of his brother. Before this event, Mendoza's image of a hero is that of the strongman, respected for his power and status. According to Mendoza's understanding, the life of heroism demands that he must destroy himself. Mendoza is determined to die for what he has done and so salvage some honor from the situation. He has reached a point of self-loathing requiring self-annihilation.

Interiorly, there is despair in all self-hatred. However, there is a further problem with self-hatred when combined with a desire for self-inflicted punishment that heads towards a tragic irony.[14] The person filled with self-hatred sets themselves up as both judge and accused, executioner and criminal. Miller states that the part of the self "who steps back from my self does so in order to examine it from the position of *superiority* which enables me to look down upon the self to be examined. I am the criminal guilty and worthy of punishment; but I am also the judge ready to become the executioner. If I experience in my role as criminal all the humiliation of being debased, I experience in my role as judge all the self-righteous and moral outrage which crime arouses in the virtuous."[15] The more painful that he makes his punishment as judge, the more confident he can be of his purity for being willing to inflict it. In as much as he sets himself up as judge, he believes in his purity and his innocence, and, from that point, is prepared to visit on himself all the hatred that he deserves. The danger with this kind of self-hatred is that the hero stands above and apart from the evil that he has become. He has not yet become entirely honest with himself and, through his actions, is unknowingly stepping back and away from the full impact of this crisis.

Third, Mendoza's tears above the falls are a sign of a transformation in his horizon. They are tears of honest and genuine shame, and those tears represent a transition in Mendoza's inner moral person. We might say that Mendoza has become honest with himself. The tears point to the mortification of shame beginning to take shape in his conscience. The experience of shame precipitates a state of crisis in him and initiates a radical rethinking of what good and evil are. Healthy shame persuades the person that taking away the life of another, in this case, his brother's life, is so serious that the wrong of not acknowledging his brother's worth becomes devastating beyond measure. One cannot gain access to the moral order except through shame's abject grief on behalf of the reality that one

14. Miller, *Way of Suffering*, 124.
15. Miller, *Way of Suffering*, 125.

has violated. Such shame ruptures our sense of being morally upright and throws in our face the fact that we have lost our moral bearing.

If we have avoided these realities, then, the final acknowledgment of them will require a humiliating contrition for all one's previous avoidances. The choice is clear: we protect ourselves from feeling healthy shame or we feel mortification. If we choose healthy shame, then we choose sorrow and mortification as the beginning of a process towards obedience to a new moral order. This distinction is a moral dialectic of contradictories at work in us. The great paradox of the moral life is that only those who are willing to undergo this most profound experience of shame are capable of being truly good. The more profound one's awareness of evil, the more tormenting one's shame will be, and the more piercing is the perception as to how far we must move to establish a new moral order.

Fourth, there is a relationship between self-esteem, disesteem, and shame. John Bradshaw names unhealthy shame as toxic shame "experienced as the all-pervasive sense that I am flawed and defective as a human being. Toxic shame is no longer an emotion that signals our limits; [rather,] it is a state of being, a core identity. Toxic shame gives you a sense of worthlessness, a sense of failing and falling short as a human being. Toxic shame is the rupture of the self with the self. *It is like internal bleeding.*"[16] Toxic shame makes someone into something evil when the shamed person has done no evil. For many years, we have concerned ourselves in western societies with the problem of unhealthy shame, in part from our awareness of disesteem. An unhealthy shame is the voice of the false self and something we ought to escape.

We discover toxic shame lurking in the recesses of a heart overdetermined by a secular culture that measures worth according to material value. We find unhealthy shame in a false religion that seeks to control people by fear. An unhealthy shame exaggerates our faults and can become a chronic affective condition, pervading our whole being. From what we know about Mendoza, his shame becomes toxic by adding the layer of self-hatred. Self-hatred robs healthy shame of its mortifying power since the self-hating person has set themselves up as both judge and criminal. Within the persona of judge/executioner, there lingers the shadow of moral superiority and perfectionism.

There is a world of difference between the shame of false conscience and the shame of real conscience. The tears of Mendoza above the falls

16. Bradshaw, *Healing the Shame*, 10.

give witness to a man who is now willing to succumb to the power of healthy shame by suffering mortification through a realization of his evil. Such mortification will require him to remain in crisis and wait for insight to emerge. With this realization comes the birth or stirring of conscience. The stirring of conscience is a starting point for acknowledging that he has victimized so many people in his life: the Guarani, his brother, his fiancée, and himself. False conscience is more an internalized code spoken by some authoritative voice other than the voice of one's heart. It represents an early stage of moral development gone wrong. False conscience approves or disapproves based on fear and the possibility of exclusion. However, with right conscience there exists the possibility of ongoing moral conversion through choosing what is truly worthwhile.

Fifth, there is a profound relationship between religious and moral conversion. Above the falls, the Guarini people recognize Mendoza as the enslaver and murderer of their people. When Mendoza arrives, beaten physically by the load he dooms himself to carry, the first and most just response of the Guarani tribesman, according to their codes, would have been to cut his throat. Instead, prompted by the tribal leader, the Guarini tribesman is directed to cut the heavy load from his neck rather than killing him in the act of retribution. For Mendoza, it is an unexpected gift of unconditional love. This gesture is a significant redemptive moment in the life of Mendoza. It is an experience of religious conversion. Mendoza does not yet know its full significance and only in the ensuing days does he seek to understand this event by reading and meditating on the Scriptures.

Putting aside for a moment the action of love shown towards Mendoza, let us explore what could be going on within his heart in the light of such a gesture. We all know that choices have exterior consequences; some foreseeable and others are unforeseeable. Choices also have interior consequences. Choices form us into a specific kind of character. One might even say that choice *is* primarily character forming and so it is very difficult for us to disassociate ourselves from our choices.[17] We will always be the person who has made that choice, and for every choice made in the past, we also make it as part of a future that we become and, in that way, are bound to it for as long as we live. It is thus clear that those schooled in the suffering that their deeds have caused, begin to feel the mysterious gravity of choice in all its incomprehensibility. To undergo

17. Miller, *Way of Suffering*, 113.

such suffering is to realize the full import of even one chosen act of evil against another. Such a realization is a profound moral accomplishment and brings about deep tearfulness and sorrowfulness, the pain of feeling that we have caused harm to others. Only when this happens can we realize the real miracle of forgiveness.

In the case of Mendoza, the specific crime against the Guarani is that he has murdered and enslaved their people, while his sin against his family is to have killed his brother. Therefore, the Guarani's act of cutting loose the heavy burden from his shoulder is even more extraordinary since Mendoza receives this unexpected act as a gift in his very character as a murderer. Up until that point, he would not have expected anything more than retribution for his multiple murders. Indeed, we notice that in his prison cell, Mendoza has become hopeless in the depth of his heart. He would never have expected divine love mediated through his victims. So, as St. Paul says, the love that embraces us while we are still sinners is genuinely unimaginable, inconceivable, and historically impossible (Rom 5:8). No rationale or logic could account for an act that amounts to forgiveness. Mendoza, the violator is shown love while still the violator. The violated who love through forgiveness, despite the painful wound inflicted by the violator, impart from their own wounded heart a new grace to the violator, which we call mercy. The victim's wound becomes a fountain of grace. This new grace helps bring about a very different horizon of love in the violated. By means of contrition, it transforms the moral horizon of the violator.

Growth in the Virtues and *The Mission*

There is a connection between moral conversion and the development of the virtues. Following the events above the falls, the film goes on to explore the religious development of Mendoza. He begins a new life through reading Scriptures and common prayer. Most especially, we find him reflecting on St. Paul's hymn to love in 1 Cor 13:1–13. He spends time getting to know the Guarani people, and he integrates himself into their daily communal life. He consents to become a postulant in the Jesuit Order. This decision requires him to accept the vows of poverty, chastity, and obedience. Later, we find him called reluctantly to demonstrate his commitment to obedience when he is asked by Gabriel to apologize to the Governor for intemperate comments against him. From previous experiences, when he worked as a mercenary for the establishment, Mendoza knew that the Governor had been behind the mass slavery of the Guarani. Mendoza has now pitched his tent with the Guarani people and seeks to expose the injustices perpetrated against them while remaining loyal to his Jesuit promises. His intemperate outburst against the Governor is a sign of his inability to grasp the realpolitik of the situation.

Later, in the final scenes of the film, when the Spanish and Portuguese soldiers are advancing with full force to attack the Guarini Camp, Mendoza must decide whether to take up arms to stop the unjust aggressors or choose the path of non-retaliation. Mendoza chooses to fight the unjust aggressor. Gabriel confesses to Mendoza earlier the reason for his choice of pacifism: he is unable to live in a world where there is no love. In the last scene of the film, we see Gabriel carrying the Eucharist in a monstrance, leading a group of Guarani Christian believers who one by one are shot dead by the soldiers. All this is observed by Mendoza who has also been shot in the heat of battle and is unable to resist any longer.

In this passage of the film, Mendoza draws our attention to the importance of the development of virtues. Prudence helps us work out how to discern good decisions in our lives. Mendoza must decide with whom he stands and what is the best path to take. He must work out whether the conflict is worth the casualties that are sure to come. Justice helps us determine what is rightfully due to each person and where fairness lies so that they can live a good life in every respect. Mendoza must adjudicate who is in the right and work out a just response to an unjust aggressor. Courage helps us do the right things in the face of danger and death. Mendoza faces the soldiers of Spain and Portugal with bravery even though outgunned. At one point during the battle, he moves to ignite the explosives that would destroy the bridge. At the same time, he sees a child in mortal danger. He chooses to help the child rather than ignite the bridge. This decision allows the soldiers to dismantle the explosives. For Mendoza, the preciousness of the children comes before a tactic of battle and his bravery is displayed.

Social Conversion and Justice

Chapter 6 examined the interrelationship between moral conversion and the building of a just society. The virtue of justice as love's fairness is vital in a moral community. Justice requires the work of just men and women. Moral conversion recognizes that serving people by building a just society and reversing the effects of social sin are centrally important if persons are to grow authentically. Conversely, both the individual egoist and those engaged in group bias are destructive of community life.

Social conversion is a form of moral conversion which makes the rights of individuals as a community its focus and so reflects the desire to build a more just society. From exploring the scale of values, we learned that Lonergan asserts the importance of both spontaneous intersubjectivity and practical intelligence for community living. He writes that "as members of the hive or herd belong and function together, so too men are social animals and the primordial basis of their community is not the discovery of an idea but a spontaneous intersubjectivity."[18] The natural manner by which people form bonds and relationships with one another influences the emergence of practical insights and this kind of intelligence, in turn, acts on feelings and motivations. Lonergan asserts "The spontaneous, intersubjective individual strives to understand and wants to behave intelligently; and inversely, intelligence would have nothing to put in order were there not the desires and fears, labors and satisfactions of individuals . . . the alternations of social tranquility and social crisis mark successive stages in the adaptation of human spontaneity and sensibility to the demands of developing intelligence."[19]

Although the term social conversion is never named as such by Lonergan, we know that Lonergan spoke about the interrelationship between the various levels of the scale of values as a framework for bringing about a just process. Following Lonergan's scale of values, Doran points out:

> For problems in the equitable distribution of vital goods can be resolved [by means of] justice only by transformations in social structures, in technologies, economies, polities, and spontaneous interrelatedness; and these transformations demand changes in the meanings and values by which people live, which changes in turn a function of the conversion of the person to authentic self-transcendence—until the individual changes nothing changes. However, that personal transformation itself depends on the gift of God's grace which is required for consistent self-transcendent performance affectively, intellectually, morally, and politically. Conversely, then, God's gift of love

18. Lonergan, *Insight*, 237.
19. Lonergan, *Insight*, 243.

effects personal transformation; such conversion shows itself in the transformation of meanings and values constitutive of culture; this transformation alone guarantees the justice of the social order, which itself is required for the equitable distribution of the earth's vital goods.[20]

The distortions within any social situation are also characterized by what Lonergan calls the shorter and longer cycles of decline, and, hopefully, by God's grace, the reversal of this decline.[21] These cycles of decline result from an overemphasis on practical intelligence and a lack of respect for the way practicality without an awareness of *people as people* negatively impacts on them. This distortion of decline occurs when the tension is broken, and practical intelligence dominates over intersubjectivity. The shorter decline takes hold when groups work against the interest of the whole for their wealth and power. The rich become separated from the poor and struggling. The longer cycle of decline comes about due to the general neglect of intelligent thinking within a significant number of a community's members over a long period, specifically through not using the full range of intelligence available to them to work out solutions to practical problems. Thus, the situation of the widening gap between rich and poor, and the unequal distribution of goods and services needed for daily existence, embedded in the social and cultural fabric of society, is an instance of the longer cycle of decline. Ultimately, the cycles of decline have their origins in one group of people claiming that their voice, their story, their contribution to the social, and cultural world are more important than those who did not share their economic and social privileges.

Social Justice and *Romero*

To demonstrate social conversion and the importance of just political processes within community, let us examine the film *Romero* (1989). The life of Oscar Romero, who accepted the position of Catholic Archbishop of San Salvador on February 22, 1977, underpins the storyline of the film. He was the first choice for Archbishop among the oligarchic families, the government, and the military of El Salvador. He was a very conservative person and influenced by the religious group, Opus Dei. He had spoken out against priests and bishops who had espoused Marxist views of social

20. Doran, "Bernard Lonergan and Daniel Berrigan," 126.
21. Lonergan, *Insight*, 249–54.

and economic change within the Salvadoran society. In 1976, while still Bishop of Santiago de Maria, he delivered, in front of a large group of believers, mostly government officials and members of the diplomatic corps, a homily attacking priests and faithful who subscribed to hate-filled and revolutionary ideas that distorted the way of Christ. Initially, Romero aligned himself with the twelve families who owned 95 percent of the wealth in the country. He also supported government policies and denied government involvement as inconclusive in the disappearance and torture of civilians.

Three incidents bring him to the threshold of conversion. First, there is a massacre perpetrated by the Las Tres Calles National Guards-men at the behest of the Astorga family, in which six civilians are shot and hacked to death. This incident places before Romero the brutality of the military and militia groups aligned with the rich. He begins to read church documents that speak of social justice. Second, he listens to the voice and stories of ordinary men and women. Widows, mothers, and daughters who describe incident after incident of fathers, brothers, uncles, and sons are taken from their home, some tortured, some muti-lated, and some never seen again. Third, he learns of the assassination of Father Rutilio Grande, a Jesuit priest who has spent his pastoral life helping the poor, and his two *Campesinos*. It is the first time that a priest dies at the hands of murderers in the country.

Jon Sobrino, a Salvadoran theologian, present on the day of Father Rutilio's funeral Mass, gives this recollection of Romero:

> Whether one actually calls it conversion or not, the radical change that took place in Archbishop Romero on the occasion of Rutilio's murder was one of the most impressive things anyone around him, including myself, had ever seen. He was fifty-nine years old at the time, an age at which people's psychological and mental structure, their understanding of their faith, their spirituality and their Christian commitment have typically hardened. Furthermore, he had just been named an Archbishop—the highest level of responsibility in the institutional church, which like any other institution, necessarily has a strong instinct for continuity and prudence, not to say out-and-out retrenchment. Finally, historical circumstances were scarcely favorable. [However,] Archbishop Romero changed, and changed radically. He refused the beautiful palace and went to live in Divine Providence Hospital, in a little room next to the sacristy. Thus, not only were the powers cheated of their hopes

for a nice, pliable ecclesiastical puppet, but the new archbishop was actually going to oppose them somehow. In store for him, of course, if he did so, was the wrath of the mighty—the oligarchy, the government, the political parties, the army, the security forces, and later, the majority of his brother bishops, the various Vatican offices, and even the US government.[22]

For Sobrino, Romero's moral deliberations reflect the impact on him of the historical events and the ethical issues they generated. First, while not approving of Father Rutilio's pastoral ministry at Aguilares, based on its political nature, Romero's horizon of questioning and understanding changes after Rutilio is murdered. Standing before Rutilio's coffin, Romero comes to appreciate that pastoral ministry, the mission of the church to the poor, and the kind of faith that Rutilio once advocated, is the true church. If Rutilio is right, Romero reasons, then he himself is wrong. He faces the question: What will I do for Christ?[23] Indeed, the religious conversion of Romero comes to be known as "Rutilio's miracle."

Second, there are varying reactions from groups within the broader church. Romero understands that his appointment has been received with skepticism and even alarm from the small faith-based communities or by anyone in tune with the theology of liberation. This theology had become the backbone of discussion through the Conference of Bishops at Medellin in 1968, and, from that point in time, had become a theological underpinning for addressing the problems associated with poverty. Romero also knows the satisfaction that his appointment has brought to the church hierarchy and the oligarchic power groups within society. Yet, in those days after Rutilio's death, the group that rallies to his side are the poor and not the rich. Some church authorities and powerful families grow in suspicion of him, attack him, and ultimately abandon him.[24] By what they say and what they do, their responses help Romero come to a transformation in his moral stance.

Third, Sobrino asserts that "the poor were effectively calling for his conversion. But in offering him light and salvation, they also facilitated that conversion. And Archbishop Romero recognized this. For me there is no doubt that is Archbishop Romero's last secret, and I shall reveal that secret. In one of his most felicitous expressions, in words of the kind that

22. Sobrino, *Oscar Romero*, 8–9.

23. Sobrino, *Oscar Romero*, 10.

24. Sobrino, *Oscar Romero*, 11.

cannot be invented, but can only come from the heart, he said "'With this people, it is not difficult to be a good shepherd.'"[25] Romero develops a pastoral closeness to the poor. From the start of his appointment, the poor show him acceptance and affection. They find no one else to defend them and so hope for an archbishop one who will stand alongside them. During this time, Romero makes his first steps that reflect a change of his horizon by denouncing in public the violence and brutality of the military and their bosses. In those days, Romero links his faith in God to the suffering poor. The identity of God becomes the God of the little ones, the poor, and the oppressed. He prays to Christ as suffering and crucified. At one point in the film, a woman confronts Romero and tells him that he speaks for all the poor such as herself. In another scene of the movie, a church building is taken over by the military and used as a barracks. Romero goes to the place and preaches to the people gathered a message that takes a stance with the dispossessed poor, the crucified poor united to the suffering of Christ on Calvary, and the poor who will contribute to El Salvador's liberation and redemption.

Following Rutilio's death, the archdiocesan chancery goes through turmoil and upset. Romero publishes a set of communications denouncing political repression and the persecution of the church, demanding that government authorities investigate the murder of priests and other lay workers. He promises to stay away from government functions until the authorities solve the crimes and the repression has stopped. In the film, we witness his courageous preaching where Romero appeals passionately to the army. He appeals to their common origins but does not hold back that the ones the military have killed are their brothers and sisters. Romero exhorts them not to follow the voice of those who command them to kill, but rather to obey the commandment which tells all not to kill. He reminds them that there is no obligation to follow an order to kill since it is against God's law. Finally, Romero makes a plea in the name of all who have suffered that the army stop their oppression.

Romero keeps his promise not to attend a single government function for three years. He also holds his pledge to close the schools for three days so that people might reflect on the Bible, Vatican II, and the documents of Medellin, through the lens of solidarity with the poor. On Sunday, March 20, he has all the churches closed and refuses to celebrate Mass in the Cathedral church. These events are portrayed vigorously in

---

25. Sobrino, *Oscar Romero*, 13.

the film. In February 1980, paramilitary forces shot Romero dead while he celebrated Mass in a hospital chapel. Just a few days before, he speaks these words to a journalist from the newspaper *Excelsior* in Mexico City: "If they kill me, I shall rise again in the Salvadoran people. I am not boasting. I say it with the greatest humility."[26]

Sebastian Moore gives an insightful account of power, poverty, and the cause of the oppressed from an interior perspective. Globally, in societies today, the rich are getting richer, and the poor are getting poorer thanks to powerful multinational groups who operate out of a predominate profit motive. Believing that God is just and truthful means that witnesses of faith must identify with the victims of history just as Romero did. Moore examines the phenomenon of the gulf between the powerful and the powerless interiorly. Moore unpacks Georg Hegel's insights regarding the master-slave relationship:

> Here is how Hegel builds up his idea. A person wants to feel more significant. He wants to feel his life is his own to enjoy, but he soon comes to realize that he cannot feel significant all by himself. He needs another, because the person is meaningless to himself in isolation. . . . Hegel is talking about a strategy used by something in us, that does not want to share, at least not yet. What is that strategy? Hegel's imaginary person employs an-other to supply the minimum of 'other-ness' necessary to enhance his own self-importance. In short, the other is the slave, the retinue, the extension of the first person. The other person is there mainly for that purpose, to be the reassuring echo of the first person's sense of his own significance.[27]

In this dynamic, Moore assesses that the slave has no sense of his own life as significance except in its task of enhancing the master's significance. The slave's subjugation cannot last forever for the slave begins to get a sense of his significance. The master resists this development and tries to keep the slave down, but the slave persists. Soon, the master is enslaved by "the necessity of enslaving the other; the Slave is the master of the situation; he has won the battle for significance."[28] The battle usually begins another cycle where the oppressed become the oppressors. Therefore, Moore suggests another approach to the use of power. Authentic power becomes "the sense of personal significance corroborated

26. Romero quoted in Sobrino, *Oscar Romero*, 99.

27. Moore, *Fire and the Rose*, 46

28. Moore, *Fire and the Rose*, 47.

by the concern of another, by another's having to take me seriously. In contrast, love is the sense of personal worth experienced as enhanced by and enhancing another. So, power and love are two modes of the working of the human drive to feel significant."[29] While the pattern established in the slave to master relationship is a distorted exercise of power, Moore asserts that this does not have to be the case if our basic human need is met and we engage the authentic structure of desire in our lives. Distorted unilateral power does not encourage mutual growing in the significance of the other but rather confrontation and animosity between parties. Moreover, the situation does not have to remain one of confrontation and animosity. Mutual understanding can transform a situation when love and power are intertwined.

29. Moore, *Fire and the Rose*, 48.

8

Affective Conversion and Feelings of Love and Commitment

THE THIRD KIND OF conversion that facilitates transformation is affective conversion. Some would say that affective conversion is a subset of moral conversion, only this time focusing on the affective quality of our relationships of love, care, and commitment. There is no doubt that affective self-transcendence and moral self-transcendence are linked closely. Lonergan asserts that people who undergo moral conversion become people "capable of genuine collaboration and of true love."[1] Moral conversion becomes the condition for the possibility of a sustained love for others. It is the quality of our love which then helps us choose and order values correctly. Dunne affirms that people deepen their friendships and expand the field of those for whom they care when "they learn to trust love itself."[2] In the order of personal discovery, it is more likely that people who have experienced the love of others will demonstrate care and concern, and so find themselves embedded in a vibrant and joyous existence.

A WHOLEHEARTED COMMITMENT TO LOVE

Chapter 2 explored how our horizon is everything that a person cares for or interests them. The conversion of our horizon is "a total opening of

1. Lonergan, *Method*, 35.
2. Dunne, *Doing Better*, 136.

one's horizon through some form of commitment."[3] Affective conversion is "a wholehearted commitment to the unrestricted range of love."[4] Since it is wholehearted, feelings respond to the highest values, orienting and motivating the person toward the release of moral self-transcendence. In this way, Lonergan directs our attention to the importance of love. He states that "self-transcendence reaches its term not in righteousness but in love and, when we fall in love, then life begins anew. A new principle takes over, and as long as it lasts, we are lifted above ourselves and carried along as parts within an ever more intimate yet ever more liberating dynamic whole. Such is the love of husband and wife, parents and children. Such again less conspicuously but no less seriously, is the loyalty constitutive of civil community, where individual advantage yields to the advantage of the group and individual safety may be sacrificed to the safety of the group. Such, finally is God's gift of his own love flooding our hearts through the Holy Spirit he has given to us (Rom 5:5)."[5]

Further religious conversion sublates affective conversion. The love of God inspires our love of others, therefore our capacity for self-transcendence becomes "an actuality when one falls in love. Then one's being becomes being-in-love. Such being in love has its antecedents, its causes, its conditions, its occasions. But once it has blossomed forth and as long as it lasts, it takes over. It is the first principle. From it flows one's desires and fears, one's joys and sorrows, one's discernment of values, one's decisions and deeds."[6] The center of affective conversion is that we make decisions and direct our choices according to the urgings of love and we move toward a shared life with one another. We are no longer limited by what kind of ethnic or racial group someone belongs to or what socio-economic standing we possess. It becomes a wholehearted movement away from egocentrism or self-absorption towards others in care and love, with the matching affective life to sustain the transformation. Love is the key to escaping the centripetal force of our persistent egocentric gravity.

Further, when such a conversion takes place, the person's care is not centered in this or that act of care, but a *dynamic* state of being-in-love with God and loving others. Love may begin in an intimate interpersonal

---

3. Dunne, *Doing Better*, 136.

4. Dunne, *Doing Better*, 136.

5. Lonergan, *Third Collection*, 169–70.

6. Lonergan, *Method*, 105.

relationship but then soon extends to others, to global citizens, and the whole of creation. Such affective conversion turns us from a possessiveness rooted in an obsessive concern for our own needs to an intimate care of others. It shapes our affective states or feelings so that, through our affective reorientation, we educate ourselves to recognize the best decisions to make, based on what our loving feelings are saying to us. It prompts us to seek out loving attentiveness, loving intelligence, loving reasonableness, and loving responsibility. It gives us confidence rooted in the quiet joy of knowing that we can commit ourselves to an excellent course of action and overcome obstacles in our efforts to care for and love others. In this way, we can speak of affective conversion as a fundamental transformation of our affective desires.

Chapter 1 explored the importance of love stories. There are the love stories of young couples, newlyweds, aging married and single people, the love of parents for their children, the love of children for their parents, the love of citizens for their community, and our love for God. Is it any wonder that so many songs in the Folk and Country tradition especially, speak to the threefold longings of the heart: the desire of home, community, and love? People separated from the ones they love often express this separation as a lament or longing for home since our home is a place or memory that cannot be snatched away without severe psychic consequences. Even when people are trying to get away from home, there is a nostalgia that speaks to a wound in the heart for something not there. Such a wound may well impel the person to seek solidarity with all the strangers of the world. For those touched by divine love we feel the longing of the communion of saints, and yet we also know the alienation, anonymity, and lack of belonging that can come from being unappreciated in a community of faith.

Musical lyrics express the ecstasy of falling in love, the pain of being betrayed, and the devastation of losing love, and the integrity of aging with someone we love. These desires are symbols of love and longing. John Denver's lyrics in his song, "Back Home Again" speak to this universal theme. The lyrics voice the thoughts of a truck driver making his way back home after considerable time on the road. To be home feels good, surrounded by family and friends, and the intimate love of couples. Alternatively, in the musical *Les Miserables* based on the novel of the same name by Victor Hugo, the song, "I Dreamed a Dream," portrays the betrayal of love. The song is a lament, sung by the anguished Fantine, who has just been fired from her job at the factory and thrown onto the streets. In the song, she thinks back to happier days and remembers both the highlights and troughs of her life. She is destitute now and bears the burden of still caring for her daughter, Cosette, who is being looked after by an unscrupulous couple who think only of the payment. Misunderstood and unjustly accused in a workplace dispute, she is forced to earn money as a sex-worker. In the song, Fantine sings of the poignancy of love smashed by abandonment. Such abandonment and lack of mercy are symbolized metaphorically as tigers that come at night with their destructive voices, tearing apart her dreams. For some people, meaningless acts of evil reach them, bring them to a breaking point, and, left to their efforts alone, leave them feeling hopeless.

The Phenomenon of Integral Love

What is the orientation of integral love? Love is a very complex phenomenon. Obviously, through the love we have and share with others, we experience a new kind of affectivity. These feelings can be passionate and intense. In the first place, we appraise others through an affective desire toward or aversion away from them. Each encounter leaves an affective memory, which is always available and relived in new but different situations. However, as explored in chapter 2, this initial appraisal in feelings is not the final word as to the worthwhileness of any desire. While this intuitive appraisal may lead to an action impulse, in the end, the value of the action is to be judged by the feeling tone of intelligence.

Conversely, loving action is not merely a matter of rationality alone. The act of love is a "passionate interpretation, judgment, decision and choice."[7] According to Walter Conn, desire and self-giving are not identical, but neither are they at odds with each other. While desire can be possessive and destructive of the other, passionate desire need not be. Love moves the person beyond themselves to become a better person. Dunne asserts that this desire to love another first opens a primary horizon that helps the lover notice what their act of love is doing to their own heart. Then, the lover is better able to understand the nature of love. Finally, the lover counts on this love to help guide their decisions and commitments.[8] This person feels like someone falling out of the will to control and into the hands of love with the promise of commitment. Affective

7. Conn, "Affective Conversion," 268.
8. Dunne, *Doing Better*, 138.

conversion reorients the whole person, and especially the pre-reflective and passionately felt desires towards conscious and intelligent decisions, choices, and commitments.[9] The conclusion is: affective conversion is centrally about both affectivity and commitment.

The Art of Loving Well

While human formation may be able to map the stages of affective and moral development, human transformation comes about because we decide to love in the concrete circumstances of life. This kind of love requires self-surrender to another, and self-surrender requires first receiving the gift of love from another, and receiving the gift of love requires the work of a community of love whose way of loving does not want to possess the person or dictate what one should decide.

Moreover, loving well is an art. First, love begins when we are touched or moved or stirred by another's goodness or beauty. Margaret Farley describes this first experience of the exchange of love in this way: "There is another aspect to my loving which makes it, in its beginning, not a matter of 'simply choosing.' That is, my love for you is first of all a response—a response to your lovableness, your value and beauty. This is the passive dimension of love. I just 'receive' your revelation of yourself as lovable. Your Self or some aspect of it must touch my mind and heart; awaken it so that I respond in love."[10] Love begins when someone acts upon us. Something about another person speaks to us, enters into us, and draws us out of ourselves. Something about the other person imprints itself on us and shapes us. We stir and awaken in response to the value of another. It begins through being vulnerable enough to receive something of another. There develops an active awareness of another's goodness.

Second, loving well is an affective affirmation of the other. To love someone is to be invited into a relationship of trust. To love someone is to be glad that the beloved we love is alive. To love someone is to devote time, attention, and energy to wanting the beloved's existence to continue. The vision of what the person is and might be in the future inspires us along the path of authentic love. In this sense, our love for one another continues what God has begun. God affirms the goodness

9. Conn, "Affective Conversion," 269.

10. Farley, *Personal Commitments*, 31.

of our existence by creating us and delights in us every step of the way. The supreme dignity of every person is carrying forward what God has begun and, in this way, bringing their beauty and goodness more fully to life. This vocation is both humbling and awesome.

Third, if loving begins by receiving the goodness of another, and continues by affirming and helping to enhance their goodness, loving well also aims for the highest possible union with the beloved. Love takes the direction of receiving the other as a different person to ourselves, to be shaped and reshaped by the other. Loving well begins in a feeling ratified through a reasonable choice to commit ourselves to the well-being of another and moves toward the flourishing of another. The act of loving contains within it both the assurance of judgments of truth and value and the attraction of desire.

Fourth, such active flourishing commits to the long haul. Such commitment to service allows for the virtue of fidelity to emerge and survive. Fidelity sets the condition for giving the loves of our life to grow, deepen, and become more resilient, protecting us from the temptation to give up on them when times get difficult. In as much as there is a commitment in fidelity, loving another may bring with it the consequence of suffering.

Fifth, loving well is hard work and requires much patience, resolve, perseverance, and energy. Love is hard work because none of us present ourselves as perfect persons to the other. The ones we love are like ourselves with their strengths and limitations. Persons do not enter an encounter completely healed of past hurts or completely free of the tendency to egocentricity. Loving requires that we must be prepared to change and to grow with the persons we love. Without this insight, our love can become inept and lazy.

Sixth, loving well requires that we have insight into persons, that is, it demands that we take time to know persons as they are, especially everything that makes them who they are and not someone else. Loving well means that we love the actual person before us and not some image of who they should be. We are committed to understanding the truth about another. Understanding comes with empathy and requires us attending to the specific needs, hopes, dreams, and ambitions of those we love.

Seventh, loving well requires that we accept the freedom of the other. Love is devoid of possessiveness, manipulation, coercion, and control. If one wants to love, then loving must be more than a projection of our insecurity and unquenchable needs. Forcing or coercing another to love turns what may have begun as true romantic love into egoism. If love is to be genuine over the long haul, we can reach out and invite people into relationship, but can only grow if the invitation is freely accepted.

Romantic and Service Love

It is vital also to examine two specific kinds of love and their importance in affective conversion: romantic love and commitment to service. First, there is romantic love. Rosemary Haughton speaks of romantic love as "passionate," evoking the sense that the quality of this love is something "in motion—strong, wanting, needy, concentrated towards a very deep encounter . . . [yet also] helplessness, suffering and [an] undergoing for the sake of the desired and, implicitly, the possibility of a tragic outcome."[11] Romantic love in the Western tradition had its emergence in the courtly love of France during the twelfth and thirteenth centuries. It made its way to Italy and especially to Florence, where it notably featured in Dante Alighieri's, *La Divina Comedia*. Dante's love for one of his central characters, Beatrice, brings a distinct Christian element into his portrayal of romantic love. Dante recognizes his true self for the first time through his love for Beatrice. Dante wants his audience to know that romantic love is bodily, sexual, and spiritual, requiring the giving of one's whole self to the other. The passionate aspect of love is that energy which aids one into embracing the unknown of this encounter towards an intensely desired wholeness, without guarantees or knowledge that this relationship will last.[12]

Haughton asserts that there are at least two essential features of romantic love learned through the prose of Dante. First, romantic love is a meeting or encounter between two persons so that the embers of love may be fanned brightly into a flame. Second, there must be an exchange of life between lover and beloved such that each is in the other. Haughton states that "the beloved is the door which, being touched, opens the way, so that the lover may enter into the new 'sphere.' It is Beatrice who opens the 'door' for Dante, but from whichever direction one looks at it there are two different roles, even if both enact both roles."[13]

11. Haughton, *Passionate God*, 6.

12. Haughton, *Passionate God*, 52.

13. Haughton, *Passionate God*, 33.

Haughton instructs that romantic love brings specific characteristics: "Particularity, singleness, a capacity for 'changing the face of reality,' a kind of 'halo' of obscure glory and, also, painfulness."[14] Through the element of particularity, she emphasizes that a person meets another through a direct encounter at a level far more profound than the level of logic. The intelligence is illuminated and strengthened through that experience. Through the element of singleness, she implies that at this point of meeting by the two, the passionate breakthrough or the whole energy of the lover and beloved focuses on this one moment. The other becomes the center of one's world. In terms of a change of reality, from the point of encounter onwards, ordinary life feels and means something very different. We feel, see, notice, understand and evaluate things differently. The halo of obscure glory signals an experience of beauty and awe before a mystery, the encounter itself having a surplus of meaning which people find difficult to describe in words and before which one expresses a degree of ignorance. Finally, there is an element of painfulness that arises out of a felt sense of incompleteness within the experience. Haughton states that the lovers experience something which has an excess of meaning and therefore is "only a glimpse of an experience which is closed to them."[15] Though there has been a genuine breakthrough to something wondrous, the opening of that breakthrough is not large enough for the excess of meaning to be discovered in the one moment.

Second, romantic love finds its way to the second kind of love, namely, dedicated service and commitment toward the other or *amour voulu*.[16] Just as the flow between lover and beloved is an exchange, so *amour voulu* is an uncompromising dedication "of that which has been freely and undeservedly received."[17] Such love is the outcome of affective, moral, and religious conversion. In love stories, men and women, knowingly or unknowingly, grounded in their love for God, offer their lives in the service of people. In chapter 4 we examined the faithful religious service that St. Augustine offered as bishop of the church of North Africa and to the wider church community through his theological writings. In the same chapter, we examined the work of Dag Hammarskjöld acting as a global citizen in his UN role, bringing the skill of mediation to bear

14. Haughton, *Passionate God*, 55.

15. Haughton, *Passionate God*, 56.

16. Haughton, *Passionate God*, 58.

17. Haughton, *Passionate God*, 58.

on international crises. We also examined the life of Vaclav Havel and his commitment to his homeland through a political ministry of public service.

The Damaging of Affectivity

While we can examine what loving well means, it is also a fact that people are wounded in their affectivity. The will to control can seriously prevent the full flourishing of our authentic feelings toward one another and God. Wendy Farley uses the older ascetic language of "passions" to name disordered desires as the habitual obstacles that take root in the human heart and block us from loving well. The insight is that there is a difference between ordered and disordered passions, life-giving and destructive desires. Disordered desires as obstacles to loving are as varied as are individual persons.[18]

The Damage of Disesteem

Chapter 2 argued for the centrality of self-esteem for our lives and so, implicitly, recognized the wounding of affectivity that arises from relationships characterized by disesteem. Living in an environment where one is disesteemed becomes an obstacle to loving well. If we are living in a distorted horizon of disesteem, then, many of our evaluations and judgments may spring from or be influenced by disesteem, felt self-hatred, and felt self-apathy. These negative feelings may cause us to act violently toward others and even toward ourselves. Note the alarming number of young people who end their own lives due to the hurtfulness of cyberbullying. Disesteem may cause us to act either with reactive rage against or co-dependently towards others. It may cause us to act with apathy toward life's offerings. It may cause us to undermine ourselves and others regularly. Our effective freedom shrinks even further. Our horizon shrinks due to a small number of concerns. This blockage amounts to a minor or even a significant psychic disorder, depending on intensity, duration, and interventions to reverse its affects.

Neil Ormerod, reflecting on the importance of self-esteem, says that "conversion can be thought of as a radical change in one's horizon, from one horizon to a dialectically opposed horizon, from a horizon

18. Farley, *Wounding and Healing*, 55.

determined by inadequate and false distorted self-esteem to one deter-mined by proper, undistorted true self-esteem."[19] For healing to happen, the person must move from the deeply felt sense of being unlovable to a deeply felt sense of being loveable. This shift is genuinely transformative. This shift will involve naming what is going on interiorly, naming certain false convictions and then, letting go of certain false attitudes, negative thoughts about and toward oneself, and negative images of self. Healing means embracing life-giving attitudes, a positive self-image, and appro-priate changes in behavior.

The Damage of Social Exclusion

There also exist specific social conditions that act as a blockage to loving well. Social exclusion and its offsprings, humiliation and demonization, are obstacles to loving well. First, social exclusion emerges when moral evil becomes a cooperative scheme. Differences between groups usu-ally invite the recognition of pluralism and, through dialogue, the pos-sibility of mutual understanding and inclusion. By contrast, exclusions often come out of an assessment of differences that go on to construct barriers to mutual dialogue, often through an illegitimate undermining of the other. Volf states that exclusion entails "taking oneself out of the pattern of interdependence and placing oneself in a position of sovereign independence."[20] The other emerges as an enemy, and we must push them away. Ultimately, social exclusion is a failure to take to oneself fully the cooperative nature of human existence, preferring instead to be mired in individual, group, and general bias.

The problem with the logic of exclusion is that people socially con-struct most ideas of identity based on some notion of otherness. If it is a distorted notion of otherness, then the sense of constructed identity will also be distorted. One insight worth bearing in mind when exclu-sion happens is that each distinct group has much in common with other groups. The challenge is to be able to discern different kinds of other-ness, to accept those that are intelligent and responsible, and reject those that are stupid and irresponsible. This discernment requires empathy. To move beyond the exclusion of the stranger requires us to ask whether we can accommodate the experience of the *stranger as a stranger*, without

19. Ormerod, *Grace and Disgrace*, 26.
20. Farley, *Wounding and Healing*, 66.

repudiating him or her or projecting onto them our fears, insecurities, and horror.[21]

Second, acts of humiliating exclusion also provide the conditions for the survival of processes that wound affectivity.[22] The more we exclude people, the more we make them feel disvalued among their peers and in society. The process of dehumanization specifically defaces the humanness of the victim, further extending the evildoer's sense of power over their victim.

An example of social exclusion, humiliation, and dehumanization is witnessed in the processes that established and maintained the Nazi death camps of World War II. This project required camp authorities to regard and depict their enemies as essentially subhuman. SS pamphlets tell the story of exclusion, humiliation, and dehumanization towards all who did not fit the Aryan profile: "From a biological view he seems completely normal. He has hands and feet and a sort of brain. He has eyes and a mouth. But, in fact, he is a completely different creature, a horror. He only looks human, with a human face, but his spirit is more powerful than that of an animal. A terrible chaos runs rampant in this creature, an awful urge for destruction, primitive desires, unparalleled evil, a monster, a subhuman."[23]

In the case of Nazi Germany, the name for Jews was *muselmanner* (literally, the man that looks like a Muslim) or the skin and bone one, the half-dead victim, the living corpse, the person who is dead yet still alive, and whose death is no longer a human death.[24] Paul Daponte states that the critical stratagem of the dehumanizing processes of Auschwitz was to strip "victims of their integrity, dignity, and identity through the implementation of camp policies aimed at eliminating a semblance of a prisoner's humanity" to bring about an efficient killing operation.[25] We could make the same assessment regarding instances of ethnic cleansing especially in the Balkan conflict of the late 1980s and early 1990s. In all situations of exclusion, humiliation, and dehumanization, we eviscerate the subjectivity of the victim.[26]

21. Miller, *Way of Suffering*, 35. Miller proposes a more authentic approach towards the stranger.

22. Jones, *Blood that Cries Out*, 36.

23. Segev, *Soldiers of Evil*, 80.

24. Daponte, *Hope*, 24.

25. Daponte, *Hope*, 26.

26. Daponte, *Hope*, 25.

LOVING WELL AND HEALING AFFECTIVITY

When we speak to affective conversion, there exists a link between loving well and the healing of emotions. Feelings have an important part to play in the assessment of values especially the value of others. Destructive feelings are a byproduct of disesteem and the conditions of social exclusion. These feelings can be healed through the ministrations of pastoral care, community solidarity, and friendship. Other destructive feelings are the byproduct of childhood victimization over a long period of time and require a mixture of professional therapeutic approaches including psychotherapy for their healing. Chapter 10 will examine destructive feelings coming out of a victimized psyche and requiring more complicated interventions. In this respect, there is a difference between destructive feelings grounded in personality and destructive feelings grounded in character flaws.

Tyrrell calls this "affectional" conversion. Existential loving is the key to healthy recovery.[27] It is only in the context of love with others that we will be willing to face our distortions, name them, claim them as our own, and tame them, moving away from damaged self-esteem. To love others presupposes in the one who loves a deep and abiding feeling of being valued and loved in oneself. It communicates to the one loved their significance and worthiness. Religious faith sublates this affectivity when we appreciate the experience of being loved as a beloved son or daughter of the Heavenly Father.

The Conditions for Healing Affectivity

Our ability to love well needs certain conditions for it to flourish. These conditions represent the interrelationship between the personal and the social. There are four conditions worth addressing: communicative communities, religious communities of fellowship, spiritual friendship, and compassionate solidarity.

Communicative Communities

If affective conversion occurs, it is because we have supported the conditions in communities that focus on building bonds of connection

27. Tyrrell, "Psychological Conversion," 245.

grounded in open communication. Communicative communities represent the most fertile ground for developing caring individuals. Communication establishes relationships of inclusion and belonging. These communities include our families, our neighborhoods, and our workplaces especially when such communities engage in the task of improving the lives of people through health, welfare, and educational services. Margaret Wheatley, commenting on the importance of the bonds of connection for communicative communities, states:

> There is no power greater than a community discovering what it cares about. Ask "What's possible?" not "What's wrong?" Keep asking. Notice what you care about. Assume that many others share your dreams. Be brave enough to start a conversation that matters. Talk to people you know. Talks to people you don't know. Talk to people you never talk to. Be intrigued by the differences you hear. Expect to be surprised. Treasure curiosity more than certainty. Invite in everybody who cares to work on what's possible. Acknowledge that everyone is an expert about something. Know that creative solutions come from new connections. Remember, you don't fear people whose story you know. Real listening always brings people closer together. Trust that meaningful conversations can change the world. Rely on human goodness. Stay together.[28]

Communities of Religious Faith

One specific kind of community is the community of religious faith. The word *ecclesia* comes from the Hebrew word, *qahal,* meaning to gather people. The description in the New Testament for people in a community of faith is fellowship or *koinonia*. Koinonia is central to the Body of Christ, and we find the expression in the Acts of the Apostles and the Pauline letters. Paul uses the expression "fellowship of the Son," "fellowship of the Holy Spirit," and "fellowship in the Gospel" (1 Cor 1:9; 2 Cor 13:13). In the Acts of the Apostles, the writer tells us that the disciples came together for teaching, prayers, the breaking of bread and fellowship (Acts 2:42).

So, the community of faith looks like any other society of people only in this case one constituted by the Holy Spirit into a fellowship. The building of the faith community requires human capacities, attitudes,

28. Wheatley, "Turning to One Another."

and skills as well as God-given grace. There exist several elements that ought to be visible. First, we should observe an enabling of trust so that the member's basic attitude to others is one of trust and trustworthiness. We should feel the expression of relationships through friendship, signaling to the other "it is good to have you around." We should be sufficiently mature to have a sense of embodiment or an at-home-ness in the body and, therefore, confidence and competence in human physicality and sexuality; and abilities in restoration and reconciliation since conflicts and disagreements will arise.[29]

Extending to both members of the community of faith and the broader community is the task of pastoral care. Neil Pembroke gives a distinctly interior dimension to the work of pastoral care. He states that pastoral care is presence, availability, and confirmation, requiring a measure of attentive listening so that the person offered care reaches up to and actualize their God-given, psychological, moral, and spiritual potentialities.[30] He grounds the practice of pastoral care in the philosophy of Martin Buber whose central insight is the importance of the I-thou relationship summed up as

> the depth that I am, the grace that I am, ultimately only has meaning in the context of my capacity to give of myself to the other. . . . When I commit myself to be available to the other, it can be said that I belong to her. The relationship of belonging is constituted through a free substitution of the other's will for my own. Far from entering into a relationship of bondage, in belonging to a person one is set free. In freely disposing myself for the other I am liberated.[31]

This description correlates pastoral care with both the conditions for and goal of affective conversion.

One of the central metaphors for the life of the Christian community of faith is that of the community of equal friends. In the context of the Last Supper, Jesus describes the nature of commitment and service through the metaphor of friendship when he gets up from the table, rolls up his clothes, and begins to wash the feet of his disciples (John 13:1–20; 15:12–17).[32] He intends to model a form of service that would avoid su-

29. Goodliff, *Care in a Confused Climate*, 147–59.
30. Pembroke, *Art of Listening*, 11–12.
31. Pembroke, *Art of Listening*, 13.
32. Au, *Way of the Heart*, 153–54.

periority in the giver and inferiority in the recipient.[33] At the rebuke of Peter, Jesus speaks a strong response since Peter is still viewing service from the perspective of the superiority of the server and inferiority of the served. To rise above this position, Jesus proposes a service grounded in mutual and equal friendship, "the free sharing of gifts among equals in a community of friends."[34]

Spiritual Friendship

Good friendships are more complicated than many think and part of the difficulty lies in our understanding of it. Aelred Squire, reflecting on twelfth-century monk Aelred of Rievaulx and his text *On Spiritual Friendship*, states that for this medieval monk, friendship remains one of the most significant goals yet one of the most challenging to achieve in one's life.[35] Aelred of Rievaulx, speaking from within a monastic community, is conscious that friendship is both important to psychological and spiritual maturity yet could be a source of harm if practiced in the wrong way. He makes a point of distinguishing between carnal, worldly, and spiritual friendship. Carnal friendship has a single aim, the mutual satisfaction of pleasure and worldly friendship has as its goal the mutual enhancement of each other's business interests. Only spiritual friendship is worthy of the name, real friendship. For Aelred, spiritual friendship is more likely to take into consideration the whole person.

Aelred's starting point is grounded in religious conversion. For him, spiritual friendship consists of two friends and "Christ between us as a third."[36] The grace of God is required to sustain friendship over the long haul since we are prone to sin and friendship is a difficult commitment to undertake. Though we enter friendship freely, it does not eliminate the difficulty of different temperaments, tiredness, anxiety, and sadness. Following the definition of friends proposed by the Roman writer Cicero, Aelred affirms that friendship is "an accord on things human and divine, accompanied by goodwill and love."[37] By good will, Aelred indicates action and by love he denotes affection. If love is a pre-condition

33. Au, *Way of the Heart*, 154.

34. Au, *Way of the Heart*, 155.

35. Squire, *Summer*, 143.

36. Rievaulx, *Spiritual Friendship* 1.1.

37. Rievaulx, *Spiritual Friendship* 1.11.

of friendship, then this means that a friend is "the guardian of love . . . the guardian of the soul itself."[38] To share the responsibility for what motivates a person to human authenticity is a grave responsibility. The keeper of the soul will be required to "bear and endure according to his ability anything wicked he sees in my soul. For the friend will rejoice with my soul rejoicing, grieve with its grieving and feel that anything that belongs to a friend belongs to himself."[39] Both passion and commitment, grounded in love, activate the good of friendship.[40]

Interpreting Aelred's writings on friendship, Squire states "we need those who can bear to know us in our worst moments to be few enough and reliable enough for us to be able to avoid the strain of being put on our mettle all the time, especially on those points about which we are the weakest."[41] Further, the friend is not afraid to correct and guide his friend "to help us to see how we are to handle ourselves in a way that will not for us be warping and to say a word of encouragement when we have got through what for us was a difficult matter."[42] Throughout life, there are many matters of great importance to our well-being and maturity which can take a long time to accomplish. Friendship depends on each other's uprightness, waiting for that maturity to come about in the friend, while, at all times, wanting the good of the friend. While gospel love may command us to love all people, whether friends or enemies, friendship is a unique form of love since "only those who can be called friends we are not afraid to commit what is on our hearts."[43] It requires keeping confidences through a loyal silence. Finally, friendship is sought not out of any personal gain or ulterior motive, nor out of some desire to feel superior over another but for the proper fulfillment of need in the other.[44] The kind of love that delivers reward is a love that gives to the other person "the intrinsic value one gives to oneself."[45]

---

38. Rievaulx, *Spiritual Friendship* 1.20.

39. Rievaulx, *Spiritual Friendship* 1.20.

40. Rievaulx, *Spiritual Friendship* 1.21–30.

41. Squire, *Summer*, 147

42. Squire, *Summer*, 147.

43. Squire, *Summer*, 148.

44. Squire, *Summer*, 149.

45. Squire, *Summer*, 149.

Compassionate Solidarity

Just as affective conversion flourishes in situations of communicative action, in fellowship, and looks for the intimacy of friendship, so too the conditions for loving well require us to mentor, witness, and exercise compassionate solidarity with those who are suffering. Chapter 7 explored the solidarity that Oscar Romero demonstrated toward the poor and the poor toward him. Solidarity is usually interpersonal but can also be national and international in its range. We can find the roots of the affective commitment of solidarity in our conviction regarding the unity of the human family. We are all brothers and sisters and under one Heavenly Father (Eph 3:14–15). Ultimately, while solidarity is an action, it is also an attitude of the heart cultivated from a horizon of care for the other. Speaking on the importance of solidarity in a fractured world, John Paul II states:

> We need *to adopt a basic attitude towards* humanity and the relationships we have with every person and every group in the world. Here we can begin to see how the commitment to a solidarity with the whole human family is a key to peace. Projects that foster the good of humanity or good will among peoples are one step in the realization of solidarity. The bond of sympathy and charity that compels us to help those who suffer brings our oneness to the fore in another way. But the underlying challenge to all of us is to adopt *an attitude of social solidarity with the whole human family* and to face all social and political situations with this attitude.[46]

The most poignant story in the Gospels which speaks to the importance of compassionate solidarity is the parable of the Good Samaritan (Luke 10:25–37). Jesus finishes responding to a lawyer's question as to how one could inherit eternal life. He tells the lawyer to love God with one's whole being and to love one's neighbor as one's self. The lawyer then asks Jesus the question: who is the neighbor? Jesus tells this parable in response to this question. On his way to Jericho from Jerusalem, a man undergoes a violent episode. He is robbed, beaten, and left half dead by the side of the road. There are five people in the parable: the Jewish victim, the Priest, the Levite, the Innkeeper, and the Samaritan. Both priest and Levite belong to a privileged group in society. They do not go to the aid of the victim, probably curtailed by rules around ritual impurity,

---

46. John Paul II, *World Day of Peace* par. 3.

since in this case the man is bleeding and is stripped naked. Finally, a Samaritan man comes along. Jews and Samaritans had been divided and sworn enemies for the best part of 500 years, each never speaking to each other, suspicious of each other, never allowing intermarriage or economic exchange. The Samaritan risks his life by stopping to aid the victim, overlooking ritual impurity, and a possible trap by the bandits to assault him. He binds the wounds of the victim and makes sure that his hospitality toward the victim continued, by paying the innkeeper to look after him.

This gospel story speaks of solidarity, hospitality, and compassion. His sense of solidarity pierces through the distorted divisions within societies in such a way that one man who is ethnically different and religiously excluded would come to the help of another man. His hospitality is both personal and practical. The essential affective virtue is compassion (v. 33). In the Greek New Testament, the word for compassion is *splagch- nizomai.* The word means "to be moved from the pit of your bowels" since the bowels were thought to be the seat of love and pity. It is the same word used by Jesus when he looks over the crowd and, moved to compassion, begins to teach them since they were like sheep without a shepherd (Matt 9:36); or when Jesus is moved to compassion when approached by a man suffering from leprosy (Mark 1:4). The virtue of compassion reaches out socially through an interior attitude of solidarity for the marginalized, as with the Samaritan in the parable.

The parable of the Good Samaritan is as much a story about the kind of inner disposition required to interact with the stranger as it is a story about the meaning of neighborliness and the transformation made possible by loving well. Chapter 1 spoke about the will to control and its deleterious impact on our ways of feeling, thinking, and deciding to act. In contrast, Miller asserts that the way of contemplation and love plants deep in us a calmer attitude to life that is not controlling, yet quite deliberate on our part. Contemplation and love allow for a welcoming of the other, free of the control of the other. This contemplative spirit gives rise to a different approach to the stranger. Miller states that "an intrinsic part of contemplation itself is my stopping at a certain time, my standing at a certain place, my gesturing to the Other in this concrete way my will- ingness to welcome. Contemplation is an example of the one act which does not point toward the production of something external to itself; the gesture of generosity toward the Other."[47] Miller also speaks of the cost of approaching the stranger with a particular open spirit, in such a way that "I leave myself unguarded; and in that sense I consent to the possibility of being wounded. I place my dreadful and groundless trust in the Stranger who approaches as wholly unknown. The heart consents to the Other before it knows anything at all about it—except that it is Other."[48]

A modern-day account of the story of the Good Samaritan and the importance of letting in the stranger as a stranger comes from the war experiences of a journalist, Chris Hedges who was a war correspondent during the Bosnian conflict from 1992 to 1995. One afternoon, Hedges sat down to speak to the Sorak family, a Bosnian Serb couple outside of the village of Gorazde. Recalling this meeting, he writes:

> I sat one afternoon with a Bosnian Serb couple, Rosa and Drago Sorak, outside of the Muslim enclave of Gorazde where they had once lived. They poured out the usual scorn on the Muslims, but then stopped at the end of the rant and told me that not all Muslims were bad. This, they said, it was their duty to admit. During the fighting in the bleak, bombed-out shell of a city that was Gorazde, where bands of children had become street urchins and hundreds of war-dead lay in hastily dug graves, a glimmer of humanity arrived for the Soraks in the shape of Fadil Fejzic's cow. The cow forged an unusual bond between Fejzic, a Muslim and his Serbian neighbors, the Soraks.[49]

Hedges goes on to describe the sporadic fighting and chaos that brought tragedy upon the Soraks in that conflict. Muslim police took the Soraks oldest son, Zoran, away for questioning. Zoran never returns. Their next eldest son is struck by a car and killed. This final death leaves the Soraks childless. Harassed by the police and townsfolk, Drago, the father of the household, is often conscripted into manual labor by the Bosnian Army. The Soraks considered fleeing. Things get worse with food shortages until only 200 Serbs are living in the town. They hide and keep away from public places to avoid the harassment of Muslim groups. All of this turned the Soraks against a Muslim-led government, which they would have been open to before the war. Always in their mind is the memory of their murdered son.

---

47. Miller, *Way of Suffering*, 28.
48. Miller, *Way of Suffering*, 29.
49. Hedges, *War*, 50.

At this part of the story, a shift in feelings happens within the Soraks. Hedges states:

> Five months after Zoran's disappearance, his wife gave birth to
> a girl. The mother was unable to nurse the child. The city was
> being shelled continuously. There were severe food shortages.
> Infants, like the infirm and elderly, were dying in droves. The
> family gave the baby tea for five days, but she began to fade. 'She
> was dying' Rosa Sorak said. 'It was breaking our hearts.' Fejzic,
> meanwhile, was keeping his cow in a field on the eastern edge
> of Gorazde, milking it by night to avoid being hit by Serbian
> snipers. 'On the fifth day, just before dawn, we heard someone
> at the door,' said Rosa Sorak. It was Fadil Fejzic in his black rub-
> ber boots. He handed up half a liter of milk. He came the next
> morning, and the morning after that, and after that. Other fami-
> lies on the street began to insult him. They told him to give his
> milk to Muslims, to let the Chetnik children die. He never said
> a word. He refused our money. He came for 442 days, until our
> daughter-in-law and granddaughter left Gorazde for Serbia.[50]

According to Hedges, the Soraks eventually leave and take over
another house a short distance away. They can no longer communicate
with Fejzic. They continue to grieve daily their sons and miss their own
home. They could never forgive those who had taken their son, Zoran.
Despite their anger and loss, they could not think badly of all Muslims
while thinking of Fejzic and his cow. Fejzic's action is a demonstration of
the power of love. This illiterate farmer's act shapes their appreciation for
humanity in a positive manner and becomes an ocean of hope for them.
They relate to Hedges that "the milk he had was precious, all the more so
because it was hard to keep animals. He gave us 221 liters. And every year
at this time, when it is cold and dark, when we close our eyes, we can hear
the boom of the heavy guns and the sound of Fadil Fejzic's footsteps."[51]

Finally, Hedges speaks to his own encounter with Fejzic. He states
that Fejzic's circumstances change as the war comes to an end: the bombs
have shattered his apartment block; he lacks heating; his cow does not
survive the war, and he has only a thin layer of clothing to protect him
from the cold. Hedges describes that when they spoke "he sat huddled in
the corner of a dank, concrete-walled room rubbing his pathetic collection of small apples, many with brown holes in them, against his sleeve.

---

50. Hedges, *War*, 51.
51. Hedges, *War*, 52.

When I told him that I had seen the Soraks, his eyes brightened. 'And the baby' he asked. 'How is she?'"[52]

The story of the relationship between Fadil Fejzic and the Sorak family is about compassion and solidarity in suffering. Compassion does not always require words. It can be a silent action by which one person can identify with the sufferings of another. As in the original story of the Good Samaritan, this story relates to the actions of a Muslim man who acts with compassion toward a Christian family and their child. The two parties of this story are both ethnically and religiously diverse from each other and caught in the context of a bloody conflict between their respective communities. Fejzic becomes the outsider in his community on account of his commitment to the Soraks. The Soraks are outsiders in the Muslim town based on their ethnicity and religious faith. Affective conversion is transformative of both, bringing them together in a bond that creates waves of hope.

Restoring Esteem and As It Is in Heaven

As It Is in Heaven is a film that helps illustrate the conditions for healing affectivity: a communicative community, friendship, compassionate solidarity, the importance of esteem, and the healing of disesteem. The specific scenes occur about halfway through the film and highlight the importance of restoring real desire and self-esteem to the life of a person. As described in chapter 4, Daniel Daréus is a successful and renowned international conductor whose life aspiration is to create music that will open people's hearts. In time, Daniel is commissioned by the local clergymen to direct and lead the church choir. Through their participation in the church choir, people reveal their inner troubles to each other and the audience. Arne is so very ambitious for the choir's success that he obsesses over tiny mistakes, failing to see that he is making significant mistakes himself. Tore is intellectually disabled and, though customarily struggling to find a place to belong, feels a beautiful sense of inclusion in the choir. Holmfrid has put up with being called "Fatso" by Arne since childhood and eventually stands up to him. Each member of the choir has their desires and aversions. Each has reached a different point of self-esteem versus disesteem.

---

52. Hedges, War, 53.

For our purposes, let us focus on Gabriella, a member of the choir, a young wife and mother, who is beaten and abused by her alcoholic husband, Connie, regularly. The abuse is a fact that is known yet ignored by many in the village and by some in the choir. Gabriella's sense of self cannot easily grow due to the emotional confusion caused by the putdowns and the violent actions of her husband. The audience does not have access to the backstory of Gabriella's life so we can only assume that she has been raised in a more or less affectionate home and that, therefore, her emotional turmoil is due to her marriage to Connie. Daniel is also aware of her situation yet is sensitive enough not to put pressure on her to leave her husband before she is ready to do so.

To raise her esteem, Daniel writes a song for Gabriella and asks her to sing it as a solo for the upcoming choir performance before the village. When first asked, Gabriella refuses. Due to the actions of her violent husband toward her, her terror forms an unworthiness and lack of confidence in her. She fears her husband's resentment and rage toward her. Her husband's reactive anger springs from the guilt of not being able to be the husband Gabriella wants him to be. She also fears her husband's jealousy turning to abusive anger at the prospect of losing her. Gabriella represents a person who is pulled by conflicting forces. She wants people to like her and wants to be fully unmasked and open before others, but she is fearful that they will not like what they see and want nothing to do with her.

The film explores the reaction of her refusal among the other members of the choir. Arne becomes very angry with her lack of courage to sing a song written especially for her. For Arne, the townsfolk's esteem of him is uppermost in his mind. He acts angrily toward her out of a fear of being judged as unsuccessful by others. Holmfrid tries to console Gabriella only to be put down by Arne. We can see that Arne tends to put others down, especially those who do not agree with him. Holmfrid reacts angrily to Arne's putdowns and reveals the emotional devastation that years of name calling by Arne have had on his person. A violent argument ensues. Through these cathartic events, Gabriella understands that no one is above feeling vulnerable, fearful, or unworthy. She agrees to perform the song.

The lyrics of "Gabriella's Song" are a homage to her heart's desires and echo the importance of self-esteem in the life of the individual. Gabriella sings of her desire to rediscover trust in life, of her desire to live life on her terms, and of a desire to believe in her goodness. We notice in the lyrics the desire for freedom, welcome, recognition, and significance. Self-esteem is something gained in a relationship with others and has its fulfillment when it moves towards another in an exchange of mutual love. Specific wants become wonderful when we desire to be for another person, in other words, to be someone for someone. The end of loving another begins in desire awakened in each of us, contrasted to the state where someone squashes desire in us. Again, there can be no hint of possessing or manipulating or controlling the other who desires us, a mistake made by Connie towards his wife. We receive the other's desiring and consent to it as a gift. Moore states that "a person who awakens my desire makes me feel good. I want this good feeling to be fully exercised in my being desired by that person. I look to the cause of my desire for the exercising of the good self-feeling in which my desire is grounded."[53] Through the lyrics and the performance of the song, Gabriella speaks the voice that is in everyone's truest heart, the desire to feel on earth what exists in heaven.

Daniel's gesture of writing the song, and asking her to perform it, is an affirmation of Gabriella's goodness. This gesture activates positive feelings within her that had been put aside but not forgotten. These positive feelings bring to self-awareness that she is desirable and a worthwhile person. As soon as Gabriella feels her goodness, her feeling for existence heightens, and she is aware of the desire to be. In the song, she sings of her desire to be free, to watch the sunrise, and to watch it set. Being desirable in the eyes of others, Gabriella is also able to desire, that is, she is enabled to see her goodness and reach out with a real desire to others. She can make better decisions in her life. From an affirmation of her existence, she moves to the essential human need: to be herself for another. Human desire is self-transcending and transforms us when we allow it to reach its real end. In other words, to feel love for another is to feel joy in the whole of one's being, empowered through oneness with the other. Moore states, "What desperately needs to be understood is that people's essential power over each other, which is the power of their beauty and goodness, cannot be thought of as the possession of each, but has to be thought of as a life-force whose interest is to unite them. My power is my partnership in the energy that unites persons in love. The essential human power is not solitary but unifying."[54]

53. Moore, *Let This Mind*, 6.
54. Moore, *Let This Mind*, 20.

Gabriella wants to abide in the self-presence of her true self and her real desire. It is simply untrue or an act of self-defeat to think that one's existence starts with emptiness and becomes trapped in a desperate attempt to fill an inner void. When we con ourselves into feeling empty, the demand for a narcissistic fix embeds itself in us. Then, manipulation and aggressive control take over. The truth is that God did not create us empty. We are created full of desire, especially with a desire to know, to value, and to love. Our desire has intentionality; that is, it intends or moves toward all that is true, all goodness, and beauty. Our intentionality finds fulfillment in love.

Miller offers some insights that correlate with Gabriella's inner transformation. He states:

> What affects us first and primordially is the primal gladness of wonder, the shudder of astonishment, the awe-full ardor of venturing into [the] mystery. The human subject is all heart. Each of us is [a] sheer vulnerability. The repressive ego, with its centripetal certainties and the pleasure-seeking id, with its centripetal addictions, are only reaction formations. These defenses we create to protect the affect-ability at the core of us. The most primordial of all affects is the self-donative passion evoked in us by the experience in our first fascinations. [We are] born praise singers. Child's play celebrates by exploring. It goes all in without desire's goal of winning. Unlike our addictions, our joys are self-transcending. [We are] ecstatic only when, transported beyond ourselves, [we are] in the throes of a goodness not subservient to us.[55]

Before this event, Gabriella's decision to join the choir demonstrates that she is implicitly searching for the gladness of wonder even though still fearful of her husband. She is kind, generous, and desiring to be with others and for others. After her solo performance, we sense the triumph of centrifugal forces in Gabriella. She glows with positivity and beauty. This shift in horizon stands in contrast to her husband who is given over to egoism, fear, and bullying. We witness in Connie, the destructiveness of centripetal forces that trap him into an addictive personality that acts out of fear.

---

55. Miller, "Desire, Passion," 11.

Affective Conversion and Dead Poets Society

Finally, the film *Dead Poets Society* illustrates the transformative power of affective conversion. In 1959, a very shy Todd Anderson began his last year of high school at Welton Academy. Welton is an elite, all-male college preparing young men for a university. Anderson is paired up with a roommate, Neil Perry, and quickly receives acceptance by Neil's friends: Knox Overstreet, Richard Cameron, Steven Meeks, Gerard Pitts, and Charlie Dalton.

On the first day of their poetry class, they are surprised by the unorthodox teaching methods of the new English teacher John Keating, a Welton alumnus who encourages his students to make their lives extraordinary, a sentiment he summarizes with the Latin expression *carpe diem*. Mr. Keating has them take turns standing on their class desk to teach the boys to look at life in a different way and from a different vantage point. He tells them to rip out the introduction of their poetry book which purports to evaluate poetry according to a mathematical formula. He invites them to display their style of walking in the school courtyard, a small exercise promoting individuality. His methods attract the attention of the strict headmaster, Gale Nolan. During the film, the audience, through many teaching vignettes, begins to appreciate the different teaching methods employed by Mr. Keating. In Keating's method, the emphasis is on understanding the felt meaning of texts through reflection on personal experience. In the case of other teachers, the emphasis is on memorization to pass the exams and thus achieve success in their subject.

Upon learning that Keating was a member of the unsanctioned "Dead Poets Society" while he was at Welton, Neil Perry restarts the club. Neil and his friends sneak off to a cave each night where they read poetry and prose verse, including their compositions. As the school year progresses, Keating's lessons and their involvement with the club encourage them to make decisions on their terms. Knox pursues Chris Noel, a girl whose family is friends with his family but who is dating a football player from a prestigious public school. Neil discovers his love of acting and gets the role as Puck in a local production of *A Midsummer Night's Dream*. This decision by Neil happens even though his domineering father wants him to entirely dedicate himself to his studies to secure his place in an Ivy League school and, ultimately, medical school. Mr. Keating helps Todd come out of his shell and encourages him to realize his potential when he takes him through an exercise in self-expression, resulting in Todd's composition of a poem spontaneously in front of the class.

Towards the end of the film, Neil has an angry conversation with his father. Neil's father discovers Neil's involvement in the play and forces Neil to quit on the eve of the opening performance. Devastated, Neil goes to Keating, who reassures him of the importance of making his decisions and encourages his love of acting as something to take seriously. Neil decides to participate in the final performance. Neil's father unexpectedly shows up at the performance. He takes Neil home and announces Neil's withdrawal from Welton and enrollment in a military academy to prepare him for Harvard. Unable to find the courage to stand up to his father, a distraught Neil commits suicide. All the boys are distraught beyond words when they learn of Neil's death with some understanding more than others the pressure that Neil suffered under his authoritarian father.

The school principal, Mr. Nolan investigates Neil's death at the request of the Perry family. Mr. Nolan comes to know about the "Dead Poet's Society" and the students who were part of it. As principal of the school and, wanting to avoid a scandal, he decides to throw all blame for Neil's death away from the school and judges that Mr. Keating's influence had been the single most unfortunate factor in Neil's death. Each of the boys is called to Nolan's office to sign a letter attesting to specific allegations against Keating, even though they know the allegations concerning Mr. Keating to be false. One of the boys is Todd, who at this juncture is still a timid and uncertain lad. Speaking to Todd with an authoritative and paternal voice, Mr. Nolan goes through a litany of false allegations concerning Mr. Keating and the poor judgment exercised by him in promoting their reckless and self-indulgent behavior. He also falsely accuses Mr. Keating of encouraging Neil to follow his obsession to act in the play and directly states that such encouragement is the sole cause of Neil's death. Todd tries to protest the truth and is reluctant to sign, but does so at the behest of his angry father as well as the school principal.

The final scene of the film arrives. Keating's poetry students are all gathered in class being tutored by Mr. Nolan for the rest of the term. At this point, Mr. Keating comes to collect his personal effects. He is allowed in but with the proviso that he performs the task quickly and silently. As Mr. Keating is about to exit the class, Todd speaks out aloud to Mr. Keating expressing his regret at signing the paper, protesting that their elders made them sign under duress. Mr. Keating acknowledges their sadness and lets them know that he does not hold them in any way responsible for his scapegoating. Mr. Nolan insists Mr. Keating leave at once.

Then, Todd initiates a gesture that turns out to be a profound moment in his life, demonstrating the power of affective conversion. He stands on his class table and cries out the words "O Captain, My Captain," signaling to Mr. Keating his affection and respect for him. Despite the continuous protestations of Mr. Nolan to get down from his desk, Todd remains firm. Soon, other boys do the same. In the final scene, we witness some boys ascending their desks turned towards Mr. Keating in solidarity with him, while others do not. They know in their hearts that this gesture will most likely carry their expulsion and Keating also knows full well the import of their actions. Seeing all this take place, and ready to leave the room, Mr. Keating turns to then and calls out "Thank you boys, thank you."

There are many insights in this film that speak to the importance of affective conversion and the destructiveness to young minds and hearts of affective wounding. First, in chapter 1, the importance of having one's voice to be able to tell one's own story was mentioned. To speak one's own story is to be empowered and transformed. Keating's approach to education tries to inculcate in his students the importance of personal inner feelings, personal experience, and human subjectivity as a primary starting point to human understanding. For him, this stands in contrast to an education grounded merely in the memorization of material, where we are learning from others but not always understanding. Learning is not only about pouring information into young heads. Learning is understanding from personal reflection and imminently generated by acts of attentiveness, intelligence, and judgment. Indeed, it is possible for a student to accomplish the very top mark in a course without learning a thing. Good learning is about eliciting curiosity and wonder in one's students so that they might ask all the relevant questions, no matter what the circumstances. Curiosity, wonder, understanding, and judgment are all interior activities of human consciousness. They are the activities of our subjectivity. If we desire to know and value the world around us, we must attune ourselves to these activities. Subjectivity and objective knowledge are linked.

Importantly, Mr. Keating demonstrates affective conversion. He affirms the self-worth of each person and the importance of authoring their own lives. Keating is communicating a deep sense of affirmation for his students in pointing to their capacity to arrive at moral judgments, choices, and actions. Keating demonstrates the care and concern of a teacher, seeking to develop his student's inner potential and capacities for sorting out right and wrong, good and evil, truth and untruth. In this way, the film contrasts Keating to other teachers, including Mr. Nolan, the school principal. Nolan's approach is to preserve the past no matter what. The students are in class to memorize facts as handed down by the great authors of the past. The students are not in class to understand the kind of questions such authors were asking that gave rise to their insights or even to query why their insights are universally significant. Indeed, Mr. Nolan is unable or unwilling to attend to the different questions present in the young minds and hearts in the class.

Second, the events surrounding the death of Neil Perry illuminates the tragedy of affective wounding. The film demonstrates a strained relationship in the Perry household with Mr. Perry exercising an authoritarian manner over both his wife and their son, Neil. There is a particular kind of integration that occurs in adolescence, a creative act which takes young people from the self that one is to another development and beyond what one was before. Neil's decision to participate in the play is an attempt to grow in personal autonomy and ego-strength while remaining faithful to the unity of the family. For this growth to occur, he needs the love of parents who can communicate to him that just being himself will do and that his choices matter.

Neil's relationship with his father has been that of the dutiful son, symbolized in his address to his father as "sir." In joining the play, Neil feels a legitimate pull toward something that might increase his self-worth and express his creativity. His father's negative reaction to this decision represents a parental love unable to enjoy itself in his son's actions. Neil's father crushes his son, rather than delighting in his son and so crushes in Neil the part of him that Neil wants to enjoy. Effectively, Neil is cajoled by his authoritarian father to suppress in himself the nascent quality of his self-love in the name of a parent identity that fundamentally communicates "you are to be a mirror of me and you cannot be yourself." This approach is grounded in an impulse to dominate on the part of the parent, even if clothed in thoughts such as "wanting the best for my child." There is little positive affectivity within Mr. Perry's horizon. For Mr. Perry, it amounts to a system of deprivation rather than a whole-hearted commitment to the promptings of love toward his son. The academic success of Neil's studies and the father's rigid structure are the stifling chains that are holding this family together. These goals for Neil's life an imposition on

Neil rather than becoming goals worth pursuing in themselves, and one suspects also imposed on Neil's mother. All of this becomes too great a burden for Neil to bear.

Third, a lack of affective conversion, as well as a lack of moral and religious conversion, underpins the scapegoat mechanism employed by Mr. Nolan and, through his instigation the parents of the students, towards Mr. Keating. Chapter 2 speaks about rivalistic desire and the destructive manner by which rivalry generates violence so that a group assumes the position of all against one to restore order. Girard calls this mindset, the scapegoat mechanism. For Mr. Nolan, the rivalry is over the hearts and minds of the students. This scapegoat mechanism stands in stark contrast with affective conversion which is a passion and commitment to love the other. It displays a strong group bias on Mr. Nolan's part which shares with the parents a set of expectations around a code of behavior for his students and the importance of school reputation above everything else. Group bias results in inertia toward changing the social structure of order and where changes are threatening to one group or individual, rivalry happens that demands a victim for harmony to return. Mr. Keating is the victim. It is quite startling to hear the voice of Todd Anderson at the end of the film, exposing in front of Mr. Nolan and his fellow students the truthful intent behind the expulsion of Mr. Keating.

Fourth, we come to the final scenes of the film and the extraordinary action of the students when they stand on their desks as an act of love and solidarity for Mr. Keating. It is also implicitly an act against a system of egoism, both individual and group, which has led to his expulsion. As Todd leads the cohort and steps up onto his desk, he proclaims aloud the opening words of Walt Whitman's famous poem of the same title, introduced to the students by Keating in an earlier class. The poem describes a ship coming back to port after a time of war to the resounding cries of jubilation, only with the Captain cold and dead upon the deck. Whitman wrote the poem following the assassination of President Abraham Lincoln. There is relief at the end of the American Civil War. America the ship has braved the storm of the division between the Union and Confederate forces. The North has won the Union, they have abolished slavery, and the people are rejoicing. However, the event seeps with grief at the death of their Captain.

Todd's naming of Mr. Keating as the "Captain" is an acknowledgment and appreciation that he has sacrificed himself to help them reorient themselves. Their combined action of appreciation is also a manifestation of the care they have for him and will surely come at a cost to their personal lives. Their action reflects the hearts and minds of young people who have embarked on a path of love through affective conversion. These students demonstrate a passion and a commitment to love in their hearts. Despite the forces of hatred and resentment against their teacher, they stand in passion and commitment to the importance of love in the world. They do not choose to act violently in the face of the injustices perpetrated against Mr. Keating. They choose to lay down their own lives and their uncertain futures for the sake of their teacher. They stand against the victimizing system. Any victimizing system is destroyed not by more violence but by the power of love and by love's ability to name the system for what is it, exposing its central lie of bringing about peace through violent expulsion. Through their actions, they expose the victim mechanism and reveal it for the evil thing that it is. The reaction of Mr. Nolan reflects this fact as he keeps calling out with rage for the students to sit down. It is as if he knows that their actions of loving resistance reveal the truth of the matter and the falseness of the scapegoat mechanism.

9

Intellectual Conversion, Knowledge, and Reality

WE NOW TURN TO intellectual conversion, the fourth of the conversions and perhaps the most difficult to understand in terms of human transformation. Intellectual conversion consists of "understanding our understanding," therefore, it requires a transformation to our understanding of the process of knowing reality. Chapter 1 quoted a statement by Richard Flanagan on the importance of and need for objective truth in our political context. Flanagan is pointing to the fact that we live in a period of global history where the possibility for the distortion of truth is higher than ever before. As in George Orwell's *Nineteen Eighty-Four*, the urgency to get the facts of the past right is not there, especially in a context where people hold the conviction that no past exists except for a knowledge of the past held by the most powerful group. On the one hand, we hear terms such as false facts and, in the same breath, alternate facts and fake news. Day by day, people working in media organizations erode the distinction between knowledge and opinion pieces. On the other hand, those working in the media continually remind us of the importance of a free press since governments often lie.

Similarly, many people equate knowledge to merely subjective attitudes or traditional prejudices. In this setting, loud voices mistakenly assert that ordinary people could not possibly know the truth. Some believe that knowledge is so embedded in a context that immanently generated knowledge is not possible except in terms of what our culture or social conventions tell us is the truth. Delving deeper, people convince us that there are no transcultural norms within human consciousness for generating real knowledge or values. On the contrary, people argue that one set of pronouncements replaces a previous set and truth in knowledge is impossible.

THE MEANING OF INTELLECTUAL CONVERSION

Lonergan states that intellectual conversion is "a radical clarification and consequently, the elimination of an exceedingly stubborn myth concerning reality, objectivity, and human knowledge. The myth is that knowing is like looking, that objectivity is seeing what is there to be seen and not seeing is what is not there and that the reality is what is out there now to be looked at."[1] Knowledge, truth, objectivity, and affirming reality are all possible and being able to arrive at the truth is very transformative even if it is a challenging process. Coming to the truth and real knowledge of a matter is one of the most critical capacities given to us by God.

Speaking out of a religious context, John Haughey ponders the relationship between the desire to know, to solve a problem, to learn, to plan for some course of action, and our religious faith:

> What end do I have in mind in my inquiry? Information and knowledge, of course. Accurate knowledge! True information! Knowledge of the truth of the reality in which I live and which I seek to understand and judge. I am scripted to know as much about reality as I can take in, which is why I am endlessly wanting to know as much as I can. It seems provable that human consciousness is the apex of God's creation. We already glorify God simply by employing it. A consciousness that is not merely functioning well but is functioning with an ongoing awareness of its Source—that is the consummation devoutly to be wished. Surely, this is what glorifies God.[2]

Our understanding of intellectual conversion can fruitfully begin by recognizing the radical difference between reality affirmed through correct understanding and reasonable judgments and an extraverted biologically oriented drive to imagine the real as "out there." Extraversion is a term that signifies our mistaken equating of reality for the object of our sensory experience, without needing the activity of questioning, understanding, and reasoning which the mind introduces. The process

1. Lonergan, *Method*, 238.
2. Haughey, *Housing Heaven's Fire*, 155.

of extraversion does not take account of questions for intelligent such as why, how, when, and where. Nor does it factor in questions for judgment or whether this understanding is true. Nor does it factor in questions for deliberation on values so that we might know what to do about the truth. It is these very questions that place us in a world of "intelligence, reason, and value, of insight, judgment, and decision."[3]

For Lonergan, the problem is that our world has a shrunken agenda about the road to truth or reality. Reality is not the same as an observation or "seeing" the truth. Truth is not what others tell us to say. Nor is the truth just what we subjectively think it to be, based on our self-assertion. Instead, we intend toward truth by questioning data, seeking insight, and correctly understanding insights based on evidence. We are more likely to be in tune with this inbuilt process through the self-appropriation of the operations within human consciousness. Therefore, a bifocal awareness is critical: the object before us and the subject who acts, the content of knowledge and the knowing process.

Equally, certain mistaken assumptions coming out of a pseudo-scientific mindset distort a correct understanding of the process of knowledge. For many centuries now, our culture has been building on the mistaken assumption that subjectivity and objectivity are two very different realities separated by an enormous chasm. This distorted assumption is, on the one hand, that subjectivity retreats into the world of feelings, intuition, imagination, dreams, and memories. Those who espouse these views claim that subjectivity does not have a place in attaining objective insights. Arising from this negative criticism of subjectivity, there arises the counter stance of subjective idealism. Subjective idealism asserts, erroneously, that once the person has gained insight, then he has already arrived at truth especially if the person holds the insights passionately. Alternatively, there also exists the mistaken assertion that objectivity is identified with tangible and measurable things "out there," that is, things that can only be touched, smelt, seen, and heard. This assertion emboldens the behaviorists and positivists of our time who argue that mental activities do not exist since we cannot observe them. People use this distortion as their justification for speaking negatively toward the possibility of truth acquired through a process of heightened interiority or heightened consciousness.

---

3. Ormerod and Jacobs-Vandegeer, *Foundational Theology*, 95.

Chapter 1 highlighted the importance of taking into account that any person who seeks to know, value, and love is already part of or implicated in reality. He does not stand back from reality like some detached observer seeking to find meaning and truth. Lonergan overcomes this supposed divide between objectivity and subjectivity, between the knowing process and what is to be known, by stating, "Genuine objectivity is the fruit of authentic subjectivity."[4] The problem, therefore, is not subjectivity as when we hear the taunt, "That's just a subjective opinion; we need to be objective." The problem is biased subjectivity. Therefore, objectivity is not the opposite of subjectivity. The opposite of objectivity is biased subjectivity. As Dunne proposes,

> Wouldn't you trust a woman of intelligence and character? Wouldn't you sit and listen closely to a man who has written beautiful poetry? Wouldn't you take seriously the reflections of people who have won the Nobel Peace Prize? This is because we trust the subjectivity of people who are unbiased—whose attention doesn't get fixated on petty things, whose concerns are as much for others as for themselves, who dig deeply into complex problems so as to heal them at their roots, [and] who are aware of the desire for holiness.[5]

Truth, or the correct affirmation of reality, comes about when one asks all the relevant questions, arrives at insights, and judges the validity of insights based on evidence. The person does not allow biases to get in the way of knowing. The person remains open to searching for more data or possible explanations and subjecting to scrutiny any suppressed feelings that may impede his ability to act on a matter. In the end, he arrives at truth through a process that requires him to be self-aware and critical, open to the meaning of what is or is not the case. This approach to truth and reality is grounded in the conviction that the world is mediated through acts of meaning.

Chapter 2 examined four levels or operations within human consciousness required for knowing and valuing anything at all. To sufficiently differentiate the existence and interrelationship of these levels requires intellectual conversion. These four levels differentiate further the natural desire to know and value. At the first level or operation of knowing, one experiences and the term "experience" has a very technical

---

4. Lonergan, *Method*, 292.

5. Dunne, "Critical Thinking," 10.

meaning.[6] When we are noticing the data of our experiences, we realize that experiences occur in ordered patterns. As indicated in earlier chapters, Lonergan addressed the variety of human experience through his notion of the patterns of experience.

The practical pattern of experience is for most people one of the dominant patterns in daily living. Morelli states that the "practical interest is *the interest to get things done*. It is not an unfocused interest in doing things but an interest in taking care of business or getting things done. Its first emergence is normally in reaction to given biological demands that announce to us what, in the first instance, needs doing. The unconscious orientation of organic life to maintain itself emerges into consciousness as, for example, feelings of hunger and thirst, the desire for pleasure and the fear of pain, fatigue, and sexual discomfort."[7] Combined with intelligence and responsibility, the response to our needs is no longer instinctual but the practical desire to meet our needs and wants and guarantee their satisfaction as "efficiently and effectively as possible."[8] From the moment we rise from our beds in the morning till the setting of the sun, our intelligence is mostly working out of a practical response to the demands of the day. We have mastered some practical concerns over years of doing them the same way, for example making our bed, preparing breakfast, and driving to work, while others require new learnings.

However, there are also patterns of experience that respond more to the urgency of technically precise demands and invitations, for example, the intellectual pattern. The intellectual pattern of experience requires a sustained and urgent focus on understanding a subject matter. Here is where intellectual conversion comes into the light. Intellectual conversion challenges us to maintain a sustained effort to attune ourselves to an intellectual pattern of experience. Morelli states that "the intellectual pattern is *the interest in complete understanding of the universe and ourselves.* It is the desire to understand that motivates the questioning with which the Wondering Mode of conscious operation begins. But it is that desire unfettered by the restrictions imposed upon our questioning by other interests."[9] For example, the science of climate change requires an intellectual pattern so that we understand the meaning of the terms to help

6. Streeter, *Foundations*, 62–63.

7. Morelli, *Self-Possession*, 193–94.

8. Morelli, *Self-Possession*, 196.

9. Morelli, *Self-Possession*, 207.

explain how scientists judge that climate change is real. The opposing voices to climate change often raise their objection based on practical observations about the weather. Skeptics deny the validity of climate change. They protest that any observer can see warmer and cooler years simply through their observation of the weather. Since they do not grasp the distinction between common sense and theoretic knowing from an intellectual perspective, they fail to appreciate the scientific argument in this field. Without employing a wholly intellectual endeavor, they will never grasp the arguments for the truth of climate change.

The second step or operation is the act of understanding.[10] We begin to question and wonder about what we have experienced. If no question emerges, the data remains inert, and no act of understanding occurs. Similarly, even when we are attentive to the data, we can avoid the pursuit of inquiry for a whole host of reasons. Understanding is not a matter of opening one's eyes, taking a good look, and merely seeing what needs to be seen "out there in the real world." Understanding is not simply a matter of formal logic and deductive reasoning where the knowledge of one premise gives rise to knowledge of another. Understanding is not simply comparing concepts. Understanding is the experience of having an insight that arrives even before we have conceptualized it and put it into a language. We accompany insight with an "aha" or "I get it" acclamation. At the moment of insight, things fall into place. We "see" the relevance or irrelevance of data. We can relate things to each other differently. We intelligently bring forth a unity in the data that we did not bring forth previously. We get the point. *We experience insight as a release of tension from wondering and inquiring. Insight is a pairing of understanding with what needs to be understood.*

Also, the question "what is it?" may give rise to two different kinds of knowing: descriptive and explanatory knowledge.[11] Descriptive knowing helps us understand the data by relating it to our senses, our feelings, and the impact that such data has on our immediate lives. Sometimes that is all we want. Someone may ask: What kind of weather is it today? A person may answer that it is looking like a sunny day. This is a descriptive piece of knowledge. However, then comes a second question such as, "Why is it a sunny day?" This question asks for a critical understanding in which terms are fundamental. Explanatory knowing consists of relating

---

10. Streeter, *Foundations*, 63–64.
11. Flanagan, *Quest for Self-Knowledge*, 127–31.

terms to each other and getting our knowing precise. Meteorologists would answer in this critical manner. The meteorologist answers using terms such as barometric pressure, isobars, high and low systems and the Southern oscillating index in which each term has a specific and precise meaning. Whether descriptive or explanatory, *the answer to our questions may only be possibly true giving rise to the third step.*

The third step or operation is judgment.[12] Typically, we must spend time mulling things over, reorganizing the data, following clues or hints, and trying to determine whether they correspond to situations we have dealt with in the past. When an insight occurs, it is a possible answer, a hypothesis, a guess, an idea, or possible relevant explanation of the data. These are the pre-conditions to understanding. However, correct understanding is made up of pre-conditions as well as post-conditions. The question "is it so?" must be applied to our guess, idea, or hypothesis. This question consists of adopting a critical attitude toward an insight much the same way that questions for understanding adopt an inquiring attitude to the data.

Judgment is a desire to establish whether our bright idea or "aha" amounts to anything and whether our understanding correctly fits the data. Judgment brings to our answer the feeling of assurance. If our answer is true, then, other things follow. If other things do not follow, then our understanding might have to be abandoned and we need to ask more questions. Attention given to post-conditions amounts to marshaling and weighing up the evidence. For example, a jury retires to the jury room to weigh up the statements by witnesses presented in the courtroom. The assumption is that if an idea is correct, we can find enough evidence to verify it or at least to verify it with some degree of possibility or probability. When we come to the point of establishing that the evidence is enough to affirm the adequacy of the insights, only then are we in a position to express a judgment. Only at this point have we come to a knowledge of the real world, the world as it exists and works. At this point we can also affirm an important and wonderful moment of self-discovery, namely, "I am a knower."[13] The affirmation of judgment reaches up to the truth, and through the truth, we can affirm what reality is or what is illusory. The truth of existence is pulling us toward itself to be known.

12. Streeter, *Foundations*, 64–65.
13. Lonergan, *Insight*, 343.

Lonergan presents four elements for arriving at a sound judgment. First, each of us must have an openness to truth and strive to overcome our fears and false thoughts.[14] The habit of truth-seeking must be uppermost in our hearts. Second, to acquire specific knowledge may require some specialized training and expertise. This search for knowledge will mean hard work on our part. We may have to master a particular skill or understanding in a given field of study. Third, the person must be prepared to engage in a self-correcting process of learning. Such a process might lead the person down many false questions, and dead-end paths until the right questions lead to knowledge and insights build upon insights.[15] One must approach the truth with a humble heart. Fourth, the person must know themselves especially the quality of their temperament. If a person judges too quickly or hesitates unreasonably or is prone to jump to conclusions or easily persuaded, then, these flaws in character must be addressed before a good act of judgment emerges.[16]

Chapter 2 explained our innate desire and chapter 6 examined moral conversion postulating that the desire to know the truth leads to doing the truth. Knowing is therefore linked to valuing and doing. There is a link between truth and inner freedom. One of the painful divorces of our modern time has been the divorce of truth from values and values from freedom. This divorce often reflects a manic desire for self-invention. The manic desire for self-invention prioritizes an identity based merely on its efforts, on what we can achieve, and on our freedom to make ourselves whatever we want to be. The danger is that we lose touch with a storehouse of wisdom or a living tradition of truth and authentic transformation stalls.

Suffice to say; intellectual conversion focuses on cognitive self-transcendence. An intellectual conversion has an important pastoral dimension. This pastoral dimension relates to countering the harmful effects of general bias explored in chapter 3. General bias rationalizes a flight from understanding and disguises itself behind "false philosophies and undignified myths of human life, considers 'the really real' to be whatever fits with short-term practical needs and desires of human beings. The

---

14. Lonergan, *Insight*, 310.

15. Lonergan, *Insight*, 197.

16. Lonergan, *Insight*, 310.

result is the gradual deterioration of the social situation and the inability of human beings to communicate on the basis of rational conviction."[17]

Now, this process of knowing is not a rigid pattern. It is an internal process we can spontaneously and naturally engage in or refuse to engage. It is a process that we engage in even if we were to seek to disprove its existence. Lonergan is trying to present us with a method for understanding our understanding. He is presenting an intellectual therapy to reverse the skepticism and relativism endemic in human knowing. Lonergan is not saying: proceed rigidly through these steps, and all will be well. He is trying to help us to notice or pay attention to what happens when we do understand. This entire process is our desire to know and is a God-given gift that orients us toward self-transcendence and, therefore, transformation. Our ability to engage and transform the world with integrity depends on our willingness to give ourselves over to this desire to know. Through these acts, we transcend, or go beyond, myths and illusions about reality and disvalues and reach the real and the good. Through these acts, we transcend the selves that we are so that we may become more authentic human beings.

Intellectual Conversion and *Dial M for Murder*

We can illustrate intellectual conversion through two films: *Dial M for Murder* (1954) and *Twelve Angry Men* (1957). Both films come out of a crime genre. William Mathews notes:

> Before a criminal process can arrive in the courtroom a great deal has to happen behind the scenes. There is the physical event of the criminal act, be it a murder or a robbery or more elusively, illegal financial transactions. This [criminal act] triggers and evokes the curiosity of the detectives. A significant difference in detective work is that unlike the suspicious crown or the DNA molecule, it involves an interaction with people, their words, deeds, acts and communications. This problem of interpreting the words of others does not occur in the data of the natural sciences! After all the relevant questions and clues have emerged and along with them a supervening insight into how they hang together, the lawyers are briefed and the case goes to court. A jury is selected, a difficult task in certain situations where biases or race enter into the case. The prosecution argues that their

17. Liddy, "Transforming Light," 157.

case meets all the relevant questions, is invulnerable to revision; the defense argues the contrary, attempts to show missed questions and oversights. Finally, there is the summing up by the judge and the handing over of the case to the jury. It becomes the collective responsibility of the jury to establish and affirm what in fact happened. There is no better experience.[18]

Dial M for Murder concerns the dark intrigue within the marriage of Mr. and Mrs. Wendice. Tony Wendice is a professional tennis player married to a wealthy socialite, Margot. However, Margot, dissatisfied with her husband's emotional distance, has an affair with an American crime writer, Mark Halliday. Tony discovers the affair, seeks to end the marriage, and decides that, in order to maintain his luxurious lifestyle, he must murder his wife to collect on the financial benefits of the marriage. Tony sets up a scheme for the murder by first contacting a former University acquaintance, Charles Swann. Swann has already engaged in criminal activity and so, using this knowledge, Wendice blackmails Swann into murdering his wife for a price. He tells Swann of her affair and shows him a letter of affection sent from Halliday to his wife, which Wendice has discovered and stolen. He tricks Swann into leaving his fingerprints on the letter. Tony offers Swann one thousand pounds to kill his wife, otherwise threatening to turn Swann into the police as Margot's blackmailer. Wendice suggests that if Swann refuses, his criminal history alone will compromise him in the eyes of the law. Swann agrees to commit the murder.

Tony explains his plan. Tony will take Mark Halliday to a party the next evening. Swann will come to the apartment, entering using Margot's latchkey which Tony has stolen already and which will lay hidden outside the door of the apartment under a stairway carpet. Swann is to take the key, open the door, enter the apartment, and hide behind the curtain of the French doors. He is to remain there until prompted by a phone call from Wendice to his wife. Swann is to kill Margot when she answers the phone. Then, he is to open the French doors, leaving signs suggesting a robbery, and exit through the front door placing the key back in its hidden space.

At around eleven o'clock that night Tony does phone, Margot does answer, but the plan goes awry in several ways. First, Swann enters the apartment but immediately puts the key back in its place under the

18. Mathews, "Self-Appropriation in Ira Progoff," 9.

carpet. Second, Tony is delayed and does not phone in time, and when Margot answers the phone, Swann is not quite in position. Third, while Swann tries to strangle her with his scarf, Margot manages to stab Swann to death with a pair of scissors that are on the desk. Tony is still on the phone and hears Margot who is still alive, pleading for help. He advises her not to call the police until he arrives. Fourth, when Wendice arrives, Tony sets about reorganizing the evidence surrounding the murder. He puts the key that he finds in Swann's pocket into Margot's purse, thinking it is the key he stole from Margot weeks before and the key Swann used to access the apartment. Tony plants the letter bearing Swann's fingerprints on his person, destroys Swann's scarf and replaces it with Margot's stocking to incriminate and frame her for the murder. He then calls the police. Fifth, the conclusion drawn by the police, given all the evidence, is that Swann was blackmailing Mrs. Wendice, and that Swann had come to the apartment, had been let in by Mrs. Wendice and that she saw this as an opportunity to kill her blackmailer. Later, Mrs. Wendice is found guilty in court for the murder of Swann.

Intellectual Conversion and Inspector Hubbard

Although all the tampered evidence seems to point toward the conclusion that Mrs. Wendice did commit the crime out of the motive of wanting to kill her supposed blackmailer, Inspector Hubbard, the hero of the story, reveals himself as a man who has attained some measure of intellectual conversion. Hubbard collects all the data, forms his hypothesis based on many insights into what might have happened, and then looks to the evidence to make a judgment as to whether his hypothesis is correct or incorrect. Peter Beer insightfully explores the human spirit of inquiry within each of us, but especially the spirit of inquiry heading in the direction of truth, objectivity, and reality in the human mind of Inspector Hubbard. He states that "the inspector, little by little, was being led to grasp the intelligible organization of the line of data, as construed by Mrs. Wendice that hinted at this—namely, that Mrs. Wendice had not been truthful, was not to be trusted and was acting suspiciously."[19]

At first, Hubbard's conclusions lead to the arrest, trial, and conviction of Mrs. Wendice based on the motive of blackmail. After the trial, however, Hubbard "became aware of some unanswered relevant questions

19. Beer, *Introduction*, 12.

that for him demanded answers."[20] He begins to attend to new data not known about beforehand. He ponders that Mr. Wendice and his wife had made out a will naming each other as beneficiaries upon the death of either one. He notes that Mr. Halliday's arrival in London could be a possible occasion for his wife's leaving him and so possibly setting in train a long-arranged plan by Mr. Wendice to murder his wife. He surmises that the plan goes awry, and his wife avoids death. Then, there is Swann's key to his apartment found in Mrs. Wendice's handbag and no key at all found in Swann's pocket. Hubbard's immediate question is: Why wasn't Swann carrying a key? Why was his key in her handbag? Further, Hubbard notes Mr. Wendice's display of suspicious behavior after the trial by making unusually large purchases.

This other set of data leads Hubbard to another hypothesis. This new hypothesis leads to the insight that Mr. Wendice planned for his wife's murder. His new insight "explained all the data prior to and following the trial."[21] These new insights unify all the data intelligently and coherently. Beer states "but coherence is only a possibility; it has to be proven! The condition that linked the hypothesis with fact would truly be fulfilled with the concrete experiential element of Wendice opening that door with his wife's missing key. It would *then* be evident that Wendice had conspired to leave his wife's key there for the assassin to use. So, it would be evident that the master criminal would be Wendice himself and not his wife. They would then know everything."[22] This hypothesis requires two questions answered to Hubbard's satisfaction: Did Mrs. Wendice know the whereabouts of her key to the apartment which Hubbard finds located under the carpet opposite the apartment door? If she did not, did Mr. Wendice know the location of the key?

Hubbard sets up two experiments to clarify the answer to these two questions. First, Mrs. Wendice is brought from prison to open her apartment with the key in her purse. The key in her purse does not match the door, and Mrs. Wendice is not able to genuinely explain why this is the case. She is innocent of the crime since she displays genuine surprise at not being able to open the door. Second, through an elaborate plan hatched by Hubbard involving switching coats and surmising about keys, Mr. Wendice comes to another realization. The key that he is using from

---

20. Beer, *Introduction*, 14.

21. Beer, *Introduction*, 16.

22. Beer, *Introduction*, 17

his wife's purse is not the right key and that Swann had opened the door and then replaced the key in its spot, which meant that it was still there. Wendice comes to the conclusion that the key he held was probably the key to Swann's apartment. Wendice goes to the place where he first hid the key, finds it, opens the door, and falls into the arms of the police.

Throughout this whole process, Hubbard reveals himself as a man transformed by intellectual conversion and so able to discover the truth. First, he is attentive to the data. A dead man is lying before him, killed by a pair of scissors. There seems to be no forced entry. There is a letter found in his pocket owned by Mrs. Wendice and of a compromising nature. Second, he seeks to tie together all the data gathered into one explanatory whole. He waits for insight and an intelligible unit in the data to emerge prompted by further questions. Third, he commits himself not just to a possible explanation of the data, but a real explanation considering all the data. It is one thing to seek understanding. It is another to judge whether our understanding is a complete explanation of the data. He proceeds from data to questions, to seeking insights that explain the data wholly, and finally seeks the conditions to verify the insights.

The orientation of his enquiring intelligence guides Inspector Hubbard that is, "a pure, detached, disinterested desire to know"[23] toward the goal of finding the truth. This desire to know is primary, and so he puts aside other tendencies, for example, the desire for a quick resolution to the case, or the conviction that he can trust his senses and his immediate verdict upon the data before him. We also notice in Inspector Hubbard certain apprehension. He considers that it would be irrational of him to proceed with his second hypothesis unless the two final questions had been answered. He can only be "rationally empowered to give consent to the real"[24] once he found the answer to those two questions to his satisfaction.

Fourth, a proper understanding of consciousness comes only through intellectual conversion. Chapter 1 gave a brief account of the three forms of consciousness. Usually, our ordinary language is a barrier to gaining insight into the meaning of consciousness. We imprecisely talk about "awareness" and "consciousness" as being equivalent to knowing something. However, when we think about ourselves curled up on the lounge watching *Dial M for Murder* on our television, we might find at its conclusion that, though we were completely engrossed consciously in the storyline, we were not even "conscious" of the time slipping by. However, no one can seriously assert that during that time we were asleep or not conscious. We were aware and conscious the whole time. The experience was real, and it happened. Until we ask questions about what we have experienced, it remains an open question as to what we know of the story. The same is the case for Inspector Hubbard.

Fifth, Hubbard's goal all along is to find the truth behind the killing. Beer asserts that Hubbard focuses on himself as an inquiring subject and so makes himself the object of inquiry, making sure to follow up any hypothesis with an experiment. This process has become second nature to him. There exists a twofold focus: one focus on his conscious acts and the other focus on the object to be known. Years of training have molded him into a fine detective. This has required him to know the difference between the insight within the hypothesis and the insight gained from experimentation upon the hypothesis. Further, Hubbard's dealings with criminals of all kinds has alerted him to the possibility of bias in others and in himself. Biases can always stymie our understanding. True objectivity is the fruit of authentic subjectivity.

Intellectual Conversion and *Twelve Angry Men*

Matthews states that it becomes the collective responsibility of any jury to establish and affirm what in fact happened, their responsibility for judgment of facts and, therefore, to understand "the sufficiency or not of the evidence offered and to make the judgment."[25] It is crucial for the juror to be self-consciously aware of himself as attentive, intelligent, reasonable and responsible. Self-conscious awareness demands of the juror a shift of focus to perceiving rather than the perceived, puzzling rather than the puzzled over, insight rather than its solution, and thinking as such rather than the thought.

Twelve Angry Men is an American courtroom drama adapted from a teleplay by Reginald Rose.[26] It is first and foremost a drama, with actors drawing the audience into the plot as they interact with one another. It is not meant to be a forensically accurate blow by blow account of a jury room. The audience knows that the purpose of the jury is to establish the

25. Mathews, "Self-Appropriation," 9.
26. Rose, "Twelve Angry Men."

truth to pass judgment on the guilt or innocence of the accused. However, the dramatic import of the film wants us to respond to what they are doing and to pronounce our approval or disapproval as an audience on them. The drama is asking us to question: what kind of system of justice and kind of jurors do we want in our society? By the end of the film, the drama brings the viewer to the understanding that we are looking for justice that is impartial, attentive to all the data, and able to come to the truth. This system of justice stands in contrast with a system ruled by bias or lazy generalities or a lack of critical thinking.

The key protagonists in the drama are the twelve members of a jury asked to come to a verdict regarding the guilt or innocence of an 18-year-old Puerto Rican man, accused of murdering his father by stabbing him with a knife. Already the question of patricide adds another layer of complexity to the crime. The violence of son against father is considered one of the most heinous of crimes in the mythic memory of Western society. In the opening scenes, the judge, speaking in a routine tone, asks the jury to retire to the jury room and deliberate on their verdict. A guilty verdict will attract the death penalty for the young man. They have just listened to many witnesses at the trial. They have understood what the witnesses have said. They must ask whether what has been spoken by the witnesses is indeed real and credible. Does the narrative offered by the prosecutor and the witnesses he has called on, prove the guilt of the boy? Alternatively, could there be a competing and credible alternative narrative of the events establishing reasonable doubt?

Uncomfortably ensconced in the jury room, without air-conditioning, and on a hot and humid night, the foreman or Juror 1 calls for a ballot. All jurors firstly vote "guilty" except for a single juror, Juror 8. He admits not knowing whether the boy is guilty or not guilty but pleads that the boy's case deserves some deliberation by them, since if found guilty, the accused may face the electric chair. This holdup in proceedings irritates some of the other jurors, who are impatient for a quick deliberation, especially Juror 7 who has tickets to the evening's baseball game starting at 8 pm, and Juror 10 who demonstrates blatant prejudice against people from slums.

At this juncture, Juror 8 suggests that the defendant's appointed lawyer did not try hard enough for his client. Later, in concert with Jurors 5 and 6, they question the accuracy and reliability of the only two eyewitnesses to the crime. Juror 8 carries into the jury room questions around the prosecution's claim that the murder weapon, a common switchblade, of which he possesses an identical copy, is rare. At this preliminary stage, Juror 8 seeks from his fellow jurors enough time to discuss the trial. They decide that all the other guilty verdicts should persuade him why his verdict is wrong. Juror 8 makes a bargain with the other jurors: if after each speaks their piece, there is still no resolution, Juror 8 would agree to vote guilty. Each speaks his piece. They hold the ballot minus Juror 8 and a new not guilty vote appears. An angry Juror 3 inaccurately accuses Juror 5, who grew up in a slum, of changing his vote out of sympathy towards slum children. This act precipitates anger between the jurors. Some claim that people are jumping to conclusions based on biased perceptions. However, Juror 9 reveals that it is he who has changed his vote, out of respect for Juror 8's request for more discussion.

From the events of the trial, to which the audience are not privy, the prosecution presented narratives as evidence to establish the guilt of the defendant. The uniqueness of the murder weapon and the account of a shopkeeper who stated that he had sold this unique weapon to the defendant, is one such narrative. The defendant's inability to remember what film he watched on the night of the murder which was to be an essential part of his alibi, is another narrative. The account of the elderly man living in a proximate apartment, who claims to have heard the boy cry out "I am going to kill you," is also offered as evidence. The man had also claimed that one second later he heard a body fall to the floor and, walking to the door of his apartment, witnessed the young boy running from the building. There is the account of the elderly lady living across the rail tracks and opposite the boy's home, who claims she watched the boy stab his father through the windows of the last two carriages of a moving train. From all these statements the jury is expected to judge whether these elements constituted a probable truth that the young boy is guilty. On the surface and at this stage, it would appear that there is enough evidence to render a verdict of guilty.

However, Juror 8 shows respect for the boy and the importance of slowing down to deliberate. As time goes on, we notice that the slowing down tactic by Juror 8 bears fruit. He is bringing other jurors to think differently about what they are doing. Other data and relevant questions motivate him and these prompt other alternative insights, concerning the guilt of the boy. Juror 8 has decided that the weapon is not as unique as made out by the shopkeeper. He questions the claim of uniqueness. He assumes a working hypothesis that the weapon is not unique during the trail. He tests out his hypothesis by taking a specific action. He purchases such a switchblade quite quickly on one of the nights of the trial period. He also describes to the other jurors how he had lived near an elevated train track and recalls how noisy the environment was when a train passed. He concludes that one of the eyewitnesses could not have heard what he thought he heard, while the elevated train was roaring past his building. His experience and insight give rise to an alternative hypothesis, now backed by an experiment, and the judgment that the senior man's testimony is probably not credible.

Lastly, Juror 8 comes into the jury room with the conviction that even if someone says, "I am going to kill you," an element raised to high prominence by the prosecution, the phrase is so common, it does not mean necessarily that the person uttering such a phrase is intending to kill anyone. The prosecution uses this insight as a second-tier piece of circumstantial evidence which adds to the primary evidence of the witnesses. For Juror 8, it is a small point but worth reappraising in the light of other data, insights, and working hypotheses already in his mind.

Finding himself in the jury room and with some openness to explore some of the issues bothering him, Juror 8 works with other jurors in testing his hypotheses through simple experiments. The first hypothesis tests the testimony of the senior man. The question is asked: Would such a man lie? What would he gain from lying? It is Juror 9 who comes up with a psychological portrait of the elderly witness. Juror 9 is a man who has engaged in an intense noticing of the elderly man during the trial, observing features that others have not picked up. Some of these include: he carries two canes; he wears a torn jacket; he is a man whom few people would have given any attention. Some of these observations lead him to the conclusion that one possible explanation for his coming to the trial is to gain recognition and feel important.

At one point, an experiment is carried out to test whether it was possible for the elderly man to walk to the door and see the boy running from the building. He claims that he got to his door within fifteen seconds of hearing the body fall to the floor in the above apartment. After Juror 8 conducts the reenactment experiment, it becomes self-evident that what the senior man has claimed could not have been the case. The hypothesis that the senior man could not have seen what he claimed, namely, the young boy running from the building in the parameters defined by the witness is at worst proved doubtful, or, at best, proved not to have occurred. Juror 8 also throws doubt over the possibility that the elderly man heard a voice saying, "I am going to kill" for ten seconds, while an elevated train roared past.

The second hypothesis concerns the testimony of the woman. New questions into new data give rise to a new hypothesis. The new question is: How can anyone see some act performed so clearly such as the stabbing death of a man when the action occurs at night, in the dark, and through the windows of an elevated train? The possibility of her testimony being accurate is further eroded when it is established that she wore glasses but did not mention putting on the glasses to make this supposed observation.

The third hypothesis seeks to test whether the boy's alibi during the time of the crime should be accepted as truthful, or judged to be untruthful, given he could not remember the names of the films. Juror 4 judges the boy's guilt based on his inability to remember the names of the films. Juror 8 carries out a simple experiment. He asks Juror 4 if he has been to the movies lately and whether he remembers the names of the films. The outcome of the experiment is that Juror 4 fails in his recall. Again, Juror 8 has shown that it could have been possible for the defendant not to recall the names of the films, given he was asked to supply an alibi while looking over the dead body of his father.

During this whole process, we see Juror 8 taking responsibility for his part in the deliberation as to the guilt or innocence of the accused. This sense of responsibility is captured eloquently also by Juror 11, a migrant from Eastern Europe who meditates on the significance of their responsibility as part of a democracy, namely, they are notified by mail to come to court to adjudicate the guilt or innocence of a fellow citizen. This view on the administration of justice stands in contrast to his own experience of living in a communist country where an elite make all judgments. In the case of Juror 8, we assume that he has listened to the evidence of each of the witnesses just like his fellow jurors. However, we note that there are other relevant questions for him that have not been satisfactorily answered by the insights presented in court.

In the jury room, Juror 8 convinces the rest of the jurors to test alternative working hypotheses to establish the possible or probable truth in the situation. During this period, some of the jurors articulate that jury deliberation is never an absolute science. Probable truth is possible even where absolute truth is not. Juror 8 also displays a moral rectitude which allows him to stand up with courage and contradict the judgment of the other jurors. He is a man who is committed to doing the right thing and part of this conviction is to find the truth of a matter. Moral conversion sublates and guides intellectual conversion.

Within this atmosphere of truth-seeking, other jurors begin to question parts of the narrative that do not fit for them. Juror 2 brings up his uneasiness about the relationship between the knife, its position in the body of the victim, and the height of the young man. He points out the somewhat awkwardness of stabbing a father with a down action when the son was much shorter than the father. In other words, it is more likely that if a stabbing killed the father by a down action, then, it was done by a taller person. Again, to test his insight, he uses an experiment. Juror 5 confirms his hypothesis by an experiment and by his background knowledge into how young men behaved with switchblades in his neighborhood when he was young.

Such attempts at clarification stand in contrast to the indifference, boredom, haste, and bias of others involved in the jury when they first gather. These barriers to truth-seeking are all factors that blind people to noticing accurately, asking other relevant questions, coming to insights, and seeking evidence leading to a reasonable judgment. The indifference is witnessed even in the attorney for the accused and the lack of vigor with which he prosecutes the case for the defendant. The boredom is witnessed in the body language of the judge, especially in his voice as he drones instructions to the jury. The haste is witnessed by a few jurors who want to speedily get things done, claiming that they have busy lives.

Racial prejudice is especially evident in Juror 10 who is convinced that people, especially Puerto Ricans, who live in such housing apartments, are inferior to other people. At a certain point, Juror 10 makes his prejudices clear, claiming that people brought up in slums cannot ever know the truth or be truthful. Meanwhile, Juror 3 suffers from dramatic bias causing an over-identification of the defendant with his son, with whom he has had a violent falling out and against whom he harbors unresolved reactive anger. To find the truth requires that we examine ourselves should we be limited by biases which might prevent us from noticing and asking other relevant questions, coming to other insights, and making judgments based on evidence, especially when the life of another is at stake.

The insights to be gained by the film *Twelve Angry Men* are twofold. First, it is possible to understand the meaning and truth of an event by noticing the data, asking questions, attempting to understand, suggesting some hypothesis based on those understandings and then testing it to arrive at a judgment of fact. Each person is oriented naturally towards reality and truth. Bias pollutes such an orientation. Equally, we can understand not only the meaning and truth of an event but also attune ourselves to our acts of noticing, understanding and judgment within human consciousness. Through this bi-focal awareness, we not only come to knowledge about the world but we also understand what we are doing when we are knowing. We begin to appreciate that knowing is not about "taking a good look." Through self-appropriation, we might more accurately notice whether bias is hampering our critical thinking.

Second, the film puts before us a challenge: How are we going to conduct our intellectual life? This question is a moral question as much as an intellectual question. We can notice, understand, and make judgments either well or poorly. Truth is a deliberate goal and value, and while there is a value in truth, individual and group bias, haste, boredom, indifference, and racial prejudice can stifle the practice of finding the truth. To eliminate all bias and indifference from our lives is to set ourselves on a path of transformation through moral integrity, intellectual conversion, and the realization that true objectivity is the fruit of authentic subjectivity.

10

Psychological Conversion
and Transformation

THIS CHAPTER WILL EXPLORE what broadly can be called psychological conversion. Psychological conversion gives prominence to the ongoing importance of healing grave psychic wounds. If psychic wounds have continuously debilitated us, brought on by a history of victimization by others, oppression by social structures, and supplemented by our distorted use of freedom, then, authenticity becomes a challenging achievement. This kind of conversion highlight the significance of our psyche, its needed transformation, and especially the place of feelings and symbols in the drama of life.

We can speak about this kind of conversion in two ways. First, we can speak about it by addressing the importance of recognizing neurotic distorted feelings and seeking their healing so that they might motivate us toward intelligent, responsible, and loving lives and, in this way, reversing specific neuroses. Bernard Tyrrell, building on the insights of Lonergan, speaks about psychological conversion in the context of healing neuroses. These often originate in childhood and constrain us toward unhelpful routines in human living.[1] Second, Robert M. Doran, with the same psychological focus, has built on Lonergan's insights and added a fifth conversion, psychic conversion, explicitly acknowledging the work of Sigmund Freud, Carl Jung, our knowledge of depth psychology, and the practice of psychotherapy.

---

1. Tyrrell, *Christotherapy II*, 110–12.

PSYCHOLOGICAL CONVERSION AND NEUROSIS

Tyrrell characterizes psychological conversion as a shift away from a neurotic way of functioning and toward a healthy functioning.[2] He differentiates between neurosis and psychosis. The radically neurotic person suffers from "massive anxiety, exaggerated fears, deep hostility, paralyzing guilt, unrecognized or unacknowledged anger, depression, debilitating tension, a sense of partial loss of control of the self and of life, and other symptoms."[3] The psychotic person "suffers from radical personality disintegration and the loss of contact with reality. Psychosis is marked by major disturbances, delusions, hallucinations, severe mood alterations in rapid succession, and other symptoms."[4] A healthy way of functioning is marked by the ability to be attentive to our feelings and images, to feel the clarity of insight, the assurance of judgment, the peace of a good conscience and the joy of being in love.

It is not easy to be attentive to our feelings since there is a difference between experiencing the feeling, on the one hand, and understanding and noticing its occurrence, on the other. This distinction highlights the importance of self-discovery and the ownership of our conscious performance as well as the difficulties and challenges of such an undertaking. If the person has gone through trauma in life, ownership of feelings is even more difficult since traumatic events have the potential to inhibit personal growth. The traumatic memory system can inhibit the consciousness of the person without the sufferer knowing it. Such systems throw the sufferer into a forgetfulness of the past and occasion a distorting influence on one's deliberations in the present.

In as much as psychological conversion is concerned to address neurosis, neurotic deformation consists of two aspects. First, a cluster of disordered affectivities can render feelings off-kilter, solidifying and sedimenting themselves within consciousness in such a way that a felt sense of being unlovable and worthless predominates. Destructive behavior and self-defeating strategies for dealing with disesteem usually accompany such distortions. Second, where there is severe repression at work, feelings are hidden and hard to identify. Repression almost always leads to destructive attitudes, unhelpful behaviors, and psychic discomfort.[5]

---

2. Tyrrell, "Psychological Conversion," 239.

3. Tyrrell, *Christotherapy II*, 55.

4. Tyrrell, *Christotherapy II*, 55.

5. Tyrrell, "Psychological Conversion," 239.

Repression drives the feelings and images so deep that it makes it hard to name them. In time, repression causes an unwillingness to face our vulnerability.

The Wounding of Terror

Farley names three grave and persistent woundings to our psychic health that may pave the way to neurosis: the wounds of terror, rage, and addiction. First, there is the wound of terror. Farley states that "when we are terrified it is hard to think and feel outside the experience of terror. It demands our complete attention, diminishes our awareness, and distorts our entire sense of reality. When we leave it out of the religious imagination, we are forced to interpret our spiritual lives as if our main problem were a strong, overweening ego dominated by impulses of pain and pleasure, when in fact so many of our difficulties arise from self-hatred, fear, anxiety and the misapprehensions that flow from these."[6]

A sense of terror and unworthiness paralyzes the most profound dimension of the person. The consequence of not coming to terms with the power of terror is to engage in unworthy and self-defeating actions. With terror, "cruel bodily practices, self-degradation, and acquiescence to unjust treatment seem to make sense when we have been made to believe we must tame the raging cesspool of lust and rage we humans have become. Cruel theologies do little to defang terror. And the beauty of the Holy Ones can be harder to discern when they are concealed behind a liturgy of judgment. It shows the incredible resilience of the human soul that it sometimes survives these poisonous cures."[7] We notice the way that women subjected to domestic violence are paralyzed from pulling away from their abusive husband. We observe the way adults become psychologically stuck in their lives due to the dictates of authoritarian parents in their childhood.

All of us feel human vulnerability at some time, often powerfully when faced with the experiences of death, decay, contingency, danger, and meaninglessness. The added layer due to terror is passivity, paralysis, or attempted invisibility. This passivity arises from a conviction that the world is inherently dangerous. Rage can also be a reaction to danger and contingency, but it differs to terror. According to Farley, terror's passivity

6. Farley, *Wounding and Healing*, 57.
7. Farley, *Wounding and Healing*, 57.

"deprives us of the occasions for self-expression, action, creativity, zest, and active self-defense."[8] Sometimes we will come across people or observe in ourselves hints of terror such as the fear of harm to oneself or others or a fear that pops up in odd places. We notice the body that is held close in as if taking up as little space as possible and a body that minimizes movement or avoids things that might make it stand out. We observe uncharacteristic passivity that suddenly appears from nowhere. We feel the passivity that chains us to deadening patterns of work or relationship, or difficulty in doing what is usually easy to do or the inability to complete a project.[9] Too much exposure to terror can also give rise to a hypersensitivity to danger, while rage seeks to claim back power through violence. With terror, we expect harm toward ourselves, and passivity becomes a way of life.[10]

The terrorized are most apparent among the afflicted, traumatized, or oppressed. The afflicted "embody a prolonged apology—for having suffered harm, for provoking the harm, for deserving the harm, for all of the imagined mistakes they make, for existence itself."[11] The deflated person "recites the familiar stanzas of impotence, reminding us of our awkwardness, inabilities, incompetence, and the dangers of visibility: 'Who are you to try such a thing?' we ask ourselves."[12] Since terror can produce false humility, it is often confused with the virtues of patience and self-sacrifice. The anxiety and preoccupation of unworthiness pin us to egocentrism. False religion often proposes that our response to terror be patience and self-sacrifice, making terror go largely undiagnosed as a wounding of affectivity.

The Wounding of Rage

Second, there is the wound of rage. Rage is very different from the emotion of anger or the spiritual power of wrath. Rage is the will to harm acted upon or not. Because of the vividness of our personal experience, rage causes us to exaggerate the harm done to us as well as the inhumanity of what thwarts and hurts us. Rage can become intoxicating. Bondage

8. Farley, *Wounding and Healing*, 60.

9. Farley, *Wounding and Healing*, 59.

10. Farley, *Wounding and Healing*, 59.

11. Farley, *Wounding and Healing*, 60.

12. Farley, *Wounding and Healing*, 60.

to rage intensifies when people discover the potency that rage gives to them. Farley states that due to the condition of constant rage we loosen

> the reins that hold us back as we experience a greater intensity of the wild, freeing intoxication of rage. It is like a balm to our battered, frustrated, humiliated soul. It restores dignity and power to our community or nation. Like other intoxicants, rage is pleasant because it gives us a rush and makes us feel vital and powerful. It is pleasant also because it shuts out what we do not want to see and numbs us to what we do not want to feel. It replaces painful feelings with pleasant ones, and it eases the confusion of life.[13]

For the ego caught in rage, we experience others as constantly threatening and obstacles. The person of rage responds to the felt sense of worthlessness by inflating their importance beyond measure.[14] Further, we achieve invulnerability when others recede from view and if that means defrauding others of their existence or claiming that they are not persons with complexities and bondages, then so be it. This state of reaction can proceed even to the point of naming the other as demonic and evil. The raging person will not suffer anything other than the raging person as the center of their universe. The distorted passion of people fuelled by rage reaches into deceit, torture, mutilation, war, and genocide.[15]

The Wounding of Addiction

Third, there exists the condition of addiction. Addiction is primarily a distorted attempt to relieve the painfulness of existence.[16] For this reason, we refer to substance abuse as the addict's addiction of choice and as their means of self-medication. Like all sentient life, we move toward those places which give us comfort and pleasure, only in addiction there is little room for intelligence and responsibility. Miller asserts:

> Pleasure is most satiating when it covers and saturates the whole flood plain of consciousness. Such pleasure has many modalities: it can be intense but short-lived (orgasm) or mellow but prolonged (the experience of being stoned). Whatever the

13. Farley, *Wounding and Healing*, 61.
14. Farley, *Wounding and Healing*, 62.
15. Farley, *Wounding and Healing*, 64.
16. Farley, *Wounding and Healing*, 65–67.

modality, the pleasure of this sort pleases by engulfing awareness. The contents of consciousness dissolve into the immediacy
of the experience. The world that is ordinarily the object of our
senses disappears. All that is order, and beyond us evaporates.
Pleasure, when totalizing, suspends the other-directed focus of
conscious living. Flooded by it we have no psychic distance from
it. That is why such pleasure is the perfect refuge—the ideal ha-
ven. It provided the absolute relief, the total escape. We can relax
in it, unwind in it, [and] sink down into it, as in a womb. We
never feel safer, more invulnerable, [and] more impenetrable,
than when we are enveloped by it.[17]

In the end, continual pleasure seeking becomes an exercise in repression and a recoiling from the world. This repression is derivative
and secondary. What we fail to appreciate is that we are always and everywhere in a condition where trauma could come over us. It is always
possible to experience that which could cause us to be anxious since what
is primary and primordial in our lives is our vulnerability. Repression is
our attempt to flee what may upset us, overwhelm us, or traumatize us.

Addiction is a powerful attraction to someone or something we believe is concretely good, even as a means to overcome some other trauma,
but that ultimately becomes an enormous harm to us. We enter the addiction cycle under the expectation that it will ease our pain and delude
ourselves into believing that it will exhilarate our hearts. We are all called
to happiness, yet embodiment and limitation point to the fact that we are
likely to experience the frustration of desire. It is this harsh paradox that
translates the desire for happiness into a hell of addiction. In the end,
the path of addiction diminishes our spiritual capacity and truncates our
relationships. We become indifferent to the harm that an object of mere
satisfaction will cause, caring only for relief. It induces us "to objectify the
things we desire: they become objects promising satisfaction and cease
to have much existence in themselves. When we relate to the world as a
depositary of satisfying objects, we become less attentive to the complexities of beauty and wonder that arise all around us all the time."[18]

The energy required to notice what is going on dissipates because
of addiction. Indeed, "addiction's preoccupation with satisfaction dead-
ens its awareness of other people as living beings, irreducible to our

17. Miller, "Addiction and Tears," 55.
18. Farley, Wounding and Healing, 65.

satisfactions."[19] Addiction also follows the pattern of rage when the addictive object requires us to sanction violence for us to obtain it. Again, rage and addiction reinforce an orientation toward egocentrism and, if it continues, a spiral down to narcissism. Consequently, the addict does not tolerate any counterclaim since addiction is the problem of compulsion. Compulsion is a suppression of our subjectivity. A compulsion is an "autonomic psychic impulse that constricts impulses to intelligence."[20] Compulsions are autonomic since their repetition follow their laws, often going unnoticed. It is difficult to predict when they will arise. They wear their deep routines into our character and, ultimately, into our personality.[21] Compulsions belong to the psyche, though often manifesting themselves in the body and behavior.[22] Compulsions "constrict impulses to intelligence" since the psyche cuts a deal with the intelligence and the deal is that intelligence will turn a blind eye to certain impulses in return for psychic comfort. The deal formalizes into a simplistic worldview which acts as the rationalization for certain impulses.[23] When compulsive desires catch us up, we rationalize our actions and suppress our intelligence, becoming attached to various behavior which in turn block the ability to achieve other real desires.

The Role of the Psyche and Psychic Energy

Robert M. Doran builds on Lonergan's insights and recognizes the transformative power of psychic conversion.[24] Doran's investigations into the role of the psyche, its relationship to the human spirit, a reappraisal of Freud's psychic censor, a reappraisal of Jung's notion of complexes, the insights of depth psychology, and the importance of grace have amounted to a lifelong and complex body of work. His insights form the basis for addressing moral impotence and the lack of willingness to achieve the good, thereby transforming our lives. The assumption is that moral choices are neither fully determined and without freedom nor completely

---

19. Farley, *Wounding and Healing*, 66.

20. Dunne, *Enneatypes*, 40.

21. Dunne, *Enneatypes*, 37.

22. Dunne, *Enneatypes*, 37.

23. Dunne, *Enneatypes*, 38.

24. Doran, *Subject and Psyche*, 240–46; *Theological Foundations*, 83–88.

freely chosen, since clearly there are unconscious factors negatively influencing our decision making.

To understand what Doran means by psychic conversion requires that we first understand the crucial role of the psyche and psychic energy in the life of the individual. For many centuries, the church provided an account of human anthropology through philosophical terms such as body and soul to explain our humanness. Lonergan suggests that a new paradigm is needed, namely, the turn to the subject. With the advent of modern psychology and the natural sciences, these older terms began to change. This change is not to say that the former terms lacked insight. However, the shift to a new terminology is an effort to more easily speak to a new cultural setting which reflects the turn to the subject, and so effect a creative collaboration between religious faith and those disciplines. The older terms for explaining an understanding of the human person did not give enough prominence to the human body, the human psyche, and the role of feelings as a pre-apprehension of values.

For Lonergan, the human person is a tripartite structure of the organism, the psyche, and the human spirit. The branches of physiology and neurology, to name a few, predominately explore the dimension of the organism.[25] Through the various branches of philosophy, human psychology, and psychiatry, researchers have explored the dimensions of the psyche, its relation to the body and its neural networks, and its relationship to the human spirit. Within human consciousness, there is a two-fold duality, consisting of a more basic dialectic, namely, a creative tension between the organically based neural network and the psyche on one hand and as a derived dialectic from the more basic one, namely, the creative tension between the psyche and the human spirit, on the other.[26] The breaking of one or both of these tensions will make it very difficult for us to live genuinely.

What is the psyche? First, Doran states that the "psyche is the sensitive stream of consciousness. It is the experience itself of the movement of life. It is the stream of our sensations, memories, images, emotions, conations, conscious bodily movements, associations, and spontaneous responses to persons, things, and situations."[27] There are multiple sources

25. Scientists and medical professionals have expertly investigated the human organism over the centuries in its various parts: the skeletal, neurological, circulatory, respiratory, lymphatic, reproductive, digestive, and endocrine systems.

26. Doran, *Theology*, 55, 70, 215.

27. Doran, *Theology*, 219.

contributing to this sensitive stream include our five senses, images stored in memories with their feelings, our creative imagination, and the filtered, selected, and provided energies of the psyche.

Second, psychic energy is already active in the womb, orchestrating the slow development of the person. The organism under the impetus of psychic energy presses forward, committing to psychic memory the feel of the interaction of its various systems even *in utero*.[28] This energy is both the instrumental cause for the start of the fetal heartbeat as well as recording the feeling tone of the mother to this heartbeat.[29] This energy rooted in the original organism *in utero* drives the impetus of cell division. In short, Streeter declares that psychic energy is the "activating form of human matter provided by ovum and sperm"[30] which unfolds into psychic sensitivity.

Third, the psyche is that energy field which draws from and influences both the organism, on one side, and the human spirit, on the other side. The neural networks of the organism have a goal and purpose, that is, representation in the psyche. The function of the psyche is toward imaging, emoting, fantasizing, and dreaming. However, to fully understand the role of the psyche, the metaphor of two feet might help. The psyche is the energetic part of the person, with a foot in the organism, that filters, selects and provides psychic representations of the neural pathways, and, with a foot in the mind, releases needed images and feelings for insight and decisions.

Fourth, the psyche stores images. What we smell, see, taste, hear, and touch, we also store in the feeling memory, accompanied often by images that trigger emotions whether they arise in dreams or daylight. Lonergan calls these feeling-laden images, symbols.[31] When these feeling laden images bridge the span of the psychic field to the first level of the human spirit, we notice their energy.

Fifth, the psyche gives emotional vitality to our thoughts, decisions, and actions. Psychic energy is the basis of human feeling and bodily sensations that integrate into more complex emotions: love, hate, joy, sadness, fear, courage, hope, despair, and anger., and, ultimately, is sublated by the higher levels of intelligence and decision. This psychic energy,

28. Streeter, *Foundations*, 50.

29. Streeter, *Foundations*, 50.

30. Streeter, *Foundations*, 50.

31. Lonergan, *Method*, 64.

though rooted in the neural network, is the most fundamental aspect in the dynamism of the human spirit not yet aware of itself. Psychic energy has a purpose and direction. Its purpose is to pattern the energy of the neural network and provide images to the human spirit. Unlike plants and animals, this psychic energy will not rest until "consciousness emerges in its distinctive *self-reflexive* human form."[32] Lonergan states that psychic energy underpins a "tidal movement" within us towards all reality and is an aspect of "the passionateness of being" which draws us to itself.[33] We are conscious of this movement in psychic restlessness, then in conscious intentionality sublating images and their feelings into knowing and valuing and, finally, in an overarching total commitment of love for others and God. This purposeful direction occurs unless something in the form of dramatic bias distorts the proper function of the psyche or something in the form of individual, group, and a general bias in the human spirit, derails the direction.

Sixth, we should not view the psyche as merely a part of the human being but rather as a dimension of the one human person with a distinct function. The functioning of images is very distinct in humans when compared to animals. Streeter asserts that "humans not only form images; they decide which images they will entertain and which they will suppress."[34] Our interests and concerns guide our choice of images and feelings. Streeter concludes that "the psychic energy, rooted in the physical and pressing forward toward the human capacity to think and choose is the ability to fuse the entire range of human operations into a unified field."[35]

THE RELATIONSHIP BETWEEN THE BODY/PSYCHE AND HUMAN SPIRIT

What people have called the *soul*, the psychology of intentionality names as psyche and the human spirit. Often science does not pinpoint the human spirit; however, the humanities and religion claim this dimension as their preserve. Our cultural distortions do not help us in the exploration of the human spirit. Often, people equate the human spirit with

32. Streeter, *Foundations*, 50.
33. Lonergan, *Third Collection*, 28.
34. Streeter, *Foundations*, 51.
35. Streeter, *Foundations*, 51.

the psyche, intellectually collapsing the exploration of intelligence and responsibility into psychology. Others reduce the human spirit to the physical and chemical levels of the organism alone, such as in some forms of neuroscience, collapsing the whole person into a set of organic patterns. There has been a great deal of criticism against the Christian faith in the past for not giving enough attention to the psyche, and for being overly rationalistic and sterile in its philosophical anthropology, tending to make disembodied rather than embodied affirmations of faith. The criticism is that Christians ought not to forget that "The Word was made flesh and dwelt among us" (John 1:14).

Robert Doran employs Lonergan's notion of dialectic to the human person.[36] The body/psyche and the human spirit are the two drivers or opposed principles of change in the human person. The body/psyche is the pole of limitation. The human spirit is the pole of transcendence. The pole of limitation is the integrator in human living. The pole of transcendence is the operator in human living. When these two poles are working in cooperation with each other, moving the person forward to greater transcendence, the person flourishes, and there exists a dialectic of contraries between the opposing principles or poles. The virtue of detachment develops to allow growth from the person one is to the person one becomes along a vector of creativity. Philosophers describe this psyche/human spirit relationship as the life principle of the person, capable of self-reflective thought and choice.

There exist healthy and unhealthy tension in this dynamic process along four directions. First, in a healthy state of affairs, the unconscious is a complex array of neural pathways in the body with their physical, chemical, and biological substratum. Psychic energy interacting with neural demands meets the constant limitation of the organism. The psyche cannot ignore these organic demands released as energy into the psyche. In other words, neural demands condition the proper functioning of the psyche. Psychic energy gives rise to feelings, symbols, and images, conscripting the energies of the neural demands into psychic representation.

Second, in an unhealthy state of affairs, there may develop a problem with the chemical base in the organism, such that psychic representation will falter. Alternatively, there is the problem of biases that conspire to

---

36. Doran, *Theology*, 179–85.

make the censor repressive.[37] If victimization toward the person has occurred especially in childhood and in a grave manner, dramatic bias is established which negatively impacts the functioning of the psyche in its relationship to neural demands. In other words, negative energies dominate and the person represses needed feelings and images out of a sense of threat or fear or anxiety. Further, there is the problem of individual and group bias. The self-regarding stance of individual bias negatively impacts the psyche's ability to choose needed images from the neural undertow. Similarly, group bias impedes the relationship of the psyche with its neural undertow.

Third, there exists a constructive and creative tension between the human spirit and the psyche in its role as censor. There relationship to each other is reciprocal. In the best of situations, intelligence and imagination work together in such a way that the psychic censor filters and selects mental representation for questions and wonder, intelligence, and correct judgment. The person moves toward greater intellectual and moral transcendence. However, there are a number of distortions that might operate to derail this process and, ultimately, the person's development.[38] If the tension breaks toward too much limitation through psychological addictions and mental disorders, then physical dependencies and other prisons of limitation emerge. The breakdown of the psyche affects negatively the human spirit. If the tension breaks towards too much transcendence, then the person's loss of intelligent self-limitation, overreaching, irresponsibility, ego-inflation, and the aberration of disordered freedom contributes to a repressive psyche. The breakdown of the human spirit affects negatively the psyche. The next chapter will explore these imbalances in greater detail.

The Psychic Censor: Constructive or Repressive?

From this understanding of the psyche and its relationship to the human spirit, we are in a better position to understand the notion of the psychic censor. The human psyche and the idea of a psychic censor came to greater prominence in the nineteenth century due to the work of Sigmund Freud. In his major work *The Interpretation of Dreams* (1899), Freud developed a theory of dreams around a general theory of what he calls mind

---

37. Doran, *Theology*, 182–83.
38. Streeter, *Foundations*, 51–53.

or psyche. It is within this context that Freud dealt with the idea of the psychic censor describing the effects of repression operating in dreams and other events. For Freud, the unconscious signified those pieces of data and facts that the person repressed, did not know, and did not want to know but that severely disordered their lives. It also represented that content which proven to be a source of inner conflict and confusion. Freud judged that this censor had a predominately repressive function, basing his assertions on his experiences of countless clients who came to his clinic suffering from all forms of psychopathology.

The censor is a vital aspect of consciousness if we want to function with some degree of control in our lives when it is sufficiently independent of the neural demands of the organism. The flow of conscious representation through feelings, images, and symbols needs controlling. We have to filter, select, and provide what comes into psychic awareness if we are to function in an orderly manner. Psychic representation into the level of experience cannot be unlimited and at the same time. We would not be able to handle the volume of images and feelings. Nor does it help to be caught up with feelings and images of gardens when our questions call for more nuanced moral reasoning (see the film *Being There*). Alternatively, there has to be some way for a scientist to concentrate on the problem at hand by selecting certain images and putting others aside.

Contrary to Freud, Lonergan has a different understanding of what is unconscious and conscious. Lonergan asserted that the unconscious aspect is the neural network and organic dimension of the person. This underlying unconscious level of neural stimuli demands representation and integration in the psyche. The desire to know, to value, and be in love is the primary direction of the self-transcending human person and so the censor functions to provide feelings and images for understanding what needs to be understood, valued, and put into loving action. Lonergan accepts the existence of the psychic censor and postulates that the censor is primarily constructive.[39] When this gatekeeper function is constructive, the negotiation between intelligence and psyche allows for images to emerge for new insights and values. The possibility of such a constructive functioning of the psychic sensor is conditioned by healthy bodily functions, on one side, as well as significant authentic living, healthy relationships, and cultural milieus of integrity, on the other side.

39. Lonergan, *Insight*, 216.

Lonergan acknowledged Freud and the insight that other factors were at work in consciousness which amounted to our "refusals to keep on taking the plunge from settled routines to an unexperienced but richer mode of living. There are the mistaken endeavors to quiet an uneasy conscience by ignoring, belittling, denying, rejecting higher values."[40] He also accepted that the censor can be repressive, distorted through biases, dramatically shaken by trauma, and deviated by gross selfishness.[41] When our censor is repressive, the person's intelligence and responsibility do not function well, and we miss the authentic direction in life. The proper images are not lined up by the psyche for insight. There is more confusion when images are repressed and feelings break away from them and seek release with other images. If this occurs consistently, even the neural network is negatively affected.[42] It follows that when we resist the operations of the spirit, the needed affectivity to grow blocks. Through engaging in a flight from understanding, procrastination toward decisions, or unloving acts, the psyche becomes more constricted and repressive.

When we deliberately suppress, we will merely avoid speaking about a topic or change the subject. In time, these mental representations will emerge again, and we will have to deal with them. When we repress without our knowing it, something which needs to emerge into consciousness is not being allowed to emerge. Repression distorts the censor and its relationship to both the human spirit and the neural demands. The distraught person suffers from a confusing and fearful confrontation with disowned or disconnected bits of consciousness and enters therapy in the hope of being finally able to live the truth. If therapy is not at hand, the feelings may attach themselves to other images making the person very confused.[43]

When speaking about the psyche, we are more in the field of personality than character. All of us can be deformed by rigid personality characteristics while unable to articulate to ourselves and others what is going on in the destructive behaviors that emerge. These include: being trapped in avoidances; being constant complaints; being attached in co-dependencies; being overcome by paranoias; subjecting others to passive-aggressiveness; and driven by our narcissistic needs. These personality

40. Lonergan, *Method*, 41.

41. Lonergan, *Insight*, 216.

42. Doran, *Theology*, 73.

43. Moran and Kelly, *Searching*, 93.

flaws are our unhelpful strategies used to deal with hurt, toxic shaming, destructive anger, hate, and unhealthy guilt. Such experiences are capable of blocking psychic energy from its more creative direction and when psychic energy blocks, there is a felt resistance to insight. When speaking of the human spirit, we are more in the arena of character formation. All of us can be deformed by an abandonment of virtue: lack of prudence, intemperance, injustice and lack of courage, ego-inflation and overreaching. These character flaws will inevitably negatively affect our psyche.

The Meaning of Psychic Conversion

With this brief exposition on the importance of the human psyche for the human spirit and its possible maladaptation, we can better understand the meaning of psychic conversion. Psychic conversion is the movement away from a repressed psychic censor and the movement toward a constructive psychic censor where images and feelings are conscripted into the services of the human spirit.[44] It is the constructive psyche which allows for a smooth flow of images and feelings into awareness, needed for understanding, judgment, decision, and action. In the latter case, through employing a constructive psychic censor, we can integrate, grow and transform our life situation as needed.[45]

Underpinning the importance of a constructive psychic sensor is the conviction that our lives need the momentum of feelings, symbols, and images. This insight grounds the fact that our life is not merely many discontinued events or acts but is, in fact, a dramatic story with irony, sorrow, pathos, romance, and lyricism. Psychic conversion, then, facilitates our ability to know what we are feeling, and how feelings are related to particular symbols, images, questions, insights, ideas and decisions. In the light of psychic conversion, the hope is that we will have enough insight to make our lives into a work of art. We will have the courage to face even those images that would disturb us and reveal to us our irresponsible and unloving actions however painful that might be.

To undertake such a task is arduous, painstaking, and requires an enormous amount of courage. It requires that we name and objectify that which circulates in the subterranean region of the psyche which may be the cause of our self-alienation and confront what expresses itself in

44. Doran, *Theology*, 66.
45. Doran, *Theology*, 85–86.

various self-destructive behaviors. We are conscious of this repressed material although we have not yet objectified it and, therefore, still do not know it. Through the process of therapy, primarily, the therapist assists the suffering person "to attend to their experience, to make sense of what surfaces, to come to a new judgment on the direction of their lives and thus to awaken a new originality and freedom of living."[46]

Psychic Wounding, Healing, and Ordinary People

The film *Ordinary People* (1980) directed by Robert Redford illustrates the importance of psychic recovery. This film demonstrates how suppression and repression can take hold over our lives, paralyzing a proper response to tragic events, and thereby straining our relationships. The film also explores what needs to occur for the unblocking of repression and the release of needed transformation.

The Jarrett family is an upper-middle-class family in suburban Chicago trying to return to normal life after the accidental death of their older teenage son, Buck, one year earlier. The parents have also faced the attempted suicide of their surviving son, Conrad, some six months previous. These two very stressful events cause some boundaries between family members to come down. When boundaries are no longer able to be maintainable, roles become confused. During the story, the audience comes to appreciate that the Jarretts live within a particular set of values and beliefs. They have held together by the belief that there is a moral order to the universe. This moral order dictates that we are masters of our destinies. We are urged as people to take control of our lives no matter what the circumstances. However, their moral universe has been turned upside down by recent events.

We enter their lives with Conrad having returned home from a four-month stay in a psychiatric hospital. Some months after Buck's drowning, Conrad attempts suicide by slashing his wrists. He does this in the family bathroom, luckily discovered by his father. Upon his return, Conrad tries to fit into home and school life but finds himself continually distracted with painful flashbacks of recent events and awkward in the presence of others. His inner pain is preventing him from acting normally and, more and more, he feels alienated from his friends and family and begins seeing a psychiatrist, Dr. Berger. Berger learns that Conrad was involved

46. Moran, *Searching*, 151.

in the sailing accident in which his older brother, Buck, whom everyone idolized, died. Buck's character is significant to the story. Buck is the son who made everyone laugh. He was a high achieving risk taker for whom the possible tragic consequences of actions did not figure as strongly in his calculations as would have been the case with Conrad. Buck's trophies from sporting achievements fill the room.

Conrad's experience in the hospital is very positive. Conrad feels unsettled at home in an atmosphere of control and stoicism after experiencing the open dialogue of the hospital. In the hospital, people did not hide secrets. Now at home, Conrad is dealing with post-traumatic stress and, possibly, survivor's guilt causing insomnia, diminished appetite, suicidal thoughts, decreased interest, decreased concentration, social withdrawal, and avoidance. At first, Conrad fears and distrusts his feelings. Finally, he disavows his feelings. He is afraid that they will overwhelm him with their painfulness. The central revelation concerning Conrad is his personality. He has been raised and strongly influenced by his mother to take control of his life. The problem with an ethic of control is the neurotic guilt and shame Conrad feels when a painful event, beyond his control, intersects into his life.

Further to this, for Conrad, taking control means not talking about the terrible incident of Buck's death or his suicide event or the overall grief of the family. Taking control means not allowing time to honestly process what is painfully felt but instead holding it in and assuming an attitude of suppression. Taking control means going back to their usual way of relating to each other as if no rupture in their lives has ever occurred. Consequently, at some level, Conrad feels personally responsible for Buck's death, guilty that he survived and angry at Buck, the elder brother, for putting him into a situation that ended so badly.

Conrad's father, Calvin, awkwardly tries to connect with and understand Conrad as well as trying to understand his wife. He has higher levels of self-giving and sublimation as well as some guilt around his son's suicide attempt. He feels the loss of his son, Buck, and profoundly fears to lose another. While his experience of life returning to normal gives him some reassurance, still deep within his psyche, he feels uneasy and becomes increasingly troubled. When he finally goes to see Dr. Berger, his presenting problem is around how Conrad is going, but he quickly realizes that he has come to see Dr. Berger for his own sake. His family is falling apart, and he feels powerless to stop the spiral of confusion. With boundaries confused, the conflicts between Beth and their surviving son are escalating. In time, he will come to realize that he is troubled by feelings of having lost the best part of his wife since the accidental death. He will identify that he feels a loss of the spark of exchange with his wife that first drew them into marriage. He declares to his wife sadly that he is not sure whether she is indeed a giving person or ever will be.

Conrad's mother, Beth, stoically holds the loss of her son, hoping to maintain her composure, and restore her family to what it once was, the usual moral order that existed before these tragic events. We learn that she does not cry at the funeral. For her, outward appearances are social essentials, and the family needs to keep control. Her husband calls her a cautious woman. Buck appears to have been her favorite, and now, because of Conrad's suicide attempt, she is even more fragile. She is suspicious of affectivity and is preoccupied with external details. Beth is determined to maintain privacy, the appearance of perfection, and normality within her family for the sake of social appearances. Beth makes some constrained attempts to bond with Conrad more for the sake of some semblance of normality returning to the home, but she gives up. Conrad senses this remoteness and at one point declares to his father that he feels no love from her.

Beth is a woman who has not yet discovered that there is no turning back to a normal existence. The events surrounding the death of one son and the mental breakdown of another have shattered her world to pieces in an irretrievable way and the moral order by which she once lived no longer exists. Beth must find a new world from the ruins of the past shattered world. Meanwhile, her desire to return to normalcy employs the mechanism of avoidance, controlling what she will allow herself to feel and not to feel. While her psyche is in that state, there will be no new feelings, no helpful images by which to imagine a new future, and no helpful insights by which to move forward.

The film reaches a dramatic point in the final act. While Conrad was in psychiatric care, he shared the space with a girl called Karen. Since their return home, they have met once for conversation. At the meeting, Conrad tries to tell Karen that he misses the safety of the hospital, but Karen does not agree. Karen expresses a high degree of optimism in the future and on departing wishes Conrad a very happy future. Karen seems to be echoing the narrative of her parents, especially her father, who is encouraging her to exercise greater will power over her negative and confusing feelings. In this way, Karen is encouraged to think positive thoughts rather than be truthful about what she is really feeling.

While Conrad's parents are away on holiday in Florida and Conrad is staying with his grandparents, something dramatic happens. He decides to ring Karen. Karen's father answers the phone and tells Conrad bluntly that Karen has suicided. Hearing of Karen's death, Conrad is confused, upset, and anxious. Conrad rushes into the bathroom where he ends up sitting on the toilet, grabbing the washbowl. Then, the flashbacks to his brother's death begin, and he is further overwhelmed by anxiety and fear. He calls Dr. Berger, and they agree to meet. Conrad finally confesses to his psychiatrist that the reason for his attempted suicide is the guilt of having survived and the guilt of failing to save his elder brother in the boating accident. He is also angry at his free-spirited brother for allowing such a dangerous situation to develop.

In this passage of the film, Conrad feels the struggle to name the unnamable feelings and to expose the falseness of his neurotic guilt. Neurotic guilt is the falseness of feeling guilty for not being the supreme human being and, in his case, Conrad's guilt for not saving his reckless brother under impossible conditions. In the final scenes of the film, we find Conrad sitting with his father in the backyard of their home, having been informed by his father that his mother has gone away. Conrad immediately blames himself for the rupture, at which point Calvin, his father, sharply rebukes him, telling him it is nobody's fault. He goes on to declare to Conrad that he has always been the son who was hardest on himself, while Buck the son who needed the most amount of discipline. In this way, Calvin tells Conrad how alike he is to his mother. The film ends with father and son affirming their love for one another.

11

The Sickness of the Psyche, the Sickness of the Spirit, and Healing

WHENEVER WE SPEAK OF psychological and spiritual development, we are talking about each person in all their complexity discovering meaning and being meaning-makers. Chapter 10 highlighted the function of the psyche and the psychic censor, and importance of the psyche as healed of neurosis and constructively working with the human spirit. This chapter will continue the insights of the previous chapter exploring the link between the sickness of the psyche and the sickness of the spirit as well as the centrality of love for healing and transformation.

THE SEARCH FOR DIRECTION

The person we become makes a difference to us and others. We are *self-determined* persons, which means that the self both shapes our world and is shaped by the decisions that we make. We cannot shape our world with integrity without being in tune with our psyche and our spirit. Whenever there is a development of feelings together with acts of intelligent inquiry, critical reflection, and responsible love, then, we are experiencing growth that is both existential and artistic. Personal integrity is the search for direction in the movement of life that is found in the gift of authenticity and in making of one's life a work of art.[1] For the Christian, such personal integrity means cooperating with and participating in the grace of God in Christ through the Holy Spirit.

1. Doran, *Theology*, 45.

We should never think that we stand alone as solitary individuals unaffected by the influences around us. Cultural attitudes and social processes mediate influences that promote the conditions for growth. Equally, the integrity of the person is crucial for shaping the integrity of culture and the integrity of the community. The integrity of the person is a felt experience just as much as it is an intellectual, moral, and religious experience. Being in touch with authentic feelings results in the person being able to more efficiently and consistently arrive at proper meaning, truth, and value, and so transform the world and oneself by being a source of love.

However, this is not the whole story. We can sadly lose our search for direction in life. The wounds of terror, rage, and addiction, the four biases and the social wounding of exclusion, humiliation, and demonization conspire to derail our direction and curtail our transformation. These deformations come through distortions within the community and through unhelpful cultural attitudes that work against the growth of families, organizations, large social groups, and nations. Disordered individual desires can also bring havoc into our lives especially when accompanied by the will to control. Sin and human evil create victims and derail development. A rejection of our innate and God-given capacity to quest for the truth brings dire consequences. The abandonment of intellectual objectivity results in communities of opinion marshaled by a will to power. The occlusion of God precludes the power of love entering lives to reverse the effects of sin.

PSYCHOPATHOLOGY: THE SICKNESS OF THE PSYCHE

Chapter 10 proposed that human consciousness is constituted by a duality: a creative tension that exists between the bodily neural network and the psyche and between the psyche and the human spirit.[2] When the creative tension between the neural network and the psyche breaks, the result is maldevelopment. The derailment can occur due to a displacement either towards the pole of limitation or the pole of transcendence. Psychopathology points to the derailment of the proper functioning of the psyche in its relationship to the neural network.[3] As a displacement towards limitation, we observe psychopathology in persons who exhibit

2. Doran, *Theology*, 84.

3. Doran, *Theology*, 180.

excessive rigidity or have a great fear of change or who suffer from chronic depression.[4] We observe it in those persons who have overwhelming anxieties about life and use this anxiety as a defensive wall to protect them from growth or confrontation. Displacement towards limitation invites fixation on the biological rhythms such that the psyche ends up trapped into fixed routines. People feel lethargic and unmotivated as if their bodily existence holds them back. People can seek to compensate for this distortion, but healing can only come about by addressing the underlying reasons. We know that in cases of chronic depression, we may need pharmacological therapy. However, drugs alone will not bring healing and, often, there is an overcompensation toward drug therapy. All healing will require insight and decision making.

Psychopathology can also be a displacement towards the pole of transcendence, especially witnessed in the minds and hearts of persons who suffer from mania.[5] Their power to accomplish tasks is so high that they move from one activity to another but without reaching goals, often unable to relate to people in a cooperative manner. They have fantastic vistas free of the salutary conservatism of the established order. They have intelligence but not the right judgment of fact or value. Their insights have ceased to be pertinent to the context. We witness this chaos in persons who are fuelled by the need to relieve anxiety, self-doubt, and felt self-disesteem. They do much activity at home, work, school, and in the broader community but always chasing that elusive sense of esteem and worthiness. Overall, psychopathology results in an inability to be attentive to the movement of life.[6]

If a person's ability to be responsible is diminished due to a dramatic victimizing of the psyche by significant others and by oppressive structures early in their formative year, then the possibility of becoming responsible is even harder to achieve. Victimization can trap people into cycles of self-destruction over long periods. If the person represses and avoids questions, then there is an unwillingness to look at the origins and the causes of psychic disruption. Often, the victims of child abuse have a terrible and painful path to walk to become survivors and many lives end in suicide.

4. Doran, *Theology*, 289.

5. Doran, *Theology*, 289.

6. Doran, *Theology*, 214–15.

The Words to Say It: Psychotherapy and the Talking Cure

To elucidate psychopathology and the importance of psychotherapy, the autobiographical account of a journey through madness by Marie Cardinal provides a fertile ground for study. The story of Marie Cardinal is an excellent example of dramatic bias and repression at work. In her case, there existed the repression of memories, images, thoughts, and feelings from childhood until she became so psychically dysfunctional that she bled uncontrollably. We may never know whether her autobiography represents a complete account of her life. What we can say is that it is her story, in her voice, and, in as much as she sought to ask all the relevant questions post-therapy, we can speak of this account as an objective body of work. Following a period of bewilderment, dysfunctionality, and lostness, Cardinal craves for relief from her suffering and answers to questions about her breakdown. It is an account by a woman experiencing mental illness and only able to break through her illness by utilizing the "talking cure." Through this process, she recounts and remembers her memories and takes responsibility for the truth revealed.

Born in Algiers of a well to do family in 1929, Marie Cardinal is raised Catholic by her mother. Her mother and father divorced in her younger years. Her older sister dies at birth, and she has an older brother. At the age of 30, with three children and married, Marie has a total mental breakdown and what she later calls "The Thing" takes over her life.[7] The symptoms include uncontrollable bleeding from her uterus, the paralysis of fear, and involuntary obsessions. She is considered mad by her family and admitted into a family run sanatorium where she receives medication and shock treatment. Marie leaves that place and seeks help from an analyst, to whom she dedicates her book with the expression "to the doctor who helped me to be born."[8] It is through these seven long years of analysis for three times a week that we become privy to her inner world about which she has little knowledge and from which she has experienced a complete loss of control until she could not move.

As "The Thing" consumes her, Marie's life becomes soulless and meaningless. With a small remnant of hope, she makes her way to the doctor. When she first arrives in those rooms, she states "Prostrate as I was, withdrawn into my own universe, how to find the words which would flow between us? How to construct the bridge which would join

7. Cardinal, Words to Say It, 7.
8. Cardinal, Words to Say It, iv.

the intense to the calm, the clear to the obscure, which could span this sewer, this river filled with decomposing matter, this treacherous current of fear, that separated the doctor and me, the others from me?"[9] It is in the analyst's room, lying on the couch in the silence, and in the thoughtful questions, that she finds the words with which to say what was happening inwardly and so finds herself once again. There, she speaks of her memories, dreams, and feelings. In time she puts into words the products of repression. The doctor listens attentively, waits for speech, and, finally, when the speech emerges, he and Marie discover another world apart from the one she knew. When she happens upon "The Thing" she discovers an unspoken existence that manifests outwardly in anxiety, depression, hallucinations, and feelings of deep dread.

According to Frances Moran, a prominent Melbourne psychotherapist, as time progresses, Marie Cardinal's knots unloosen, the stranglehold upon her mind unravels, and she can think without fear of her thoughts and how they might lead toward the unspeakable and unthinkable "Thing."[10] She discovers within herself much that is conscious but unknown. Though she resists the revelation of these thoughts, finally, she comes to an open door and then with great resistance sits on the couch one day and tells the analyst about the "tube" and the "eye."[11] Both are significant sub-elements of "The Thing." The image of the "tube" acts like a devouring black hole in her life and with it a plethora of associations hidden in some memories too traumatic to relive. The "eye" has come up early in the process of analysis, and when pressed to give it a meaning, she tells the doctor that it reminds her of her father, but she is reluctant to expand. Here is Marie at 34 years and terrified by an incident that had occurred when she was a child. In speaking of the "eye," she recalls a train ride when she is four years old, of having to take a pee, or crouching down above a hole and the fear of being sucked into the hole between her legs. Cardinal also relates going for a walk with her father when she was two years old. She recalls squatting and watching a jet of water flowing from her. She can relate that she hits her father when he photographs her taking a pee. Marie is finally contextualizing the "eye." Further, she relates incidents of violence between herself and her brother and how her rage

9. Cardinal, *Words to Say It*, 3.

10. Moran, *Searching*, 24–25.

11. Cardinal, *Words to Say It*, 147–49, 152.

is met with a cold shower by her mother, repressing her reaction of rage, and from then on turning rage into tears.

Overall, the task of analysis is to find out where she stands concerning the desires of her parents since "The Thing" began amid the painful breakdown of their marriage. Especially, after the divorce of her parents, Cardinal has to deal with the struggles of her mother. Since her mother is grief-stricken by the divorce, Marie tries to be the perfect child for her mother, continuously in search of something that would overcome her inability to make her mother completely happy.[12] Apart from this and embedded in her memory is the knowledge that her mother had tried numerous times to abort her by crude methods which, for Marie, translates to her mother's desire for her nonexistence. When she is finally able to articulate this, Marie can come to terms with her own self-loathing and the self-hating feelings of being a nobody. There are also numerous dreams that relate to her mother, the instructions generally that women in her life have taught her about the power of men, and her incident of being finger raped at the age of 12. She finds in herself a deep fear of the power of men and a deep fear of her vulnerability in the face of this power.

Moran presents an insightful interpretation of Cardinals' life story. She detects three significant moments of recovery and transformation for Cardinal. First, Cardinal's life is such that, while living in the practical present, her psychic past is unknown to her. This past gives shape to a great deal of what she negatively feels in the present. The needed recovery requires a disengagement from all self-destructive attempts to become all that her mother wants of her and so to cease "to live out of the feeding ground of her mother's own troubled state of mind. To contextualize herself within the complex of her history was the only means by which she could extricate herself from the tentacles of its hold of her."[13] Remembering is, therefore, vital to the process of healing.[14] Until this remembering happens, the anxiety of thinking that she would never exist in her own right or ever be herself, fills her mind. Revealing this personal history is the start since from that history the analysand and the analyst can uncover and unknot the past and then re-position with a new set of desires. In other words, transformation can begin.

12. Moran, *Searching*, 43.

13. Moran, *Searching*, 48.

14. Moran, *Searching*, 49.

Second, Marie is obliged to find a new truth.[15] This revelation into her person is not the truth of science or mathematics. It is a lived existential truth and so goes beyond the simple biographical details concerning the events of her life. In her disoriented condition, she is no longer mature and assertive. She is a person in the making, scared and dangling over an agonizing abyss, looking into the darkness. While she has grown used to her distorted emotional world, a new and unexplored world is revealed through analysis which brings its own set of fears. She needs to find her truth and no longer kowtow to the need to please others and their stories about her. Once she discovers her truth, moving forward means yoking herself to the truth and the "constraint of truth."[16] Moran concludes that "when in the yoke of truth analysands learn differently in the face of truth that persists in its uncompromising presence in their life. Through the gradual process of coming to terms with its insistence they learn to speak with truth."[17] This yoke of truth is indeed a hard-won security which leads all people under the talking cure to the truth about themselves and to "a subjectivity that is a truth-filled presence."[18]

Third, with this new subjectivity, Marie is no longer a passive object. She has repositioned herself as the subject of her action. Marie can be, for the first time, a person of responsibility. As a subject, she comes into existence slowly, intermittently, and surprisingly.[19] To arrive at this place, Marie must accept there is a "price to be paid" which amounts to "the loss of who she struggled to be for others"[20] in all its futility. In her new subjectivity, she discovers that she existed and "treatment terminated when I felt capable of taking responsibility for my thoughts and actions, whatever they may be."[21] The psyche may not know what images or feelings to repress, but it does have an animal apprehension of these mental representations which become unacceptable due to the impediments of fear, insecurity, and anxiety. This journey by Cardinal is a process of psychic conversion. This conversion opens the way for the clarity of insight, the assurance of judgment, and the joy of love. It takes an enormous amount

15. Moran, *Searching*, 58–60.
16. Moran, *Searching*, 62–63.
17. Moran, *Searching*, 66.
18. Moran, *Searching*, 67.
19. Moran, *Searching*, 75.
20. Moran, *Searching*, 79–80.
21. Cardinal, *Words to Say It*, 175.

of courage for her to regain her life and not allow these fears to hold her back.

Pneumopathology: The Sickness of the Spirit

If this is our understanding of psychopathology, what do we mean by pneumopathology? If the measure for human flourishing and authentic transformation is the capacity of the person to be attentive, intelligent, reasonable, responsible, and in love, then, human deformation comes about when people are unloving, irresponsible, unreasonable, unintelligent, and inattentive. In as much as these deformations take root in people's lives, we have the beginning of a pneumopathology or the pathology of the human spirit.

Pneumopathology is manifested in the refusal of insight, ego-inflation, delusions of power, abusive tendencies, over-reaching, moral renunciation, the abandonment of virtues and lovelessness. In terms of the deformation within consciousness, there can be a displacement towards limitation and transcendence. The oversights of Ernest Becker represent an example of displacement toward the pole of limitation. According to Kelly, Ernest Becker claims that the manifestations of modern culture in consumerism, exploitative sex, preoccupation with youthfulness, and hyperactivity are the result of the denial of death.[22] Our possession and absorption of these deformations drive us towards pneumopathology. There is evidence to show that this correlation rings true. There is also much insight into Becker's solution: a humbler awareness or acknowledgment of our death, that is, an acceptance that we are creatures of limitation and bound for the grave.

However, while Becker deals with the denial of death insightfully, he fails to allow other intelligent questions in the face of human mortality. One of his oversights is his denial of God. Kelly asserts that Becker cannot allow himself to ask other relevant questions. Critiquing Becker, Kelly asks: Is death the destruction of the rich world of meanings that Becker has explored? Is release from repression nothing more than the release into a world in which every human life is finally meaningless? Is all the brave creativity of human freedom nothing more than a posture against the onset of final darkness?[23] Blocking the full power of these ques-

22. Kelly, *Touching the Infinite*, 54–58.
23. Kelly, *Touching the Infinite*, 52.

tions into our lives ultimately leads to the replacement of the model of self-transcendence by the model of self-fulfillment and self-realization.[24] Chapter 3 briefly mentioned the bias of secularism. An authentic spirit is difficult to attain in a culture and community whose radical forgetfulness encompasses the repression of God. In such a society, there exists an abdication of the responsibility to discover our ultimate direction. Such a position plays into the hands of those who would stand over people as oppressors, threatening them into submission, and signaling that the primary thing they must worry about is whether they will die or not. The issue of our physical death becomes the defining limit of our lives. It effectively eliminates the possibility of all subversive action based on the intelligible, the true, and the good, witnessed by so many authentic people of goodwill. Becker's oversight is thus an example of a pneumo-pathological imbalance towards the pole of limitation.

Just as pneumopathology can be a displacement toward limitation, so it can also be a displacement towards transcendence. We observe such displacement in those persons who overreach or engage in ego-inflation. The pages of history are replete with examples of people who believed the things written about them and became megalomaniacs. Such people often use the adulation of others to dominate and control. More modestly, it can also be witnessed in the way people overwork because they are emotionally caught up in a consumerist model of existence or hold affluence as the badge for having been successful in life. This conviction distorts reality in such a way that consumerist oriented people do not attend to questions concerning the needs of the disadvantaged and the poor. Though they receive the esteem of success among their peers, ego-inflated persons are often shallow and selfish. We assess that this distortion underlies the lives of people whose use of power turns into a form of spiritual, emotional, sexual, or physical abuse toward those they have promised care.

There are also subtler forms of the pathology of the spirit. We detect this pathology in the lives of people of learning and science who engage in experimentation for the sake of scientific knowledge without moral consideration. They put aside moral issues that accompany scientific truth. They are prepared to put aside the primacy of the dignity of persons for the sake of getting results. The premise is that in some way they are above accountability and, implicitly this is their starting point.

24. Doran, *Theology*, 282.

More broadly, we evaluate the pathology of the spirit in those who engage in practices of self-abuse in the name of achieving greater wellbeing. It can happen that a person who, though responsible in many aspects of their life, engages in drug taking as a recreational way of feeling better to handle the overreaching and ego-inflation in their lives.

Pneumopathology and Psychopathology: An Illustration

It is also the case that pneumopathology can be the condition for the development of psychopathology. For this reason, the sickness of the spirit is more radical than the sickness of the psyche. We practice all kinds of avoidances when moral renunciation and lovelessness rules our lives. This sickness in the long run has a damaging and repressive effect on our psyche. Created from the novel by Oscar Wilde, the film, *The Picture of Dorian Gray* (1945), tells the story of Dorian Gray who embarks on a life of hedonism, moral renunciation, and dark cruelty. He fears the inevitability of aging and is willing to do anything to remain youthful.

At the beginning of the story, Dorian receives a painting of himself from Basil Hallward and notices that, for every period of aging and every act of cruelty performed by him, the image of the himself in the painting changes. The aging progresses, the acts of cruelty multiple, and the deformations in the painting render his image unrecognizable. By contrast, his physical appearance remains youthful. In the last scenes, having outlived all his peers, the audience finally witness outwardly in the colors and contours of the painting his condition of moral renunciation. The painting turns into an ugly and grotesque comparison to what he was as a younger and responsible man. The painting is a representation of Dorian's psychic repression and moral renunciation working against his journey of authenticity. The story highlights the moral truth that each of us could very well end up with a malfunctioning psyche when moral renunciation forms in us the anxiety of losing power, the threat of being discovered, and the fear of being vulnerable.

Pneumopathology and *The Godfather* Trilogy

Francis Ford Coppola's *The Godfather* trilogy presents us with a portrait of increasing pneumopathology within the main protagonist, Michael Corleone. The trilogy centers on the Corleone family, an Italian mafia organization based in New York. It is an example of the pathology of the spirit but not without subtle victimizations in early childhood. While the audience learns about the machinations of this crime group and their efforts to protect their power base, we also observe the intimate events and relationships within the family: weddings, birthdays of old and young, family meals, times of grief, endearing gestures one to another, petty jealousies and slights, domestic violence and patriarchy, and codes of conduct.

In the first of the trilogy, simply named *The Godfather*, the storyline focuses on Michael's rise to the commanding position of Godfather of the Corleone family. In the second film of the trilogy, the storyline focuses on the backstory of Michael's father, Vito Corleone, and his rise to power. This intimate and personal history intermingles with ongoing problems that Michael, in the present, faces with people seeking to wrestle power away from him, as well as Michael's efforts to secure and expand his family's business interests in Nevada. The third film of the trilogy focuses on the ongoing problems that beset Michael. He removes the family from its gambling interests and tries to legitimatize his business dealings by getting involved with the Vatican Bank and gaining a place at the table in the prestigious European business, *Immobiliare*.

In the first film, Michael is introduced to the audience as a returned World War II decorated veteran who has a girlfriend, soon to be fiancé, Kay Adams. Michael is determined to be himself and not participate in the family business which is built on gambling, prostitution, illegal alcohol, and favors to people who ask the godfather for help. He asserts to his future wife, Kay, after explaining to her what his family does, that there exists an enormous difference between what his family does and who he is. His father's hope is that with a college education behind him, Michael will one day become a Senator or Governor. He does not want Michael to have to deal with the dirty work of the family business. The consequence of such dealings is to be always looking over one's shoulder, anxious that envious enemies will wrestle away power through violence, to acquire greater power and greater wealth. Euphemistically, they assess any death of an enemy through the simple phrase: "It's business, not personal." By the end of the first film in the trilogy, so many family members and their "soldiers" have been killed, and all are deeply affected by the carnage.

Michael's descent into a greater pathology of the human spirit begins after the attempted assassination of his father. Vito Corleone has refused to share his political and police contacts with the other crime families who are seeking to grow their business into the area of narcotics, an expansion that Vito opposes. Individual members of the other families decide to kill him. He is gunned down by assassins while purchasing some fruit, but he survives the assassination. Michael finds out through reading a newspaper, a symbol that Michael has truly disconnected himself from the family business. He leaves Kay, with whom he is doing Christmas shopping, and joins the family in their grief. Later, Michael goes to see his father and is worried immediately for the lack of security around his father, especially since the police guard outside his father's hospital room has left. He goes into his father's hospital room and promises to look after his father. This symbolic act of bonding elicits a tear from his father and from that moment on Michael is wholly committed to his father, to the mafioso lifestyle, and the business. In the same hour, Captain McCluskey, a senior New York policeman, who is on the corrupt payroll of the enemies of the Corleone family, attacks Michael. It is a symbol of Michael's initiation in the way of violence that would soon characterize his whole way of life. In time, it becomes clear that his love for his father does not solely motivate his change of mind. Michael is ambitious to prove himself as the son of his father.

Michael is now part of the family conferences. At this point, another level to Michael's socialization into violence begins. His older brother Sonny is still keen to keep him at a distance from the violence of the business. However, when the enemy criminal, Sollozzo, is found to be the person who instigated the hit on their father and Luca Brasi, the strongman for the Corleone family, a plan is hatched to kill Sollozzo and McCluskey at a meeting organized by Sollozzo. Michael volunteers to be the assassin for efficient and practical reasons. He carries out the assassinations without hesitation. We observe the disappointment in Vito Corleone's face when he discovers that Michael is now part of the web of violence. Michael, meanwhile, is taken to Sicily for his protection where he meets his future bride, Apollonia. She is courted by Michael in a traditional Sicilian manner and marries him as a pure virgin. Their marriage is short lived when Michael's enemies, discovering that he is in Sicily, attempt to kill Michael but instead murder his young wife.

Michael returns to New York shattered and, within a year, meets up with Kay and asks her to marry him, promising that the family business would be legitimate within five years. However, there are still vendettas to be settled by Michael. In time, one by one those responsible for Vito's attempted assassination, as well as those who have conspired to assassinate

Sonny successfully, are murdered for their parts in the assassination plot. With the help of his father, Michael works out who is pulling strings behind the scene. Finally, Michael's father dies, and there are three sons left: Tom, Fredo, and Michael. Michael receives increasing pressure by the other families to take the kind of action that would avoid war between the families which has, by this stage, produced many dead soldiers.

In the famous baptism scene, we find Michael in church at the baptism of his nephew. He is the godfather to his nephew, Carlo and Connie's newly born son. A plan formulated beforehand progresses at Michael's instigation. The plan is to assassinate those who have visited violence or betrayal on the family. At the same time that Michael is professing his Christian faith, which includes believing in God the Father, Son, and Holy Spirit and renouncing the devil and all his evil ways, Michael's orders are carried out and one by one his enemies are killed simultaneously. The baptism of his nephew in the waters of salvation corresponds to the immersion of Michael in the waters of violence, ego-inflation, and overreaching. In that one period, he brings about the murders of several people. Philip Tattaglia and the woman with whom he is sharing a bed at the time die in a hail of bullets. Don Emilio Barnisi and his bodyguard die also. They kill Moe Greene in Las Vegas who refused to sell his casino to the Corleone family. They assassinate Sal Tessio who conspired with Barnisi to bring down the family. Carlo Rizzi, Michael's brother-in-law, who was part of the plot to kill Sonny. His descent into violence, ego-inflation, and overreaching is complete. At work in Michael's mind and heart is a powerful rationalization process which is grounded in a distorted code of conduct, characterized by disvalues such as a deference to power often described as respect, family honor, and an eye for an eye mentality, narrowly interpreted to justify revenge, payback, and assassination. The code that he lives by is a rationalization for the evil that he does.

Michael and his father subscribe to the conviction that society is corrupt and people are corrupt and corruptible. The worldview dominating their lives is that society is constituted by so many people who are gripped by ego-inflation and over-reaching. For example, Jack Woltz, head of a movie studio, will not give Johnny Fontane his needed start in the film industry. He is angry at the way one of Woltz's leading ladies fell in love with Fontane and abandoned her film opportunities. Woltz rages at how these events made him appear in the eyes of his peers. In a very memorable scene, Woltz wakes one morning to find the severed head of his favorite champion horse placed alongside him in bed, a demonstration by the Corleone family of ruthless power.[25] Then, there is the belligerent New York Police Captain Mark McCluskey who is on the corrupt payroll of Sollozzo. Judges and politicians are already receiving bribes from Vito Corleone so that his interests continue without impunity. There is the Las Vegas casino owner, Moe Greene, whose empire has flourished due to his criminal and villainous activities in his youth, together with his friend Hyman Roth, and from finances supplied illegally by the Corleone family. Later in the second film of the trilogy, we come across the lustful, avaricious, and corrupt Senator Geary. In the third film, we are privy to the corruption wrought by Archbishop Gilday, Fredrick Keinszing, Lucio Lucchesi, and Don Altobello, who conspire to defraud Michael of hundreds of millions of dollars.

According to Mark Malvasi, the protagonists of the film "are driven by lust, anger, greed, vanity, and prejudice, easily losing their tempers and getting unnecessarily carried away. Unless he has power or powerful friends, a man who finds himself in such a depraved and perilous world is alone, isolated and vulnerable."[26] Michael implicitly follows the ideas of Machiavelli's *The Prince*, namely, that a ruler must be prepared to be a beast if he is to survive his enemies, stubbornly pursuing vendettas against those who have acted against him. He must exact violent payback without compunction. That payback must also extend to family members, if necessary. Michael orders the death of Carlo, his brother-in-law but he lies to Kay when asked about his involving.

In the second film of the trilogy, Michael's rage against his wife Kay reaches a fever pitch when he finds out that she has had an abortion, thus denying him a son. He has his brother Fredo murdered for his unwitting part in an earlier assassination attempt on his family. He has Roth's lieutenant Johnny Ola assassinated. He later settles the score with Roth who is behind the plot to murder Michael. We leave Michael at the end of the second film, sitting in the garden of his Lake Tahoe home, alone and in the cold. In Malvasi's assessment, Michael's rationalizations, though couched in the language of keeping his family safe from the horrors of the world, have failed utterly.[27]

---

25. In Mario Puzo's book, *The Godfather*, we also learn that Woltz is a child molester.

26. Malvasi, "Tradition and Modernity," 2.

27. Malvasi, "Tradition and Modernity," 13.

In the third film of the trilogy, set in the late 1970s, the film opens at the house on the shores of Lake Tahoe, abandoned and now a distant memory. Michael has dispossessed himself of all his gambling establishments and is living in New York. We are taken to a religious ceremony to honor Michael for his philanthropic works toward the church in Sicily. Michael is still determined to become legitimate and so remove all danger toward his immediate family. Sadly, Michael has not realized this plan. In a meeting of the combined crime families where Michael declares to them that he is going his own way, Joey Zasa sets up an assassination of all the assembled. Michael survives this massacre, only to suffer a diabetic attack. The shock and stress in his life leave him in a permanent type 1 diabetic condition. During his stay in the hospital, his now right-hand enforcer Vincent Mancini, Sonny's son born out of wedlock, achieves payback on Joey and his henchmen during an Italian Religious Festival in New York, at the orders of Michael's sister, Connie. The circumstances are a mirror image of Vito Corleone's first murder of Fanucci, the extortionist, at a similar festival in New York, many years before.

After recovering, Michael goes to Sicily where he attends the premiere performance of his son, Anthony, in the opera *Cavalleria Rusticana*. While in Italy, he tries to secure his legitimate business interests. Michael meets up with Cardinal Lamberto who persuades Michael to have his confession heard. Michael confesses all and feels remorse when he tells this good priest that he ordered the assassination of his brother, Fredo. Sadly, Michael has discovered that all his evil deeds, though based on the Mafia code, have not been able to bring peace to his conscience. The excellent minister of God warns Michael that, while he may be redeemed, his wish to be extricated from the violent deeds of his past will surely elude him. Afterward, in a touching scene of reconciliation, Michael explains to Kay, for whom he still holds loving feelings, the reasons for his past actions. He states that he loved his father but swore not to be like him. Michael relates to Kay that the decision to help his father and the children was a response to danger. He acknowledges his love for Kay and the family yet he regrets the estrangement from them. It is clear from this monologue that Michael is reframing the tragic circumstances of his life in terms of being a victim of the poor decisions of others. Michael cannot be honest with himself and take responsibility for his contribution to the history of violence, ego-inflation, and overreaching.

Later, when it becomes clear the person directing the deeds of Joey Zasa, Michael surrenders his title as Godfather to Vincent Mancini, anticipating that Vincent will enact further payback. Unrealistically, he hopes that his family will be safe from all harm. However, the events of his personal history, his family's history, and the cycle of violence in New York, Nevada, and Sicily fold around him like so many tentacles. While Vincent orders the death of Archbishop Gilday, Lucchesi, Keinszing, and Altobello for their part in defrauding Michael and plotting his downfall, they, in their turn, have had the new Pope assassinated and a hit placed on Michael.

In the final scenes, Michael screams aloud and uncontrollably on the steps of the opera house as an assassin's bullet, meant for him, kills his beautiful daughter Mary. The plot line of the opera, which they have just enjoyed dramatically acted on stage, is mirrored on the opera house steps, but this time with Michael unable to step out of a heartrending and personal tragedy. We leave Michael sitting, an old man in his Sicilian garden, remembering the three wonderful women in his life: his daughter Mary, his first wife Apollonia and his second wife, Kay, all who had given him the gift of a waltz at various joyful periods of his life. He dies alone with his family relationships saturated in grief. He and Kay have lost their daughter. Anthony has lost his sister to violence. Connie has lost her brother to grief which we could rightly assume will be a barrier between them. Vincent has lost Mary whom he loved and has learned that vendettas bring about unintended harmful consequences. It would seem that nothing can bring the family back together again. Despite his best efforts to find redemption for himself and his family, Michael's life is embedded too thickly in a history of violence and egoism, both predating his birth and to which he has contributed, and from which there is no easy escape.

Healing the Sickness of the Psyche

Lonergan's insights into the biases and Doran's use of the term complex, taken from Jungian psychology, help to explain what is involved in the healing of the psyche and human spirit. First, complexes are compositions of energy with a purposeful orientation. They are units within the psyche with a focus of energy, content, meaning, and value.[28] As positive units of energy, they can positively aid the human spirit in finding direction in life. If the psyche is healthy, this normally means that the

28. Doran, *Theology*, 307.

conscious subject is in touch with the complexes. If the psyche is unhealthy, it means that the conscious subject has lost contact with the complexes and they have assumed an independent life. We no longer sense
that they are there. Conversely, these independent complexes negatively
interfere with, subvert, derail, and block the flow of energy needed for
direction in life. They become rigid and self-defeating patterns in human consciousness.[29] Doran states that such distorted complexes act in
such a way that our psychic energy becomes "blocked, fixed in inflexible
patterns, driven by compulsions, plagued by obsessions, weighed down
by general anxiety or specific fears, resistant to insight, true judgment,
and responsible action."[30] One ends up being "dragged through life rather
than walking through life upright."[31]

Second, these negative complexes come about through victimization by others and through self-victimization. From general bias through
to group and individual bias and into dramatic bias, there is an increasing
victimization at work, beyond the responsibility of the person affected
and not of the psyche's doing.[32] Such victimization has both the sickness
of the psyche and the sickness of the human spirit conspiring against
each other. A person may have suffered a narcissistic complex due to the
predominance of dramatic bias and victimization in childhood, leading
that person to become a consummate narcissist. Such narcissism conspires against the human spirit and the needed insights for responsible
loving. Alternatively, a person may engage in so much irresponsible action over a long period through self-centeredness, exacerbated by habits
of addiction, in such a way that there exists an increasing degree of psychic inability.[33]

Third, the consequence of victimized darkness is a sustained period
of a lack of reflection. We engage in repression and refuse to be attentive
to our darkness. We adopt a position of avoidance, rationalization, and
denial. We go on doing the practical things of life that help us to function, but we do not look at the questions that would lead us to deepen
our sense of purpose and direction. Unwilling to ask essential questions,
we formulate answers that do not address the issue of authenticity. We

29. Doran, *Theology*, 229.

30. Doran, *Theology*, 229.

31. Doran, *Theology*, 230.

32. Doran, *Theology*, 232–35.

33. Doran, *Theology*, 233–34.

engage in moral renunciation and capitulate to darkness based on the assertion that there is nothing that one can do about it. It is, in the long run, a form of self-destruction. Overall, moral relativism and moral impotence take hold in our minds and hearts.

Fourth, in attempting to bring healing to the victimized complex, there is a vicious circle operating that must be overcome. The distorted complexes are not providing the needed images and feelings for insight and so are preventing self-transcendence. However, self-transcendence is what is needed to move the person to the position of a compassionate negotiation and overcoming of the complex. One even finds that the more one attempts to move beyond the victimized complex the stronger the complex becomes. The person's future would seem to be heading towards a life of victimization by others and self.

Fifth, therefore, healing must come from beyond this vicious cycle paralyzing our lives by means of a compassionate negotiation of these victimized complexes.[34] Here is where divine love enables such a negotiation. Religious conversion is a radical change in our horizon from a horizon determined by the forgetfulness of or the refusal of the love of God to a horizon that is healed by the love of God. Through religious conversion, a person comes to the rest of being-in-love with God. This love is the self-communication of God in grace. It is the operative grace of God freely given to us even before we may ask for grace. It is the experience of the love of God poured into our hearts through the gift of the Holy Spirit (Rom 5:5). It is also the cooperative grace of God that makes us partners with God in Christ and, through the Holy Spirit, partners in ongoing acts of sanctification. This grace constitutes us and the world according to the mind of Christ. The cross and resurrection of Christ redeem us, and Christ calls us into discipleship that patterns our life on the life of the Crucified and Risen Lord. It is a love that brings our restless compulsions to rest and gifts us with the theological virtues of faith, hope, and love. This conversion is ongoing and needs to grow in a community of faith.

Sixth, the gift of love will meet those needing healing in different ways.[35] For those who are derailed through psychic inability and suffer the severe effects of psychopathology, this love comes as gentleness and compassion. The cause of their inability is beyond themselves in the distortions of community and culture. They do not need the further

34. Doran, *Theology*, 239, 242–43.
35. Doran, *Theology*, 244.

victimization of harsh distorted religion which judges them sinners awaiting the punishment of God or, worse still, a false interpretation of their sickness as being a punishment for their sinfulness.[36] They need healing through acceptance before they can come to experience sorrow for any other victimizing tendencies. They need to befriend their complexes and help the energy move from the complex into the service of the whole person. Listening and attentive therapy is vital for healing.

Seventh, for those derailed through their progressive misdirection, due to character flaws and irresponsibility, the experience of love will be felt differently. This kind of love will come as a judgment that seeks to help them recognize the gravity of their irresponsible actions and empowers them on a course of action that will help them show contrition, a willingness to make amends, and, where necessary, the willingness to approach their self-victimized darkness. Even when approaching their darkness, there is a need for compassion toward oneself.[37]

Eighth, if people are to be healed the issue of the relationship between divine love and human love must be addressed. Can human love alone sustain a relationship that seeks to meet people in their inability and unwillingness, in the sickness of spirit and the sickness of the psyche? Human love alone can never be completely free of the distortions of community and culture and, therefore, will inevitably fail the person. Therefore, human love must be a participation in the love of God for the healing of persons to be sustained.[38] Only a love that is willing to relinquish control over how healing progresses within victims can run the full course of healing. It must be a love that is willing to be self-giving and to walk the extra mile. Walking the extra mile is not the same as the victimization of co-dependency. What distinguishes co-dependency from authentic self-giving is that for the co-dependent, acts of care arise from feelings of disesteem, rather than being a response of genuine compassion. Co-dependents strive to overcome their painful feelings by proving to others that they are worthy of being loved.

Ninth, through the power of healing love our feelings point us more accurately towards true values.[39] Again, moral conversion moves our horizon from what is merely satisfying or pleasurable to values and it is not

36. Doran, *Theology*, 247–48.

37. Doran, *Theology*, 248.

38. Doran, *Theology*, 244.

39. Doran, *Theology*, 248–49.

a single event in the life of a person. As Lonergan states authenticity is a withdrawal from inauthenticity and the withdrawal is never complete and always precarious. In time one adheres spontaneously to values, and so priorities transform into a more integral scale of values where all values count. One begins to feel oneself more and more a source of personal value. One even assumes responsibility for the havoc that one has caused in the lives of others.

Tenth, the values of insight and truth are among the values to which a consciousness healed by love can respond.[40] We grasp truth through inquiry and critical judgment into ourselves and the world. To live in the truth may require a greater self-scrutiny. The assurance of inquiry and reflection means that we can wait for judgment to emerge without jumping to conclusions. Since we desire truth, we become more attentive to our feelings. Love helps us not to be afraid of our feelings. We give an enthusiastic reception to the images needed for insight. We experience symbols in dreams that confirm our direction towards meaning, truth, and value.

Universal Willingness and Healing the Spirit

If ego-inflation and overreaching are such a corrupting influence on our human story, what needs to happen to bring about inner peace and healing? First, the integrity of the human person is grounded in a universal willingness. Universal willingness is a level of human integration and development that allows for a creative tension between the psyche and the human spirit through a detachment that reaches into all areas of life.[41] It is the achievement of a lifetime. Universal willingness is a habitual orientation to decide and act according to the moral good that is intelligently grasped, reasonably affirmed, and according to the scale of values.[42] There exists a radical difference between willfulness and universal willingness.

Complementing Lonergan, Gerald May asserts that the attitude of willfulness sets oneself apart from the fundamental essence of life in an attempt to master, direct, control, or otherwise manipulate human existence. Willfulness ignores or even seeks to destroy wonder. It is the

---

40. Doran, *Theology*, 249–51.

41. Doran, *Theology*, 189.

42. Doran, *Theology*, 197.

attitude that often grounds the destructive forces in life. By contrast, willingness requires:

> [the] surrendering of one's self-separateness, an entering into, an immersion in the deepest processes of life itself. It is the realization that one is already part of some ultimate cosmic process and it is a commitment to participation in that process. More simply, willingness is saying yes to the mystery of being alive in each moment. Willfulness is saying no, or perhaps more commonly, "Yes, but . . ." It is obvious that we cannot say yes to everything we encounter; many specific things and situations in life are terribly destructive and must be resisted. But willingness and willfulness do not apply to specific things and situations. They reflect instead the underlying attitude one has toward the wonder of life itself.[43]

Second, willingness is impossible to achieve by one's energies and lights alone. It has both a religious and moral aspect. It is grounded in the experience of transcendent mystery when the love of God is poured into our hearts by the gift of the Holy Spirit. This experience is not of our own making but is the gift of God calling us into partnership with the transcendent measure of all meaning, truth, and value. At its core it is the felt experience of being valued as God values us, that is, with unconditional love and the engagement of a partnership with God.[44] Willingness has a moral aspect. This experience of being loved facilitates moral conversion that leads us to choose positive values according to an integral scale of values and to understanding the order of the world as made by God. We feel a pull in our hearts towards appreciating and enhancing the world by good deeds. Questions of deliberation, judgments of values, and decisions become easier for us.

Third, universal willingness facilitates the possibility of intellectual conversion and an openness to questions for intellectual inquiry and critical judgment. We feel a natural pull to be open to unrestricted questions and to make sense of our lives and the world, through exploring and questioning all the data and a willingness to find evidence for our insights.[45] We desire to eliminate illusion and live in the truth of reality. Universal willingness facilitates the possibility of psychological conversion so that human affectivity heals through positive self-esteem. It

43. May, *Will and Spirit*, 6.
44. Doran, *Theology*, 200.
45. Doran, *Theology*, 200.

facilitates psychic conversion so that the repressed censorship changes into the constructive censorship enabling us to filter and select correct images with their feelings for insight.

Fourth, willingness makes way for the virtue of detachment and universality. Detachment means that there is sufficient degree of inner freedom in our lives that helps us achieve sustained performance in our desire for self-transcendence. Within the Christian Tradition, many writers and mentors characterize the gift of detachment and equanimity as spiritual freedom from sin and disordered inclinations, enabling one to commit oneself completely to God and others. Willingness is universal since we are drawn to meet the problem of evil, in all of its manifestations, through a hopeful partnership with the love of God made visible in Jesus Christ.[46]

Fifth, universal willingness takes the person in the direction of authenticity. We achieve authenticity through the sustained effort to give ourselves to our natural orientation toward meaning, truth, and value. Willingness orients the person into a developing path of both integration (self-realization) and transformation (self-giving and outward), that is, the path of the self-transcending subject.

46. Doran, *Theology*, 204.

12

The Interplay of Conversion and Ecology

PREVIOUS CHAPTERS NOTED THAT often there is more than one kind of conversion at play if the process of transformation is to be holistic in the lives of people. Sustained moral and affective conversion requires religious conversion due to the presence of sin in the world. Reflecting on Franz Jägerstätter, religious conversion grounded his moral stance on war and military service. Pondering on the life of Oscar Romero, religious conversion authenticated the socio-political stance that he took and for which he was martyred. It is also the case that religious and moral conversion ground the possibility of intellectual conversion, by which we grasp reality and the objectivity of values. Self-victimization often requires the power of God's love to deal with one's inner darkness. It is also the case that God's love helps the therapist or spiritual director continue to guide the person along the difficult path of healing with patience and perseverance. This chapter will address the interplay of these conversions by exploring ecological conversion.

WHAT IS ECOLOGICAL CONVERSION?

People have called the problem and threat of climate change the single most important moral challenge of our time. In response, governments of the world, including the Australian government, have signed an international treaty called the United Nations Framework Convention on Climate Change. The agreement addresses the problems surrounding aspects of our ecological crisis.[1] Under this treaty, the Inter-governmental Panel on Climate Change (IPCC) has been formed to provide governments with the best possible scientific advice. In 1994, the IPCC concluded that we face the following consequences in the coming decades if our mistreatment of the environment goes unchecked. First, more severe and frequent natural disasters like cyclones, floods, and droughts will increase in severity. Second, patterns in ocean currents that transfer energy between the Polar Regions and the equator will change, slow down, or cease to circulate. Third, global temperatures could rise by as much as 5 degrees Celsius (estimated range of 1.4–5.8 degrees Celsius) over the next century, but increases could be higher than this in specific regions. Fourth, the Arctic ice cap will thin out and will melt further over the coming decades causing a rise in sea levels, affecting low lying island nations (such as Tuvalu and Kiribati in the South Pacific) and bring about the sea water encroachment of freshwater. Similarly, communities living on coastal river plains (such as in Bangladesh) are vulnerable to rising sea levels. Fifth, developing countries will suffer disproportionately from rapid climate change, in part because of their geography and in part because they lack the resources to respond. Sixth, human suffering in our region will increase from maladies such as heat stress and the spread of insect-borne tropical diseases south of the equator.

Seventh, geographic and seasonal patterns of rainfall will alter. Harvests in some of the world's principal food crops could drop over the next 100 years resulting in food insecurity. Farmers in tropical areas will be forced into higher and cooler mountainous areas, intensifying pressure on forests and wildlife habitat, as well as on the quality and quantity of water supplies. Eighth, many species will be unable to adapt or disperse to better suited locations because of the speed of climate change. Individual species may become extinct, and indeed entire ecosystems may vanish as their climatic niche disappears as habitats are lost or fragmented. Invasive weed species may overcome native plants and animals. In the special report issued in October 2018 on the impacts of global warming, the members of the committee reiterated that ongoing scientific research has only verified the 1994 findings and greater action towards addressing the deleterious effects of climate change needs to be taken immediately.[2]

1. United Nations, "United Nations Framework."
2. IPCC, "Special Report," 1–26.

Chapter 2 presented an understanding of conversion in terms of a set of cumulative decisions resulting in a shift from inauthenticity to authenticity. These possible transformations in the horizon of each person make themselves felt in communities and cultures and seek to overcome the distortion of sin and bias. They seek to orient us along the path of meaning, truth, value, beauty, and love when it comes to assessing how humans are to live in relationship to the natural world. Ecological conversion directs our feeling, thinking, valuing, and doing toward a path that will reverse actions that are causing a degradation of the environment, which threatens the whole planet including flora, fauna, and human ecosystems.

In the Catholic Christian tradition, the importance of ecological conversion has been encouraged by successive Popes. In more recent years, Pope Francis has released his comprehensive document *Laudato Si'*, the title words coming from the Canticle of Creation, a poem and prayer by St. Francis of Assisi. The implications of the Pope's statement are massive and multi-dimensional. If holistic human transformation requires a multiplicity of conversions, religious, moral, affective, intellectual and psychic, then a comprehensive understanding of ecological conversion requires addressing each one of these conversions as it pertains to our relationships with the natural world.

THE NATURAL WORLD AND RELIGIOUS CONVERSION

Chapter 3 spoke about religious conversion as a falling in love with God who has first loved us. Religious conversion is the movement from a radical lovelessness to a wholehearted loving of God and all that God has created and sustains in being. Lonergan remarks that religious faith places

> all other values in the light and the shadow of transcendent value. In the shadow, for transcendent value is supreme and incomprehensible. In the light, transcendent value links itself to all other values to transform, magnify, [and] glorify them. Without faith the originating value is man, and the terminal value is the human good man brings about. But in the light of faith, originating value is divine light and love while the terminal value is the whole universe. So, the human good becomes absorbed in the all-encompassing good. Where before an account of the human good related men to one another and to nature, now man's concern reaches beyond man's world to God's

world. Men meet not only to be together and to settle human affairs but also to worship. Human development is not only in skills and virtues but also in holiness. The power of God's love brings forth a new energy and efficacy in all goodness, and the limit of human expectation ceases to be the grave.[3]

Ecological conversion, therefore, understands God's love of us and our love of God as the ground of the relation between Creator, creature, and created. All that God creates is good just because God creates it. The creation reflects the glory of God and so potentially reveals God. God's creation is sacramental. The story of Moses and his encounter with the burning bush in the Book of Exodus symbolizes the sacramentality of life and creation.

> Moses was keeping the flock of his father-in-law Jethro, the priest of Midian; he led his flock beyond the wilderness, and came to Horeb, the mountain of God. There the angel of the Lord appeared to him in a flame of fire out of a bush; he looked, and the bush was blazing, yet it was not consumed. Then Moses said, "I must turn aside and look at this great sight, and see why the bush is not burned up." When the Lord saw that he had turned aside to see, God called to him out of the bush, "Moses, Moses!" And he said, "Here I am." Then he said, "Come no closer! Remove the sandals from your feet, for the place on which you are standing is holy ground." He said further, "I am the God of your father, the God of Abraham, the God of Isaac, and the God of Jacob." And Moses hid his face, for he was afraid to look at God. (Exod 3: 1–6)

First, we notice that Moses experiences a blazing tree which remains unharmed. The tree ablaze symbolizes the divine presence. Rainer Maria Rilke once stated that some mystics see all things ablaze with the divine fire. The holiness or unimaginable Otherness of God dwells amid his people and creation. A person or event does not stop being itself or existing according to its nature while it reflects the presence of the divine. The mystery is that God enlivens all things. We are encouraged to see God in all things.

Second, sacramentality is central to any understanding of Christianity. The pivotal sacramental moment of God in human history is the person of Jesus, for in Jesus the full plan of the Father is realized. Jesus is the living symbol of the Father's love in the world made present to

---

3. Lonergan, *Method*, 116.

humanity. The church is the sacramental community of Christ which re-members and is remembered by Christ. Since Jesus is the definitive mo-ment of God in history, the followers of Jesus are called to participate in the mission of Christ, an ongoing process of overcoming evil with good. Through the Spirit of Christ, we receive the gift of religious faith that appreciates all that Christ appreciates and has created. We are encour-aged by the gift of religious hope confident that God will bring about what God has planned for creation despite the forces of evil and other enormous barriers. Our valuing of God enables us to act with integrity and care toward the creation given to us by God for our sake.

Third, the fact that God communicates the divine mystery through human embodiment never fails to challenge us. The disciples experience Jesus' resurrection by seeing the wounds in his hands and his side. One of the reasons why this does not sit well with us is that we pre-reflectively and erroneously pit the material against the spiritual, the lower form against the higher form, and embodiment against the spirit. The mystery of the incarnation, the religious affirmation that Jesus is fully divine and fully human, asserts that we cannot become spiritual without the mate-rial. The spiritual is a higher integration of the material. The spiritual sublates the material. Fundamentally, sacramentality states that all reality is potentially the bearer of God's presence and the instrument of God's action. With the Psalmist we can pray: "the heavens are telling the glory of God; and the firmament proclaims his handiwork" (Ps 19:1).

Fourth, human beings need to cultivate a new sacramental imagi-nation, since the old imagination has become jaded by an overly ratio-nalistic scientific mindset, aided by the fast pace of city living, and by a calculative mentality that seeks to evaluative the natural world solely in terms of usefulness. A calculative mentality stands in stark contrast to appreciating creation as sacramental. To acquire a new sacramental imagination, we need to slow down, feel the difference between walk-ing on sand, grass, the forest floor, or on smooth granite that has been warmed by the sun's rays. We have to listen to the birds in the trees and the wind blowing across the canyons. Acquiring a sacramental imagina-tion means taking off the dullness of routines and being reinvigorated by new symbols.

The Natural World and Moral Conversion

Moral conversion changes the criterion of our decisions and actions from mere satisfaction to what is truly worthwhile and valuable. As far as the ecological crisis is concerned, choosing satisfactions over positive values means continuing to subscribe to patterns of behavior that serve our comfort while bringing harm to the natural and human world. According to Neil Ormerod and Cristina Vanin, the implications for an ecological conversion can be more precisely formulated by attending to the ecological aspects of the scale of values.[4] The scale of values presents us with an explanatory structure for a proper preferential relationship between values. The scale of values helps us "to unpack a range of ecological implications that confront the morally converted subject."[5]

Ormerod and Vanin begin with vital values. Vital values relate to all those elements of human living that help nourish our health and vitality: food production, fresh drinking, water reservoirs, and land for farming. The ecological crisis of our time has affected each of these critical elements adversely. Science has established a link between climate change and depleted food production. Increasingly extreme weather occurrences such as cyclones, floods, and droughts are severely affecting our ability to produce food. Toxic chemicals used to maximize production are finding their way into the water tables and creating other health problems for our citizenry.[6] The toxic consumption patterns of First World countries harm Third and Fourth World countries with oceans becoming filled with plastic and fish supplies depleting. It is the world's poorest who are most affected by these changing conditions.[7] Again, the impact on the biosphere negatively affects us all.

Social values concern the social arrangement within societies which provide the conditions for the delivery of vital values consistently and over a long period. These social arrangements include the use of technology, economy, and political persuasion. If the food supply is being affected, water reserves are drying up, and the environment is becoming more toxic, it is a sign that the good of order to deliver vital values has broken down. A commitment to the good of order that will reverse these devastating impacts will require a moral conversion to ground a better

4. Ormerod and Vanin, "Ecological Conversion," 336.

5. Ormerod and Vanin, "Ecological Conversion," 344.

6. Ormerod and Vanin, "Ecological Conversion," 336–37.

7. Francis, "Laudato Si'" par. 20–52.

use of technology, the economy, and the political realm. Technologies that harm the environment must be named, and alternative technologies created, even if they do not deliver as much profit in the short term. Economies that rely on fossil fuels for tax incomes ought to be reconsidered. Governments that supply benefits to fossil fuel companies, though scientists know that fossil fuels increase the level of harmful greenhouse gases, have the effect of not only disfiguring the functioning of the economy but also damaging the environment. Political leaders who make such decisions are capitulating to technological and economic circumstances and are advocating that in terms of decision making, the economy is the dog that wags the tail of the political community.

It is clear that the social order requires critique and direction, and so we come to the role of cultural values. Cultural values have a role to play in the dynamic of ecological conversion. Culture is a set of meanings and values that provide direction to our lives. Cultures potentially bring integrity to social arrangements so that we all have a better chance to grow into fully human persons. What is less understood is that there has been an enormous cultural shift in the past 2000 years in the West and indeed over the whole planet, concerning cultural forms in themselves. To explore the magnitude of this shift, the insights of Eric Voegelin postulate the cultural shift within societies and their history by speaking about three main typologies that influence cultural self-understanding: cosmological, anthropological, and soteriological.[8] When we talk about typologies, we are dealing with significant tendencies within society. No one society purely reflects any one kind of cultural typology and, indeed, sub-cultures may be numerous at any one time.

The cosmologically constituted cultural type that gives rise to cosmologically oriented societies adheres to the cycles and rhythms of the cosmos. The integrity of the individual comes from the integrity of the group, and the integrity of the group comes from its ability to conform to the rhythms of nature and be in tune with the cosmos. These societies have not yet thought about a divine radically beyond the world nor have they distinguished between natural and divine realities. They grasp all these realities as a unified whole.[9] We notice the reliance on a form of cosmic participation and a close connection between the human world and the natural world.

8. Ormerod, *Public God,* 29–31.
9. Hughes, *Transcendence,* 71.

Indigenous culture, such as the Australian Aborigines whose cultural presence for the past 80,000 years has been part of the history of Australia, is cosmological in form. Moreover, Ormerod notes "human destiny is viewed as subject to cosmic forces beyond their control, and human flourishing requires our conformity to the cosmic order. Hunter-gatherer peoples such as Australian Aboriginal peoples and the First Nation peoples of North America display these features, as do more settled rural and agricultural societies. This pole of cultural dialectic remains a permanently valid source of meaning and value for any society. Taken on its own, however, it tends to fatalism, pantheism, the stifling of the individual, and a static conception of the social order that is trapped within a static cosmic order."[10] Traditional leadership or authorities become the gatekeepers for society legitimated by reference to long-standing traditions. In such societies, people tend to orient their lives according to the seasons of the year and the cycles of the day. Mythology and ritual seek to represent the order of truth found in the cosmos.

In the Old and New Testaments, for example, we are dealing with people who were predominately shaped by cosmological elements. The fate of Israel is tied up with the right use of kingship according to the covenant, yet the kings fail to eliminate the high places and their pagan temples. The calamities that followed, both human and natural, are interpreted by the prophets as divine judgments on the kings and the people. As we walk through the gospels, we witness Jesus casting out evil spirits who have taken possession of people. The world of Jesus' time allowed for a multiplicity of beings with powers. Jesus and the early church did not automatically reject this worldview. They instead spoke about other spiritual beings, such as divine messengers as well as evil beings who seek to deceive people away from the worship of the one true God.[11]

By contrast, the anthropologically constituted cultural type adheres to the priority of the individual to change society. Thus, society gains its integrity from the individual, and the individual gains integrity through human reason and our ability to make decisions and choose the right direction. The emphasis is on the individual having the responsibility to follow the dictates of reason. Ormerod states that human existence "is ordered not by cosmic forces but by reason. For example, we can see some of the transition from the cosmological to the anthropological pole in the

10. Ormerod, *Public God*, 30.
11. Ormerod, *Re-Visioning the Church*, 236

shift from monarchies—as bearers of a divine right to rule based on the arbitrary privilege of birth—to democratic republican structures where majority rules and meritocracy prevails."[12]

In the Axial period (800–200 BCE), when the anthropologically constituted cultural elements began to emerge, the *cosmos* started to become the world, the universe, creation and the theatre of history, differentiated from the divine. This differentiation in meaning reached a new level by the industrial revolution and beyond. In anthropologically constituted societies dominant in the west for the past 600 years, there emerges a different understanding of cosmos, one that distinguishes the body from the soul, the finite from the infinite, immanence from transcendence and good from evil.[13] However, Glen Hughes notes that with this shift there remains a need to account for the sacramental presence of divine reality within finite reality since "nothing in this discovery negated the human experience of the oneness of reality."[14] What emerges is a conceptual autonomy of the finite and the infinite without a complete separation since the finite participates in the life of the infinite.[15] Even with the anthropological shift, it follows that some symbolic evocation of the divine presence within created reality continues to be healthy for human living, attested to in the sacramental character of certain places, things, and persons.[16] Without these symbolic evocations, we run the risk of draining the natural world of eternal significance, perpetuating a disenchantment, and negating the relationship between God, humans, and creation that was there from the beginning.[17]

The third of the cultural typologies is the soteriological influence. Soteriology is the experience of salvation, God's entry by grace into human history. Soteriology is the basis of religious conversion. We are currently at that point in human history where we have witnessed all three typologies. The gospel of Jesus Christ grounds the genuinely cultural meanings and values that inform our lives. The genuinely religious transcends or goes beyond the cultural to the extent that religion orients human beings

---

12. Ormerod, *Public God*, 30.

13. Hughes, *Transcendence*, 157.

14. Hughes, *Transcendence*, 157.

15. Hughes, *Transcendence*, 160.

16. Hughes, *Transcendence*, 161.

17. Hughes, *Transcendence*, 162.

toward divine mystery which transcends all cultural achievement and grounds all meaning, truth, goodness, and holiness.

The cosmological and the anthropological are two poles or principles within the identity of culture. They are another instance of a dialectic of contraries. When the tension maintains, and the insights and symbolizations of each principle are recognized, a dialectic of contraries endures in a both/and relationship. When the tension breaks and one principle dominates over the other, there occurs a dialectic of contradictories. Only the genuinely religious can ground the anthropological orientation in culture and help us to have a greater openness to the insights of cultures with cosmological tendencies. It is the soteriological influence which gives us the ability to find a taut creative tension between the best insights of both the cosmological and anthropological orientations. In other words, we in the West need to listen to the insights of Indigenous people if we are to reverse the devastating effects on our natural world.

Sadly, we find ourselves within a cultural form in the West that approximates a dominant anthropological principle and, according to Ormerod and Vanin, at the same time a "denigration of primal cultures that remain living witnesses to cosmological meanings and values."[18] We, therefore, negate the wisdom they hold out to us. Coupled with this is our own "cultural alienation from the rhythms and cycles of nature so that the natural world is seen simply as a point of extraction (mining and agribusiness) and a site for dumping our waste."[19]

This deforming outcome could be described as a hyper-anthropological tendency in which personal over-reaching and human ego-inflation damages our approach to all life, human and natural. Due to this deformation, we become estranged from the natural world and allow a technological paradigm and economic interests to rule our decision making in terms of how we live on the planet. The decisions of hyper-affluent people in First World countries fail to address and even contributed to the rising poverty of people in Third and Fourth World countries. Pope Francis pleads for a cultural revolution that will "recover the values and great goals swept away by our unrestrained delusions of grandeur."[20] Such an approach highlights an important truth: we are all interconnected.

---

18. Ormerod and Vanin, "Ecological Conversion," 341.

19. Ormerod and Vanin, "Ecological Conversion," 341.

20. Francis, "Laudato Si'" par. 114

Cultures and societies change because of persons of integrity. Personal value points to the importance of self-transcending persons who undergo conversion in their lives toward "ecological sustainability, of protecting our common home even though this may involve self-sacrifice in terms of lifestyle and life options."[21] One of the fundamental desires of the human mind and heart is consistency between knowing the truth and doing the truth, and in this case, "between knowing the environmental damage being done and the actions we need to take to diminish our personal contribution to that damage." This consistency must penetrate every aspect of our lives: "our food choices, travel options, forms of housing . . . patterns of energy consumption and so on."[22]

As cultural agents of change, each of us working individually or in groups must challenge and reverse two kinds of cultural deformations. The first cultural deformation is consumerism by which we measure our worth by our identification with the products we purchase. This deformation stands in dialectical opposition to a culture of intelligent self-limitation. The consumerist distortion not only goes against our inner dignity as children of God that He loves, but also manufactures in us a disordered desire for material goods as a way of satisfying our longings. Such consumerism means that the environment will become sick in direct proportion to the "violence in our own hearts, wounded by sin."[23]

The second cultural deformation is a widespread malaise that accompanies a culture of self-fulfillment. This deformation stands in dialectical opposition to an attitude of thankful generosity and thankful thinking. This deformation is grounded in the bare soil of competitive individualism dominated by an attitude that human life measures worth, solely by economic outputs and inputs, and fuels an anxiety concerned to fulfill one's needs for immediate gratification.[24] These factors become systemic with the enthronement of the commodity as central to our societies.

When it comes to finding a way forward, Pope Francis speaks about "ecological virtues." These virtues translate into practical habits and we evaluate their worth from our TV screens in programs such as the *War on Waste*. This program provides a number of practical insights to combat

21. Ormerod and Vanin, "Ecological Conversion," 343.

22. Ormerod and Vanin, "Ecological Conversion," 343.

23. Francis, "Laudato Si'" par. 2.

24. Gallagher, *Struggles of Faith*, 87.

ecological destruction: recycling water, reducing the use of plastic, carpooling, planting more trees, and reducing electricity consumed. Even all of these together as practical approaches will not be enough to stop environmental degradation. However, they will give us enough self-esteem to go on looking for more comprehensive solutions to this massive crisis.

The Natural World and Intellectual Conversion

Chapter 9 explained the meaning of intellectual conversion as a shift in the criteria for knowing from one that is dominated by extraversion to truth grasped through making an intelligent grasp of the data and a reasonable affirmation grounded in weighing the evidence. Ormerod and Vanin state four different ways that intellectual conversion can be critical to ecological conversion.

First, "intellectual conversion helps support moral conversion by allowing us to understand and affirm the full reality of values."[25] If we have been able to shift the criteria of our actions from mere satisfaction and agreeableness to real values, then we will intelligently affirm a scale or preference of values. The possibility of coming to an objective understanding of values increases through moral conversion. Without this objectivity of values, the claim that one's ecological statements are no less true that those opposed to them, becomes the argument of the day. Paraphrasing the words of Richard Flanagan in chapter 1, the truth reduces to arbitrariness, and the ability to enact the consequences of one's opinions depends on having the most power.

Second, "intellectual conversion facilitates the shift from descriptive to explanatory knowing."[26] Descriptive knowing is concerned with common sense knowledge, that is, a knowledge that practically relates to us. Explanatory knowing leads to knowledge which can grasp the complexity of systems and is more theoretical. It relates terms to each other so that we can explain structures within reality. It is counterproductive to try and understand the complexities of the climate systems through common sense knowing when what is required is more technical and explanatory knowledge.

Third, "intellectual conversion can contribute to the currently intense debates concerning the role of and nature of science, which has

25. Ormerod and Vanin, "Ecological Conversion," 344.
26. Ormerod and Vanin, "Ecological Conversion," 344.

arisen in relation to the overall debate on climate change."[27] The scientific community has been ill-prepared for the politicization of science that has occurred in the climate change debates. The inability of scientists to describe their findings in easy to understand terms also creates barriers in people to a full acceptance of these findings. Scientists have a role in reaching up to scientific objectivity through the scientific method, but they also have a role in communicating these findings in a way that persuades the ordinary person.

Fourth, "intellectual conversion is essential for the healing of the distortions present in our hyper-anthropological culture."[28] Our culture in the West prizes reason, yet we have distorted the meaning of reason through the single lens of usefulness that serves the block of domination and power in our societies. Reason and persuasion must be the tools of politicians, not unilateral power. One of the principal indications of intellectual conversion concerns the way we explain the ecological emergence and survival of systems within the biosphere. Any practical ethics that might inform public policy must endeavor to guide human action by rational persuasion and responsible love and consider the human and the non-human in all their rich complexity. This conversation requires politicians and other persons of power involving themselves in the complexity of the issues.

Lonergan's account of the order of the natural world helps us understand the relationship between the natural and human world, so that we are better able to tackle the enormous task of reversing the ecological crisis. Lonergan calls this process, emergent probability. Emergent probability tries to explain how classical laws and statistical laws reveal the "intrinsic intelligibility" of the universe. Classical laws are those laws that capture the necessary and causal functioning of the universe, for example, the law of gravity, Newtown's laws of motion, and the laws of thermodynamics. They avoid observing data other than what is relevant to universal insights. Statistical laws are those laws that capture the probable occurrence of events, their coincidence, their emergence, and their survival. Statistical laws reveal why novelty and change exist in systems. These laws deal with the data of concrete situations, the frequency of occurrence, and its relationship to the other dynamics around events.

27. Ormerod and Vanin, "Ecological Conversion," 345.

28. Ormerod and Vanin, "Ecological Conversion," 345.

Lonergan moved away from a Darwinian emphasis on evolution to the emergence and survival of things through their being part of schemes of recurrence.[29] There are two kinds of schemes of recurrence: natural and human. The notion of a scheme of recurrence helps us to grasp the relationship between regularity and the conditions needed to sustain regularity. A thing does not just emerge in isolation but emerges within an already existing system depending on that system for its survival. Its survival depends on many conditions being fulfilled. Each scheme connects to other schemes in a complex interconnected whole. We might represent the scheme in this way: if A occurs, then B occurs, and if B occurs than C . . . until we are back to A. For B to occur then, the probability of its survival is dependent on the probability of some other scheme that destroys, replaces, changes or otherwise interferes with its integral functioning. The recurrence of other conditions influences each reaction in the system. These interacting systems and the conditions for each element of the system can be very complicated. The more we can understand the complexity of interacting systems and their schemes of recurrence, the more we can predict how changing one or many elements of schemes may adversely affect the whole environment. Such knowledge requires a sustained dedication to intellectual patterns of experience and an openness to theoretical and explanatory ways of knowing.

For example, the complex system which makes up the circulation of the water on our planet conditions the possibility of the nitrogen cycle of plants. These systems condition the possibility for the digestive systems of animal life to arise. We can now begin to appreciate the meaning of emergent probability and schemes of recurrence for the ecological health of the planet. Things emerge within a system due to novelty, and if that emerging event is to survive, then the conditions for its survival needs to be repeated over and over again. Emergence is dependent on the continuing functioning of prior schemes. At the same time, development cannot progress until later schemes have transformed the previous schemes. The relationship between prior and later schemes is delicate. Emergence is probable since the random accumulation of conditions occurs around frequencies, that is, how many times and how often conditions occur for elements within the scheme to establish themselves. Once a cycle sets itself at one level into a recurrent scheme, then, there is an increased probability for the emergence of the next level in the recurrent scheme.

29. Dalton, *Theology for the Earth*, 143–47; Lonergan, *Insight*, 141, 144–62.

This account of the emergence and survival in the physical universe are two components in an account of natural processes that highlight both the complexity and the fragility of the natural world. It goes some way to explaining how human actions can interfere with natural cycles. When the conditions for the survival of elements in the scheme are harmfully affected, the whole scheme of recurrence can be potentially affected. It is this kind of understanding that implicitly grounds the finding of the scientific community, especially when they correlate climate change with the rise of greenhouse gases.

Finally, when we speak of human schemes of recurrence, we are alluding to human insight, whether practical, reflective, or deliberative insights. Practical insights grounded in judgments of truth and value maintain the schemes of human living and are responsible for transformative new schemes in our cities and our natural world. Their emergence and survival depend on acts of intelligence and wise choices.

Following Lonergan, many thinkers have grounded their insights regarding ecological conversion in the interconnection of human and non-human worlds, through exploring the notion of schemes of recurrence and its relationship to novelty and change.[30] Charles Hefling puts the general orientation of Christian ethics toward environmental matters in this way:

> The earth (is) a single organically interdependent ecological system, within which even the self-directed course of human civilization . . . is only one element. . . . It would follow that decisions to alter the cycles and patterns and ongoing processes that are actually occurring at a given time will be right or wrong depending on how they affect not the human race in isolation, much less any particular group or individual, but the being and functioning of the whole. Such an argument is entirely consonant with the theological affirmation . . . that what God creates, sets in order, approves, and loves is in the first instance not any particular being or kind of being but the dynamically interrelated entirety of finite being. Accordingly, to set the common good, not simply of human society but of the earth, ahead of any particular good is to take responsibility for co-creating what God creates. But such a responsibility demands intelligence. Adequately to understand the actual circumstances and probable consequences of any human act or practice that alters what is

30. Crysdale and Ormerod, *Creator God*, 19–39.

called the balance of nature—which is to say, any act or practice whatever—is clearly an enormous task.[31]

The Natural World and Psychic Conversion

If our imagination regarding the earth is not wholesome, then our decisions on behalf of ourselves and the earth will also be unwholesome. For Lonergan, symbols are vital to human living. Symbols help the human psyche to set up an internal communication between mind and heart as well as between our conscience and the body.[32] For example, when we take a newborn child into our arms, there is a joy released in us and that joy points towards the preciousness and value of human life. The child is a symbol of something precious: the preciousness and vulnerability of life. Further, the child's birth communicates to the believer the wonder and greatness of God. The child actualizes in us a meeting with God through its symbolic power. Pope Francis has made it very clear that we are not to be disconnected from the natural world but interconnected, joined in "a splendid universal communion."[33] We sustain this feeling of interconnection can only through a symbolism which changes the way we feel about the natural world.

Most people would agree that science has dramatically improved the living standards of humanity. Health care, communications, mechanical, and virtual technology have advanced beyond our wildest expectations and have improved our ability to grow food, create tools, heal bodies, and build our cities. While science has an essential place in shaping our understanding of the world and how we are to live in it, the body of knowledge discovered in science cannot bear the weight of human meaning that humankind has put on its shoulders. However, as early as the eighteenth century, the aberrant myth about the cosmos or universe as a machine, specifically, a clock with its physical scientific laws, had other spinoffs in the human and social world. People began to imagine the giant machine of nature guided by the Great Engineer, while scientists viewed nature as a factory of labor and a storehouse of raw materials for human use. Thomas McPartland notes that "when the cosmos is a machine of matter in motion, operating according to mathematically

31. Hefling, "Creation," 253–54.
32. Lonergan, *Method*, 66–67.
33. Francis, "Laudato Si'" par. 221.

determined mechanical laws, then the polis is . . . a machine to be con-structed, refined and reformed by Enlightenment social engineering."[34] Utilizing such a myth, "scientific progress would propel moral progress," and a virtuous society would be created spontaneously, modeled on the precision of geometry resulting in a culture that does "not seem to do justice to the evil propensities of unredeemed humanity," often leading to an all-encompassing commitment to practicality alone.[35]

This symbol of the cosmos as machine reflects an understanding of the created order; both non-human and human determined solely by laws systematically worked out by science. This approach substitutes a practical reason guided by genuine human values by an approach to reason underpinned by calculative thinking. There can be no doubt that the machine as a symbol for organic life has a valid place in understand-ing the natural world. Machine metaphors employed in synthetic biology leading to expressions such as "genetically engineered machines" and "genetic circuits" highlight how the organism functions.[36] The problem is an over-emphasis on the machine metaphor that prioritizes the eth-ics of instrumental rationality. Such an ethic is concerned more with the means of achieving practical desired results, and not with questions such as ultimate value, interconnections, and the purposefulness of creation. Both machine symbolism and instrumentalism fall short of and stand in stark contrast to the idea of a cosmos that reflects the goodness and glory of God and a cosmos that has finality built into it by the Creator. The predominance of the machine symbolism, which leads to a machine imagination, grounds disordered attitudes that have much to do with our current ecological crisis.

For these reasons, the symbolism of mother, the web of connection, and the importance of home are a necessary corrective to the domination of the machine symbol. Songwriters employ such symbols powerfully in the lyrics of our favorite songs. In his song, *Wild Montana Skies*, John Denver tells the tale of a man in tune with the natural world. He begins as an orphan boy and is raised by his uncle to love and work the land. It is through his love and knowledge of the wilderness and the land that he learns his identity. Though he travels to the city to find work, he later comes back to the land for there exists something in the wilderness that

---

34. McPartland, *Lonergan*, 128.

35. McPartland, *Lonergan*, 129.

36. Boldt, "Machine Metaphors," 1–3.

he finds unique. The "wild wind" was his brother, the "wild Montana sky" gives him a sense of home, and he discovers that his true vocation is to listen and speak for the wilderness. Our feelings and memories are immediately drawn to Indigenous communities, such as the Australian Aborigines, who speak about the earth as a mother and their home being "country," a shorthand term for their close relationship to the natural world from which derives laws and social customs, sustenance, and a purpose for living.

Pope Francis in *Laudate Si'* uses the symbol of communion, "our common home," who is like "a sister with whom we share our life and a beautiful mother who opens her arms to embrace us."[37] He grieves the fact that "the earth, our home, is beginning to look more and more like an immense pile of filth."[38] He affirms hearts filled with "tenderness, compassion and concern for our fellow human beings" since all in life is interconnected. This kind of heart gives rise to the conviction that "this sense of fraternity excludes nothing and no one . . . since every act of cruelty towards any creature is contrary to human dignity."[39] Further, our humanity is grounded in elements of the natural world found in our bodies[40] in such a way that "nature cannot be regarded as something separate from ourselves or as a mere setting in which we live. We are all part of nature, included in it and thus in constant interaction with it."[41] This symbolic imaginative corrective highlights the importance of the bonds of connection. In this way, we find the motivation to engage in an ethical reflection and a collective action that restores balance. By so doing, we also come to the aid of our brothers and sisters who suffer from economic and technological poverty. For Pope Francis, environmental justice, social justice, and food shortages are part and parcel of the same problem, namely, overconsumption in the First World, the quest for unlimited profits, hearts full of greed, and the lack of intelligent self-limitation.

For Pope Francis, the mentor for ecological conversion is the Italian medieval saint, Francis of Assisi. Here is where religious conversion heals psychic distortion through an imagination that prizes the communion of all things in God and the sacramentality of life. By reading the writings

37. Francis, "Laudato Si'" par. 1.

38. Francis, "Laudato Si'" par. 21.

39. Francis, "Laudato Si'" par. 92.

40. Francis, "Laudato Si'" par. 2.

41. Francis, "Laudato Si'" par. 139.

of St. Francis, imitating his love of the poor, and his love for all creatures of the natural world, and seeking his prayerful intercession, Pope Francis hopes that all people of religious faith might give themselves to the path of ecological conversion.[42] Through the trusting act of prayer and the imitation of the saints, our imagination for God's purpose in creation and our part within creation inspires us to reverse the effects of human evil perpetrated on the natural world. We become like Francis of Assisi, drawn to God through creation, "protectors of God's handiwork" through "a loving awareness that we are not disconnected from the rest of creatures, but joined in a splendid universal communion."[43]

According to Yeongseon Kim, at the heart of a renewed Franciscan eco-spirituality are several elements to help bring about an ecological conversion. First, Francis of Assisi was always keenly aware of God's self-emptying in Jesus to assume the condition of a servant.[44] In his own life, Francis sought to be a servant to all and a master to none. This aspect of his spiritual toolbox correlates well with proper stewardship of creation that renounces a superiority of human over non-human, a separation of humans from the rest of creation, and a perception of nature as merely a useful resource. This "downward movement" of richness to poverty is also evident in Francis's renunciation of power, wealth, domination, and possessions. He chose for himself and his followers to be poor and to find companionship with the poor.

Second, the life of Francis of Assisi is a movement from exclusion to inclusion. He includes the lepers, the despised of the society of his time.[45] He includes Sultan Malik al-Kamil and his Muslim fellow believers, considered to be unbelieving profaners in medieval Christian society. His encounter with the Sultan at Damietta affects him profoundly, leading him to implore his fellow brothers not quarrel, judge, or argue with people of different faiths, especially Muslims, but rather practice being meek, peaceful, and humble, always being courtesy and gentle toward them.

Third, a true ecological conversion in the spirit of Francis extends love to all creatures.[46] Francis eloquently expresses these movements of

---

42. Francis, "Laudato Si'" par. 1, 10–12, 66, 87, 91, 125, 221.

43. Francis, "Laudato Si'" par. 220.

44. Yeongseon, "St Francis," 54.

45. Yeongseon, "St Francis," 62–66.

46. Yeongseon, "St Francis," 68–72.

the heart in the Canticle of Creatures. All creatures share a common fate with human beings. All are contingent and one day will decay and pass away. Francis chooses to call them "brother" and "sister" reflecting the importance of this relationship to humans, their relationship among themselves, and the whole universe.

13

Ecological Conversion
and *The Lord of the Rings*

IN THE WORLD OF cinema, there is emerging a vast array of films addressing the impact of climate change and the broader problem of environmental degradation. Two films that immediately come to mind in the documentary genre are *An Inconvenient Truth* and *Gasland*. *An Inconvenient Truth* is a 2006 American documentary directed by Davis Guggenheim about the former United States Vice President Al Gore's campaign to educate citizens about global warming. *Gasland* is a 2010 American documentary written and directed by Josh Fox. The film focuses on communities in the United States affected by natural gas drilling and, specifically, a method of horizontal drilling into shale formations known as hydraulic fracturing or 'fracking.' The film is a critical mobilizer for the anti-fracking movement.

By contrast, in Australia, the ABC production of *War on Waste* hosted by Craig Reucassel guides viewers into owning the problem of waste in our cities. We create waste through the use of excessive plastic and other petroleum-based products that are making their way into our oceans and waterways. The proliferation of coffee cups in a coffee obsessed society increases waste products. People discard plastics and other chemical components of mobile phones regularly for newer versions. We are finding it harder and harder to recycle other computer technology-based products. Reucassel tries to offer some small step but practical solutions for reducing our carbon and waste footprint. In this chapter, rather than choose one of the documentaries that speak to environmental issues, we turn to the fantasy trilogy, *The Lord of the Rings*.[1]

Ecology, *The Lord of the Rings*, and *Laudato Si'*

These films present viewers with a choice since the trilogy of *The Lord of the Rings* was first written in fictional prose by J. R. R. Tolkien and only subsequently translated into film. In this process, the rich descriptive resonance of the prose has been cut back to deliver a tight screenplay. According to Kelly, Tolkien would have considered the film version of his narrative a far diminished form for communicating the fantasy story. His preferred form of communication was always the narrative word.[2] Nevertheless, the story belongs to the genre of fairy-story in which the human imagination reigns and where awakened desire is the ground on which one stands.[3] Fantasy fiction immediately draws the viewer to the kind of stories characteristic of mythological texts in which the hero must accept a moral quest and face multiple dangers before achieving the quest, undergoing a personal transformation, and returning to contribute in a new way to society.

Tolkien's masterful creation brings the reader into the realm of *Faerie*, an enchanted world where we discover reality in all its depth. In this trilogy, the specific stories of this fairy realm are those surrounding the inhabitants of Middle Earth in the Third Age, when the Dark Lord Sauron rises to dominate the inhabitants of Middle Earth, the quest to destroy his ring of power, and the various communities and characters whose lives are deeply impacted by these events. Ecological themes and virtues may be both explicit and implicit, but they abound. The screenplay carries a message of integral ecology and sharply contrasts this worldview to ecocide. An exploration of the protagonists will help describe the ecological vision comparing its spiritual and moral insights to those presented by Pope Francis in *Laudato Si'*.

1. The Trilogy includes three separate works: *The Fellowship of the Ring*; *The Two Towers*; and *The Return of the King*. The three prose volumes were published in the 1950s.

2. Kelly, *Thinking Faith*, 233.

3. Kelly, *Thinking Faith*, 231–32.

The Lady Galadriel and the Elves

The Lady Galadriel and the Elves are a group within the trilogy who are said to be the designated stewards of the Third Age. The Third Age is the period in which the events of Middle Earth and the final thrust by Sauron for complete power becomes central to the lives of all who live in that period and place. The first film in the trilogy, *The Fellowship of the Ring*, begins with a prelude spoken by Lady Galadriel whom the audience has yet to meet. She describes the mood or disposition of this Third Age in dark tones. In foreboding words, we pick up the sensitivity of the Elves and the Lady Galadriel to the stirrings within the natural world of Middle Earth, either for good or for evil. The Lady is keenly in tune with the dark mood of Middle Earth, a mood she senses through the sound of the earth, the taste of the water, and the smell in the air. Here is a sensitive being who is attuned to the natural world through every fiber of her person, in such a way that any decision made for good or evil she feels through nature, such is the level of interconnection between herself, others, and nature.

The Lady alerts us to the wretched darkness that has come over the whole land after the forging of the Great Rings in the Second Age. The rings are nineteen in all, given variously to Elves, Dwarves, and Men. However, one secret ring is forged by the Dark Lord Sauron to control all the other rings and into that ring Sauron has poured all his malice and cruelty in order to dominate the land and all its inhabitants. One by one, the lands fall to his power until the last alliance between Men and Elves is formed to stop him and regain freedom for Middle Earth. An alliance against Sauron fight their last battle on the slopes of Mount Doom. Though King Elendil is struck down by Sauron, still his son Isildur, King of Gondor, fights Sauron and cuts off his ring finger, thus defeating him on the slopes. Isildur takes the ring and, with Elrond, goes to the molten cave of Mount Doom, the only place where they can destroy the ring. Instead of destroying it, Isildur chooses to keep it, his mind already clouded by the evil of the ring. Later, Orcs ambush and kill him and the ring falls into a river. It is the fate of the ring that will be become a dominant theme throughout the trilogy. The ring symbolizes the worst of dominating and subjugating power. It represents a deformation of the will to control taken to its absolute limits.

In the first film, we are in the period of the Third Age, and we pick up the story with Elves feeling their inability to stem the tide of evil. Later on, the Fellowship, a party chosen at Rivendell to make sure the ring of power is destroyed, come upon the woods of Lothlorien. There is found the beautiful city of Caras Galadhon, home to the Elves, located in the Mallorn forests, the tallest trees of Middle Earth. At first sight, the film introduces the audience to a feeling for the city itself characterized by an interconnection between the natural world and the beings who inhabit it. In this Third Age, there are three Elvish Kingdoms, and two of them located among trees. Lothlorien, set among the trees, is beautiful just because the Elves love the trees. At the center of ecological conversion is a love for the natural world.

At one stage, Frodo, the ring bearer, offers the ring to the Lady Galadriel. Frodo is yet to feel in his body and psyche the full debilitating effects of the ring and so is able at this stage to give it away. The Lady gives Frodo an insight into what would happen if she were to take possession of the ring. She tells Frodo that upon receiving the ring, she would start to change into a treacherous and powerful being, uncaring for others. At the epicenter of all ecological destruction is the desire to dominate and control. Even someone as good and pure as the Lady Galadriel would become treacherous and terrible to all creation, natural and non-natural, were she to possess the ring.

Throughout Pope Francis's *Laudato Si'*, the reader is introduced to the notion of ecosystems having an intrinsic value independent of their usefulness. The Elves witness to an interdependence akin to a sacred wholeness, especially in their beloved and beautiful Mallorn forests. The Elves prove themselves to possess such a tenderness to the natural world and, by standing with the armies of Rohan at Helms Deep, demonstrate their love for men even when their time has come to an end, and could have quite easily sailed to their Eternal home without involvement in the affairs of men. In the words of Francis:

> A sense of deep communion with the rest of nature cannot be real if our hearts lack tenderness, compassion and concern for our fellow human beings. It is clearly inconsistent to combat trafficking in endangered species while remaining completely indifferent to human trafficking, unconcerned about the poor, or undertaking to destroy another human being deemed unwanted. This compromises the very meaning of our struggle for the sake of the environment. It is no coincidence that, in the canticle in which Saint Francis praises God for his creatures, he goes on to say: "Praised be you my Lord, through those who give pardon for your love." Everything is connected. Concern for the environment thus needs to be joined to a sincere love for

our fellow human beings and an unwavering commitment to resolving the problems of society.[4]

Treebeard, the Ents, and Fangorn Forest

Among the plant kingdom, there are the Ents: Treebeard, his fellow Ents, and their home in Fangorn Forest. In the second film of the trilogy, *The Two Towers*, the audience is introduced to the Ents and Treebeard. Ents are very ancient beings whose physical appearance is similar to trees. When Merry and Pippin meet Treebeard, they mistaken him for a tree up until he turns to speak to them. The Ents share a relationship with the other trees of Fangorn Forest. What is more important to the drama of the film is that they have not met Hobbits before, which immediately put Merry and Pippin at a disadvantage.

At one-point, Merry calls Treebeard, a shepherd of the forest. To call Treebeard a shepherd is significant since there are qualities of shepherding realized in Treebeard that empower him to overcome evil. These qualities include integrity, nurturance, and courage. Treebeard is already aware of the evil at work in his beloved forest. He describes the actions of Orcs in the forest in terms that reflect his sensitivity to the pain that the trees are experiencing at their hands. The actions of the Orcs are putting Fangorn on the path of environmental destruction in the service of the Dark Lord and his co-conspirator Saruman. The wood of the forest is being used to forge armaments for their evil purposes without regard for the destruction of living beings. Treebeard describes the impact on the psyche of the plants in terms of reactive anger fomenting within them at the disregard shown them. Here is a witness to environment degradation bringing about a backlash from the natural world.

Finally, the Ents decide to lead Merry and Pippin out of the forest but without getting involved in the fight at hand. Treebeard asserts that it is not their war. As Treebeard is instructed by Merry and Pippin to take them south, he becomes aware of the ecological devastation at first hand and realizes what is at stake. Treebeard feels for the first time the impact of evil on his friends and neighbors in the forest and knows that neither he nor the brotherhood can remain separated from the events of Middle Earth. For Treebeard, the forest is their common home; a place shared by Ents, other trees and all kinds of creatures that look to it for their survival.

---

4. Francis, "Laudato Si'" par. 91.

These had become his friends, and now their home had been destroyed by those who should have known better. He gathers his fellow Ents for the assault on Isengard.

The Hobbits and Hobbiton

The setting of Hobbiton and the life of the Hobbits who dwell there is a scene of pastoral harmony. Our first meeting with the Hobbits and their Shire is at the beginning of the first film in the trilogy. They are a group who love to work with their hands, growing their fruit trees and vegetables. It would seem that their style of agriculture is sustainable and self-sufficient. The primary value of nature is felt to be its beauty and nurturance and not merely some brute usefulness.

Departing from the text of the novel, the screenwriters do not include the destruction of the Shire found at the end of the third book in the trilogy, *The Return of the King*. In the prose version, the Hobbits return to the Shire to find it manipulated and destroyed at the hands of Saruman's cohort. However, we do get a feeling for the tremendous love that Frodo and, by association, the other Hobbits have for the Shire when, in Lothlorien, Frodo is invited to look into a basin of water by the Lady Galadriel. The Lady tells him that the images from the water might reveal both the events of the past and the future. In the water, Frodo sees the Shire in ruins, buildings burning, bodies lying dead, Orcs enslaving the Hobbit folk, and their beloved natural world turned to ruin. Frodo is left horrified at the sight of these foreboding events, so much does he love his home. His compassion for the Shire is deep. It is the memory of the Shire that sustains Frodo and Sam when they are exhausted and vulnerable within the land of Mordor. Sam, in a spirit of encouragement reminds Frodo of the orchards in bloom, the birds nesting in the hazel thicket, the summer barley, and the first of the strawberries. The natural beauty of the Shire is ever on his mind

Sauron and Saruman

The malevolent figures of Sauron and Saruman and their destructive impact on the environment cast a darkness over the whole story. There was a time when both Sauron and Saruman were not evil. Sauron is an ancient figure who goes back to the First and Second Age. However, then, he enlisted the help of the Elves of Eregion to create the Rings of Power, while secretly forging the one Ring on Mount Doom to dominate all the other nineteen rings. By the Third Age, his whole reason to live is to dominate and increase in power. Throughout the films, Sauron separates himself by physical proximity from the one ring, but no one can ultimately separate him from the one ring of power. He has no physical human shape, no face, no voice, and no corporeal existence. He takes the form of the flaming eye looking out over the lands from his territory of Mordor and beyond, searching for his ring, while his ring searches for him.

Sauron is a symbol of evil, seemingly unredeemable and wholly given over to the pursuit of dominating power, willing to enslave or kill all who are in his path. His actions are worked out according to an instrumentalization of rationality. For Sauron, reason has become synonymous with abusive power and not with intelligent living. The materials of nature are forged to manufacture the ring only so that it might rule and dominate the other rings for him. There is a legitimate place for the usefulness and practical application of knowledge. However, such knowledge becomes a weapon in Sauron's hands to overpower and dominate. In the first film, Gandalf reads to Frodo the fiery letters written into the inner band of the ring in the elvish tongue. Gandalf is well aware of their evil intent when spoken in the original tongue and so translates the words into the common tongue for Frodo. The message is centrally concerned for the domination of others.

The evil of Sauron is also represented in his servants, the Nine Nazgul, led by the Lord of the Nazgul known as the Witch King of Angmar. The Lord Nazgul lives in his tower at Minas Morgul. The Nazgul were once men but have since lost the minds of men and by the power of Sauron are given over to the evil of the ring. They live solely to focus on the one ring of power. Not only have the deformations of Sauron's actions taken shape in these evil servants, but his actions also reflect on the land of Mordor itself, where Sauron's and the Lord Nazgul's fortress are located. The devastation of Mordor, stripped of most flora and fauna and its putrid smell of death, covers the land until the slopes of Mount Doom, from which emerge seas of molten lava. This ashen environment is an image of ecocide. Evil destroys the natural landscape. It is no wonder that Aragon, Isildur's heir, the rightful king to the Throne of Gondor calls Mordor, "the Black Land." According to Doron Darnov, Mordor seems to have little of the machinery and factories of war-making when seen by Frodo and Sam, until Tolkien tells us that the great slave-worked fields were to be found to the south of Mordor. Frodo and Sam see the remains of mines and forges but only as remnants of land long since stripped of its agricultural basis through mistreatment and abuse.[5] Mordor is the final stage to which Saruman's Isengard is heading.

The other antagonist akin to Sauron is the wizard Saruman, who through the first two parts of the trilogy progressively becomes corrupted by the power that Sauron offers him and turns to evil through fear of not being able to stop Sauron. In the shadow of the Orthanc Tower, especially in the second film of the trilogy, Saruman advances his pretensions to power by building an army of Orcs, crossing Orcs with Elves who had previously been captured and tortured and Orcs with Goblins. Around the walls of Orthanc, Saruman builds a large factory complex to manufacture all manner of weaponry to assist him in his war against Middle Earth on behalf of Sauron. He breeds a faster and stronger version of Orcs than even Sauron has produced. They can live in the light of day, and they feed on human flesh. Saruman states his intentions: the destruction of the forests, the erection of the machinery of war, and the overcoming of all opposition. Nature has no intrinsic value for Saruman. Nature is reduced to a source for industrial fuel, while technological progress harnesses the elements of nature for the sake of war. In both the actions of Sauron and Saruman, we witness the making of a deformed political society where the military complex is the first order of the day. Pope Francis states that "once we lose our humility and become enthralled with the possibility of limitless mastery over everything, we inevitably end up harming society and the environment."[6]

Both Sauron and Saruman represent what *Laudato Si'* calls the "dominant technocratic paradigm."[7] Their use of power is never considered by them in terms of responsible and reasonable choice but instead through a will to dominate others. This dangerous quest for power drives their desire for knowledge and the technical manipulation of the environment. Sauron and Saruman lust for complete power over Middle Earth and will use all technological means to attain it. Sauron channels this lust through the one ring itself. The ring is his greatest technological weapon. It is apparent that the distorted value of supreme domination and power at the center of Sauron's choices serves only to enslave and

5. Darnov, "Mind of Metal and Wheels," 13–14.

6. Francis, "Laudato Si'" par. 224

7. Francis, "Laudato Si'" par. 104.

bend everyone's will to his interests. Sauron is a pure representation of individual bias. His actions carry a moral lesson for us all regarding the environment: recovering from ecological disaster requires that we examine the direction, goals, meaning, and social implications of technological and economic growth.[8] Unless we are transformed in our minds and hearts by beginning to feel, understand, and value the interconnection of everything on the planet, "life gradually becomes a surrender to situations conditioned by technology, itself viewed as the principal key to the meaning of existence."[9] Sauron and Saruman are so drenched in the stench of domination that they cannot engage in simple daily gestures which break with the violence, exploitation, and selfishness. In the end, a world of exacerbated consumption is at the same time a world that mistreats life in all its forms.[10]

The Dwarves

From the very beginning of the trilogy, Gimli, son of Balin, part of the race of Dwarves comes into the story. Gimli comes to Rivendell to join the quest and becomes part of the fellowship. The dwarves are worth mentioning for they come from a race of great rulers, miners, and artisans of the mountain halls. Their origins go back to a pre-history and the beginnings of time when Aule, keen to taste the joy of having children to pass on his lore and crafts, and impatient or unwilling to allow Iluvatar to work out what to do next, creates the dwarves. When Iluvatar discovers this, he accedes to the pleas of Aule to spare the Dwarves. However, from that time on the relationship between dwarf and nature is very different from the relationship between the children of Iluvatar and nature. Thus, the Dwarves live under the mountain rather than on the surface of Middle Earth.

In the Second Age, Sauron gives the Dwarves three rings of power, and though they do not come directly under the spell of the one ring, nevertheless, the three rings linked to the one ring feed their ambition and greed for wealth. During the Third Age, the greed of the Dwarves leads them to mine for mithril but to an unsafe depth below the mountain. They awake the Balrog in Moria, an ancient creature who breathes

8. Francis, "Laudato Si'" par. 109.

9. Francis, "Laudato Si'" par. 110.

10. Francis, "Laudato Si'" par. 230.

fire from its mouth as well as wielding a sword of fire. The Balrog drives the Dwarves out of their home and slays their leader, King Durin VI, and so the Balrog is after that episode called Durin's Bane. It is a reminder of how a lack of respect for the natural world can give way to an even worse unintended consequence such as the non-recovery of the natural world.

The disastrous outcome for the Dwarves is symbolic of the failure to live by the practice of intelligent self-limitation. There is no denying that the Dwarves need mithril to make coats to act as physical protection. However, Pope Francis could have been talking to the Dwarves when he states that "we need also to think of containing growth by setting some reasonable limits and even retracting our steps before it is too late."[11] Such excess has an effect on other parts of the world, and though this is more difficult to understand in the context of Middle Earth, certainly in a more general sense, lowering consumption levels and aspiring to levels of sufficiency will have its positive effect on other parts of the world. What needs to change is an inner attitude of "moderation and the capacity to be happy with little."[12]

Gandalf the Wizard

The other protagonist of central importance is Gandalf the Grey. In the Third Age, Gandalf is sent to Middle Earth to protect it from the domination of Sauron and to facilitate the coming together of an alliance that would engage in "the battle of our time." He is not a king or steward of any kingdom, but he is resolute to defend all the inhabitants of Middle Earth and stand beside all who care for Middle Earth. His care extends to the human and natural world. His stewardship consists of looking after or holding in trust that which he is sworn to care. He finds a simple delight in visiting the Shire, fraternizing with his Hobbit friends, and being in an environment of calm and beauty where the natural world and Hobbit folk live in harmony. As a wizard, he communicates with Treebeard and understands the anguish and anger of the Forest destroyed at the hands of Saruman. In the final scenes of *The Return of the King*, Gandalf receives a reward for his stewardship by being allowed to sail with the Elves to the undying lands of Valinor, relinquishing his role of steward in the new Age of Men.

11. Francis, "Laudato Si'" par. 193.
12. Francis, "Laudato Si'" par. 222.

The Men of Rohan and the White Tree

Many other protagonists in the trilogy highlight the wonderful relationship between humans and nature. The world of Rohan led by men, called Rohirrims, meaning "horse-lords," reveals the symbiotic relationship between men and their horses. The horse is more than a beast of burden, in stark contrast to the dragons that bear the Wring Wraiths. The breeding and riding of horses became an art form for these people.

There is also the White Tree of Gondor. The White Tree of Gondor stands as a symbol of the health of Gondor in the Court of the Fountain in Minas Tirith. The White Tree also appears as a part motif upon Gondor's flag and throughout its heraldry. It has a very symbolic meaning for the people of Gondor, their king, and their future. The Tree is originally planted as a sapling brought back to Minas Tirith long ago. However, when Sauron captures Minas Tirith in a previous age, he destroys the tree. This destroyed tree stands in the courtyard as a symbol of his continuous dark power. At the end of *The Return of the King*, when Sauron is defeated, the old dead tree is removed, and a new sapling discovered by King Aragon on the slopes of Mindolluin is planted, signifying a new era of peace and harmony among the people of Gondor and all others in Middle Earth. Its growth holds out the guarantee that all sins of the past, especially the commitments by the people of Gondor, are forgiven, and a new age has begun.

Other Hobbits

There are also the hobbits, Frodo and Samwise Gamgee, the loyal friend to Frodo. We do not pick up from the film what Frodo feels or thinks about the pastoral aspects of the Shire. We know that he loves the Shire, especially for its simplicity and nurturance. What we do know is that Frodo is a Hobbit of exceptional moral character: loyal to friends, self-sacrificing, merciful to Gollum, committed to the good, and determined to finish the quest. Frodo must shift from a Shire-focused love of the land to a Middle-Earth focus.

Samwise Gamgee is at heart a pastoralist. His mind turns ever towards his beloved Shire where the seasons beckon the preparation of the soil and the planting of new crops until their harvest. It becomes one of the great strengths of the trilogy to be invited into the lives of such humble people as the Hobbits, the lowly of the world, tasked with such great burdens for the sake of the whole of Middle Earth. Tolkien weaves lowly characters of minimal social status into the story to demonstrate courage in the face of unbeatable odds. The destruction of the ring of power comes about by the mediation of those of little importance. Such humility of heart is somewhat cultivated, in their case, through a pastoral relationship with the land. Pope Francis would have been speaking of such communities when he wrote:

> Love for society and commitment to the common good are outstanding expressions of a charity which affects not only relationships between individuals but also "macro-relationships, social, economic and political ones." That is why the church set before the world the ideal of a "civilization of love." Social love is the key to authentic development: "In order to make society more human, more worthy of the human person, love in social life—political, economic, and cultural—must be given renewed value, becoming the constant and highest norm for all activity." In this framework, along with the importance of little everyday gestures, social love moves us to devise larger strategies to halt environmental degradation and to encourage a "culture of care" which permeates all of society.[13]

Gollum

Finally, there is the character of Gollum. At the beginning of the third film of the trilogy, *The Return of the King*, the audience understands for the first time some of the backstory of Gollum and the friendship between Deagol and Smeagol. One day they ware fishing together and following a strange series of events, Deagol finds the ring of power. Smeagol immediately desires the ring for himself, claiming the ring for his birthday. They disagree. Finally, Smeagol kills Deagol and takes the ring. This act of homicide and the possession of the ring turns Smeagol into Gollum who ends up living under the mountain in darkness, avoiding the sunlight and growing used to the dark. Originally, Smeagol belongs to a branch of Hobbits. Now, after many years with the ring, Smeagol become Gollum has morphed into a pathetic physical figure, lacking moral sensibility, and driven by an inordinate desire to regain the ring since losing it to

---

13. Francis, "Laudato Si'" par. 231.

Frodo's uncle, Bilbo Baggins, years before. Gollum is a character to be pitied having lost most of what we might call integrity and dignity.

Though Gollum helps Sam and Frodo to find a path to Mordor, most of the time he intends to have them killed so that he might possess the ring. He does not desire the power of the ring to dominate others, but he desires the mistaken greatness of the ring to sustain his failed esteem. It would be correct to say that it is the ring who manipulated Gollum so that it could get back to Sauron. Gollum has no unique relationship with the natural world, except as a source of food for him, especially in fresh fish. He prefers to live in a darkened cave until necessity drives him out. He is familiar with some of the hideous sites on Middle Earth, including the tunnel of Shelob, yet it does not upset him. He has no care for the beauty of Lothlorien or the pastoral peace of the Shire or the impending evil that will cover the land if Sauron is victorious. His mind and heart are thoroughly addicted to the greatness of the ring.

There can be no doubt that sustainable natural and human environments are created by persons who love the natural world and acknowledge its intrinsic value. Though the human person is the most valuable of all creatures that God has created, faith impresses even more on each of us, the responsibility to care for our common home. Pope Francis gives the matter of ecological integrity an interiorly based source. He sates:

> Inner peace is closely related to care for ecology and for the common good because, lived out authentically, it is reflected in a balanced lifestyle together with a capacity for wonder which takes us to a deeper understanding of life. Nature is filled with words of love, but how can we listen to them amid constant noise, interminable and nerve-wracking distractions, or the cult of appearances? Many people today sense a profound imbalance which drives them to frenetic activity and makes them feel busy, in a constant hurry which in turn leads them to ride rough-shod over everything around them. This too affects how they treat the environment. An integral ecology includes taking time to recover a serene harmony with creation, reflecting on our lifestyle and our ideals, and contemplating the Creator who lives among us and surrounds us, whose presence "must not be contrived but found, uncovered."[14]

14. Francis, "Laudato Si'" par. 225.

Touchstones of Ongoing Transformation

THROUGHOUT THIS BOOK, THERE has been an effort to construct a framework for understanding human transformation from an interior perspective, preferring to speak about human transformation as a series of conversions: religious, moral, affective, intellectual, and psychological/ psychic. While these conversions do not follow any specific or strict order when experienced in the concreteness of living, they do necessarily build on and interact with one another. These processes of transformation are not without their challenges in a cultural and social milieu characterized by an occlusion to the presence of divine mystery, an assessment of values in terms of individual emotional preferences, a hesitancy to acknowledge the possibility of objective truth, an individualistic ethos that obstructs the bonds of community, and the prevalence of psychic wounding.

Bernard Lonergan and those who have found in his insights the ground on which to build their own house of love have been the principal mentors of this book. To better explain human transformation, the insights for a possible framework come from the turn to the subject, an examination of subjectivity, and human consciousness. With this starting point, we come to know the dynamic structure of human consciousness, the patterns of experience, the realms of meaning, and notions such as horizon, conversion, dialectic, and sublation. This turn also helps us understand human desire especially the unrestricted desire to know, value, and the fulfillment of desire in being-in-love with God. Values and feelings are essential dimensions of this framework and a preference in the scale of values. Affectivity and relationships of love are vital to transformation. The structure of the human person as an organism/psyche and human spirit helps give an explanatory anthropology that establishes a creative collaboration for the healing of psychic wounds. These insights reveal an understanding of human transformation that will help in making our lives a work of art.

We do not merely transform on one occasion in our life journey. Transformation is an ongoing reality until the day we die. Nor is any one event of transformation complete for us. Transformation happens in moments, usually unexpectedly and through intimations and infrequently in bright flashes. Stephen Covey, the author of several works on leadership, speaks about the seven habits of effective people. The second habit is to "begin with the end in mind."[1] This principle encourages us to articulate where we are heading. This principle is concerned to impress upon the person the importance of imagination and the ability to plot a new course of action when we know the end. The end of transformation is to become authentic authors of our own lives despite distorting choices and negative influences beyond our own choices that may have already had an unhelpful impact on us. It is concerned to highlight the importance of a mature conscience for responsible living and loving actions. All the conversions reach up to the end of personal and communal authenticity as they shape our interior humanity.

The Restless Heart

What are some crucial features of ongoing transformation? First, in the fourth century CE, St. Augustine spoke of human restlessness, not so much prompted by agitation at the lack of a spiritual home, but as a religious insight concerning where individual desiring is heading. He states "You stir man to take pleasure in praising you, because you have made us for yourself, and our heart is restless until it rests in you."[2] This spiritual insight points to the affirmation that all our longing, feeling, imagining, desiring to know, to value, and to do the good reaches up to and finds fulfillment in God. For this reason, to get in touch with our true inner self is to get in touch with one's restlessness or inner loneliness that will only find rest in God.

---

1. Covey, *Principle-Centered Leadership*, 42.
2. Augustine, *Confessions* I.i.1 (3).

According to Sebastian Moore, there are three ways to come to terms with this inner loneliness or restlessness.[3] The first way postulates the sadness of the person who does not advert to a favorable orientation of this inner loneliness and instead interprets it as a lingering discontentment. This ascertain goes up: life is ultimately dissatisfying, and we have to live with this realization, snatching what comfort we can along the way through whatever can give us pleasure. The second way postulates that a person notices and awakens to this inner loneliness and seeks a remedy for it in another person, say a spouse or close friend, a remedy that will never be fully satisfied since no person can sustain another completely. Our contemporary songs are often a homage to this kind of expectation we place on human love. The third way awakens in us the realization that this deep and inescapable feeling of restlessness is not without reason. Through an act of trust, a measure of patient attention, and an awareness of our vulnerability, we go in search of God, the mysteriously desiring and desired One, who is the source and terminus of our inner loneliness. God leads us to love our neighbor as ourselves.

THE DESIRING PERSON

Second, the vast undiscovered territory waiting to be traveled will require us to value the process of desiring and value our subjectivity. This desiring is not some power by which to control one's life or the lives of others. This desire does not amount to an exercise in religious hoarding or one-upmanship. It is not a desire for the acquisition of insights for the sake of spiritual elitism. This desire is not a desire to have more to fill one's empty spiritual well, nor is it a matter of behaving like a spiritual consumerist. This desire is not a pursuit toward acquiring spiritual knowledge to make ourselves invulnerable to the sorrows and loves of life. This desire is not a means to avoid making a serious moral inventory of our lives, or to engage in self-protection by amassing some power over others or by feeling ourselves better than others.

Lonergan speaks to the five imperatives of the human spirit: be attentive, be intelligent, be reasonable, be responsible and be loving.[4] We

---

3. Moore, *Inner Loneliness*, 14–15.

4. Lonergan, *Method*, 55, 321. Lonergan mentions the first four of the imperatives, but a proper reading of his work reveals the importance of being-in-love with God and others as the apex of the imperatives.

are asked to attune ourselves to the inbuilt desire of the human spirit. This inbuilt desire is central to being human whenever we are engaged in the task of self-transcendence whether religious, moral, intellectual, and affective. This desire is the ground from which to measure the goodness or otherwise of all our other particular desires. This desire invites us to self-discovery and discovery of the world. This desire will ground us and will constitute us. The surprising element is that any attempt to refute these imperatives employs these very activities in consciousness to do the refuting. While it is true that we are all unique, coming from very diverse backgrounds, formative experiences, and ways of life with different starting points shaping us along many paths, nevertheless, we all stand on common ground. This common ground is a set of imperatives that unite us in one common humanity. The desiring human spirit is the starting point to transformation, and its fulfillment is knowing reality, affirming values, doing the good and being-in-love with God and others.

The Place of Wonder

Third, the person learns to recognize all reality with a heart full of wonder. Wonder surprises us making us curious and filling us with inner silence and joy. When we experience beauty, a kind of wonder fills us, and we cry out how marvelous things are. Wonder leads to awe, reverence, and a veneration for higher things. At times, wonder generates the response of amazement, moving us to re-examine our ideas and beliefs. In this sense, wonder is a doorway from the known to the unknown. The unknown cannot be possessed, however the unknown beckons us and directs its passionate pull on us. By questions for intelligence, we wait upon insights to help us understand. By questions of judgment, we desire to validate our insights and make an affirmation of reality. By questions of deliberation, we aspire to find out what is valuable. By questions of action, we desire to become the best person we can be.

Jerome Miller talks about allowing ourselves to be caught in the "throe" of wonder, inquiry, and questioning.[5] To be caught in the throe of wonder is to stand at the threshold of something unknown and unable to be tightly controlled. Francis Bacon speaks of wonder as a kind of knowledge that breaks us, aligning it to the German word, *wunde* or wounding. Miller insists that the wound or breach that wonder creates requires some

5. Miller, *In the Throe of Wonder*, 23–31.

repair. The unknowns toward which wonder points have the potential to rupture or deconstruct our life toward a transformed horizon. The unknown may cause fear in us. However, Miller states, it is "not fear as a paralyzing terror beyond, rather, fear at an inability to picture just where opening this door might lead. I am held spellbound by a future unknown beyond the door."[6] Through wonder, we adopt the heart of a seeker with no destination except the unknown, yet we stand uncertain at the doorway between the known and the unknown. When caught in the throe of wonder, Miller states "we do not stand motionless; we are held fast in the throe of an ambivalence between the known and the unknown, the same and the other, the past and the future."[7] Wonder may cause us to *wander*: away from old habits, settled routines, established norms, and positions, and, so for its part, wonder can be subversive.

Describing the experience of wonder, Gallagher states:

> You will be sitting quietly in a chair and suffer an attack of wonder, simply because you are alive. One moment seems boringly ordinary and the next it is suddenly and rapturously extraordinary. One moment you are sitting there with your daily but undramatic nihilism, where nothing seems very special, and the next a chink in your armour lets in a flood of novelty. You break out of the tiny theatre in which your own familiar plot is being played. This is the blessing of the sunrise of wonder. Indeed, my main worry about people is that they might stay prisoners, stuck within all that seeming boredom. I wonder about their not wondering enough.[8]

Gallagher also names gratitude as the first fruit of wonder. Gratitude leads to humility. He is alluding to the importance of thankful feelings, thankful thinking, and thankful acting. If the stance of wonder can bring us to a point where we affirm that we are alive, then what a gift that is. The path of wonder can be an adventure toward something more. Sadly, many people do not open themselves to the gift of wonder. They fear change or an unsettling of their homeostatic equilibrium. People, therefore, call wonder a childish pursuit, impractical, and self-indulgent. They prefer to remain in their set routines and their spiritual contraction. They prefer to be the total masters of their destiny, thinking that there is

6. Miller, *In the Throe of Wonder*, 35.
7. Miller, *In the Throe of Wonder*, 36.
8. Gallagher, "Attack of Wonder," 1.

nothing but themselves and their thoughts. Above all, we do not want to suffer the process of transformation.

SELF-DISCOVERY

Fourth, questions and wondering invite us to a life of self-discovery through appropriating ourselves. Self-discovery is only possible through insight. It is, however, crucial to realize that we do not start with a clean slate in this process of self-appropriation. Lonergan signals the importance of conversion for transformation. We already live in communities with their true insights as well as their biases and errors. These errors include what we think we are doing when we are knowing, valuing, choosing, and acting. Lonergan asserts that transformative self-discovery involves "a matter of pulling out the inadequate ideals that may be already existent and operative within us. There is a conflict, there is an existential element, there is the question of the subject, and it is a personal question that will not be the same for everyone."[9] We also appropriate ourselves when we live and work among communities. We grow in self-knowledge through the response of others to our words and deeds. We learn through the powerful example of authenticity in others that causes us to want to act in the same way. We appropriate ourselves in the quiet of prayer and humble surrender to the mystery of God, reflecting on the wisdom of our living tradition of faith for us, society, and culture.

GOING TO THE DEPTHS

Fifth, Jesus invited the disciples by the Sea of Galilee in these words: "Put out into the deep water and let down your nets for a catch" (Luke 5:5). Going deeper uncovers, through interiority, a vast unchartered territory within us. The German theologian Paul Tillich, using the spatial metaphor of "surface" and "depth," diagnoses the malady of our time in this way:

> Most of our life continues on the surface. We are enslaved by the routine of our daily lives, in work and pleasure, in business and recreation. We do not stop to look at the height above us or the depth below us. We talk and talk and never listen to the voices speaking to our depths and from our depth. We accept ourselves

9. Lonergan, *Understanding and Being*, 17–18.

as we appear to ourselves, and do not care what we really are. Like hit and run drivers, we injure our souls by the speed with which we move on the surface; we miss therefore, our depth and our true life. And it is only when the picture we have of ourselves breaks down completely, only when we find ourselves acting against all the expectations we had derived from that picture, and only when an earthquake shakes and disrupts the surface of our self-knowledge, that we are willing to look into a deeper level of our being. . . . He who knows about depth knows God.[10]

Tillich identifies the potential transformation that awaits the person who is willing to keep on examining the depth of their being and person. Living at the depth challenges us to face our ignorance, wishful thinking, and self-deception.[11] Specifically, it stands in contrast to the cultural tendency that values the appearance of the body over the presence of being, frenetic activity over noticing and quiet reflection, the insatiable urge to have more rather than to become more, and the impulse to accumulate information over the wisdom to integrate knowledge into a worthwhile life.

According to Roy, our self-examination of the depth reveals a threefold dynamism in the human person when it comes to matters of religious faith. The three dynamics are affective fulfillment, the search for meaning, and an aspiration for truth.[12] By affective fulfillment, Roy presents the vital dimension of affectivity and emotions in relation to religious faith. This affective dimension asks: How can our deepest desires be satisfied? How can our behavior be consistent with our purposes? Are we ultimately significant?[13] This dimension focuses our attention on the metaphor of the heart of flesh, the affective disposition of feeling free, and an imagination which is a bridge between the historical texts and personal commitment. This dimension correlates to Gallagher's escape stories. Affective fulfillment indicates that people do not come to faith through proofs for the existence of God but more through something inwardly felt, living, and personal.

By the search for meaning, Roy presents the vital dimension of reflection and a quest for making sense of our religious faith. This reflective dimension asks: How do we know that God exists and life is worthwhile?

10. Tillich, *Shaking of the Foundations*, 55–56.
11. Roy, *Three Dynamisms of Faith*, 165–77.
12. Roy, *Three Dynamisms of Faith*, 158
13. Roy, *Three Dynamisms of Faith*, 159.

How do we understand conversion? In what way do the words of the pre-modern text of Scripture speak to the post-modern concerns of today? What is the difference between meaningful suffering and meaningless suffering? Can there be redemption for the sinner and in what way does redemption impact the victim? This dimension correlates to Gallagher's quest stories. The search for meaning is akin to sitting at the crossroad, receiving a revelation and then translating it so that it speaks to the cultural milieu of today.[14]

By an aspiration for truth, Roy presents the crucial dimension of surrender, trust, obedience, and commitment to God.[15] The aspiration for truth asks: What is it about the voice of Christ that speaks with authority? To whom are we invited to surrender? What will this surrender mean for us in all the aspects of our life? God ceases to be a good idea but becomes the Reality that transforms our lives. Lonergan asserts that all love is self-surrender. Only from within a living commitment does religion come alive.[16] Love, reflected in the depth of our commitments, dismantles our horizon and introduces something entirely new. This dimension correlates with Gallagher's love stories.

Each of these dimensions of faith is important. Each is in a constant process of interaction. For an authentic living, there must exist a healthy interaction between these three dimensions. If one dimension dominates over the other two, errors are likely to occur. If two dimensions gang up through some alliance against the third dimension, deformations of faith are more likely to occur. Our life at the depth is a process of vigilance and patience as we recognize all three dimensions and the different voices that they speak to human wholeness throughout the varying circumstances of our story.

The Spirit of Suffering

Sixth, questions and wondering invite us into a spirit of suffering. Usually when we speak of suffering, immediately our attention is drawn to pain in our bodies and relieving it. Following this, there is the kind of pain inflicted on bodies that would make victims and victimizers. Our propensity to fill human history with victims is part and parcel of our

14. Gallagher, *Faith Maps*, 151.

15. Roy, *Three Dynamisms of Faith*, 159.

16. Gallagher, *Road Maps*, 157.

descent into meaninglessness. The victimizing of children or adults cannot possibly be anything but destructive. Such victimization usually does not test character, educate, or bring about some other good. Indeed, many people who have suffered such torment never recover.

Speaking to a more intelligent and responsible spirit of suffering, Miller states that "I suffer when the other ruptures my boundaries, but this rupture cannot occur without my permitting it. And this means that I suffer only when I will to undergo this rupture. Suffering is a *human act* and thus, in a sense, an accomplishment. But it is an act which accomplishes nothing for the self who 'does' it. In 'doing' it, I undo what would have been accomplished had I exercised my will to control."[17] A spirit of suffering points to a habit of heart responding to any event of complexity and unease in life, in which we can deliberately take account of a process that potentially helps us to grow. More centrally, when we suffer something, we give our consent that this event will get under our skin, penetrate to the heart, requiring us to let our defenses down, and inviting us to abandon the will to control.

There can be no doubt that adopting the spirit of suffering is very challenging. Miller adds:

> Only when one allows oneself to be affected, wounded, (and) moved by something loveable-that passion is born. Passion alone enlivens us and makes us participants in the world. But we cannot produce it ourselves. We cannot fabricate or engineer it. It's awakened in us when something beautiful or sublime moves us all the way down and stirs us to tears. Passion isn't subject to control. Passion is suffered. To be fully alive is to be caught in the throes of the world, to be overcome by its poignancy, to give oneself to it in impassioned celebration. To live fully is to spend oneself to death for what is dearest. Suffering is a mortal wound. . . . It happens at the beginning. The dying grief one suffers at the end is the last breath of ardor.[18]

Miller gives voice to a significant insight that brings together wonder and suffering. Openness to wonder implies that each of us consents to be wounded and disrupted by insights and by the practical decisions that follow the disruptions of our world. We are prepared to let them have an impact on us. Opening oneself to disruption, we decide to be patient in the face of these world-shattering events so that the heart might open

17. Miller, *Way of Suffering*, 31–32.
18. Miller, "Terminal Patience," 45.

to what is even more precious. To suffer a disruption of our world means that the very core of our being is affected.

There is also a link between authentic religion and suffering. We find the link in a conversation recounted between Francis of Assisi and Brother Leo, in a set of writings called the *Fioretti*, attributed to Francis. On a day in winter, Francis and Brother Leo are walking from Perugia to Assisi and along the way Francis asks Leo where perfect joy is to be found. The conversation goes on for the next three kilometers with Francis saying that perfect joy is not this and not that when Leo, somewhat frustrated asks: "Father, I pray you for God's sake tell me wherein is perfect joy." Francis replies:

> When we shall have come to St Mary of the Angels, soaked as we are with the rain and frozen with cold, encrusted with mud and afflicted with hunger, and shall knock on the door, if the porter should come and ask angrily, "Who are you?" and we replying: "We are two of your brethren," and he should say back to us, "You speak falsely; go on your way" (Francis even goes on to describe how the porter comes out and physically assaults them for persisting in their knocking)—if we should bear all these things patiently and with joy, thinking on the suffering of our Saviour, as which we ought to bear for love of him, Brother Leo write that it is in this that there is perfect joy. . . . Brother Leo, above all the graces and gifts of the Holy Spirit which Christ has given to his friends, is the grace of conquering oneself and suffering willingly for the love of Christ all pain, ill-usage, and calamity. Because of all the gifts of God, we can glory in none, seeing they are not ours, but God's. But in the cross of tribulation and affliction we may glory in, for these are ours; and therefore, says the Apostle, "I will not glory save in the cross of our Lord Jesus Christ."[19]

Chapter 3 offered the insight that there is a destructive kind of suffering that throws a blanket of meaninglessness over the lives of people. The only way to overcome it and find new meaning is to absorb it and turn it to good. Francis is fully aware that such a stance is impossible without religious and moral conversion and this book has argued also to the importance of affective and psychic conversion. Miller states that the most tragic condition of the human spirit is one "surrounded by a network of defenses, nothing can enter it or emerge from it. Nothing can move it to

---

19. Francis quoted in Squire, *Asking the Fathers*, 232.

praise or grief because a tourniquet has been placed on the arteries that are supposed to circulate the affections. The perfectly protected heart is closed, like a clenched fist. Since nothing is allowed to move it, nothing can become dear to it—nothing can matter to it. The heart's tight grip on life makes it moribund."[20] The opposite of suffering disruptions to one's world is to engage in avoidance, repression, or denial of these disruptions. Avoidance makes possible our taking control of whatever has the potential to bring about transformation. We would rather be in control and keep at bay all that touches what is most vulnerable in us.

EMMAUS: A MODEL OF TRANSFORMATION

Seventh, there exists one model of transformation, among many, that comes from the Gospels and concerns undergoing conversion into a community of love. It is the post-resurrection story in Luke 24:13–25. We meet these two disciples walking along a road to the village of Emmaus. Jesus comes and walks alongside them though we are told that they do not recognize him. Indeed, we are told that "something prevented them from recognizing him" (v. 14). This lack of sight could be described in various ways. On one level, grief and desolation have the ability to stress a human being that they forget, do not hear things correctly, and do not pick up the clues that are part of the ordinary course of human relating. At another level, the lack of recognition stems from the oversight that confuses suffering and death with the impotence of God. After all, God is supposed to be all powerful. Consequently, their inability to see Jesus is spiritual blindness. Grace has to be part of the practical solution if they are to recognize Jesus. Through religious conversion, God opens their eyes to see again and to recognize that God had been with them all along even if they did not know it.

Jesus, sensitive to their pain and confusion, begins to ask them questions. He asks: "What matters are you discussing as you walk along?" (v. 17). They begin to talk, to tell their story in their voice, and to name what is confusing them. We hear those two disciples saying, "our hope had been that he would be the one to set Israel free" (v. 21). There are some who speculate that the telling of their story required many tearful interruptions, outbursts of anger, and feelings of helplessness. We receive the shorthand version in the gospel. In other words, they tell the story of

20. Miller, "Terminal Patience," 45.

their awakened desire and its collapse into desolation and grief, mixed with moral guilt.

Jesus begins to speak and says something very significant: "Was it not ordained that the Christ would suffer and enter into his glory?" (v. 26). The meaning of these words speaks to a new religious interiority, while at the same time turning on its head our current world political order. The Christ of God was bound to suffer. Why? A strong case could be made for reading the Bible as a painful process by the people of God in recognizing the illusions of domination and the power of Empire, the delusion of surrounding self with security without limits or avoiding suffering by surrounding one's life with the pretense of success. To trust in the security of armaments or power or success is idolatry. Idolatry sacrifices everything to these idols. The disordered desire for these idols even sacrifices people. Whether we are individuals, governments, groups, or international bodies, it is possible through our social structures to sacrifice people and ourselves on the altars of our malice, hatred, apathy, disesteem, and self-rejection. Alternatively, fidelity to God means living a different way: an openness to grace, the power of community without domination, creativity, healing, security within intelligent self-limitation, and success shared between people.

Now from within the whole story of Israel, there arises a gigantic leap in understanding as to how domination and the alienation can be overcome through fidelity to God. That leap takes the form of the Suffering Servant. Israel is to be God's light to other nations through the life of the Suffering Servant in the here and now. The servant humbly turns everything upside down so that things can be the right side up. This servant draws attention to all that distorts our felt sense of who we are, what we think, and how to authentically live. Pride, envy, jealousy, self-centeredness, narcissistic self-importance, self-deception, lovelessness, and isolation from one another distort the correct direction of desire since desire is love trying to happen. If things are to be right again, it will not be without personal suffering. The task of the servant brings upon himself personal ridicule, humiliation, and even persecution from others. The servant suffers because he is living from the deep-down truth of things and people. These people do not want to live by the deep-down truth of things since they feel fearfully threatened. So, we hear Caiaphas say of Jesus: "Better that one man dies for the nation than that the whole nation is destroyed" (John 11:50).

On the one hand, the death of Jesus shows how far humankind is prepared to go to stop life from taking a loving, responsible, and creative path. The darkness of the human heart is laid bare in the cross. We are capable of killing the Innocent One (James 5:6). The human heart is capable of such darkness that it would destroy the Lord of life (Acts 3:15). The death of Jesus becomes yet another example of our ability to make victims of people but in this case the completely innocent victim, Jesus. It means that our human history we speak of and teach our children, emphasizing achievements, heroism, and progress, is only one side of the story. There is another side to this history, and it is a dark underbelly of victimization. This underbelly is the history of meaningless human suffering. It is a history of suffering that feels like a blanket of meaninglessness thrown over the human condition and out of which we mourn the breakdown of people, cultures, and whole societies. We need transformation.

On the other hand, Jesus feels this history of human suffering in his body, psyche, and the human spirit. What matters to him is the history of suffering people. Following Jesus through the gospels, we realize that his identification with suffering humanity did not come only toward the end in Gethsemane. Even in the beatitudes, he pronounces blessed those who mourn, who are poor in spirit, those who hunger and thirst after justice, those who are persecuted for the cause of right, and who are abused on account of him (Matt 5: 1–11). Evil is a dark foreboding aspect of his whole life. The solution that Jesus offers is not one of meeting force with force, power with more significant physical power. Jesus' practical solution to breakdown is to subvert it from within. Transformation happens when the deep-down truth of people is restored. For this solution to come about, Jesus becomes the victim, the forgiving victim. His wounds heal the people and, most especially, the fountain of life flows to us from his wounded side. We overcome evil from within through self-sacrificing love. The disciples on that road are yet to understand the full significance of his death. It would seem that they are yet to grasp that the One to set Israel free is also the Suffering Servant of God. Until they meet the risen Lord, they are incapable of understanding the way that God deals with the problem of evil and how God responds to the history of suffering people with all their helplessness and hopelessness.

Finally, they arrive at Emmaus, and the gospel text speaks those most important words: "He made as if to go on" (v. 28). It is a gesture of freedom on the part of Jesus. Jesus gives them a choice to invite him in or not. When God is transforming our lives, God does not force us. It is their invitation to Jesus that completes the beginning of something new, bringing to a climax and fulfillment all that Jesus had spoken of as he walked with them. At the table, he takes the bread, says the blessing, and breaks it, and their eyes are opened, and they recognize him (v. 31). What has happened? Their desire had been awakened in the days of fellowship in Galilee and made void and empty in the days that followed the death of Jesus. This desolation of desire is now transformed into the knowledge of a love more powerful than death, goodness more powerful than evil. Jesus has risen with the transforming gifts of forgiveness, healing, and peace.

The Emmaus story began with Jesus coming alongside these two failing and failed disciples at the point of their most profound grief. He listens to their story with reverence and does not rush in with the truth. Then, Jesus offers a more in-depth vision of their story and the whole human story. He respects their freedom. They invite him in, and he breaks bread. They are now a company, a word coming from two Latin words "cum" and "panis" meaning to share bread with another. He shares bread with them: the bread of his word, the bread of his felt presence, and the bread of new vision. We witness to both a story of human transformation and a map about how we might best live out transformed lives.

Bibliography

Alison, James. *Knowing Jesus*. Springfield, IL: Templegate, 1993.

Arcamone, Dominic. *Religion and Violence: A Dialectical Engagement through the Insights of Bernard Lonergan*. Eugene, OR: Pickwick, 2015.

Au, Wilkie. *By Way of the Heart: Towards a Holistic Christian Spirituality*. New York: Paulist, 1989.

Augustine. *Confessions*. Translated by Henry Chadwick. New York: Oxford University Press, 1991.

Beer, Peter. *An Introduction to Bernard Lonergan: Exploring Lonergan's Approach to the Great Philosophical Questions*. Glen Waverley, Victoria, Australia: Sid Harta, 2010.

Benson, Bruce Ellis. "Friedrich Nietzsche (1844–1900)." In *Religion and European Philosophy: Key Thinkers from Kant to Zizek*, edited by Philip Goodchild and Hollis Phelps, 173–83. London: Routledge, 2017.

Boldt, Joachim. "Machine Metaphors and Ethics in Synthetic Biology." *Life Sciences, Society, and Policy* 14 (2018). Online. https://lsspjournal.biomedcentral.com/articles/10.1186/s40504-018-0077-y.

Boone, Mark. *The Conversion and Therapy of Desire: Augustine's Theology of Desire in the Cassiciacum Dialogues*. Eugene, OR: Pickwick, 2016.

Boyle, Susan. "I Dreamed a Dream." *I Dreamed a Dream*. Sony Music, 2009. CD.

Bradshaw, John. *Healing the Shame That Binds Us*. Deerfield, FL: Health Communications, 1988.

Byrne, Patrick H. "Moral Conversion: The Stripping Away of Self-Delusion." *The Lonergan Review* 7 (2016) 10–48.

———. "The Passionateness of Being: The Legacy of Bernard Lonergan, SJ." In *Finding God in All Things: Celebrating Bernard Lonergan, John Courtney Murray, and Karl Rahner*, edited by Marco Bosco and David Sagama, 35–51. New York: Fordham University Press, 2007.

———. "Ressentiment and the Preferential Option for the Poor." *Theological Studies* 54 (1993) 213–41.

Capon, Victor. *Changing the Mind: The Bible, the Brain, and Spiritual Growth*. Eugene, OR: Cascade, 2016.

Cardinal, Marie. *The Words to Say It*. Cambridge, MA: VanVactor and Goodheart, 1983.

Conn, Walter E. "Affective Conversion: The Transformation of Desire." In *Religion and Culture; Essays in Honor of Bernard Lonergan, SJ*, edited by Timothy P. Fallon and Philip Boo Riley, 261–76. Albany, NY: State University of New York Press, 1987.

Covey, Stephen R. *Principle Centred Leadership*. London: Simon and Schuster, 1990.

Cronin, Brian. *Phenomenology of Human Understanding*. Eugene, OR: Pickwick, 2017.

Crysdale, Cynthia S. W. *Embracing Travail: Retrieving the Cross Today*. New York: Continuum, 2000.

———. *Transformed Lives: Making Sense of Atonement Today*. New York: Seabury, 2016.

Crysdale, Cynthia, and Neil Ormerod. *Creator God, Evolving World*. Minneapolis: Fortress, 2013.

Dadosky, John D. *The Eclipse and Recovery of Beauty: A Lonergan Approach*. Toronto: University of Toronto Press, 2014.

———. "The Proof of Beauty: From Aesthetic Experience to the Beauty of God." *Analecta Hermeneutica* 2 (2010) 1–15.

Dalton, Anne Marie. *A Theology for the Earth: The Contributions of Thomas Berry and Bernard Lonergan*. Ottawa: University of Ottawa Press, 1999.

Daponte, Paul. *Hope in an Age of Terror*. Maryknoll, NY: Orbis, 2009.

Darnov, Doron. "'A Mind of Metal and Wheels': Technology, Instrumental Reason, and Industrialization in *The Lord of the Rings*." *UC Berkeley Comparative Literature Undergraduate Journal* 5.2 (2015). Online. https://ucbcluj.org/a-mind-of-metal-and-wheels-technology-instrumental-reason-and-industrialization-in-the-lord-of-the-rings.

Denver, John. "Back Home Again." *The Essential John Denver*. Sony BMG Music Entertainment, 2007. CD.

———. "Wild Montana Skies." *The Essential John Denver*. Sony BMG Entertainment, 2007. CD.

Doran, Robert M. "Bernard Lonergan and Daniel Berrigan." In *Faith, Resistance, and the Future: Daniel Berrigan's Challenge to Catholic Social Thought*, edited by James L. Marsh and Anna J. Brown, 119–31. New York: Fordham University Press, 2012.

———. *Intentionality and Psyche*. Vol 1. of *Theological Foundations*. Marquette Studies in Theology 8. Milwaukee: Marquette University Press, 1995.

———. *Subject and Psyche: Ricoeur, Jung, and the Search for Foundation*. Washington, DC: University Press of America, 1977.

———. *Theology and the Dialectics of History*. Toronto: Toronto University Press, 1990.

Dunne, John S. *The Way of All the Earth: Experiments in Truth and Religion*. Notre Dame, IN: University of Notre Dame Press, 1972.

Dunne, Tad. "Critical Thinking I: Bias." *Still Learning* (blog), November 26, 2014. http://stilllearning.sienaheights.edu/uploads/1/8/6/3/18634728/critical_thinking_-_bias.pdf.

———. *Doing Better: The Next Revolution in Ethics*. Milwaukee: Marquette University Press, 2010.

———. "Faith, Charity, Hope." *Lonergan Workshop* 5 (1985) 49–70.

Eliot, T. S. *Four Quartets*. London: Harcourt, 1971. Online. http://www.columbia.edu/itc/history/winter/w3206/edit/tseliotlittlegidding.html

———. *The Poems and Plays, 1909–1950*. Orlando, FL: Harcourt and Brace, 1967.

———. "The Social Function of Poetry." 1945. Online. http://tseliot.com/preoccupations/religion.

Erling, Bernhard. *A Reader's Guide to Dag Hammarskjöld's "Waymarks."* 1999. Reprint, St Peter, MN: Gustavus Adolphus College, 2010. Online. http://www.daghammarskjold.se/wp-content/uploads/2014/08/rg_to_waymarks.pdf.

Farley, Margaret. *Personal Commitments: Beginning, Keeping, Changing.* San Francisco: Harper & Row, 1986.

Farley, Wendy. *The Wounding and Healing of Desire: Weaving Heaven and Earth.* Louisville: Westminster John Knox, 2005.

Flanagan, Joseph. *Quest for Self-Knowledge: An Essay in Lonergan's Philosophy.* Toronto: University of Toronto Press, 2002.

Flanagan, Richard. "Fredrich and Flanagan: The Con-Man and His Ghost-Writer." *Conversations,* October 16, 2017. Online. http://www.abc.net.au/radio/programs/conversations/conversations-richard-flanagan/9032374.

———. "On Love Stories and Reza Berati." *Guardian,* February 26, 2014. Online. https://www.theguardian.com/world/2014/feb/27/on-love-stories-and-reza-barati.

Francis. "Christian Hope—9. The Helmet of Hope (1 Thess 5:4–11)." February 1, 2017. Online. https://w2.vatican.va/content/francesco/en/audiences/2017/documents/papa-francesco_20170201_udienza-generale.html.

———. "Laudato Si." May 24, 2015. Online. http://w2.vatican.va/content/francesco/en/encyclicals/documents/papa-francesco_20150524_enciclica-laudato-si.html.

"Gabriella's Song—As It Is In Heaven." *Yahoo! Answers,* October 27, 2015. Online. https://answers.yahoo.com/question/index?qid=20080219015948AAkxHYx&guccounter=1.

Gallagher, Michael Paul. "An Attack of Wonder." *Thinking Faith,* November 25, 2011. Online. https://www.thinkingfaith.org/articles/20111125_1.htm.

———. "Christian Identity in a Postmodern Age: A Perspective from Lonergan." In *Christian Identity in a Postmodern Age,* edited by Declan Marmion, 145–61. Dublin: Veritas, 2005.

———. *Dive Deeper: The Human Poetry of Faith.* London: Darton Longman & Todd, 2001.

———. *Faith Maps: Ten Religious Explorers from Newman to Joseph Ratzinger.* London: Darton Longman & Todd, 2010.

———. *Free to Believe: Ten Steps to Faith.* London: Darton Longman & Todd, 1987.

———. *St Therese and Atheism.* Dublin: Carmelite Community, 1998. Online. http://www.plaything.co.uk/gallagher/pastoral/St_Therese_and_Atheism.html.

———. *Struggles of Faith.* Dublin: Columba Press, 1990.

Girard, Rene. *Deceit, Desire, and the Novel.* Baltimore: John Hopkins University Press, 1966.

———. *The Girard Reader.* Edited by James G. Williams. New York: Crossroad, 1996.

———. *I See Satan Fall Like Lightning.* Translated by James G. Williams. Maryknoll, NY: Orbis, 2001.

Goodliff, Paul. *Care in a Confused Climate: Pastoral Care and Postmodern Culture.* London: Darton Longman & Todd, 1998.

Gregson, Vernon. "The Desire to Know: Intellectual Conversion." In *The Desires of the Human Heart: An Introduction to the Theology of Bernard Lonergan,* edited by Vernon Gregson, 16–35. New York: Paulist, 1988.

Hammarskjöld, Dag. *Markings.* Translated by W. H. Auden and Leif Sjoberg. London: Faber and Faber, 1965.

Haughey, John C. *Housing Heaven's Fire: The Challenge of Holiness.* Chicago: Loyola University Press, 2002.

Haughton, Rosemary. *Love.* Baltimore, MD: Penguin, 1970.

————. *The Passionate God*. New York: Paulist, 1981.

Havel, Vaclav. "Forgetting We Are Not God." *First Things* 51 (1995) 47–50. Online. https://www.firstthings.com/article/1995/03/forgetting-we-are-not-god.

————. *Letters to Olga*. Translated by Paul Wilson. London: Faber and Faber, 1999.

————. "Speech Delivered at Stanford University, Palo Alto, California, September 29, 1994." *Multidisciplinary Association for Psychedelic Studies* 5.3 (1995). Online. http://www.maps.org/news-letters/v05n3/05346vac.html.

Hedges, Chris. *War Is a Force that Gives Us Meaning*. New York: Anchor, 2003.

Hefling, Charles, Jr. "Creation." In *The New Dictionary of Catholic Social Thought*, edited by Judith A. Dwyer, 249–54. Collegeville, MN: Liturgical, 1994.

Herzog, Tamar. "Guaranis and Jesuits: Bordering the Spanish and the Portuguese Empires." *ReVista: Harvard Review of Latin America* 14.3 (2015) 50–51. Online. https://revista.drclas.harvard.edu/book/export/html/579116.

Hughes, Glenn. *A More Beautiful Question: The Spiritual in Poetry and Art*. Columbia, MO: University of Missouri Press, 2011.

————. *Transcendence and History: The Search for Ultimacy from Ancient Societies to Postmodernity*. Columbia, MO: University of Missouri Press, 2003.

Hunt, Anne. *The Trinity and the Paschal Mystery: A Development in Recent Catholic Theology*. Collegeville, MN: Liturgical, 1997.

Intergovernmental Panel on Climate Change (IPCC). "Special Report: Global Warming of 1.5° C." https://www.ipcc.ch/sr15.

Jägerstätter, Franz. *Letters and Writings from Prison*. Translated by Robert A. Krieg. Edited by Erna Putz. Maryknoll, NY: Orbis, 2009.

John Paul II. "Development And Solidarity: Two Keys to Peace." January 1, 1987. Online. https://w2.vatican.va/content/john-paul-ii/en/messages/peace/documents/hf_jp-ii_mes_19861208_xx-world-day-for-peace.html.

Jones, James W. *Blood that Cries Out from the Earth: The Psychology of Religious Terrorism*. Oxford: Oxford University Press, 2003.

Kelly, Anthony P. *Eschatology and Hope*. Maryknoll, NY: Orbis, 2006.

————. *The Resurrection Effect: Transforming Christian Life and Thought*. Maryknoll, NY: Orbis, 2008.

————. *Thinking Faith: Moods, Methods, and Mystery*. Adelaide, Australia: Australian Theological Forum, 2017.

————. *Touching the Infinite*. Australia: Collins Dove, 1991.

Kim, Sr. Yeongseon. "St Francis of Assisi and Ecological Conversion." *Catholic Theology and Thought* 78 (2017) 47–89. Online. http://j-stt.catholic.ac.kr/DATA/STTBOOK/1489732553484.pdf.

Lamoureux, Patricia, and Paul Wadell. *The Christian Moral Life: Faithful Discipleship for a Global Society*. Maryknoll, NY: Orbis, 2010.

Lawrence, Frederick. "The Ethics of Authenticity and the Human Good." In *The Importance of Insight: Essays in Honor of Michael Vertin*, edited by John Lipsay and David Lipsay, 127–50. Toronto: University of Toronto Press, 2007.

Lewis, Helen. "Seeing Bergen-Belsen through My Father's Camera." *Conversations*, June 21, 2018. Online. http://www.abc.net.au/radio/programs/conversations/conversations-helen-lewis/9872242.

Liddy, Richard M. *Transforming Light: Intellectual Conversion in the Early Lonergan*. Collegeville, MN: Liturgical, 1993. Online. http://lonergan.org/wp-content/uploads/2002/10/LiddyLight.pdf.

Lonergan, Bernard. *Collection*. Edited by Frederick E. Crowe and Robert M. Doran. Vol. 4 of *Collected Works of Bernard Lonergan*. Toronto: Toronto University Press, 1993.

———. *Insight: A Study in Human Understanding*. Edited by Fredrick E. Crowe and Robert M. Doran. Vol. 3 of *Collected Works of Bernard Lonergan*. Toronto: Toronto University Press, 1997.

———. *The Lonergan Reader*. Edited by Mark Morelli and Elizabeth A. Morelli. Toronto: University of Toronto Press, 1997.

———. *Method in Theology*. Toronto: University of Toronto Press, 1996.

———. *Philosophical and Theological Papers, 1958–1964*. Edited by Robert C. Croken and Robert Doran. Vol. 6 of *Collected Works of Bernard Lonergan*. Toronto: University of Toronto Press, 1996.

———. *A Second Collection*. Edited by Robert M. Doran and John D. Dadosky. Vol. 13 of *Collected Works of Bernard Lonergan*. Toronto: University of Toronto Press, 2016.

———. *A Third Collection*. Edited by Robert M. Doran and John D. Dadosky. Vol. 16 of *Collected Works of Bernard Lonergan*. Toronto: University of Toronto Press, 2017.

———. *Topics in Education*. Edited by Frederick E. Crowe and Robert M. Doran. Vol. 10 of *Collected Works of Bernard Lonergan*. Toronto: University of Toronto Press, 1993.

———. *Understanding and Being*. Edited by Frederick E. Crowe and Robert M. Doran. Vol. 5 of *Collected Works of Bernard Lonergan*. Toronto: Lonergan Research Institute, 1990.

MacIntyre, Alasdair. "A Culture of Choices and Compartmentalization." Lecture delivered at the Notre Dame Center for Ethics and Culture, University of Notre Dame, October 13, 2000. Online. https://brandon.multics.org/library/macintyre/macintyre2000choices.html.

Malvasi, Mark. "Tradition and Modernity in 'The Godfather.'" *The Imaginative Conservative* (blog), September 28, 2015. Online. http://www.theimaginativeconservative.org/2015/09/timeless-essays-tradition-and-modernity-in-the-godfather.html.

Marsh, James L. "Self-Appropriation as a Way of Life." In *Meaning and History in Systematic Theology: Essays in Honor of Robert M. Doran, SJ*, edited by John D. Dadosky, 311–29. Milwaukee: Marquette University Press, 2009.

Matthews, William. "The Fragmented Self/Subject." *Journal of Macrodynamic Analysis* 3 (2003) 205–223.

———. "On Memoir, Biography, and the Dynamism of Consciousness." *Lonergan Workshop* 23 (2009) 307–328.

———. "Self-Appropriation in Ira Progoff and Bernard Lonergan." *Divyaddan Journal of Philosophy and Education* 25.1 (2014) 1–18. http://williamamathews.com/images/PDF_Publication/2014ProgoffLonerganSelfRR.pdf.

May, Gerald. *Will and Spirit: A Contemplative Psychology*. New York: Harper & Row, 1982.

McCarthy, Michael H. *Authenticity as Self-Transcendence: The Enduring Insights of Bernard Lonergan*. Notre Dame, IN: University of Notre Dame Press, 2015.

McClendon, James, Jr. *Biography as Theology: How Life Stories Can Remake Today's Theology*. New York: Abingdon, 1974.

McPartland, Thomas. *Lonergan and the Philosophy of Historical Existence*. Columbia, MO: University of Missouri Press, 2001.

Melber, Henning. *Dag Hammarskjöld and Conflict Mediation*. Mediation Arguments 10. Hatfield, South Africa: Center for Mediation in Africa, University of Pretoria, 2016. Online. https://www.up.ac.za/media/shared/237/Mediation%20 Arguments/7521-up-cma-melber-mediation-arguments-hr-revised.zp81380.pdf.

———. "Suez and the Congo—Hammarskjöld's Lasting Legacy." *Dag Hammarskjöld Foundation*, August 22, 2016. Online. https://www.daghammarskjold.se/suez-congo-hammarskjolds-lasting-legacy.

Miller, Jerome A. "Addiction and Tears." In *Sobering Wisdom: Philosophical Explorations of Twelve-Step Spirituality*, edited by Jerome A. Miller and Nicholas Plants, 53–64. Charlottesville, VA: University of Virginia Press, 2014.

———. "All Love Is Self-Surrender." *Method: Journal of Lonergan Studies* 13 (1995) 53–81.

———. "Desire, Passion, and the Politics of Culture." *Montréal Review*, May 2014. Online. http://www.themontrealreview.com/2009/Desire-Passion-and-the-Politics-of-Culture.php.

———. *In the Throe of Wonder: Intimations of the Sacred in a Post-Modern World*. Albany, NY: State University of New York Press, 1992.

———. "Terminal Patience: A Philosophical Meditation." *The Newman Rambler* 12.1 (2018) 39–46. https://newmancentre.org/wp-content/uploads/2016/01/Jerome-A-Miller.pdf.

———. *The Way of Suffering: A Geography of Crisis*. Washington, DC: Georgetown University Press, 1988.

———. "The Way of Suffering: A Reasoning of the Heart." *Second Opinion* 17 (1992) 21–33.

———. "Wound Made Fountain: Towards a Theology of Redemption." *Theological Studies* 70 (2009) 525–54.

Miller, Mark T. *The Quest for God and the Good Life: Lonergan's Theological Anthropology*. Washington, DC: Catholic University of America Press, 2013.

Moore, Sebastian. *The Contagion of Jesus: Doing Theology as If It Mattered*. London: Darton Longman & Todd, 2007.

———. *The Fire and the Rose are One*. New York: Seabury, 1980.

———. *The Inner Loneliness*. London: Darton Longman & Todd, 1982.

———. *Jesus the Liberator of Desire*. New York: Crossroad, 1990.

———. "Jesus the Liberator of Desire: Reclaiming Ancient Images." *Cross Currents* 40 (1990) 477–98.

———. *Let This Mind Be in You: The Quest for Identity through Oedipus to Christ*. London: Darton Longman & Todd, 1985.

Moran, Frances, and Tony Kelly. *Searching for the Soul: Psychoanalytical and Theological Reflections on Spiritual Growth*. Strathfield, New South Wales, Australia: St Paul's, 1999.

Morelli, Mark. *Self-Possession: Being at Home in Conscious Performance*. Chestnut Hill, MA: Lonergan Institute, 2015.

Nelson, Alex. "Imagining and Critical Reflection in Autobiography: An Odd Couple in Adult Transformative Learning." *Adult Education Research Conference* 33 (1997). Online. http://newprairiepress.org/aerc/1997/papers/33.

O'Collins, Gerald. "The Beauty of Christ." *The Way* 44 (2005) 7–20.

O'Donnell, James. *Augustine: A New Biography*. New York: HarperCollins, 2005.

Ormerod, Neil. *Creation, Grace, and Redemption*. Maryknoll, NY: Orbis, 2007.

———. "Desire and the Origins of Culture: Lonergan and Girard in Conversation." *The Heythrop Journal* 52 (2013) 784–95.

———. *Grace and Disgrace: A Theology of Self-Esteem, Society, and History*. Sydney, Australia: E. J. Dwyer, 1992.

———. *A Public God: Natural Theology Reconsidered*. Minneapolis: Fortress, 2013.

———. "Questioning Desire: Lonergan, Girard, and Buddhism." *Louvain Studies* 36 (2012) 356–71.

Ormerod, Neil, and Christiaan Jacobs-Vandegeer. *Foundational Theology: A New Approach to Catholic Fundamental Theology*. Minneapolis: Fortress, 2015.

Ormerod, Neil, and Cristina Vanin. "Ecological Conversion: What Does It Mean?" *Theological Studies* 77 (2016) 328–52.

Pembroke, Neil. *The Art of Listening: Dialogue, Shame, and Pastoral Care*. London: T&T Clark, 2002.

Ratzinger, Joseph. "The Feeling of Things, the Contemplation of Beauty." August 24, 2002. Online. http://www.vatican.va/roman_curia/congregations/cfaith/documents/rc_con_cfaith_doc_20020824_ratzinger-cl-rimini_en.html.

Rievaulx, Aelred. *On Spiritual Friendship*. Translated by Lawrence C. Braceland. Edited by Marsha L. Dutton. Collegeville, MN: Liturgical, 2010.

Rose, Reginald. *Twelve Angry Men*. New York: Penguin, 2011.

Rosenberg, Randall. *The Givenness of Desire: Concrete Subjectivity and the Natural Desire to See God*. Toronto: University of Toronto Press, 2017.

Roy, Louis. *Engaging the Thought of Bernard Lonergan*. London: McGill-Queens University Press, 2016.

———. "Human Desires and Easter Faith." In *Jesus Crucified and Risen: Essays in Spirituality and Theology in Honor of Dom Sebastian Moore*, edited by William P. Loewe and Vernon J. Gregson, 53–66. Collegeville, MN: Liturgical, 1998.

———. *The Three Dynamism of Faith: Searching for Meaning, Fulfillment, and Truth*. Washington, DC: Catholic University of America Press, 2017.

Segev, Tom. *Soldiers of Evil: The Commandments of the Nazi Concentration Camps*. New York: Berkeley, 1987.

Silf, Margaret. *Landmarks: An Ignatian Journey*. London: Darton Longman & Todd, 1988.

Sobrino, Jon. *Oscar Romero: Memories and Reflections*. Maryknoll, NY: Orbis, 1990.

Squire, Aelred. *Asking the Fathers*. London: SPCK, 1973.

———. *Summer in the Seed*. New York: Paulist, 1980.

Streeter, Carla Mae. *Foundations of Spirituality: A Systematic Approach the Human and the Holy*. Collegeville, MN: Liturgical, 2013.

Taylor, Charles. *A Secular Age*. Boston, MA: Belknap, 2007.

———. "Spirituality of Life and Its Shadow." *Compass* 14 (1996) 10–13.

Tekippe, Terry J. *Bernard Lonergan: An Introductory Guide to Insight*. New York: Paulist, 2003.

Therese of Lisieux. *Story of a Soul: The Autobiography of St Therese of Lisieux*. Translated by John Clarke. Washington, DC: Institute of Carmelite Studies, 1975.

Thornhill, John. *Modernity: Christianity's Estranged Child Reconstructed*. Grand Rapids: Eerdmans, 2000.

Tierney, Clement. *The Sacrament of Penance and Reconciliation*. Sydney, Australia: E. J. Dwyer, 1983.

Tillich, Paul. *The Shaking of the Foundations*. Eugene, OR: Wipf & Stock, 2011.

Tyrrell, Bernard J. *Christotherapy II: The Fasting and Feasting Heart*. New York: Paulist, 1982.

———. "Psychological Conversion, Methods of Healing, and Communication." *Lonergan Workshop* 6 (1986) 239–60.

United Nations. "United Nations Framework Convention on Climate Change." May 9, 1992. https://unfccc.int/resource/docs/convkp/conveng.pdf.

Voegelin, Eric. *The New Science of Politics*. Chicago: University of Chicago Press, 1960.

Webb, Eugene. *The Self Between: From Freud to the New Social Psychology of France*. Seattle: University of Washington Press, 1993.

Wheatley, Margaret. "Turning to One Another." 2002. Online. http://www.swaraj.org/shikshantar/expressions_wheatley.pdf.

Zantovsky, Michael. *Havel: A Life*. Toronto: University of Toronto Press, 2015.

Index

Nelson, Alex
  telling our story and, 11–12
Nietzsche, Fredrich, 123, 125
  passionate commitment and,
    126–27

Ordinary People, 236–39
Ormerod, Neil
  on freedom and values, 33
  on disesteem and conversion,
    179–80

pneumapathology, 247–49
  The Godfather Trilogy and, 249–55
Power, Katherine Ann, 135–36
prudence, virtue of, 143
psyche
  censorship of, 233
  healing and, 255–59
  human spirit and, 232
  organism and, 228
  psychic energy and, 229–30
  The Picture of Dorian Gray and, 149
psychopathology, 241–42

recurrence, schemes of, 275
religious experience
  affectivity and, 62
  affective conversion and, 172
  development and,
  prayer and, 63
  realms of meaning and,
  supernatural and, 62
religious conversion
  beauty and, 119–22
  belief and, 117–18
  charity and, 116–17
  Christian discipleship and, 106
  faith and, 115
  forgiveness and, 110–15
  hope and, 115–16
  moral conversion and, 140–41,
    150–56
  trust and, 118–19
  victim and, 77–80
responsibility, xii, 2, 14, 46–47, 50, 78,
  99, 186, 214

Rilke, Maria Rainer, 20
Romero, 165
Romero, Oscar
  Sobrino and, 166–67
  social conversion and, 167–69
Roy, Louis
  faith as affectivity, 301
  faith as aspiration for truth, 302
  faith as search for meaning, 301–2
  on religious experience, 60–61
  on types of consciousness, 5–6

scale of values. See Lonergan, on scale
  of values
secularism, 76
self-appropriation
  as unimaginable, 10
self-knowledge. See self-appropriation; self-discovery; self-
  sufficiency; will to control
shame
  healthy and unhealthy, 160
sickness
  of the psyche, 242–43
  of the Spirit, 249
Silf, Margaret
  moods within consciousness,
    146–47
sin, 71–73
  as cultural, 73
  as personal, 72
  as social, 73
  as social exclusion, 180–81
  Old Testament and, 71–72
Streeter, Mae Carla
  forgiveness and, 110–12
  psychic energy and, 229–30
stories
  escape, 16–17
  existential truth, 19–20
  love, 21
  my voice, 13–14
  quest, 17–18
  responsibility and, 11
symbol
  machine, 278
  organism, 278–79

www.ingramcontent.com/pod-product-compliance
Lightning Source LLC
Chambersburg PA
CBHW060327100426
42812CB00003B/903